Judicial Review: Law and Procedure

AUSTRALIA AND NEW ZEALAND
The Law Book Company Ltd
Sydney: Melbourne: Perth

CANADA AND U.S.A.
The Carswell Company Ltd
Agincourt, Ontario

INDIA
N.M. Tripathi Private Ltd
Bombay
and
Eastern Law House Private Ltd
Calcutta and Delhi
M.P.P. House
Bangalore

ISRAEL
Steimatzky's Agency Ltd
Jerusalem: Tel Aviv: Haifa

MALAYSIA: SINGAPORE: BRUNEL
Malayan Law Journal (Pte.) Ltd
Singapore

PAKISTAN
Pakistan Law House
Karachi

For Jane

Foreword

Judicial review was the boom stock of the 1980s. Unaffected by recession, the boom has roared on into the 1990s. The ancient power of the court to see that public powers are lawfully exercised had been rejuvenated and reinvigorated. Abuses of public power can now be redressed more effectively than at any time in our long history.

Inevitably, this great surge of activity has given rise to a mass of decided cases. Some of them deal with procedural questions, concerning such matters as the choice between judicial review and ordinary action, or the standing of the applicant, or delay. Many others deal with issues of substance, above all the vital but sensitive borderline, probed and explored in many authorities, between the role of the decision-maker and the role of the judge. As the cases multiply, some lines of argument are blocked but new avenues of contention appear. Save in the most straightforward cases, there are few easy answers, few obvious solutions.

This book gives an invaluable bird's eye view of this very important and fast-developing jurisdiction—invaluable, because the bird is experienced, discriminating and sophisticated, alive to the potential pitfalls, alert to the fault-lines in existing authority, intelligently critical. Even the seasoned campaigner will do well to keep a copy of the book in his knapsack. And the prudent judge will have a copy within easy reach.

Royal Courts of Justice   T.H. BINGHAM
London   Master of the Rolls

October 1995

Preface

Judicial review has come a long way since the appearance of the first edition of this work.

My interest in the subject was awakened by the House of Lords' rulings in *O'Reilly v. Mackman* and *Cocks v. Thanet District Council* which promised to put public law firmly on the juridical map.

That promise has been amply fulfilled. In the decade since this book was last published the scope of judicial review has widened dramatically. In part this is due to judicial expansionism. Cases such as *R. v. Panel on Take-Overs, ex p. Datafin*, and *M v. The Home Office* illustrate the extent to which our judges are prepared to apply administrative law principles to an increasing range of public bodies including, for practical purposes, the Crown itself. But the growing influence of Europe cannot be over-estimated. Both Community law and the European Convention on Human Rights are infiltrating the case law with the relentlessness of an incoming tide, and provoking reappraisal of the methods by which executive review is conducted.

This edition seeks to focus on these and other developments. It also takes account of the fast-moving changes in procedure which practitioners in this jurisdiction ignore at their peril. As before the emphasis is practical. Despite this, however, the aim is to clarify rather than to over-simplify.

Part 3 has been greatly expanded. There is a new chapter on commercial judicial review, and new sections on judicial review in the areas of tax, mental health, community care, coroners, education and broadcasting and communications. The remaining chapters and sections on substantive judicial review have, inevitably, been heavily updated as a result of the avalanche of new decisions. These daunting tasks have been undertaken by four practising barristers: Jenni Richards, Sean Wilken and Alan Maclean (all of 39 Essex Street), and by Craig Barlow of Bedford Row Chambers. The responsibility, however, for any errors in content, or infelicities of style, or syntax rests with me alone.

I am, as always, indebted to my wife and children for their forbearance and support during the lengthy gestation of this edition. My publishers have shown the tolerance of saints.

The law is stated as at September 30, 1995.

RICHARD GORDON Q.C.
39 Essex Street, London WC2

September 1995

Contents

Table of Cases

Table of Statutes

Table of Statutory Instruments

Rules of the Supreme Court

PART 1

LAW

1. THE REMEDY OF JUDICIAL REVIEW

NATURE AND SCOPE

Judicial review is the means by which the High Court exercises a supervisory jurisdiction over inferior courts, tribunals or other public bodies.[1] It is a specialised remedy in public law.

The distinction between public and private law is not easy to draw.[2] It is separately considered at paras. 1–003 and 1–004. Many have doubted the utility, or even existence, of such a distinction.[3] There remain, nonetheless, broad considerations of policy justifying the creation of a separate regime for certain grievances against public bodies. Most notable, perhaps, is the desirability of protecting administrative decision-making from vexatious litigants and delay.

In reviewing a particular decision[4] the court is concerned to evaluate fairness. The essential function of judicial review (albeit in the context of natural justice), was well put by Lord Hailsham L.C. in *Chief Constable of North Wales Police v. Evans*[5] where he stated:

> "It is important to remember in every case that the purpose ... is to ensure that the individual is given fair treatment by the authority to which he has been subjected and that it is no part of that purpose to substitute the opinion of the judiciary or of individual judges for

---

[1] Including individuals charged with public law functions. Note that the County Court has no jurisdiction to make an order of mandamus, certiorari or prohibition: County Courts Act 1984, s.38(3)(a), as substituted by s.3 of the Courts and Legal Services Act 1990. While s.1(1)(b) of the C.L.S.A. empowers the Lord Chancellor to make provision conferring jurisdiction on county courts in relation to proceedings in which the High Court has jurisdiction, subs (10) excludes judicial review.

[2] See generally Beatson, " 'Public' and 'Private' in English Administrative Law" [1987] 103 L.Q.R. 34; Carr, "Public Law and Private Law: A study of the Analysis of, and use of, a Legal Concept"; Eekelaar/Bell, *Oxford Essays in Jurisprudence* 3rd series (1987), Chap. 3. For a procedural analysis, see The Rt. Hon. Sir Harry Woolf, "Public Law—Private Law: Why the Divide? A personal view" [1986] P.L. 220, 230; Anthony Tanney "Procedural Exclusivity in Administrative Law" (1994) P.L. 51; Sandra Fredman and Gillian Morris "The Costs of Exclusivity: Public and Private Re-examined" (1994) P.L. 69.

[3] For a good summary of the arguments see Carol Harlow, " 'Public' and 'Private' Law: Definition without Distinction" [1980] 43 M.L.R. 241.

[4] This is shorthand since it is not always a "decision" that is reviewed but, *e.g.* a failure to perform a public duty.

[5] [1982] 1 W.L.R. 1155.

1

that of the authority constituted by law to decide the matters in question."[6]

Procedure

1–002   As a remedy, judicial review is governed by a specific procedure and it must, therefore, be carefully distinguished from other forms of process such as appeal, case stated and habeas corpus (see Chap. 6).

The court exercises control by making one or more of three prerogative orders, namely certiorari, prohibition and mandamus.[7] Since the 1977 reforms (for which see below) it is now possible for an applicant to be awarded a declaration and/or injunction as well as, or instead of, the prerogative orders. An action for damages may also lie if one of the above remedies has been applied for.[8]

Procedure is contained in the relevant provisions of the Supreme Court Act 1981[9] and in rules of court. Order 53 of the Rules of the Supreme Court is devoted to "applications for judicial review". Other rules are, expressly or impliedly, incorporated into that Order.[10]

There is both civil and criminal jurisdiction. In general, civil applications are heard by a single judge of the Queen's Bench Division[11] whereas criminal cases[12] are determined by a two- (or occasionally three-) judge Divisional Court. The avenues of appeal differ according to whether the matter is civil or criminal.

Applicants or respondents (including their legal advisers) who experience difficulty in respect of procedure should contact the Crown Office.[13] It is there that applications for judicial review and all supporting documents are required to be filed. The Crown Office is also responsible for listing.

WHAT IS PUBLIC LAW?

1–003   All developed legal systems seek to control the actions of public bodies. For this purpose, many countries have evolved a clear distinction between

---

[6] *ibid.* at p. 1160.

[7] Note that habeas corpus, a prerogative writ, has a wholly separate procedure.

[8] Probably it is necessary for one of the other remedies actually to have been granted. See *Davy v. Spelthorne B.C.* [1984] A.C. 262, *per* Wilberforce L.J. at p. 277; *cf. R. v. Northavon D.C., ex p. Palmer* (1994) 6 Admin. L.R. 195 (leave granted to seek "academic" declaration on which to follow a parasitic damages claim).

[9] *i.e.* ss.29–31 and s.43.

[10] Ord. 53, r. 8 contains instances of express and implied incorporation.

[11] Note, though, that complex or sensitive cases are directed to be heard by a two- or three-judge Divisional Court of the Queen's Bench Division.

[12] It is by no means always obvious what constitutes a "criminal cause or matter".

[13] Room C315, Royal Courts of Justice (tel: (0171) 936 6205).

public and private law, with specialised administrative courts and a separate corpus of legal principles to cope with misuse of public power.[14]

Dicey's statement that English law recognises no distinction between public and private law derives from the fact that the same courts decide administrative and private grievances and the same rules of law are applied.[15]

This does not, however, begin to deal with the problem of defining the subject matter of the remedy of judicial review under Order 53 where case law since *O'Reilly v. Mackman*[16] and *Cocks v. Thanet D.C.*[17] has tended to emphasise the contrast between private law rights, which are enforceable by action, and rights in public law which may afford *locus standi* to seek a remedy by way of judicial review.[18] The question is of increasing importance since courts are now striking out actions that ought to have been begun under Order 53 as an abuse of process.

Cases suitable for Order 53

In the light of the developing procedural distinction between private and public law, two propositions seem clear.

First, a peripheral public element will not be sufficient to bring a case within Order 53 if it is principally concerned with the enforcement of private law rights.[19] Secondly, a plaintiff or defendant in a private law action may challenge a public body's decision rather than commence separate judicial review proceedings where such challenge is in aid of existing private law rights.[20]

It would, however, be unwise to conclude that private law has no place in Order 53 applications. Particular difficulties can arise where public and private law issues are mixed. Can it be said that in such instances an applicant is obliged to select a public law remedy or vice versa? Is it not somewhat artificial to seek to impose the deadening status of private law on a complex set of facts merely because there is a plaintiff with a private law cause of action? As has been observed: "It would be a strange definition of public law which excluded the vindication of private law rights from its ambit."[21]

The reality of judicial review is that the court decides, on a policy basis, which interests are to prevail so as to enable its supervisory jurisdiction to be exercised. This is made necessary because, although the *actio popularis* is unknown in English law, there is a continuing need for judicial control of

1–004

---

[14] *cf., e.g.* the French "Conseil d'Etat" and the doctrine of "detournement de pouvoir".

[15] See A. V. Dicey, *Introduction to the Study of the Law of The Constitution* (1st ed., 1885).

[16] [1983] 2 A.C. 237.

[17] [1983] 2 A.C. 286.

[18] See, *e.g.* *O'Reilly v. Mackman*, n. 16 above, *per* Lord Diplock at p. 275. For a cautionary note, *cf. Davy v. Spelthorne B.C.*, n. 8 above, *per* Lord Wilberforce.

[19] *Davy v. Spelthorne B.C.*, n. 8 above; *R. v. East Berkshire Area Health Authority, ex p. Walsh* [1985] Q.B. 152.

[20] *Wandsworth L.B.C. v. Winder* [1985] A.C. 461; *Roy v. Kensington and Chelsea and Westminster Family Practitioner Committee* [1992] 1 A.C. 624.

[21] See Cane [1984] P.L. 17.

public misuse of power.[22] In practice, procedural rules and substantive principles under Order 53 are governed predominantly by the court's view of the permissible limits of judicial intervention in cases savouring of misuse of public power.

To an extent this analysis is circular and does not provide a conceptual definition of "public law". From a practitioner's point of view, however, it is important to recognise that the more a case involves actionable rights, the less will the court be likely to categorise it as suitable for the judicial review machinery. The absence of a common law remedy makes it more probable that the case will be designated as one involving public law and, hence, suitable for the Order 53 procedure. As a general rule, if the court wants to exercise control it is more likely to accord *locus standi* to an applicant.[23] Beyond this it is unsafe to speculate on the ambit of public law. For the purpose of Order 53 it is a moving target, approachable best through the case law. A number of subject areas are examined in Part 3.

An understanding of the relationship between public law and Order 53 is essential to predicting when judicial review must be used and when it may be dispensed with. This question is considered below after a brief discussion of the history and development of judicial review.

JUDICIAL REVIEW: THE OLD REMEDY

1–005   Before 1977 the modern remedy did not exist. The applicant seeking to challenge a decision of a public body had an alternative. He could apply for the grant of the prerogative orders under a special procedure governed by the old Order 53. Instead he might choose to bring an action claiming a declaration or injunction, provided that he could establish that some private right was infringed or special damage suffered.[24] Without this, declaratory or injunctive relief could be obtained only by means of a relator action with the consent of the Attorney-General.

Disadvantages

1–006   This artificial division of remedies meant that different standing rules applied according to the procedure employed. If the applicant sought a prerogative order, *locus* was wider since special damage or infringed private law rights were never necessary constituents of proving an interest under the old Order 53.

Procedure dictated other differences. In an ordinary action there was an automatic right to discovery, cross-examination and general interlocutory

---

[22] See generally Craig, *Administrative Law* (3rd ed., 1994) at pp. 499 *et seq.*

[23] There is an overlap between according *locus standi* and exercising discretion to refuse a remedy. See Chap. 2.

[24] See especially *Gouriet v. Union of Post Office Workers* [1978] A.C. 435. See also, *e.g. Benjamin v. Storr* (1874) L.R. 9 C.P. 400. In these circumstances of course damages might also be available, whereas such remedy could not have been obtained under the former Ord. 53.

relief which was absent from the existing prerogative order machinery. In an action the time limits were those of the normal periods of limitation whereas the prerogative orders were subject to more stringent controls. For certiorari there was a specific time limit of six months.

With the increasing importance of declarations and injunctions in the administrative context,[25] there was a growing case for assimilating all the remedies in public law under one head.

In addition, the existing procedure for the prerogative orders was proving inadequate to cope with the number of cases coming before the courts.[26] The position pre-1977[27] may be summarised as follows:

(a) An *ex parte* application was made for leave to apply for the prerogative orders to a Divisional Court consisting (usually) of three judges.
(b) If leave was granted the substantive application was subsequently heard, *inter partes*, again before a Divisional Court.

The problem was delay. By the end of 1979, there were more than 700 Divisional Court cases outstanding. Cases designated as non-urgent took in excess of two years to come on for hearing.[28] Such a backlog meant that, too often, applications at the preliminary stage were insufficiently considered. This resulted in unnecessary cases coming before the court on the full hearing and consequent additional delay.

The need for reform

Reform was urgently needed. The minimum requirements were for: **1–007**

(a) flexibility in the range of powers available;
(b) a streamlined procedure to ensure consistency as between the remedies and to reduce delay;
(c) some increased degree of expertise.[29]

Wider questions could be posed. Should there be a formal procedural separation between public and private law? Was there a need for increasing the scope of the existing remedies? These and related matters exercised the attention of the Law Commission almost from its inception in 1965.

---

[25] Especially the declaration. See in particular I. Zamir and Woolf *The Declaratory Judgment* (2nd ed. 1993) Ch. 1. Note its role in *Pyx Granite Co. Ltd. v. M.H.L.G.* [1960] A.C. 260.
[26] Due largely to a conscious widening of the permitted categories of administrative challenge.
[27] Note however that the 1977 reforms did not make the practical changes necessary to combat delay. This did not occur until the development of the Crown Office List; see para. 1–018 below.
[28] These figures are from Blom-Cooper, "The New Face of Judicial Review: Administrative Changes in Order 53" [1982] P.L. 250, 253.
[29] Because of the developing need for specialisation. *ibid.* at pp. 252–254.

INVOLVEMENT OF THE LAW COMMISSION

1–008   After several years of preliminary discussion the Law Commission, in 1969,[30] recommended to the Lord Chancellor that a Royal Commission or committee of comparable status should be constituted to undertake an inquiry to consider the following issues:

(a) How far are changes desirable with regard to the form and procedures of existing judicial remedies for the control of administrative acts and omissions?

(b) How far should any such changes be accompanied by changes in the scope of those remedies—
   (i) to cover administrative acts and omissions which are not at present subject to judicial control; and
   (ii) to render judicial control more effective, *e.g.* with regard to the factual basis of an administrative decision?

(c) How far should remedies controlling administrative acts or omissions include the right to damages?

(d) How far, if at all, should special principles govern—
   (i) contracts made by the administration; and
   (ii) the tortious liability of the administration?

(e) How far should changes be made in the organisation and personnel of the courts in which proceedings may be brought against the administration?

The response of the Lord Chancellor (delivered later in the year) was to say that the time was not right for such a wide-ranging inquiry. Instead he invited the Commission to "review the existing remedies for the judicial control of administrative acts and omissions with a view to evolving a simpler and more effective procedure".

The Law Commission reports

1–009   Although initially attempting to broaden the scope of its reference by including a study of time limits, ouster clauses and damages,[31] the Law Commission finally concluded that its inquiry was limited to answering the first of the five questions set out above. Its report on "Remedies in Administrative Law" published in March 1976[32] expressly excluded consideration of the remaining issues.

The Law Commission's principal positive recommendations were as follows:

(a) there should be a new procedure for administrative law challenges being subsumed under the general heading "applications for judicial review";

---

[30] See Law Comm. No. 20, Cmnd. 4059.
[31] Law Comm. Working Paper No. 40 (1971).
[32] Law Comm. No. 73, Cmnd. 6407.

(b) the remedies available were to include, in appropriate cases, declaratory and injunctive relief;

(c) there should be provision for an interim declaration in Crown proceedings;

(d) declarations and injunctions should, if judicial review was sought, be obtainable only on public law grounds[33];

(e) damages should be capable of being awarded in the new procedure not as an independent remedy but as ancillary to an application for one of the other remedies[34];

(f) *locus standi* should be subject to the test of whether an applicant had a "*sufficient interest*" to proceed;

(g) the new regime should be set out in a "Procedure for Judicial Review Act".[35]

Narrow though the final proposals were they have, at least, provided a basis for the revitalisation of administrative law procedure. Although the Law Commission emphasised that it was not proposing an exclusive remedy, the assemblage of the public law remedies under one head, which has been accepted, makes it (in practice) more difficult for declarations and injunctions to be claimed in public law cases outside Order 53.[36]

In some respects the Law Commission was not bold enough. It was content to leave preliminary and substantive applications to be dealt with by a full three-judge Divisional Court. No proposals were put forward for developing a more specialised personnel.[37] Fortunately the Commission's positive recommendations have been supplemented by quite separate changes in procedure (for which see below). Much of this additional reform is the result of "the simple expedience of the fiat of judges and officials".[38] It is no less effective for that.

SOURCES

The current provisions relating to the remedy of judicial review are principally contained in the 1977 and 1980 amendments to Order 53.[39] Substantially the same changes recur in section 31 of the Supreme Court   **1–010**

---

[33] This is a paraphrase. Nonetheless the Law Commission's criteria for controlling the circumstances where declarations and injunctions should be available on judicial review, adopted in Order. 53, r. 1(2), amount to this. See para. 3–021.

[34] *i.e.* any loss suffered should flow from an existing cause of action. To have proposed a separate remedy would be to answer item (c) of the 1969 submissions (see para. 1–008 above).

[35] The 1976 Report (n. 32) above contained a draft Bill in these terms.

[36] See, *e.g.* Michael Purdue, "The New Separation of Public from Private Law" [1983] 80 L.S.Gaz. 2357–2359.

[37] Arguably both these matters fell outside the ambit of the limited remit.

[38] Blom-Cooper, n. 28 above at p. 261.

[39] See S.I. 1977 No. 1955; S.I. 1980 No. 2000.

Act 1981. In addition, the introduction of a specialised Crown Office List has added a distinctive flavour to the judicial review machinery.[40]

The interrelationship between Order 53 and the 1981 Act is not entirely clear. The Act may have been passed to accord with the Law Commission's proposal that reforms should be embodied in an Act of Parliament.[41] There may also have been the desire to give statutory force to delegated legislation.

There are no express conflicts between Order 53 and the Supreme Court Act. Two possible areas of difficulty, however, are the respective provisions relating to delay[42] and the extent to which claims for declarations and injunctions in public law cases must be made by way of an application for judicial review.[43]

In the event of conflict, the Act should prevail over the Order, being both later and possessing direct statutory authority. In practice the courts have not interpreted them differently.

THE PRESENT REGIME

1–011   Most of the Law Commission's recommendations have been implemented. The salient features of the existing regime are set out below.

A full range of remedies

1–012   Order 53 now covers "applications for judicial review" rather than (as formerly) being restricted to an application for certiorari, prohibition and mandamus. The main effect of this is to incorporate, in the same procedure, the remedies of declaration and injunction[44] (Ord. 53, rr. 1 and 2; S.C.A. 1981, s. 31(1) and (2)).

Application for leave

1–013   As before, it is necessary to obtain preliminary leave before making a substantive application for judicial review. Broadly, this is obtainable provided that the applicant can show: (i) an arguable case on merits; (ii) *locus standi*; and (iii) that he has not delayed unduly (see Ord. 53, rr. 3(1), 3(7) and 4; S.C.A. 1981, s. 31(3) and (6)).

---

[40] See para. 1–018.

[41] See, *e.g.* the Lord Chancellor's statement at 415 H.L. Official Report, ser. 5, col. 1230.

[42] *cf.* Ord. 53, r. 4 with s.31(6) and (7) of the S.C.A. 1981. See also para. 2–032.

[43] *cf.* Ord, 53, r. 1(1) and (2) with s.31(1) and (2) of the S.C.A. 1981. See also paras. 6–002 *et seq.*

[44] In line with the Law Commission's proposals these remedies may still, in theory, be sought on public law grounds in an action outside judicial review. However, subsequent case law has limited the instances in which an applicant may now claim these remedies outside Order 53. See paras. 6–002 *et seq.* Note, too, that where an independent remedy is claimed on judicial review, damages may also be sought.

Civil and criminal cases

There is now a clear distinction between civil and criminal matters. The **1–014** procedural differences were principally introduced by the 1980 amendments to Order 53. Essentially the updated rules provide for:

(a) *Ex parte* "paper" applications for leave to apply for judicial review. In both civil and criminal cases such applications are determined by a single judge of the Queen's Bench Division (Ord. 53, r. 3(2) and (3)).

(b) An oral *ex parte* application for leave where the applicant requests it or by way of a renewed application where leave is initially refused by the single judge or granted on unacceptable terms. In civil cases this will take place before a single judge sitting in open court, unless there is a specific direction (which is unusual) that determination be made by a Divisional Court. In criminal cases the oral hearing takes place before a Divisional Court (45) (Ord. 53, r. 3(4) and (5)).

(c) A full hearing if leave is granted. This will be *inter partes* after service of the appropriate documents before substantially the same tribunal as on an oral *ex parte* application. Thus, civil cases are normally heard by a single judge in open court. Occasionally a hearing may be directed to a judge in chambers or, more often, to a Divisional Court. In a criminal case or matter a Divisional Court is the proper forum (Ord. 53, r. 5(1) and (2)).

Interlocutory orders

The 1977 amendments have removed a number of disadvantages that **1–015** used to face applicants in judicial review proceedings. There is, additionally, an increased range of orders available to the court. In particular:

(a) Post-1977, there is specific provision for discovery, interrogatories and cross-examination (Ord. 53, r. 8(1)).

(b) There is also power to make an unspecified number of interlocutory orders (Ord. 53, r. 8(1)).[45]

(c) The court has wide powers to permit amendment and use of further affidavits (Ord. 53, rr. 3(6) and 6(2)); to order proceedings to continue as if they had been begun by writ (*ibid.*, r. 9(5)); and to allow representations by persons who have not been made parties to the proceedings (*ibid.*, r. 9(1)).

Delay

More restrictive rules have been introduced to deal with an applicant's **1–016** delay in presenting his application. The Law Commission recommended that there should be no specific time limit for delay and that relief should not be refused on that ground unless the court considered that the granting

---

[45] *Sed quaere* whether the range of permitted interlocutory applications is similar to that prevailing in ordinary actions. See para. 8–009.

of relief would cause substantial prejudice or hardship to any person or would be detrimental to good administration. The 1977 amendments to Order 53 introduced a specific time limit of three months for certiorari alone, thereby reducing the pre-existing limit (for that remedy) of six months. The 1980 revisions have, however, imposed more draconian limits. Order 53 (as finally amended) now provides that:

> "4—(1) An application for leave to apply for judicial review shall be made promptly and in any event within three months from the date when grounds for the application first arose unless the Court considers that there is good reason for extending the period within which the application shall be made."[46]

Sufficient interest

1–017   Instead of the disparate rules that formerly prevailed as to *locus standi*, the Law Commission's recommendations have been accepted. The test is now whether an applicant has a "sufficient interest in the matter to which the application relates" (Ord. 53, r. 3(7); S.C.A. 1981, s.31(3)).[47]

The Crown Office List

1–018   One of the most far-reaching practical innovations in judicial review procedure will probably be seen as the creation of the Crown Office List.

The effect of the 1980 amendments was, in practice, to create a partial administrative list since most civil judicial review cases would, henceforth,[48] be heard by a single judge of the Queen's Bench Division with expertise in administrative law.[49]

This process has been extended by a Practice Direction made in July 1981.[50] Paragraph 1 thereof creates a Crown Office List consisting not only of judicial review cases but also of other cases with an administrative law element.

The consequences of the Crown Office List on the machinery of judicial review have been:

(a)   To facilitate the creation of clear principles of substantive law and procedure.

(b)   The establishment of guidelines as to when judicial review should be sought.[51]

(c)   Swifter determination of applications for leave and full hearings.

---

[46] But *cf.* s.31(6) of the S.C.A. 1981 which is couched in different terms. For detailed comparison of the two provisions, see para. 2–032.

[47] See Chap. 4. *Sed quaere* whether the test is uniform.

[48] *i.e.* as from January 1981.

[49] Not dissimilar from the Commercial List. See Blom-Cooper, n. 28 above at p. 259.

[50] *Practice Direction (Q.B.D.) (Trial: Setting Down Action: London)* [1981] 1 W.L.R. 1296.

[51] The relationship between judicial review and other forms of process is not always clear. See Chap. 6.

AN EXCLUSIVE REMEDY?

Neither Order 53 (as amended), nor section 31 of the Supreme Court **1–019**
Act 1981 makes judicial review an exclusive remedy. Indeed, the Report of
the Law Commission on Remedies in Administrative Law expressly
advised against so doing. However, the decisions in *O'Reilly v. Mackman*[52]
and *Cocks v. Thanet D.C.*[53] introduced a measure of doubt as to the
circumstances in which public law disputes could be resolved other than by
way of judicial review.

Prior to 1977 (it will be recalled), an applicant seeking redress for alleged
infringement of public law "rights" could proceed in three ways, namely:

(a) under Order 53 itself (for a prerogative order);
(b) by means of a relator action brought in the name of the
Attorney-General, subject to his leave (for declarations or
injunctions);
(c) by action where private rights were infringed or special damage
suffered (for declarations or injunctions).[54]

Where prerogative orders are sought, Order 53 remains the sole
procedure available. The real problem facing applicants lies in determining
whether to commence claims for declarations and injunctions by action or
by way of application for judicial review.

In *O'Reilly* the House of Lords struck out three actions brought in the
Queen's Bench Division by prisoners seeking a declaration against a Board
of Visitors in respect of certain findings and penalties, as being an abuse of
process. It was held that the correct procedure was by way of application
for judicial review. A similar conclusion was reached in the context of the
Housing (Homeless Persons) Act 1977[55] in *Cocks v. Thanet D.C.*

Lord Diplock, in *O'Reilly v. Mackman*, emphasised the difference in
procedure that prevailed before the 1977 amendments; most notably the
absence of discovery or cross-examination. Having regard to what were
clear disadvantages facing applicants under the old Order 53, he concluded
that:

"it could not be regarded as an abuse of the process of the court,
before the amendments made to Order 53 in 1977, to proceed against
the authority by an action for a declaration of nullity of the impugned
decision with an injunction to prevent the authority from acting on it,
instead of applying for an order of certiorari, and this despite the fact
that, by adopting this course, the plaintiff evaded the safeguards
imposed in the public interest against groundless, unmeritorious or
tardy attacks upon the validity of decisions made by public authorities
in the field of public law".[56]

---

[52] [1983] 2 A.C. 237.
[53] [1983] 2 A.C. 286.
[54] See *Gouriet v. Union of Post Office Workers*, n. 24 above.
[55] Now contained in the Housing Act 1985.
[56] *O'Reilly v. Mackman*, n. 52 above at p. 282.

Post-1977 the position was (in the view of the House of Lords) very different. Not only were the above disadvantages removed but the new remedy also contained:

"a procedure by which every type of remedy for infringement of the rights of individuals that are entitled to protection in public law can be obtained in one and the same proceedings".[57]

For these reasons Lord Diplock observed that as a "general rule" it would be contrary to public policy and an abuse of process to permit a dissatisfied applicant to proceed by way of an ordinary action and thereby "evade" the provisions of the amended Order 53, which are designed to afford safeguards for public authorities in the field of public law where such applicant was seeking to establish that a decision of a public authority infringed rights to which he was entitled under public law.[58]

Exceptions to Order 53

1–020   In *O'Reilly*, the House of Lords accepted that the remedy of judicial review was not exclusive. Nonetheless, Lord Diplock postulated only very limited exceptions to the above-mentioned "general rule". He held that:

"there may be exceptions, particularly where the invalidity of the decision arises as a collateral issue in a claim for infringement of a right of the plaintiff arising under private law, or where none of the parties objects to the adoption of the procedures by writ or originating summons. Whether there should be other exceptions should, in my view, at this stage in the developments of procedural public law, be left to be decided on a case to case basis."[59]

This formulation left the law in a perilously ambiguous state. Apart from the consensual exception, which must, in practice, be extremely rare,[60] applicants were in the unenviable position of having to predict the court's attitude to complex questions of collaterality and public policy. Just how difficult the task could be is shown by the case law that has developed on the collateral challenge exception. This is separately considered in the context of the relationship between judicial review and action.[61]

At present the courts appear to have retreated from the logic of *O'Reilly v. Mackman* and *Cocks v. Thanet D.C.* and to favour allowing proceedings involving public law issues being litigated outside Order 53, provided that

---

[57] n. 52 *ibid.* at p. 283.

[58] n. 52 *ibid.* at p. 285.

[59] n. 52 *ibid.* at p. 285. For cases illustrating the general rule see *Wessex Water Authority v. Farris* [1990] 30 R.V.R. 78; *Ali v. Tower Hamlets L.B.C.* [1993] Q.B. 407.

[60] A rare instance occurred in *Gillick v. West Norfolk and Wisbech Area Health Authority* [1986] A.C. 112, a case commenced prior to *O'Reilly*. Contrast *R. v. Durham City Council, ex p. Robinson, The Times,* January 31, 1992 (*held*: it is not possible to create public law jurisdiction by consent).

[61] See Chap. 6.

some private law right is also being asserted.[62] However, there are still no expressly defined exceptions beyond Lord Diplock's categories and the law remains uncertain.

Cases involving substantial factual dispute are, prima facie, more suitable for trial by action than judicial review.[63] It remains to be seen, however, whether the courts will continue to take that view, having regard to the wider use of cross-examination theoretically envisaged under Order 53. The raising of public law issues in a private law forum seems inherently unobjectionable where either private law rights are at stake or a criminal charge is being pursued. Unhappily, the courts have still not resolved many of the difficulties (see paras. 6–002—6–006). Finally, it has been suggested that cases requiring special expertise might be more suitable for trial by action rather than judicial review.[64]

It is to be hoped that the evolutionary approach favoured by Lord Diplock in *O'Reilly v. Mackman* will eventually produce a greater degree of clarity as to the type of case which must be determined by recourse to the judicial review procedure. In the meantime, having regard to the strict time limits appertaining to Order 53, it will be a brave applicant who commences a claim involving a predominantly public law element by action rather than by application for leave to apply for judicial review.

THE JUSTICE-ALL SOULS REVIEW

In 1978, soon after the implementation of the above mentioned reforms **1–021** of Order 53, a committee comprising members of JUSTICE and All Souls College, Oxford, was established, on an unofficial basis, to undertake "a full-scale examination of the existing deficiencies in the administrative law of the United Kingdom".[65]

The Committee's report ("Administrative Justice – Some Necessary Reforms") was published in 1988. The recommendations go much further than those of the Law Commission in 1976, although they have not been implemented.

The Committee's principal suggestions for reform in relation to judicial review are as follows:

    (a) *O'Reilly v. Mackman* should be reconsidered by the House of Lords. Parliament should decide whether there are any circumstances in which a plaintiff should be obliged to use Order 53 and be debarred from proceeding by action or originating summons.

[62] See, *e.g. Roy v. Kensington and Chelsea Family Practitioner Committee* [1992] 1 A.C. 624. *Mercury Communications v. Director General of Telecommunications, The Times,* February 10, 1995.
[63] See *R. v. I.R.C. ex p. Rossminster* [1980] A.C. 952 at pp. 1025–1026, *per* Lord Scarman; *R. v. Jenner* [1983] 1 W.L.R. 873.
[64] See, *e.g. Re Tillmire Common, Heslington* [1982] 2 All E.R. 615.
[65] The words are taken from a JUSTICE-All Souls Discussion Paper dated April 1981 referred to at p. 1 of "Administrative Justice – Some Necessary Reforms" (Oxford 1988).

(b) The term "public law" should cease to be used as the key to identifying those cases which can appropriately be dealt with by Order 53 procedure.

(c) The requirement to obtain leave to apply for judicial review should be abandoned.

(d) The delay provisions in Order 53 should be repealed and the matter solely governed by the test laid down in section 31(6) of the Supreme Court Act 1981.[66]

(e) There should be statutory grounds for judicial review.

(f) There should be a more liberal attitude than at present to discovery, interrogatories and cross-examination under Order 53.

(g) Proceedings wrongly commenced by writ should be able to be ordered to continue as if begun under Order 53.

(h) All questions of standing should be decided by the court. The judge should have regard to the whole circumstances of the case and ask himself whether the action is justifiable in the public interest in the light of these circumstances.

The above proposals provide a starting point for discussion. Their very comprehensiveness shows how much more development is likely to occur in this area of law in the future.

TOWARDS THE FUTURE: THE LAW COMMISSION REVISITED

1–022   In June 1991 the Lord Chancellor approved, by way of inclusion in the Law Commission's fifth programme of law reform, a recommendation of the Commission to the following effect:

"(a) that the procedures and forms of relief available by way of judicial review be examined, with particular regard to:
(i) the effect of the decision in *O'Reilly v. Mackman* [1983] 2 A.C. 237;
(ii) the current position on time limits governing judicial review;
(iii) the circumstances and form in which interim relief should be available;
(iv) discovery and the principles applicable to its grant;
(v) whether the rules as to standing require further development;
(vi) whether claims for restitution should be able to be joined in applications for judicial review;
(vii) the extent of the power to award costs;
(viii) the right of appeal against the refusal of a substantive application for judicial review;

---

[66] For which, see para. 2–032.

> (ix) whether there should be a power in the High Court in relation to proceedings before inferior courts, tribunals and other bodies, to substitute its own order for that impugned;
>
> (b) that the procedures governing statutory appeals and applications to the High Court from the decisions of inferior courts, tribunals and other bodies, should be examined, and in particular whether there should be special Crown Office rules of procedure."

It is apparent that the Law Commission's remit was wider than that accorded to it in 1969. From the practitioner's perspective the most significant aspect of this remit is that it engaged not merely the judicial review procedure but also other forms of process, often raising issues of public law, with which judicial review can become confused and which are also processed in the Crown Office. The different procedures have developed piecemeal and there is not always consistency of logic. The relationship between these procedures and Order 53 is separately considered.[67]

On October 26, 1994 the Law Commission published its long awaited proposals.[68] An extract of these proposals and draft forms suggested by the Law Commission is reproduced in Appendix F.

OUTLINE OF THE RECOMMENDATIONS

The Commission's recommendations fall into two broad categories. **1–023**
These are:

(1) Procedural reforms.
(2) Public interest reforms.

(1) Procedural reforms

The most important of the Law Commission's recommendations are these:

> (1) Formerly, improperly commenced judicial review proceedings could be converted to writ actions but there was no equivalent machinery for converting a writ action into proceedings for judicial review. The Law Commission now recommends that there should be.
>
> (2) It is proposed that the term "leave to apply for judicial review" should be removed. Instead, there is to be a "preliminary consideration" stage. This will be conducted on paper. Oral hearings will only be permitted in exceptional cases where interim relief is sought or such hearing is considered by the Crown Office or a nominated judge to be desirable in the interests of justice.
>
> (3) As part of the preliminary consideration the nominated judge may, where he considers it appropriate, issue a "request for

---

[67] See Chap. 6.
[68] *Administrative Law: Judicial Review and Statutory Appeals*, Law Com. No. 226, H.C. 669.

information" to the proposed respondent. Where this occurs, the Crown Office will be requested to send a copy of the applicant's Form 86A and the applicant will be required to supply a copy of the affidavit in support together with the exhibits thereto. The proposed respondent will have 14 days to answer the request. The answer will be supplied to the applicant who will then have a further 10 days to respond. The judge may, thereafter, order an oral hearing or reach a decision on the submitted information.

(4) There will, as previously, be a right to renew the application for leave for oral hearing, but the Law Commission recommends that there should be express provision for the making of costs orders against the unsuccessful party on such renewed hearing.

(5) The test for whether the case should proceed beyond the preliminary consideration stage is no longer whether the case is arguable but, rather, whether there is a serious issue which ought to be determined.

(6) The current time limit for judicial review should, as before, consist of an outer time-limit of three months with an overriding requirement of promptness even within that period. An application ought not to be allowed to proceed to a substantive hearing unless the applicant has exhausted all alternative legal remedies or demonstrates that judicial review is an appropriate remedy. For this reason, the court should take account of the fact that an alternative remedy was being pursued as a good reason why an application made after 3 months should be allowed to proceed to a substantive hearing.

(7) Claims for restitution, debt and interest should be allowed to be included in an application for judicial review on the same private law basis as damages may, currently, be sought.

(8) Interim relief should be able to be granted before the preliminary consideration of an application has been concluded.

(9) There should be no changes to the scope of the discovery rules under Order 53.

(10) The names of the remedies available on judicial review should be changed to reflect modern terminology. In future (apart from declarations and injunctions) there should be quashing orders, prohibiting orders and mandatory orders.

(11) Applicants should only be required to pursue judicial review proceedings where the matter is solely one of public law.

(12) Homelessness cases should be taken out of judicial review. There should be a right of appeal on a point of law to a court or independent tribunal.

(2) Public interest reforms

The Law Commission's principal recommendations are as follows:

(1) An applicant's standing should not be confined to "sufficient interest". The test for standing should be whether the court is

satisfied that the applicant has been or would be adversely affected, or the High Court considers that it is in the public interest for him to make the application.

(2) Unincorporated associations, such as pressure groups, should be allowed to make applications for judicial review in their own name.

(3) The Court should have power to grant both interim and advisory declarations. Advisory declarations should only be granted where the point concerned is one of general public importance.

(4) Costs should be available from central funds where a case is allowed to proceed to a substantive hearing on the basis of a public interest challenge or an advisory declaration.

(5) Legal aid should be able to be granted where the Legal Aid Board considers that there is a wider public interest in having the matter heard.

2. THE PROCESS OF REVIEW

GROUNDS FOR REVIEW

2–001   This chapter is concerned with the process by which the High Court reviews the decisions of public bodies under Order 53.

In *Council of Civil Service Unions v. Minister for the Civil Service*[1] ("the G.C.H.Q. case"), Lord Diplock observed[2] that:

> "one can conveniently classify under three heads the grounds on which administrative action is subject to control by judicial review. The first ground I would call 'illegality', the second 'irrationality' and the third 'procedural impropriety'. That is not to say that further development on a case by case basis may not in course of time add further grounds."

Before turning to the specific heads of review adumbrated by Lord Diplock, as well as other possible grounds that have emerged since the G.C.H.Q. case, it is necessary to deal with some distinctions that may give rise to confusion.

A preliminary distinction: errors of law and fact

2–002   Most errors of law are now susceptible to judicial review. The same is not, and has never been, true of mistakes of fact. Generally, if a public body gives undue weight to a particular piece of evidence this will not, by itself, afford a remedy under Order 53.

As Lord Brightman observed in *R. v. Hillingdon L.B., ex p. Puhlhofer*[3]:

> "Where the existence or non-existence of a fact is left to the judgment and discretion of a public body and that fact involves a broad spectrum ranging from the obvious to the debatable to the just conceivable, it is the duty of the court to leave the decision of that fact to the public body to whom Parliament has entrusted the decision-making power ...".

To this latter principle, however, there are some important qualifications which, in practice, tend to blur the conceptual distinction between errors of law and fact. Thus:

---

[1] [1985] A.C. 374.

[2] *ibid.* at p. 410. See, also, *per* Lord Roskill at pp. 414E–H and 415B–C. To similar effect see *R. v. Secretary of State for the Environment, ex p. Nottinghamshire C.C.* [1986] A.C. 240, *per* Lord Scarman at p. 249D–E; *R. v. Secretary of State for the Home Department, ex p. Brind* [1991] 1 A.C. 696 at p. 750D, *per* Lord Roskill.

[3] [1986] A.C. 484 at p. 518D–E.

(a) Whilst erroneous findings of fact may fall within an authority's jurisdiction[4] and, hence, not be obviously amenable to judicial review, reliance upon an erroneous factual conclusion may itself offend against principles of legality or rationality.[5]

(b) If there is no evidence to support a conclusion, there is a necessary error of law in the decision reached.[6] It has been cogently argued that the expression "no evidence" does not mean a complete lack of evidence but covers any case where the assembled evidence is not reasonably capable of supporting the finding.[7] If that is correct, the precise point at which an error of fact becomes assimilated to one of law may, in many instances, be difficult to determine.[8]

(c) A decision-maker is not, necessarily, empowered to reach erroneous findings of fact about matters relevant to the existence of his jurisdiction "for otherwise [he] could by [his] own error give [himself] powers which were never conferred . . . by Parliament."[9] The High Court has shown itself to be especially zealous of correcting errors of jurisdictional fact in matters relating to the liberty of the subject[10];

Two obsolete distinctions

For a long time it was believed that judicial review did not lie in either of **2–003** the following circumstances:

(a) in respect of errors of law made within jurisdiction,[11] except where the error was apparent on the face of the record[12];

(b) where a public body was acting administratively as opposed to judicially.[13]

Both these distinctions have lost their practical effect.[14] The reasons for

---

[4] See especially *R. v. Nat Bell Liquors Ltd.* [1922] 2 A.C. 128 at p. 152, *per* Lord Sumner. Note though that this is a decision of the Privy Council and is therefore *obiter*.

[5] Lord Brightman in *Puhlhofer*, n. 3 above makes this clear by adding to the cited extract "save in a case where it is obvious that the public body, consciously or unconsciously, are acting perversely." See, also, *e.g. R. v. Legal Aid (No. 10) Area Committee, ex p. McKenna* [1990] C.O.D. 358.

[6] See, especially, *Edwards v. Bairstow* [1956] A.C. 14. Note, too: *Din (Taj) v. Wandsworth L.B.C.* [1983] 1 A.C. 657 at p. 664H *per* Lord Wilberforce; *R. v. Hillingdon L.B.C. ex p. Islam (Tafazzul)* [1983] 1 A.C. 688 at p. 708D and G *per* Lord Wilberforce, and at p. 717G *per* Lord Lowry.

[7] See Wade and Forsyth, *Administrative Law*, (7th ed., 1994) at p. 312.

[8] For a contrary view, defending the "analytic integrity" of *Edwards v. Bairstow*, n. 6 above, see Emery and Smythe, "Error of Law in Administrative Law" [1984] 100 L.Q.R. 612 *et seq.*

[9] See Wade and Forsyth, *op. cit.* n. 7 above, at p. 286.

[10] *R. v. Secretary of State for the Home Department, ex p. Khawaja* [1984] A.C. 74, overruling *R. v. Secretary of State for the Home Department, ex p. Zamir* [1980] A.C. 930.

[11] See, *e.g. Racecourse Betting Control Board v. Secretary of State for Air* [1944] Ch. 114.

[12] *R. v. Northumberland Compensation Appeal Tribunal, ex p. Shaw* [1952] 1 K.B. 338.

[13] See, *e.g. Franklin v. Minister of Town and Country Planning* [1948] A.C. 87.

[14] For the relevant case law see paras. 3–005—3–007.

this are discussed in para. 3–005, in the context of the development of the prerogative order of certiorari.

Errors of law susceptible to judicial review

2–004   The modern position appears to be as set out by Lord Denning M.R. in *Pearlman v. Governors of Harrow School*,[15] where he stated that:

> "No court or tribunal has any jurisidction to make an error of law on which the decision of the case depends. If it makes such an error, it goes outside its jurisdiction."

So, too, in *R. v. Hull University Visitor, ex p. Page*,[16] Lord Browne-Wilkinson clarified that:

> "the mere existence of a mistake of law made at some earlier stage does not vitiate the actual decision made: what must be shown is a relevant error of law, i.e. an error in the actual making of the decision which affected the decision itself."[17]

ILLEGALITY

2–005   In one sense, all the grounds justifying the use of judicial review constitute an attack on the basis of contended illegality.[18]

Illegality in its narrower form, however, describes a straightforward excess of public powers. The question for determination is whether the respondent has clearly done something that was not permitted by statute or otherwise in public law.[19] If so, judicial review will lie.

In the G.C.H.Q. case Lord Diplock defined illegality as meaning that "the decision-maker must understand correctly the law that regulates his decision-making power and must give effect to it".[20]

Thus understood, analytically, illegality as a discrete head of judicial review is founded on the closely related principles of *ultra vires* and irrelevancy.

---

[15] [1979] Q.B. 56. See also: *Re Racal Communications Ltd* [1981] A.C. 374 at 383, *per* Lord Diplock.

[16] [1993] A.C. 682.

[17] n. 16 at p. 702D.

[18] For the relationship between procedural impropriety and illegality, see *e.g. Ridge v. Baldwin* [1964] A.C. 40 at p. 80, *per* Reid L.J.: "The body with the power to decide cannot lawfully proceed to make a decision until it has afforded to the person affected a proper opportunity to state his case."

[19] Consider, e.g., *R. v. Coventry Airport, ex p. Phoenix Aviation The Times*, April 17, 1995 (no power in a public authority to submit to unlawful pressure groups and, thereby, subvert the rule of law). Excess of jurisdiction can of course occur by a refusal to exercise jurisdiction at all. See *R. v. Clerkenwell Metropolitan Stipendiary Magistrates, ex p. D.P.P.* [1984] Q.B. 821.

[20] See n. 1 at p. 410F. See, also, *per* Lord Roskill *ibid.* at p. 414F–G.

Illegality: ultra vires

Many instances of illegality are encompassed by the doctrine of *ultra*   **2–006**
vires, which has been called "the central principle of administrative law"[21]
and restricts a public authority from acting outside its powers. Examples of
the *ultra vires* doctrine in operation include the following:

(a) In *Padfield v. Minister of Agriculture, Fisheries and Food*[22] the
    Minister's refusal to refer a complaint to a Committee of
    Investigation was held to be unlawful as being contrary to the
    policy and objects of the relevant statute.
(b) In *R. v. Committee of Lloyd's, ex p. Posgate*[23] the Committee of
    Lloyd's was held to have exceeded its powers in requiring the
    suspension of an underwriter contrary to the Lloyd's Act 1871.
(c) In *Brunyate v. I.L.E.A.*,[24] I.L.E.A.'s removal of school governors
    because of their failure to support I.L.E.A.'s educational policy
    was held to be unlawful as usurping the governors' independent
    function under the relevant statute.
(d) In *R. v. Thames Magistrates' Court, ex p. Clapton Cash and
    Carry*,[25] it was held that the magistrate had erred in law in ordering
    the destruction of food "unlikely to become" unfit for human
    consumption, but had power only to order the destruction of food
    which was unfit for human consumption.

As the above examples illustrate, the ambit of *ultra vires* is, largely,
dependent on statutory construction[26] as applied to the facts of each case,
and few general rules can be laid down. The doctrine is further considered
in relation to local authorities (see Chap. 12).

Illegality: irrelevancy

The classic exposition of the irrelevancy principle is that laid down by   **2–007**
Lord Greene M.R. in *Associated Provincial Picture Houses Ltd. v. Wednesbury Corp.*[27] The case involved consideration of the discretion of local
authorities under a statutory power to allow cinemas to open on Sundays.

---

[21] See Wade and Forsyth, *op. cit.*, n. 7 above at p. 41.
[22] [1968] A.C. 997, especially at p. 1030B–D and pp. 1032G–1033A, *per* Lord Reid; p.
1054G, *per* Lord Pearce; p. 1060G, *per* Lord Upjohn. *Padfield* has been identified as a
"landmark" case (see: *O'Reilly v. Mackman* [1983] 2 A.C. 237 at p. 280A, *per* Lord
Diplock) but it is, on analysis, a facet of the *ultra vires* principle.
[23] *The Times*, January 12, 1983.
[24] [1989] 1 W.L.R. 542.
[25] [1989] C.O.D. 518.
[26] The process of statutory construction now permits reference to Parliamentary materials
where (a) legislation is ambiguous, obscure or leads to an absurdity; (b) the material relied
upon consists of one or more statements by a minister or other promoter of the bill together
with (if necessary) such other Parliamentary material necessary to understand such
statements and their effect; (c) the statements relied upon are clear (see: *Pepper v. Hart*
[1993] A.C. 593).
[27] [1948] 1 K.B. 223.

In the course of his judgment Lord Greene made statements of principle that have been accepted as being generally applicable to the Order 53 review process.

As to irrelevancy he said this:

> "the Court is entitled to investigate the action of the local authority with a view to seeing whether it has taken into account matters which it ought not to take into account, or conversely, has refused to take into account matters which it ought to take into account."[28]

Irrelevancy may take many forms. Apart from expressly considering extraneous matters, the respondent may omit relevant factors in arriving at his decision. Usually, indeed, the adherence to irrelevance implies the omission of relevance. Sometimes a perfectly legitimate consideration may be given undue prominence so that, in context, it becomes irrelevant.[29] Decisions taken in bad faith (happily rare) or for improper purposes[30] are often treated as an independent head of review but they are, also, part of the irrelevancy principle. Frequenctly, of course, the fact of irrelevancy may render a decision irrational under the residual category in *Wednesbury* (see below).

Generally, decisions are treated with a degree of latitude where allegations of irrelevance are made in Order 53 applications. Thus, the omission of a single relevant factor will often not be enough to justify judicial review.[31] Also, where it is argued that a power has been used for an improper purpose the court is likely to examine whether the stated or dominant purpose has been achieved and, if so, may refuse relief.[32] Probably the more open-ended the discretion, the more difficult it will be to establish irrelevancy.[33]

The fact that a consideration may be relevant does not mean that a

---

[28] n. 26 above at pp. 233–234.

[29] See, *e.g. R. v. Police Complaints Board, ex p. Madden* [1983] 1 W.L.R. 447 (over reliance on "fairness"); *South Oxfordshire D.C. v. Secretary of State for the Environment* [1981] 1 W.L.R. 1092 (over reliance on long-expired planning permission as "vitally material consideration").

[30] See, *e.g. R. v. Ealing L.B.C., ex p. Times Newspapers Ltd.* (1986) 85 L.G.R. 316 (held: local authority ban on provision of certain resources to libraries was unlawful since motivated by ulterior political object which was irrelevant to statutory duty); *Congreve v. Home Office* [1976] Q.B. 629 (held: discretionary power of licence revocation abused where used as a threat to extract money which the Executive was not empowered to demand).

[31] See *R. v. Barnet and Camden Rent Tribunal, ex p. Frey Investments Ltd.* [1972] 2 Q.B. 342. Or, *semble*, the taking into account of a single irrelevant factor if the decision would have been the same. See: *R. v. Broadcasting Complaints Commission, ex p. Owen* [1985] 2 W.L.R. 1025; *R. v. Secretary of State for Social Services, ex p. Wellcome Foundation Ltd.* [1987] 1 W.L.R. 1166.

[32] See *R. v. Brixton Prison Governor, ex p. Soblen* [1963] 2 Q.B. 243. Though, *aliter* if the unauthorised purpose was dominant; see *Hanks v. Minister of Housing and Local Government* [1963] 1 Q.B. 999; *R. v. I.L.E.A., ex p. Westminster C.C.* [1986] 1 W.L.R. 28.

[33] *R. v. Criminal Injuries Compensation Board, ex p. Thompstone* [1984] 1 W.L.R. 1234. For a striking example in the field of planning law see *R. v. Westminster City Council, ex p. Monahan* [1990] 1 Q.B. 87. (held: financial considerations are relevant to the determination of a planning application).

decision-maker is, necessarily, required to take it into account. In this context Lord Scarman, in *Re Findlay*[34] cited, with approval, the observation of Cooke J. in *Creednz Inc v. Governor-General*[35] that:

"What has to be emphasized is that it is only when the statute expressly or impliedly identifies considerations required to be taken into account by the authority as a matter of legal obligation that the court holds a decision invalid on the ground now invoked. It is not enough that a consideration is one that may properly be taken into account, nor even that it is one which many people, including the court itself, would have taken into account if they had to make the decision .... There will be some matters so obviously material to a decision on a particular project that anything short of direct consideration of them by the ministers ... would not be in accordance with the intention of the Act."

With that caveat in mind, the following cases illustrate the irrelevancy principle as a form of illegality:

(a) In *Roberts v. Hopwood*[36] a borough council overpaying its staff was motivated by irrelevant philanthropic concerns and was, in effect, making gifts rather than paying wages. The House of Lords also held that the authority had failed to consider relevant matters such as the costs of living and comparable wages paid by other authorities.

(b) In *R. v. Lewisham L.B.C., ex p. Shell U.K. Ltd*[37] the respondent council's boycott of Shell's products because of their South African connection was held to be unlawful by reason of irrelevant considerations or motives.

(c) In *R. v. Barnet L.B.C., ex p. Pardes House School Ltd*[38] a Divisional Court held that the Council had erroneously omitted a relevant consideration, namely the educational policy contained in the Development Plan, when disposing of land under section 123 of the Local Government Act 1972.

[34] [1985] A.C. 318 at pp. 333H–334C.
[35] [1981] 1 N.Z.L.R. 172 at p. 183. The borderline between a material error of law on the one hand (sufficient to justify review) and the exercise of discretion with possible immaterial error of law (insufficient to justify review) is exemplified by decisions such as *R. v. Independent Television Commission, ex p. T.S.W. Broadcasting Ltd, The Times*, March 30, 1992 and *R. v. Hillingdon L.B.C., ex p. Puhlhofer*, n. 3 above.
[36] [1925] A.C. 578. So, too, moral and ethical objections to staghunting do not confer an unfettered discretion under s.122 of the Local Government Act 1972; see: *R. v. Somerset C.C., ex p. Fewings, The Times*, March 23, 1995 (ban on staghunting quashed).
[37] [1988] 1 All E.R. 938.
[38] [1989] C.O.D. 512.

IRRATIONALITY

2–008   Not all errors of law are properly classifiable as being straightforward breaches of the *ultra vires* and irrelevancy principles.[39] Yet all material errors of law made by public bodies in the course of reaching their decision are liable to judicial review.[40]

It is in respect of such cases that the principle of irrationality, or inherent unreasonableness, first enunciated in *Associated Provincial Picture Houses Ltd. v. Wednesbury Corp.*,[41] has particular importance. As to this, Lord Greene M.R. observed, in *Wednesbury*, that even if a decision-maker has not ostensibly breached the irrelevancy principle:

> "it may still be possible to say that, although the local authority have kept within the four corners of the matters which they ought to consider, they have nevertheless come to a conclusion so unreasonable that no reasonable authority could ever have come to it. In such a case, again, I think the Court can interfere."[42]

In the G.C.H.Q. case,[43] Lord Diplock, discussing irrationality, said this:

> "By 'irrationality' I mean what can now be succinctly referred to as 'Wednesbury unreasonableness' .... It applies to a decision which is so outrageous in its defiance of logic or of accepted moral standards that no sensible person who had applied his mind to the question to be decided could have arrived at it. Whether a decision falls within this category is a question that judges by their training and experience should be well equipped to answer, or else there would be something badly wrong with our judicial system."[44]

Irrationality, in this sense, plainly includes other heads of review such as decisions that are *ultra vires*, or based on a misdirection of law or arrived at on the basis of "no evidence",[45] in circumstances where the excess of power complained of also reflects irrationality.

Additionally, however, there is the completely unreasonable or perverse decision-making envisaged by Lord Greene M.R. in *Wednesbury*, where no

---

[39] For the fluidity of conceptual classification, even within those categories, see, *e.g.* Taylor "Judicial Review of Improper Purposes and Irrelevant Considerations" (1976) 35 C.L.J. 272. See, also [1987] P.L. 368, J. Jowell and A. Lester.

[40] See *Re Racal Communications Ltd* [1981] A.C. 374 (*per* Lord Diplock).

[41] See n. 27 above.

[42] See n. 27 above at p. 234.

[43] See n. 1 above.

[44] *ibid.* at p. 410G–H. See, also, *per* Lord Roskill at p. 414G. Whilst the determination of whether a decision is irrational is a matter of law to be determined objectively (see, *e.g. R. v. Secretary of State for the Environment, ex p. Hammersmith & Fulham L.B.C.* [1991] 1 A.C. 521, *per* Lord Bridge at p. 593E), that is by no means the same as inviting the Court to substitute its own "objectively reasonable" decision (see: *R. v. Secretary of State for the Home Department, ex p. Brind* [1991] 1 A.C. 696, *per* Lord Ackner at pp. 757H–758B).

[45] For the meaning of this expression, see para. 2–002 above.

discrete error of law can be identified, as exemplified by the decision to dismiss a teacher because of the colour of her hair.[46]

The modern doctrine of irrationality goes somewhat further than this. Now that most misdirections of law are categorised as jurisdictional error,[47] a number of cases turn on sophisticated statutory construction before a conclusion of unreasonableness is, *ex post factor*, arrived at.

In general, courts are no longer deterred by subjectively worded statutes leaving discretion to the decision-maker, and seem prepared to expand *Wednesbury* to increase control over public power. The following cases illustrate the borderline between reasonable and unreasonable decision-making in this sense:

(a) In *Lonrho plc v. Secretary of State for Trade and Industry*[48] the House of Lords upheld decisions of the Secretary of State to withhold publication of a report by inspectors appointed by him to investigate alleged fraud in connection with a take-over bid, and his decision not to refer a merger to the Monopolies and Mergers Commission. In both instances it was held that the Secretary of State's decision had been exercised rationally and on advice after consideration of all the arguments.

(b) In *Wheeler v. Leicester City Council*[49] a Council resolution to ban Leicester Rugby Football Club from its property for not putting pressure upon three of its players not to participate in a tour of South Africa was held to be irrational in the *Wednesbury* sense.[50]

(c) In *R. v. Liverpool JJ., ex p. R.M. Broudie & Co. (a firm)*,[51] a clerk's refusal to supply duplicate legal aid orders was considered to be *Wednesbury* unreasonable.

(d) In *R. v. St Albans Crown Court, ex p. Cinnamond*[52] a disqualification of 18 months for careless driving was quashed as being irrational on the basis that the sentence exceeded the ambit of discretion to such an extent that there was a necessary error of law.

(e) In *Backhouse v. Lambeth L.B.C.*[53] rent increases from £7 to £18,000 were held to be wholly unreasonable when made for the purpose of evading certain statutory provisions.

[46] This was the example that Lord Greene M.R. gave based on the decision in *Short v. Poole Corp.* [1926] Chr. 66. For a modern instance see *Ogwr B.C. v. Baker* [1989] C.O.D. 489.
[47] See para. 3–005.
[48] [1989] 1 W.L.R. 525. See, also, *R. v. Ministry of Defence, ex p. Smith, The Times*, June 13, 1995 (*held*: ban on homosexual servicemen was not irrational).
[49] [1985] A.C. 1054.
[50] See n. 49 at p. 1079B, *per* Lord Roskill. The challenge also succeeded under the head of *ultra vires*.
[51] *The Times*, April 6, 1994.
[52] [1981] Q.B. 480.
[53] (1972) 116 S.J. 802. *cf.*, though, *Luby v. Newcastle under Lyme Corp.* [1964] 2 Q.B. 64 at p. 72 (held: increase of rents not reviewable merely because of failure to discriminate between different tenants' means); *Smith v. Cardiff Corp. (No. 2)* [1955] Ch. 159 (held: rents not reviewable even though they subsidised tenants at ratepayers' expense).

Unlawful limitation of discretion

2–009   The illegality and irrationality grounds for judicial review regulate the manner in which a body, amenable to review, exercises its public law powers.

Three further principles circumscribe the way in which discretionary powers may be exercised. Breach of any of these principles may result in a decision being held to be unlawful or irrational.

The principles are that:

(a) Discretion must not be fettered.

(b) Decision-making must not be delegated unless delegation is authorised.

(c) A decision-maker must not adhere to a fixed policy without regard to the circumstances of the individual case.

Fettering discretion

2–010   It is well established that discretion lies only with the person entrusted with it and that it must be freely exercised. Failure to observe these principles is both an abuse and a fettering of such discretion.

The usual manifestation of this problem is where improper delegation occurs (para. 2–011), or where the decision-maker blindly follows a particular policy without regard to the individual case (para. 2–012). A quite different situation arises where a public body incurs obligations (or apparent obligations) in private law and then argues that it is constrained to act in a certain way. This differs from the principles discussed below, in that discretion is not generally purported to have been exercised. Much of the case law is concerned with local authorities and is, therefore, separately examined in Chapter 12.

It is also a fettering of discretion for a public body to find itself not to exercise a statutory power. This occurred in *R. v. Secretary of State for the Home Department, ex p. Fire Brigades Union*[53a] where the Secretary of State was held to have his discretion by formulating a non-statutory Criminal Injuries Compensation Scheme rather than (as he was required to do) continue to consider exercising the power to implement the statutory scheme under the Criminal Justice Act 1988.

Improper delegation of decision-making

2–011   The prohibition against unauthorised delegation is illustrated by the facts of *Barnard v. National Dock Labour Board*.[54] A docker was suspended from work without pay in the course of a trade dispute. The power of suspension was exercised by the port manager rather than by the London Dock Board to whom such power had been lawfully delegated. The House

---

[53a] [1995] 2 W.L.R. 464. The House of Lords (per Lord Browne-Wilkinson) also considered this to be an abuse of prerogative power.

[54] [1953] 2 Q.B. 18.

of Lords granted a declaration to avoid the suspension on the basis of improper delegation by the Dock Board to the port manager.

To similar effect is the Divisional Court decision in *R. v. Director of Public Prosecutions, ex p. Association of First Division Civil Servants.*[55] There, it was held that a scheme whereby non-qualified lawyers became responsible for the screening of most summary offences was unlawful because it resulted in cases not being dealt with by the Crown Prosecution Service under s.3(2) of the Prosecution of Offences Act 1985, one of the main purposes of which was to bring an independent legal mind to bear on each prosecution. As such there had been unlawful delegation by the D.P.P.

Many other cases exemplify the rule in its straightforward application.[56] There are, nonetheless, important qualifications. Thus:

(a) In numerous instances delegation is permitted by statute, either expressly or by necessary implication. This is especially so in the sphere of local authority decision-making (see para. 12–003).

(b) A public authority may rely heavily on conclusions reached by a subordinate body.[57]

(c) In some limited instances the courts have come to accept that it is impracticable to apply the delegation rule literally. In *Att.-Gen., ex rel. McWhirter v. I.B.A.,*[58] for example, it was held that members of the I.B.A. did not have to view every programme to comply with its statutory discretion relating to television output.

(d) Ministers of the Crown are, perhaps, *sui generis.* In the absence of contrary statutory intent[59] the High Court is unlikely to order judicial review of a decision because the relevant minister has not made the decision personally.[60] Even here, however, delegation by a minister is probably subject to challenge on the basis of irrationality.[61] The attempt to systematise classes of cases which a minister is obliged to decide personally has been deprecated.[62] It is not, however, permissible for one minister to transfer decision-making, as it were laterally, to another minister.[63]

---

[55] (1988) 138 New L.J. 158.

[56] See, *e.g. Vine v. National Dock Labour Board* [1957] A.C. 488; *Ratnagopal v. Att.-Gen.* [1970] A.C. 974; *Allingham v. Minister of Agriculture* [1948] 1 All E.R. 780; *R. v. Liverpool City Council, ex p. Professional Association of Teachers* (1984) 82 L.G.R. 648.

[57] As, *e.g.* in *R. v. G.L.C., ex p. Blackburn* [1976] 1 W.L.R. 550, and the earlier decision in *Mills v. L.C.C.* [1925] 1 K.B. 213, *cf., Ellis v. Dubowski* [1921] 3 K.B. 621.

[58] [1973] Q.B. 629.

[59] As, *e.g.* in the Immigration Act 1971, s.13(5).

[60] See, especially, *Carltona Ltd v. Commissioners of Works* [1943] 2 All E.R. 560; *R. v. Secretary of State for the Home Department, ex p. Oladehinde* [1991] A.C. 254; *R. v. Secretary of State for the Home Department, ex p. Doody* [1994] 1 A.C. 531.

[61] *R. v. Secretary of State for the Home Department, ex p. Oladehinde*, n. 60 above; *R. v. Secretary of State for the Home Department, ex p. Doody,* n. 60 above.

[62] *Re Golden Chemical Products* [1976] Ch. 300.

[63] *Lavender & Son Ltd v. M.H.L.G.* [1970] 1 W.L.R. 1231.

Adherence to a fixed policy

2–012   Decisions are often taken against a background of general policy. If the policy is lawful and is applied fairly, judicial review will not be appropriate.[64] As Lord Scarman observed, in the context of the Home Secretary's parole policy, in *Re Findlay*[65]:

> "the most that a convicted prisoner can legitimately expect is that his case will be examined individually in the light of whatever policy the Secretary of State sees fit to adopt provided always that the adopted policy is a lawful exercise of the discretion conferred upon him by the statute. Any other view would entail the conclusion that the unfettered discretion conferred by the statute upon the minister can in some cases be restricted so as to hamper, or even to prevent, changes of policy."

The courts have, however, frequently shown themselves prepared to investigate the formulation and application of particular policies with a view to determining whether there is an operative fetter, as the following cases amply demonstrate:

(a)   In *R. v. Forest Betting Licensing Committee, ex p. Noquet*,[66] an unannounced policy of a licensing committee of insisting that an applicant for a betting office licence must have a legal interest in the premises was not justified by statute. Accordingly, the committee's discretion to adjourn the application had been fettered by adherence to a policy which was unlawful and the decision to adjourn for a legal interest to be shown was quashed.

(b)   In *R. v. Chief Constable of South Wales, ex p. Merrick*[67] a Divisional Court held that a policy, adopted by the police, to restrict access to a solicitor by a person remanded in custody was unlawful as interfering with a common law right of access supplemental to the statutory scheme under the Police and Criminal Evidence Act.

(c)   In *R. v. Oxford, ex p. Levey*[68] the Court of Appeal, whilst upholding the formulated policy of the Chief Constable of policing Toxteth, suggested that there were circumstances in which a policy ought to be reconsidered in the light of experience.

---

[64] A policy will not be quashed as unlawful where the evidence shows only that such policy might offend the law in individual cases, depending on the method of its implementation. See *R. v. Hammersmith and Fulham London Borough Council, ex p. N.A.L.G.O.* (1991) I.R.L.R. 249. See, also: *R. v. Law Society, ex p. Reigate Projects* [1993] 1 W.L.R. 1531.

[65] n. 34 above at p. 338E–F. *Re Findlay* was a case where the parole policy was held to be lawful. In *R. v. Secretary of State for the Home Department, ex p. Doody* n. 60 above, however, the House of Lords held that the policy was being *applied* unfairly.

[66] *The Times*, June 21, 1988. Another instance of a policy held to be unlawful as being outwith the relevant statutory criteria is afforded by *R. v. Secretary of State for the Environment, ex p. Lancashire C.C., The Times*, February 3, 1994.

[67] (1994) 144 N.L.J. 423.

[68] October 30, 1986 (unrep.).

(d) In *Sagnata Investments v. Norwich Corp.*[69] the Court of Appeal held that there was no factual basis for a policy that was formulated on the premises that amusement arcades would be harmful to young persons and, on that ground, upheld the applicants' claim for licences.

(e) In *R. v. Port of London Authority, ex p. Kynoch Ltd.*,[70] Lord Bankes considered the legality of applying an otherwise lawful policy. He stated as follows:

"There are on the one hand cases where a tribunal in the honest exercise of its discretion had adopted a policy, and, without refusing to hear an applicant, intimates to him what its policy is, and that after hearing him it will in accordance with its policy decide against him, unless there is something exceptional in his case . . . if the policy has been adopted for reasons which the tribunal may legitimately entertain, no objection could be taken to such a course. On the other hand there are cases where a tribunal has passed a rule, or come to a determination, not to hear any application of a particular character by whomsoever made. There is a wide distinction to be drawn between these two classes."

(f) In *Stringer v. Minister of Housing and Local Government*[71] Cooke J. observed that a policy may be susceptible to judicial review if reliance thereon prevents consideration of "all the issues which are relevant to each individual case as it comes up for decision." This notwithstanding, there may be cases where a policy is sufficiently well established as to approximate to a rule.[72]

(g) Sometimes, departure from a lawful policy may itself be unlawful. In *R. v. Secretary of State for the Home Department, ex p. Ruddock*,[73] for example, Taylor J. held that the Secretary of State was bound by a duty of fairness not to depart from published guidelines on the issuing of warrants for telephone tapping, albeit that the applicant was unaware of the terms of such guidelines. This is, in a sense, the converse of policy operating as a fetter on discretion and connotes that policy can occasionally act to circumscribe discretion, or at least to set limits on the extent to which discretion may be exercised without affording an opportunity to an applicant of making representations as to why existing policy ought not to be altered.[74]

---

[69] [1972] 2 Q.B. 614.

[70] [1919] 1 K.B. 176 at p. 183.

[71] [1970] 1 W.L.R. 1281 at p. 1298.

[72] See Lord Reid in *British Oxygen Co. Ltd. v. Minister of Technology* [1971] A.C. 610 at p. 625D–E.

[73] [1987] 1 W.L.R. 1982. See, also, *R. v. Secretary of State for the Home Department, ex p. Asif Khan* [1984] 1 W.L.R. 1337; *Council of Civil Service Unions v. Minister for the Civil Service* [1985] A.C. 374.

[74] This type of policy application is really a species of natural justice or fairness. See below at paras. 2–026.

PROCEDURAL IMPROPRIETY

2–013   Non-observance of natural justice is a separate basis for judicial review. It may be invoked even though a decision is reasonable within the *Wednesbury* criteria.

In *Kanda v. Government of Malaya*[75] Lord Denning M.R. observed that:

"The rule against bias is one thing. The right to be heard is another. These two rules are the essential characteristics of what is often called natural justice. They are the twin pillars supporting it. The Romans put them in the two maxims: *nemo judex in causa sua*, and *audi alteram partem*. They have recently been put in the two words, impartiality and fairness. But they are separate concepts and are governed by separate considerations."

This formulation is primarily related to the notion of a fair hearing. It should be borne in mind, however, that the developing doctrine of legitimate expectation,[76] and the expansion of the duty to give reasons,[77] are both species of natural justice which may extend its boundaries to enable challenge to be made in respect of most types of administrative unfairness.

Moreover, the expression "procedural impropriety" is not itself coincident with a breach of natural justice. Lord Diplock explained his preference for this term in the G.C.H.Q. case[78] as follows:

"I have described the third head as 'procedural impropriety' rather than failure to observe basic rules of natural justice or failure to act with procedural fairness towards the person who will be affected by the decision. This is because susceptibility to judicial review under this head covers also failure by an administrative tribunal to observe procedural rules that are expressly laid down in the legislative instrument by which its jurisdiction is conferred, even where such failure does not involve any denial of natural justice."[79]

The rule against bias

2–014   Undoubtedly biased (or potentially biased) decisions are susceptible to judicial review. Bias may occur, principally, in the following ways:

(a) if a disqualified person participates; or
(b) where the case is prejudged; or
(c) where an interested party has private access to the adjudicator.

---

[75] [1962] A.C. 322 at p. 337.
[76] See para. 2–026.
[77] See para. 2–025.
[78] See n. 1 above.
[79] *ibid.* at p. 411A–B.

Disqualified persons

A disqualified person is someone who has a direct pecuniary interest in **2–015** the subject matter[80] or who, having some other interest whether indirectly pecuniary or otherwise, is biased, or likely to be biased,[81] in favour of one side or the other.[82] The smallet pecuniary interest may disqualify,[83] but not one that is purely speculative or fanciful.[84]

A good example of an indirect pecuniary interest is afforded by *Metropolitan Properties Co. (F.G.C.) Ltd. v. Lannon.*[85] There, the chairman of a rent assessment committee was a solicitor whose father had an outstanding dispute against landlords who were party to an unconnected application before the committee. In the father's dispute the chairman's firm acted on his behalf. Certain decisions of the committee fixing rents were quashed on the basis that there was a real likelihood of bias in the eyes of the reasonable man.

Prejudging

There is a danger of prejudging if initial bias is shown,[86] or if an **2–016** adjudicator has, in the past, expressed clear views about live issues in the current application.[87]

In general, magistrates should not be made aware of any outstanding charges against a defendant or of the fact that he may be awaiting sentence in respect of different offences.[88] If justices know of a defendant's antecedent history they are not automatically deprived of jurisdiction but it is desirable that the case be determined by a differently constituted bench.[89] In *R. v. Downham Market Magistrates' Court, ex p. Nudd*[90] a Divisional Court held that mere knowledge of a defendant's convictions does not necessarily preclude the court from trying the case but that it would be wrong for magistrates to proceed where the previous convictions were disclosed to the court in a way which might lead to bias or a suggestion of bias in the minds of the public.

---

[80] *Dimes v. The Proprietors of the Grand Junction Canal* (1852) 3 H.L.C. 759. In cases of direct pecuniary interest "the law raises a conclusive presumption of bias", see *R. v. Sunderland JJ.* [1901] 2 K.B. 357 at p. 371, *per* Vaughan Williams L.J.

[81] For the standard of "likelihood" applied by the courts, see para. 2–018.

[82] *Metropolitan Properties Co. (F.G.C.) Ltd v. Lannon* [1969] 1 Q.B. 577.

[83] See, *e.g. R. v. Rand* (1866) L.R. 1 Q.B. 230.

[84] As, *e.g. R. v. Burton, ex p. Young* [1897] 2 Q.B. 468.

[85] n. 82 above. See, also, *R. v. Cambridge JJ., ex p. Yardline and Bird* (1990) Crim.L.R. 733, (*held*: if there is any possibility that a member of a magistrates' court might be seen by a disinterested observer to be unable impartially to do justice by reason of his association with one of the parties, that member should not sit. If he is in doubt he should declare his interest and should, generally, withdraw if invited so to do).

[86] *R. v. Halifax JJ., ex p. Robinson* (1912) 76 J.P. 233.

[87] *R. v. Kent Police Authority, ex p. Godden* [1971] 2 Q.B. 662.

[88] *R. v. Liverpool City JJ., ex p. Topping* [1983] 1 W.L.R. 119.

[89] *R. v. McElligott, ex p. Gallagher* (1972) Crim.L.R. 332.

[90] (1988) 152 J.P. 511. See, also, N. Spencer in (1986) 150 J.P. 356.

Access to the adjudicator

2-017   Decisions may be susceptible to judicial review on the ground of bias if the prosecutor is present whilst the adjudicator deliberates or if he gives his evidence privately.[91]

An adviser to the adjudicator, such as a justices' clerk, may also render a decision amenable to review for bias in circumstances where there is improper involvement in the adjudication. There appears, however, to be a two-stage process of enquiry. Not only must there be a real danger of bias on the part of the adviser, there must also exist a real danger of such bias having infected the views of the decision-maker adversely to the applicant.[92]

The test for bias

2-018   It is the danger of bias, rather than *de facto* bias (which is very difficult to prove), that the courts seek to guard against.[93]

Until the House of Lords' decision in *R. v. Gough*,[94] the case law indicated a broad division between those favouring judicial intervention if there is a "reasonable suspicion" of bias[95] and those which required a "real likelihood".[96]

Although it has been doubted whether there is, in fact, any substantive difference between the two tests,[97] the formulation now adopted in *Gough* favours that of "real danger". In that case, Lord Goff put it in this way:

> "Having ascertained the relevant circumstances, the court should ask itself whether, having regard to those circumstances, there was a real danger of bias on the part of the relevant member of the tribunal in question, in the sense that he might unfairly regard (or have unfairly regarded) with favour, or disfavour, the case of a party to the issue under consideration by him."[98]

---

[91] *R. v. Leicestershire Fire Authority, ex p. Thompson* (1979) 77 L.G.R. 373; *R. v. Barnsley Metropolitan B.C., ex p. Hook* [1976] 1 W.L.R. 1052; *Cooper v. Wilson* [1937] 2 K.B. 309.

[92] *R. v. Gough* [1993] A.C. 646, at pp. 664C and 670G, *per* Lord Goff.

[93] *R. v. Gough*, n. 92 above at pp. 659D–660A, 661H, 668C, *per* Lord Goff; pp. 672H–673A, *per* Lord Woolf. As stated above, however, different considerations arise in the case of a direct pecuniary interest where the very fact of such interest raises a conclusive presumption of bias; see n. 80 above.

[94] n. 92 above.

[95] See, especially, *R. v. Sussex JJ., ex p. McCarthy* [1924] 1 K.B. 256 at p. 259 (*per* Lord Hewart C.J.); *Hannam v. Bradford Corp.* [1970] 1 W.L.R. 937 at p. 941 (*per* Sachs L.J.); *R. v. West Yorkshire Coroner, ex p. Smith (No. 2), The Times*, November 6, 1982; *R. v. Liverpool JJ., ex p. Topping*, n. 88 above.

[96] See, especially, *R. v. Barnsley Licensing JJ., ex p. Barnsley and District Licensed Victuallers' Association* [1960] 2 Q.B. 167; *Hannam v. Bradford Corp.*, n. 95 above at p. 946 (*per* Widgery L.J.); *Metropolitan Properties (F.G.C.) Ltd. v. Lannon*, n. 82 above; *Steeples v. Derbyshire C.C.* [1985] 1 W.L.R. 256.

[97] *Hannam v. Bradford Corp.*, n. 95 above at pp. 941, 949, *per* Sachs and Cross L.JJ.; *R. v. Liverpool City JJ., ex p. topping*, n. 88 above. Contrast, though, Staughton J. in *Tracomin S.A. v. Gibbs Nathaniel (Canada) Ltd.* [1985] 1 Lloyd's Rep. 586.

[98] n. 92 above at p. 670F. This test was applied in *Rees v. Crane* [1994] 1 All E.R. 833. See, also *R. v. Wilson, The Times*, February 24, 1995.

The "real danger" test achieves something of a reconciliation between the above-mentioned alternative formulations. It appears to be a lower threshold requirement than "likelihood", approximating, rather, to a "real possibility" of bias.[99]

Bias is determined by recourse to all the facts and not by reference merely to the hypothetical reasonable man.[1] It is probable that there must be some operative prejudice before the High Court will accede to a challenge on the ground of bias.[2]

Excluding bias

Exceptionally, it may be that the rule against bias is excluded either by express statutory intent[3] or by necessary implication.[4] Statutory provisions that prevent a decision from being invalid "by reason only" of a particular disqualification are construed restrictively so that such a decision will not be capable of being reviewed merely because of the disqualification but will be if there is a real danger of bias.[5]

2–019

Bias and Order 53

An application under Order 53 may be refused if no objection was taken to bias.[6] When applying for judicial review the applicant should, if the issue of bias is raised, state in his affidavit in support of the application that he was, at the time, unaware of any particular disqualification on the part of the decision-maker.[7]

2–020

Procedural fairness

The right to a fair hearing shifts according to various factors including, as appropriate, "the circumstances of the case, the nature of the inquiry, the rules under which the tribunal is acting, the subject matter that is being dealt with".[8] It is clear that the implication of rules of fairness is not so much a process of statutory construction but, rather, the supplying by the judges of the legislative omission.[9]

2–021

---

[99] See *R. v. Gough*, n. 92 above, at pp. 668C–D, and 670E–F *per* Lord Goff; p. 671B–C, *per* Lord Woolf.

[1] *R. v. Gough*, n. 92 above at p. 670D–E, *per* Lord Goff.

[2] See, *e.g. R. v. Grimsby Borough Quarter Sessions, ex p. Fuller* [1956] 1 Q.B. 36 at p. 41.

[3] See, *e.g.*, L.G.A. 1972, ss.82 and 94; Licensing Act 1964, s.193(6).

[4] As, most typically, where a decision can only be made by a person who is in breach of the rule; see *Dimes v. The Proprietors of the Grand Junction Canal*, n. 80 at pp. 787–789.

[5] *R. v. Barnsley Licensing JJ.* [1960] 2 Q.B. 167.

[6] *R. v. Nailsworth Licensing JJ., ex p. Bird* [1953] 1 W.L.R. 1046.

[7] *R. v. Swansea JJ.* (1913) 49 L.J.N. 10.

[8] *Russell v. Duke of Norfolk* [1949] 1 All E.R. 109 at p. 118 (*per* Tucker L.J.). For similar observations see *R. v. Gaming Board, ex p. Benaim* [1970] 2 Q.B. 417; *Payne v. Lord Harris of Greenwich* [1981] 1 W.L.R. 754; *Bushell v. Secretary of State for the Environment* [1981] A.C. 75; *Lloyd v. McMahon* [1987] A.C. 625.

[9] See *Cooper v. Wandsworth Board of Works* (1863) 14 CB(NS) 180, *per* Byles J., approved in *Ridge v. Baldwin* [1964] A.C. 40; *Durayappah v. Fernando* [1967] 2 A.C. 337; *Wiseman v. Borneman* [1971] A.C. 297.

In the leading case of *Ridge v. Baldwin*[10] the House of Lords held that a Chief Constable dismissed from his office without any opportunity to put his case or without notice of the proposal to dismiss him or details of the basis of such proposal, had been treated unfairly and that the rules of natural justice had been ignored.

From that and other decisions it appears that the essential core of procedural fairness, excluding lack of bias, consists of:

    (a) the right to knowledge of the opposing case; and
    (b) a fair opportunity to answer the charges.[11]

These aspects of procedural fairness are developed generally at paras. 2–022 to 2–024 below. A number of different situations are then examined which illustrate several manifestations of the requirements of procedural fairness in particular contexts. In *Ridge v. Baldwin*, Lord Reid emphasised that the overall test was what a reasonable man would consider to be fair in the particular circumstances.[12]

Notice

2–022   Generally, a defendant is entitled to notice of allegations so that he has an adequate opportunity of being heard.[13] In *R. v. Thames Magistrates' Court, ex p. Polemis*,[14] for example, a conviction of a pollution offence was quashed where the charge was heard only hours after the summons was served. However, the requirement of notice is not a technical one and may be unnecessary where there is no prejudice occasioned by failure to give such notice[15] or, perhaps, where conduct by a defendant makes the giving of notice impracticable.[16]

In an important decision of the House of Lords in *R. v. Secretary of State for the Home Department, ex p. Al-Mehdawi*[17] it was held that the negligence of the applicant's solicitors, which deprived him of notice of his appeal for leave to remain in the United Kingdom, did not enable him to raise natural justice so as to challenge the decision of an Immigration Appeal Tribunal in circumstances where there was not fault on the part of the tribunal.

It is, however, still unclear whether, absent fault by legal advisers or by

---

[10] n. 9 above.

[11] See, *e.g. Ridge v. Baldwin*, n. 9 above at p. 132, *per* Lord Hodson; *John v. Rees* [1970] Ch. 345; *Kanda v. Government of Malaya*, n. 75 above.

[12] See n. 9 above at p. 65. For a modern application see *R. v. Secretary of State for Education, ex p. S., The Times*, January 26, 1994.

[13] For relevant statements of principle see: *De Verteuil v. Knaggs* [1918] A.C. 557 at p. 560; *Ridge v. Baldwin*, n. 9 above at pp. 113–114; *O'Reilly v. Mackman* [1983] 2 A.C. 237 at p. 279G.

[14] [1974] 1 W.L.R. 1371.

[15] See, *e.g. Davis v. Carew-Pole* [1956] 1 W.L.R. 833.

[16] See *De Verteuil v. Knaggs*, n. 13 above at p. 561, *per* Parmoor L.J.

[17] [1990] 1 A.C. 876, distinguishing *R. v. Leyland JJ., ex p. Hawthorn* [1979] Q.B. 283. *cf.*, though, *Majorpier v. Secretary of State for the Environment and Southwark L.B.C.* (1990) 59 P. & C.R. 453, (*held*: in a case involving questions of administrative procedure, as in a

the applicant himself, challenge by way of judicial review will lie in circumstances where (for example) notice of the hearing has been properly given but has not been received by the applicant.[18]

Detail of opposing case

The right to notice implies giving sufficient detail of the opposing case to provide a fair opportunity to the affected person of preparing his own case. This principle has been applied in many different factual situations.

2–023

In *Fairmount Investments Ltd. v. Secretary of State for the Environment*,[19] for example, it was held to be unlawful to rely on a recommendation which was based upon what the inspector had seen at his site inspection but which had not been disclosed to objectors as raising quite different issues from those ventilated at the inquiry.

To similar effect is the decision in *R. v. Secretary of State for Transport, ex p. Phillipine Airlines Inc.*,[20] where the Secretary of State's curtailment of flight permission was quashed because of his failure to give notice of the proposed new basis of allocating permission.

There is usually a duty to disclose relevant material in the possession of the decision-maker to the affected party.[21] Thus, in *R. v. Huntingdon D.C., ex p. Cowan*[22] Glidewell J. granted certiorari against a licensing authority which had failed to inform applicants of police and other objections so as to enable them to make full representations in support of their application for an entertainment licence. In *R. v. Westminster Assessment Committee, ex p. Grosvenor House (Park Lane) Ltd.*,[23] the Court of Appeal quashed a rating assessment when the same had been determined on the basis of a valuer's report which had not been disclosed.[24] The Secretary of State, hearing an appeal against a local authority's assessment of a child's special education

---

public inquiry, the general rule that a party is bound by the acts of his legal advisers is not necessarily to be applied in the same way and regard may be paid to the position of the lay client personally and not simply to that of his legal advisers as his representatives.)

[18] The point was left open in the earlier decision of the House of Lords in *R. v. Diggines, ex p. Rahmani* [1986] A.C. 475. See, especially, at p. 477F, *per* Lord Scarman. The question of principle is, of course, wider that the giving of notice and was there expressed by Lord Scarman as whether a decision-maker who has acted lawfully and without procedural impropriety is susceptible to judicial review in circumstances where there is, nonetheless, infringement of a rule of natural justice. See, also, *R. v. Leyland JJ., ex p. Hawthorn* n. 17 above; *R. v. Harrow Crown Court, ex p. Dave* [1994] 1 W.L.R. 98; *R. v. Hastings & Bexhill General Commissioners, ex p. Goodacre* [1994] S.T.C. 799.

[19] [1979] 1 W.L.R. 1255.

[20] *The Times*, October 17, 1984.

[21] For a concise statement of principle, see *Wiseman v. Borneman* [1971] A.C. 297 at p. 309G–H, *per* Lord Morris; p. 320B–C, *per* Lord Wilberforce.

[22] [1984] 1 W.L.R. 501.

[23] [1941] 1 K.B. 53.

[24] See, also, *R. v. Army Board of Defence Council, ex p. Anderson* [1992] Q.B. 169 (*held*: in considering a complaint of unlawful racial discrimination by a serving soldier, the Army

needs is required both to disclose expert additional evidence received by him and to permit and consider further submissions thereon.[25]

Exceptionally, the court has not insisted on the disclosure of relevant material[26] but this is usually for reasons of public policy.[27]

The principle enshrined in this paragraph covers not merely specific information or material uniquely available to the decision-maker but extends, also, to an approach to be taken to the case by the adjudicator but which the applicant has not been alerted to.[28]

Fair hearing

2–024　　That the conduct of a hearing must be fair is a reflection of the deeper principle that a party is entitled to present his case fully. There are often statutory rules of procedure for tribunals, inquiries and courts but in the absence thereof the procedure will largely depend on the nature of the adjudicating body in question.[29]

It has been said that "a 'hearing' will normally be an oral hearing."[30] Certainly, a denial of an oral hearing may offend against procedural fairness where there is the possibility "that if the applicant had had an oral hearing ... further matters could have been advanced on his behalf."[31] However, in many instances the opportunity to make written representations will suffice, provided that the demands of fairness are met.[32] Licensing authorities, for example, frequently decide on paper;[33] a student may be sent down from university without an oral hearing, provided that he has an opportunity to know the accusation and to answer it in writing.[34]

There is, as yet, no clear right to be granted legal representation but, in a prison discipline case, Webster J. observed that there may be situations

---

Board must show the complainant all the material seen by it); *R. v. Secretary of State for Health, ex p. Gandhi* [1991] 1 W.L.R. 1053 (*held*: where a medical practitioner appealed to the Secretary of State against a refusal to appoint him he was entitled to see reports made by a family practitioner committee and a medical practices committee unless some public interest immunity or overriding third party confidentiality prevailed).

[25] *R. v. Secretary of State for Education, ex p. S, The Times,* January 26, 1994.

[26] See, *e.g. R. v. Secretary of State for the Home Department, ex p. Gunnell* [1985] Crim.L.R. 105; *R. v. Secretary of State for the Home Department, ex p. Mughal* [1974] Q.B. 313; *R. v. Monopolies and Mergers Commission, ex p. Matthew Brown plc* [1987] 1 W.L.R. 1235.

[27] As, *e.g.* in *R. v. Kent Police Authority, ex p. Godden* [1971] 2 Q.B. 662 (confidential medical report). See, also, *R. v. Association of Futures Brokers and Dealers, ex p. Mordens* [1991] C.O.D. 40 (no statutory or agreed power to order discovery).

[28] See, *e.g. Mahon v. Air New Zealand Ltd* [1984] A.C. 808; *R. v. Mental Health Review Tribunal, ex p. Clatworthy* [1985] 3 All E.R. 699.

[29] *Local Government Board v. Arlidge* [1915] A.C. 120 at p. 132, *per* Viscount Haldane L.C.

[30] See, *e.g.* Wade and Forsyth *Administrative Law* (7th ed., 1994) at p. 537.

[31] See *R. v. Immigration Appeal Tribunal, ex p. Mehmet* [1977] 1 W.L.R. 795 at pp. 804–805, *per* Slynn J.

[32] See, *e.g. Lloyd v. McMahon,* n. 8 above; *R. v. Law Society, ex p. Curtin* (1994) 6 Admin. L.R. 657; *R. v. Army Board of the Defence Council, ex p. Anderson* n. 24 above.

[33] *R. v. Huntingdon D.C. ex p. Cowan,* n. 22 above.

[34] See *Brighton Corp. v. Parry* (1972) 70 L.G.R. 576. Note, too, that natural justice in this form applies equally to a decision to expel a pupil from school; see *R. v. Governors of London Oratory School, ex p. Regis* (1989) 19 Fam. Law 67.

where, having regard to the seriousness or complexity of the charges, "no [authority], properly directing itself, could reasonably decide not to allow ... legal representation."[35]

On a related note, in *R. v. Leicester City JJ., ex p. Barrow*,[36] the Court of Appeal held that fairness dictated that a party of full capacity conducting proceedings in person should be afforded all reasonable facilities to enable him to exercise his right of audience, including the assistance of a friend to give advice and take notes, unless in the interests of justice, and exercising its power to maintain order and regulate proceedings, the Court ordered otherwise.

It has been held that, on an oral hearing, the decision-maker should consider all relevant evidence, inform the parties of the evidence to be considered from whatever source, allow witnesses to be called and cross-examined and permit argument on the case.[37]

There is a large measure of discretion in how a tribunal or court regulates its own procedure generally so that, for example, the number of witnesses may sometimes be restricted "where ... it would be quite unnecessary to call so many witnesses to establish [a] point.[38] The discretion is, of course, not absolute. For example, in *R. v. Cambridge JJ. and Chief Constable of Cambridgeshire Constabulary, ex p. Peacock*,[39] a Divisional Court held that although justices were responsible for the conduct of their own court, fairness demanded that they entertain an application by the defendant for the removal of handcuffs during the hearing.

Provided that the decision-maker behaves fairly it will, in practice, be difficult to institute a challenge under Order 53. Put the other way, anything that restricts or appears to restrict the ability to present one's case is likely to be held to be a breach of procedural fairness and, thereby, susceptible to judicial review.

---

[35] *R. v. Home Secretary, ex p. Tarrant* [1985] Q.B. 251 at p. 287. See also: *R. v. Board of Visitors of H.M. Prison, The Maze, ex p. Hone* [1988] A.C. 379; *Enderby Town Football Club Ltd v. Football Association Ltd* [1971] Ch. 591; *Maynard v. Osmond* [1977] Q.B. 240; *R. v. Rathbone, ex p. Dikko* [1985] Q.B. 630; *R. v. Tower Hamlets L.B.C., ex p. Khatun, The Independent*, October 1, 1993.

[36] [1991] 3 W.L.R. 368. See, also, *R. v. Teesside JJ., ex p. Nilsson* (1990) J.P.N. 772. (*held*: a "Mackenzie friend" has no right to address the court or to concur in the trial proceedings).

[37] See *R. v. Deputy Industrial Injuries Commissioner, ex p. Moore* [1965] 1 Q.B. 456 at p. 490 *per* Diplock L.J. On failure to hear relevant evidence see: *R. v. Clerkenwell Magistrates', ex p. Bell* (1991) Crim.L.R. 468. On the right to cross-examination see, especially, *Osgood v. Nelson* (1872) L.R. 5 H.L. 636 at p. 646; *Nicholson v. Secretary of State for Energy* (1978) 76 L.G.R. 693; *R. v. Gartree Prison Visitors, ex p. Mealy, The Times*, November 14, 1981; *Bushell v. Secretary of State for the Environment* n. 8 above at p. 116D, *per* Lord Edmund-Davies; *R. v. Birmingham City Juvenile Court, ex p. Birmingham City Council* [1988] 1 W.L.R. 337.

[38] See *R. v. Hull Prison Visitors, ex p. St. Germain (No. 2)* [1979] 1 W.L.R. 1401 at p. 1406, *per* Geoffrey Lane L.J.

[39] [1993] C.O.D. 19.

Duty to give reasons

2–025   The House of Lords' decision in *R. v. Secretary of State for the Home Department, ex p. Doody*,[40] whilst not laying down a general duty to give reasons, appears to require reasons in the majority of cases where a public law decision-maker is potentially susceptible to judicial review in order that an applicant may know whether an error of law has occurred.[41]

In *Doody*, Lord Mustill said:

> "I accept without hesitation ... that the law does not at present recognise a general duty to give reasons for an administrative decision. Nevertheless, it is equally beyond question that such a duty may in appropriate circumstances be implied ... ."[42]

A duty to give reasons was implied in *Doody* on alternative bases. The case involved the policy adopted by the Home Secretary, in relation to mandatory life sentence prisoners, of imposing a notional tariff on such prisoners in the interests of retribution and deterrence before referring their cases to the Parole Board. Given that context, and the fact that other prisoners serving discretionary life sentences know the term of, and reasons for, their sentences as soon as they are sentenced, Lord Mustill held that fairness required the Home Secretary to give reasons if he departed from the recommendation of the judiciary as to tariff.[43]

However, Lord Mustill also observed as follows:

> "To mount an effective attack on the decision, given no more material than the facts of the offence and the length of the penal element, the prisoner has virtually no means of ascertaining whether this is an instance where the decision-making process has gone astray. I think it is important that there should be an effective means of detecting the kind of error which would entitle the court to intervene, and in practice I regard it as necessary for this purpose that the reasoning of the Home Secretary should be disclosed."[44]

Lord Mustill's second basis for requiring reasons in *Doody* is, at least potentially, capable of extending to all administrative decisions amenable to the judicial review jurisdiction. Such was, clearly, the view of Sir Louis Blom-Cooper Q.C. in *R. v. Lambeth. B.C., ex p. Walters*,[45] who considered that English law had now arrived at the point where there was:

> "At least a general duty to give reasons whenever the statutorily

---

[40] [1994] 1 A.C. 531, approving the Court of Appeal's reasoning in *R. v. Civil Service Appeal Board, ex p. Cunningham* [1991] 4 All E.R. 310.

[41] For analyses of the effect of the decision in *Doody* see: N.R. Campbell (1994) P.L. 184; R. Gordon and C. Barlow (1993) N.L.J. 1005.

[42] n. 40 above at p. 564E–F.

[43] n. 40 at pp. 564G–565F.

[44] n. 40 at pp. 565G–565H.

[45] (1993) 26 H.L.R. 170. See, in a similar context, Sir Louis Blom-Cooper Q.C. in *R. v. Islington L.B.C., ex p. Trail, The Times*, May 27, 1993 (*held*: reasons are a valuable form of self-discipline).

impregnated administrative process was infused with the concept of fair treatment to those potentially affected by administrative actions."

Notwithstanding *Walters*, it is premature to assume that the courts will, in all judicial review cases, imply a duty to give reasons. This was impliedly disavowed both by Lord Mustill in *Doody*, in the above-cited extract, and by the Court of Appeal in its earlier decision in *R. v. Civil Service Appeal Board, ex p. Cunningham*.[46] Walters, itself was disapproved by the Court of Appeal in *R. v. Kensington and Chelsea Royal London Borough Council, ex p. Grillo*.[46a] Moreover, since *Doody*, Sedley J. has held, in *R. v. Higher Education Funding Council, ex p. Institute of Dental Surgery*,[47] that the logic of *Doody* is not to require reasons in all Order 53 cases but, rather, where a decision appears aberrant or where the subject matter is particularly highly regarded, such as personal liberty. In context, Sedley J. rejected the submission that there was a duty to give reasons for the exercise of a purely academic judgment.

The growing case law on reasons appears to support Sedley J.'s analysis. Decisions affecting personal liberty such as the classification of prisoners,[48] or the reasons for refusing to recommend release on parole,[49] now invariably require reasons. So, too, do those decisions which call for explanation.[50] Further, "as a rule" a professional judge should provide reasons for his decision.[51]

Reasons provided must be adequate and intelligible.[52] Adequacy and intelligibility depend on the context. For example, in *R. v. Legal Aid Area No. 8 (Northern) Appeal Committee, ex p. Parkinson*,[53] it was held that a legal aid area committee could be required to give extended reasons for their decision to refuse legal aid, particularly in cases of considerable public interest and importance and particularly in the face of a clearly favourable opinion from counsel. However, in the context of planning decisions the House of Lords has held, in *Save Britain's Heritage v. Number 1 Poultry Ltd.*,[54] that on a challenge to the adequacy of the Secretary of State's

---

[46] n. 40 above at p. 319, *per* Lord Donaldson of Lymington M.R.
[46a] *The Times*, May 13, 1995.
[47] [1994] 1 W.L.R. 242. *cf.*, also, *R. v. English Nursing Board, ex p. Roberts* [1994] C.O.D. 223 (*Held*: English Nursing Board is under no duty to give reasons for its decisions).
[48] *R. v. Secretary of State for the Home Department, ex p. Duggan, The Times*, December 9, 1993.
[49] *R. v. Secretary of State for the Home Department, ex p. Pegg, The Times*, August 11, 1994.
[50] See, *e.g.*, *Civil Service Appeal Board, ex p. Cunningham*, n. 40 above at p. 322, *per* McCowan L.J.; *R. v. Secretary of State for the Home Department, ex p. Sinclair* [1992] C.O.D. 287. *cf. R. v. Solihull Metropolitan Council Housing Benefits Review Board, ex p. Simpson, The Times*, January 5, 1994.
[51] See *Eagil Trust Co. Ltd. v. Pigott-Brown* [1985] 3 All E.R. 119 at p. 126, *per* Griffiths L.J. See, also: *R. v. Knightsbridge Crown Court, ex p. I.S.C. Ltd.* [1981] 3 W.L.R. 640 at p. 648; *R. v. Harrow Crown Court, ex p. Dave* [1994] 1 W.L.R. 98; *R. v. Snaresbrook Crown Court, ex p. Lea, The Times*, April 5, 1994.
[52] *Re Poyser and Mills Arbitration* [1964] 2 Q.B. 467 at p. 478; *Westminster City Council v. Great Portland Estates Plc* [1985] A.C. 661 at p. 673.
[53] *The Times*, March 13, 1990.
[54] [1991] 1 W.L.R. 153.

reasoning the burden of proof is on the applicant to show that he has been substantially prejudiced by the deficiency in the reasons.

A failure to give any reasons,[55] or reasons which are themselves less than adequate or intelligible,[56] may lead to the inference that a decision is unlawful. Finally, it may be that once proceedings for judicial review have been commenced, a respondent decision-maker is obliged to provide reasons so as "to explain fully what has occurred and why."[57]

Legitimate expectation and general "fairness"

2–026   Natural justice implies that a respondent acts fairly.[58] Whilst fairness encompasses all the situations outlined above it is not now considered to be co-extensive with a hearing or formal decision.[59]

The notice of "legitimate expectation" has, in particular, greatly extended the boundaries of natural justice to the point where it can be said to approximate to a requirement of (at least) procedural administrative fairness in a wide variety of contexts.

The concept was first formulated by Lord Denning M.R. in *Schmidt v. Secretary of State for Home Affairs*[60] where he observed:

> "The speeches in *Ridge v. Baldwin* [1964] A.C. 40 show that an administrative body may, in a proper case, be bound to give a person who is affected by their decision an opportunity of making representations. It all depends on whether he has some right or interest or, I would add, some legitimate expectation, of which it would not be fair to deprive him without hearing what he has to say."

Since *Schmidt*, legitimate expectation has been widely utilised. It was expressly recognised by the House of Lords as founding standing in both *O'Reilly v. Mackman*[61] and *Re Findlay*.[62] More important, however, was the way in which Lord Diplock approached legitimate expectation in *Council of Civil Service Unions v. Minister for the Civil Service*.[63] He stated that:

> "To qualify as a subject for judicial review the decision must have consequences which affect some person (or body of persons) other

---

[55] *Padfield v. Minister of Agriculture, Fisheries and Food* [1968] A.C. 997 at pp. 1032G–1033A; 1035G–1054A; 1061G–1062A; *R. v. Secretary of State for Trade and Industry, ex p. Lonrho Plc* [1989] 1 W.L.R. 525 at pp. 539G–540B.

[56] *R. v. Criminal Injuries Compensation Board, ex p. Cummins* [1992] C.O.D. 297.

[57] *R. v. Lancashire C.C., ex p. Huddleston* [1986] 2 All E.R. 941 at p. 945, *per* Lord Donaldson of Lymington M.R.

[58] *R. v. Secretary of State for the Home Department, ex p. Hosenball* [1977] 1 W.L.R. 766, *per* Lane and Cumming-Bruce L.JJ.

[59] For example, an applicant ought not to be exposed to the prospect of a real risk of prejudice or injustice where such will occur by having to deal with two sets of proceedings raising substantially the same issues; see: *R. v. The Institute of Chartered Accountants in England and Wales, ex p. Brindle* (unrep. December 21, 1993).

[60] [1969] 2 Ch. 149 at p. 170.

[61] [1983] 2 A.C. 237.

[62] [1985] A.C. 318.

[63] [1985] A.C. 374 at pp. 408–409. See, also, *R. v. I.R.C., ex p. M.F.K. Underwriting Agents Ltd* [1990] 1 W.L.R. 1545.

than the decision-maker, although it may affect him too. It must affect such person either:

    (a) by altering rights or obligations of that person which are enforceable by or against him in private law; or

    (b) by depriving him of some benefit or advantage which either

        (i) he had in the past been permitted by the decision-maker to enjoy and which he can legitimately expect to be permitted to continue to do until there has been communicated to him some rational grounds for withdrawing it on which he has been given an opportunity to comment; or

        (ii) he has received assurance from the decision-maker that it will not be withdrawn without giving him first an opportunity of advancing reasons for contending that they should not be withdrawn.

(I prefer to continue to call the kind of expectation that qualifies a decision for inclusion in class (b) a 'legitimate expectation' rather than a 'reasonable expectation', in order thereby to indicate that it has consequences to which effect will be given in public law, whereas an expectation or hope that some benefit or advantage would continue to be enjoyed, although it might be entertained by a 'reasonable man', would not necessarily have such consequences.)"

Lord Diplock's analysis of legitimate expectation in *G.C.H.Q.* was supplemented in the same case by the observations of Lord Fraser[64] who pointed out that such expectation may arise by an express promise or, by implication, from past practice.

The case law since *G.C.H.Q.* shows that the concept has, primarily, been applied in a procedural manner so as to ensure that no adverse decision will be taken, in circumstances where the doctrine is relevant, without first giving the affected party an opportunity of making representations.

Instances involving express promise occurred in *Att.-Gen. (Hong Kong) v. Ng Yuen Shiu*[65] where an illegal immigrant to Hong Kong was held to have a legitimate expectation that his case would be dealt with on its merits as the governor had promised, and in *R. v. Liverpool Corp., ex p. Liverpool Taxi etc. Association*[66] where taxi drivers had a legitimate expectation of consultation prior to the issue of licences in circumstances where such consultation had been expressly promised. In order for a promise to have this effect it must be clear and unambiguous,[67] and the applicant must have made full relevant disclosure prior to its being obtained.[68]

---

[64] *ibid.* at p. 401.

[65] [1983] 2 A.C. 629. Note, also, P. Jackson in (1983) 99 L.Q.R. 499.

[66] [1972] 2 Q.B. 299.

[67] *R. v. I.R.C., ex p. M.F.K. Underwriting Agents Ltd*, see n. 63 above at pp. 1567D–E, 1569G–H, 1572D and 1575A.

[68] *R. v. I.R.C., ex p. M.F.K. Underwriting Agents Ltd*, n. 63 above at pp. 1569E–G, 1570A–B, 1575B–C. See, also: *R. v. I.R.C., ex p. Matrix Securities Ltd* [1994] 1 W.L.R. 334.

More common are the "past practice" cases where legitimate expectation of consultation or fair hearing has been upheld to ensure, *inter alia*, that school reorganisation was not carried out without parents being adequately consulted,[69] that prisoners should have the opportunity of a fair hearing before loss of remission for disciplinary offences,[70] and that the employees in G.C.H.Q. should be consulted before being prevented from continuing to have union representation.[71]

It is not clear whether legitimate expectation is a solely procedural concept. Two modern decisions show that the doctrine comes close to permitting the conferment of a substantive benefit as opposed, merely, to the right to procedural safeguards in appropriate circumstances.

In *R. v. Secretary of State for the Home Department, ex p. Khan*[72] the Secretary of State was held by a majority of the Court of Appeal to be bound by a circular limiting the ambit of his discretion to turn down an application for entry clearance for a child. Parker L.J. went so far as to suggest that a new policy could only be adopted against the recipient of the circular after considering whether the overriding public interest demanded it. Similarly, in *R. v. Secretary of State for the Home Department, ex p. Ruddock*[73] it was held that the Secretary of State's published criteria for regulating telephone tapping created a legitimate expectation that they would be observed.

Neither of the above decisions goes as far as to prevent a public body from resiling from a previously stated (or implied) policy. This would, indeed, be inconsistent with the principle that there cannot be a fettering of discretion by policy or estoppel.[74] They do, nonetheless, imply that protection may, as a species of natural justice, now be accorded so as to ensure that undertakings, assurances or past practices are required to be honoured, subject to contrary public interest.[75]

---

[69] See *R. v. Brent L.B.C., ex p. Gunning* (1985) 84 L.G.R 168.

[70] *R. v. Hull Prison Visitors, ex p. St Germain* [1979] Q.B. 425, approved in *O'Reilly v. Mackman*, n. 13 above.

[71] Legitimate expectation here was somewhat short-lived, since judicial review was refused on the ground of national security; see para. 2–027.

[72] [1984] 1 W.L.R. 1337.

[73] [1987] 1 W.L.R. 1482.

[74] See para. 2–010, and note, especially, *Birkdale District Electricity Supply Co. Ltd v. Southport Corp.* [1926] A.C. 355, at p. 364, *per* Birkenhead L.J.; *R. v. Secretary of State for Health, ex p. United States Tobacco International Inc.* [1992] 1 Q.B. 353 above at pp. 368E, 369B, *per* Taylor L.J.

[75] See C. Forsyth in "Provenance and Protection of Legitimate Expectations" (1988) C.L.J. 238. In *R. v. Secretary of State for Transport, ex p. Richmond-upon-Thames L.B.C.* [1994] 1 W.L.R. 74, however, Laws J. held that, notwithstanding the *Khan* and *Ruddock* cases, legitimate expectation was a concept ensuring no more than procedural protection. Contrast, though, *Sedley J.* in *R. v. Ministry of Agriculture Fisheries & Food, ex p. Hamble Fisheries (Offshore) Ltd*, 1994, unrep. (*held*: Legitimate expectation could confer substantive protection and was the product of 'fairness in public administration') and, to similar effect, Dyson J. in *R. v. Governor's of Haberdashers' Aske's Hatcham College Trust, ex p. T, The Times*, October 19, 1994.

Nothing in the original formulation of legitimate expectation appears to require detrimental (or any) reliance by the applicant on a particular past practice or assurance so as to afford grounds for judicial review. However, in *R. v. Jockey Club, ex p. RAM Racecourses*,[76] Stuart-Smith L.J. suggested that it was a necessary ingredient. This was endorsed by the Divisional Court in *R. v. Lloyd's of London, ex p. Briggs*,[77] and seems to have been accepted by the courts, in practice, as a requirement.[78]

Fairness, in modern administrative law, is confined neither to the application of traditional principles of natural justice on the one hand, nor to legitimate expectation on the other. There are factual situations which fit into neither category yet which the courts have held to justify invoking the supervisory jurisdiction of the High Court.[79]

Limitations on natural justice

There exist some limitations on the availability of natural justice. It seems **2–027** not to apply at all to legislative acts[80] and may be excluded where considerations of national security are involved.[81] Further, the court may find that there is a statutory intention to exclude natural justice,[82] or to restrict its protection to the appeal stage of a particular procedure.[83] Procedural propriety may also have limited application in situations where emergency powers are being exercised.[84] Its application is not, however, limited to parties to the decision.[85]

Apart from these instances it is sometimes said that natural justice will not protect an applicant where the decision would, in any event, have been the same so that there is no prejudice.[86] However, this may mean no more than that establishing a breach of natural justice requires that some prejudice be proved. In *R. v. Chief Constable of the Thames Valley Police*,

---

[76] [1993] 2 All E.R. 225 at pp. 236j–237a.

[77] (1993) 5 Admin L.R. 698 at p. 710B–G, *per* Leggatt L.J.

[78] See, *e.g., R. v. I.R.C., ex p. Matrix-Securities Ltd.*, n. 68 above at p. 346G–H, *per* Griffiths L.J.

[79] As, *e.g. R. v. Secretary of State for Health, ex p. United States Tobacco International Inc.* [1992] 1 Q.B. 353; *R. v. I.R.C., ex p. Preston* [1985] A.C. 835.

[80] *Bates v. Lord Hailsham of St Marylebone* [1972] 1 W.L.R. 1373.

[81] *Council of Civil Service Unions v. Minister for the Civil Service*, n. 63 above. See, also: *R. v. Secretary of State for the Home Department, ex p. Cheblak* [1991] 1 W.L.R. 890 (*Held*: court will not probe reasons advanced for national security priority).

[82] As, *e.g. in R. v. Wells Street Magistrates Court, ex p. Albanese* [1981] 3 W.L.R. 694.

[83] See, *e.g., Calvin v. Carr* [1980] A.C. 574; *Lloyd v. McMahon* [1987] A.C. 625.

[84] See, *e.g., R. v. Birmingham City Council, ex p. Ferrero* [1993] 1 All E.R. 530; *R. v. Life Assurance and Unit Trust Regulatory Organisation, ex p. Ross* [1993] Q.B. 17; *R. v. Secretary of State for Transport, ex p. Pegasus Holdings (London) Ltd* [1988] 1 W.L.R. 990.

[85] *R. v. Life Assurance and Unit Trust Regulatory Organisation, ex p. Ross*, n. 84 above at pp. 49A, 50E–G; *R. v. Liverpool Corp., ex p. Liverpool Taxi Fleet Operator's Association*, n. 66 above at p. 307. *cf. Cheall v. APEX* [1983] 2 A.C. 180 at pp. 190B–D, 191E.

[86] See, *e.g. Glynn v. Keele University* [1971] 1 W.L.R. 487; *Malloch v. Aberdeen Corp.* [1971] 1 W.L.R. 1578.

ex p. Cotton[87] the Court of Appeal held that there was no such thing as a technical breach of natural justice or fairness and that an applicant had to show that there was a substantive breach. In *John v Rees*[88] Megarry J. pointed out how difficult it was, in practice, to show that a decision flawed by procedural impropriety would, inevitably, have been the same.

PROPORTIONALITY

2–028   European law contains a principle known as proportionality which requires "a reasonable relation between a decision, its objectives and the circumstances of a given case."[89] In *Council of Civil Service Unions v. Minister for the Civil Service*[90] Lord Diplock referred to it as a possible prospective basis of challenge on judicial review. As Wade has observed,[91] "It is clear that the principles of reasonableness and proportionality over a great deal of common ground."

In *R. v. Secretary of State for the Home Department, ex p. Brind*[92] the House of Lords, by a majority, held that proportionality in domestic law does not go as far as its European counterpart.[93] Lord Lowry, in particular, considered that importation of European proportionality into domestic law would constitute an abuse of the High Court's supervisory function and jeopardise stability and certainty, as well as greatly increasing the number of judicial review applications. He also thought that judges were not equipped with the requisite knowledge and expertise to embark on an investigation of administrative reasonableness involving a lower threshold test than *Wednesbury* irrationality.

The speech of Lord Roskill, in *Brind*, suggests, nonetheless, the possibility of proportionality being considered in the future as an independent head of judicial review in an appropriate case.[94] In *R. v. Secretary of State for the Home Department, ex p. Pegg*,[95] Steyn L.J. left open the prospect of retention of proportionality as a separate basis for challenge in a case

---

[87] (1990) I.R.L.R. 344.

[88] [1989] 2 W.L.R. 1294.

[89] See J. Jowell and A. Lester "Proportionality: Neither Novel nor Dangerous" in *New Directions in Judicial Review* (1988) at pp. 51 *et seq.*, where the European jurisdiction is well summarised. Consider, *e.g.* Case 261/81 *Rau v. De Smedt* [1987] E.C.R. 3961; Case C-331/88 *R. v. MAFF, ex p. FEDESA* [1990] ECR 1–4023.

[90] n. 63 above at p. 410E.

[91] See Wade and Forsyth, *op cit.* n. 30 above at p. 403.

[92] [1991] 1 A.C. 696.

[93] *ibid.* at p. 751E–F, *per* Lord Templeman; p. 759D, *per* Lord Ackner; pp. 762D–E, 766C–767G *per* Lord Lowry. See, also, *R. v. General Medical Council, ex p. Colman* [1990] 1 All E.R. 489; *R. v. Secretary of State for the Environment, ex p. NALGO* (1993) 5 Admin. L.R. 785.

[94] *ibid.* at p. 750D–F. See, too, *R. v. Secretary of State for Transport, ex p. Pegasus Holdings (London) Ltd*, n. 84 above, *per* Schiemann J.

[95] n. 49 above.

raising issues of personal liberty, and the principle seems to be applied in practice where a sentencing decision is susceptible to judicial review.[96]

In all cases involving Community law the European principle of proportionality must be applied in its discrete form.[97]

EUROPEAN CONVENTION ON HUMAN RIGHTS

The relevance of the European Convention on Human Rights to judicial review proceedings was considered in *R. v. Secretary of State for the Home Department, ex p. Brind*.[98] In *Brind* the Home Secretary had imposed a broadcasting ban on terrorists. The applicant sought judicial review of the ban arguing, *inter alia*, that it infringed the provisions of the Convention relating to freedom of expression.

2–029

The House of Lords, in dismissing the applicant's appeal against the refusal of judicial review, held (on this head of argument) as follows: (a) the Convention was not part of English domestic law; (b) in most cases, therefore, English courts would not be concerned with the Convention's terms; (c) the sole exception was where the terms of primary legislation were capable of bearing two meanings: in such event (but only in such event) the court would presume that Parliament intended to legislate consistently, rather than inconsistently, with the Convention.[99]

In the Court of Appeal judgments in *Derbyshire C.C. v. Times Newspapers Ltd*,[1] it was clarified that similar principles apply to interpretation of the common law. If the common law is unclear then recourse may be had to the European Convention but, otherwise, there is no presumption that the common law is consistent with the terms of the Convention. The speeches in the House of Lords did not deal with the materiality of the Convention to the issue of whether a local authority could institute libel proceedings and may be taken to have approved, *sub silentio*, the approach adopted by the Court of Appeal.[2]

The European Convention may also engage the courts in more 'anxious scrutiny' of the way in which executive discretion is exercised than under conventional Wednesbury criteria.[2a] In a community law case it is arguable

---

[96] See, *e.g. R. v. Highbury Corner JJ., ex p. Uchendu, The Times*, January 28, 1994; *R. v. Tamworth JJ., ex p. Walsh, The Times*, March 3, 1994.

[97] *Thomas v. Chief Adjudication Officer* [1991] 2 Q.B. 164.

[98] See n. 92 above.

[99] *ibid.*, especially at pp. 747H–748F *per* Lord Bridge; 760D and 761H–762A, *per* Lord Ackner *cf. R. v. Miah* [1974] 1 W.L.R. 683 at p. 694 where Lord Reid observed that it was hardly credible that Parliament would legislate contrary to the Convention.

[1] [1992] Q.B. 770.

[2] See [1993] A.C. 534. Consider, also, *Rantzen v. Mirror Group Newspapers* [1993] 3 W.L.R. 953.

[2a] See *R. v. Secretary of State for the Home Department, ex p. McQuillan, The Independent*, September 23, 1994.

that the European Convention must be complied with by the decision-maker.[2b]

EUROPEAN JUDICIAL REVIEW

2–030   Where Community law is infringed, judicial review lies to correct a decision-maker's public law default, whether it consists of an abuse of power[3] or breach of duty.[4] Infringement of a solely private law right is, as with a domestic law case, justiciable not in judicial review but in private law proceedings.[5] Directives may be relied upon by individuals only against the State or an emanation of the State.[6]

There may, now, be circumstances in which a public law breach of community law gives rise to a claim for damages in judicial review proceedings. In *Francovich and Bonifaci v. Italy*[7] the European Court of Justice held that it was a general principle of Community law that Member States pay compensation for damage occasioned to individuals by a breach of Community law. In context it held that where a Member State fails to fulfil its obligations under Article 189(3) of the EEC treaty to take all measures necessary to achieve the result prescribed by a directive, there is a right to compensation where three conditions are met. These are that:

(a) the result prescribed by the directive entails the grant of rights to individuals;

(b) it should be possible to identify the content of such rights by the provisions of the directive;

(c) there is a causal link between the breach of the State's obligation and the harm suffered by the injured parties.

In *Bourgoin SA v. MAFF*,[8] the Court of Appeal had held that a breach of Article 30 of the EEC Treaty did not afford any cause of action beyond that conferred by a breach of statutory duty or misfeasance in public office. The decision in *Francovich* suggests, however, that an additional cause of action, whether aptly described as an innominate tort or as a right to damages sounding in public law, now lies wherever a breach of Community law has occurred.

The grounds for judicial review, outlined above, are all potentially available in respect of a public law breach of Community law.[9]

[2b] *R. v. Secretary of State for the Home Department, ex p. Payne* [1995] Imm. A.R. 48.

[3] *Bourgoin S.A. v. Ministry of Agriculture, Fisheries and Food* [1986] Q.B. 716.

[4] *R. v. Minister of Agriculture, Fisheries and Food, ex p. Bell Lines and An Bord Bainne Co-operative (Irish Dairy Board)* [1984] 2 C.M.L.R. 502.

[5] See, *e.g.*, *Garden Cottage Foods v. Milk Marketing Board* [1984] A.C. 130.

[6] Case 152/84 *Marshall v. Southampton and South-West Hampshire Area Health Authority (Teaching)* [1986] Q.B. 401. Emanations of the State would appear to encompass most respondents to applications for judicial review; see case C-188/89 *Foster v. British Gas Corp.* [1991] 2 W.L.R. 258.

[7] [1991] ECR 1–5357.

[8] n. 3 above.

[9] See, *e.g. Bourgoin v. MAFF*, n. 3 above (illegality); *Stoke-on-Trent City Council v. B. & Q. plc* [1991] Ch. 48 (irrationality); *R. v. Secretary of State for the Home Department, ex p. Santillo* [1981] Q.B. 778 (procedural impropriety).

Where appropriate, substantive Community law principles, such as proportionality, must be applied even where domestic law does not recognise a particular head of challenge.[10] The same is true of domestic procedural rules or judicial practices which, in a case involving community law, must be disapplied in so far as they impede the full effectiveness of Community law rights.[11] This is, however, to be distinguished from the principle that, absent Community legislation or Court ruling, it is for the national courts to lay down their own remedial rules, such as limitation periods, provided that such rules are no less favourable than those applicable to domestic claims and that they do not make it virtually impossible to secure the remedy.[12]

Although the European Court of Justice has not commented on the three-month limitation period for judicial review under RSC Order 53, r. 4 it appears to be the case that time does not run thereunder until a directive has been properly implemented into national law, so that a challenge could be mounted at any time prior to such implementation.[13]

In a case where a breach of Community law is alleged, the national court must decide the question of law itself rather than determine the issue by reference to whether the decision-maker was reasonable to take a particular view of the law.[14] This may engage the court in a degree of fact-finding inapposite to most domestic applications for judicial review.[15] Community law is construed purposively and with full reference, where necessary, to preambles and preparatory measures.[16] The European Court of Justice has, in Case C-106/89 *Marleasing SA v. La Comercial Internacional de Alimentacion SA*,[17] clarified that all national legislation (whether prior or subsequent) must, so far as possible, be interpreted in conformity with the terms of any relevant directive. *Marleasing* has been construed by the

---

[10] See n. 97 above, and text.

[11] See: *R. v. Secretary of State for Transport, ex p. Factortame (No. 2)* [1990] E.C.R. 1–2433; [1991] 1 A.C. 603 (*held*: national courts have jurisdiction to grant interim relief to disapply a national law to protect putative rights in Community law); Case 106/77 *Amministrazione delle Finanze dello Stato v. Simmenthal SpA* [1978] E.C.R. 629. The approach of the High Court towards the grant of interim injunctive relief in a European context is separately considered at para. 8–012.

[12] See, *e.g.*Case 33/76 *Rewe-Zentralfinanze G v. Landwirtschaftskammer fur Saarland* [1976] E.C.R. 1989; Case 45/76 *Comet BV v. Produktschap voor Siergewassen* [1976] E.C.R. 2043.

[13] See Case C–208/90 *Theresa Emmott v. Minister for Social Welfare* [1991] E.C.R. 1–4269. This is, presumably, why the applicant was allowed to proceed in *R. v. Secretary of State for Employment, ex p. Equal Opportunities Commission* [1994] 2 W.L.R. 409 with no point being taken on delay. Note, however, the C.A. ruling in *R. v. Customs & Excise Commissioners, ex p. Eurotunnel plc, The Independent*, February 23, 1995 (*Held*: leave to apply for judicial review of three orders implementing EC directives set aside because applicants had not acted promptly).

[14] See, *e.g., R. v. MAFF, ex p. Bell Lines Ltd*, n. 4 above; *R. v. Secretary of State for Social Services, ex p. Schering Chemicals Ltd* [1987] 1 C.M.L.R. 277; *R. v. MAFF, ex p. Roberts* [1991] 1 C.M.L.R. 555.

[15] See *R. v. MAFF, ex p. Bell Lines*, n. 4 above at p. 511, *per* Forbes J.

[16] See Case 67/79 *Waldemar Fellinger v. Bundesanstalt fur Arbeit, Nuremberg* [1980] E.C.R. 535 at p. 550 (Advocate-General Mayras); *R. v. London Boroughs Transport Committee v. Freight Transport Association Ltd* [1991] 1 W.L.R. 828 at pp. 839A–841B (Commission Green Paper used as aid to interpretation).

[17] [1990] E.C.R. 1–4135.

47

House of Lords as imposing a general obligation on English courts to interpret national law consistently with Community law generally as far as possible.[18]

Declaratory relief appears to be potentially available, subject to an applicant's standing, to determine whether primary legislation is compatible with Community law even in the absence of the conferment of directly effective rights on the applicant.[19]

Cases with a Community law element may need to be referred to the European Court of Justice under Article 177 of the Treaty during the course of the judicial review proceedings. This is separately considered at para. 6–013.

CRITERIA FOR THE REFUSAL OF RELIEF

2–031   Even if an applicant under Order 53 is otherwise entitled to relief, the court may, in its discretion, refuse it. This will mainly occur if there has been undue delay in pursuing the application, but residual principles of discretion will also be examined.

Undue delay

2–032   Undoubtedly the court may refuse an application for leave to apply for judicial review, or relief on any substantive application, by reason of an applicant's delay.

Order 53, r. 4(1) prescribes that an application for leave to apply for judicial review "shall be made promptly and in any event within three months from the date when grounds for the application first arose unless the Court considers that there is good reason for extending the period within which the application shall be made."

This must be read in conjunction with section 31(6) of the Supreme Court Act 1981 which states that where the court considers that there has been undue delay in applying for judicial review it may refuse to grant leave to make the application for any relief sought, "if it considers that the granting of the relief sought would be likely to cause substantial hardship to, or substantially prejudice the rights of, any person or would be detrimental to good administration."

The respective provisions are not easy to reconcile because although section 31(7) of the 1981 Act expresses subsection (6) to be without prejudice to any Act or rule of court which has the effect of limiting the time within which an application for judicial review may be made, Order 53,

---

[18] *Webb v. Emo Air Cargo (UK) Ltd.* [1993] 1 W.L.R. 49, at p. 59G, *per* Lord Keith *cf.* the analysis of this decision by Nigel Gravells in "European Community Law in the English Courts" (1993) P.L. pp. 44 *et seq.*

[19] See *R. v. Secretary of State for Employment, ex p. Equal Opportunities Commission,* n. 13 above. *Quaere* whether Turner J.'s ruling in *Wychavon D.C. v. Secretary of State for the Environment, The Times,* January 7, 1994 that a local authority, not being an individual, could not rely upon the provisions of an unimplemented EC Directive survives the *EOC* case.

r. 4(3) provides that the preceding paragraphs "are without prejudice to any statutory provision which has the effect of limiting the time within which an application for judicial review may be made."

The approach of the court to applications for leave to apply for judicial review has been elucidated by the decisions of the Court of Appeal in *R. v. Stratford on Avon D.C., ex p. Jackson*[20] and of the House of Lords in *R. v. Dairy Produce Quotas Tribunal, ex p. Caswell.*[21]

In *Jackson* the court held as follows:

(a) The fact that an application for leave has been made within three months does not mean that it has been made "promptly".[22]

(b) Judicial review is more than a *lis inter partes*. Accordingly, cases in private law on, for example, the renewal of writs do not assist in deciding whether to grant an extension of time for leave to apply for judicial review. The question is whether, on the facts, there is good reason to extend time.

(c) Whether there has been "undue delay" within the meaning of section 31(6) of the Supreme Court Act 1981 falls to be determined objectively. Where there is non-compliance with Order 53, r. 4(1) because an application is either not made promptly or within three months, there is "undue delay". It then becomes a matter for the court's discretion as to whether (i) to extend time under Order 53, r. 4 or (ii) to refuse leave to apply for judicial review or to refuse the relief sought under section 31(6) of the 1981 Act. Section 31(6) criteria may be applied either at the leave or full hearing stage, but if this issue involves substantial enquiry into the merits then it is usually preferable to leave section 31(6) consideration until the full hearing.

In *Caswell* the House of Lords approved the *Jackson* approach to delay at the leave stage and upheld the following general tests at that stage:

(a) At the leave stage the judge must refuse leave if the application is not made promptly or within three months at the latest, unless the applicant shows good reason, in which case the judge may grant an extension.

(b) Even if the judge would otherwise have granted an extension he may still refuse leave if he is of the view that the granting of relief would be likely to cause substantial hardship or prejudice or be detrimental to good administration because "section 31(6) simply contains particular grounds for refusing leave or substantive relief, not referred to in rule 4(1), to which the court is bound to give effect, independently of any rule of court."[23]

[20] [1985] 1 W.L.R. 1319.
[21] [1990] 2 A.C. 738.
[22] Consider, *e.g. R. v. Swale B.C., ex p. Royal Society for the Protection of Birds* [1990] C.O.D. 263; *R. v. Independent Television Commission, ex p. TV NI Ltd, The Times,* December 30, 1991; *R. v. Secretary of State for Health, ex p. Alcohol Recovery Project* [1993] C.O.D. 344.
[23] n. 21 above at p. 747F, *per* Lord Goff.

(c) In practice the judge will normally grant leave if good reason is shown and leave the question of substantial hardship, etc. to be argued at the full hearing.

It should be noted that "good reason" for extending time under Order 53, r. 4 includes (but is not synonymous with) "good excuse". For example, in *R. v. Home Secretary, ex p. Ruddock*[24] the importance of the point of law at stake was held to be a good reason to extend time. In *Jackson*, time taken to obtain legal aid was held to constitute a good reason.[25] The Court of Appeal held, in *R. v. Greenwich L.B.C., ex p. Patterson*,[26] that a possession order expressed "not to be enforced without leave" was a holding order not requiring the seeking of leave to apply for judicial review prior to its being sought to be enforced.

Where there is no excuse for delay and there is no other reason for extending time, the court will be reluctant to do so even if the case is otherwise meritorious. In *R. v. Tavistock General Commissioners, ex p. Worth*,[27] for example, Webster J. held that default on the part of a professional (albeit non-legal) adviser did not constitute good reason for extending time under Order 53, r. 4. Leave granted to apply for judicial review may be set aside in circumstances where it is plain, on analysis, that there was no good reason to extend time for the making of the application for leave.[28]

In practice, a meritorious case, brought within three months of the decision complained of, will usually succeed at the leave stage. However, as Simon Brown J. held in *R. v. Swale B.C., ex p. Royal Society for the Protection of Birds*,[29] even a finding at that stage that the applicant has acted "promptly" does not prevent the court from refusing relief at the full hearing on the ground of "undue delay". At the full hearing there is, following *Caswell*, every possibility that the discretion to refuse relief on the ground of undue delay may now bite wholly independently of merit. Even if relief is not refused, the relief granted may be tailored to the fact of delay.[30]

The applicants in *Caswell* were farmers who had been allocated insufficient milk quota by the Dairy Produce Quotas Tribunal. They were ignorant of the judicial review procedure, as were their professional (non-legal) advisers. They allowed over two years to elapse before applying under Order 53. The point of law on which their complaint rested had probably been misapplied by the tribunal in up to about 3,400 cases. Leave was granted to apply for judicial review.

The case was heard at first instance by Popplewell J. who decided the merits in the Caswells' favour but ruled against them on delay. He was upheld by the Court of Appeal and by the House of Lords who approved

---

[24] [1987] 1 W.L.R. 1482.
[25] See, also *Re Wilson* [1985] A.C. 750 at p. 755B.
[26] [1994] C.O.D. 132.
[27] [1985] S.T.C. 564.
[28] *R. v. Redbridge L.B.C., ex p. G* [1991] C.O.D. 398.
[29] n. 22 above.
[30] See, *e.g., R. v. Rochdale M.B.C., ex p. Schemet* [1993] C.O.D. 113.

the following parameters in applying the section 31(6) test at the full hearing:

   (a) Notwithstanding the grant of leave it is still open to the court hearing the substantive application to refuse relief on the ground of substantial hardship, prejudice or detriment.

   (b) It is, however, not open to an applicant who has had to obtain an extension of time to argue that there has been no undue delay. The fact that the application for leave was not made promptly or within three months at the latest, carries with it the inevitable consequences of undue delay, even where the applicant has shown good reason for extending time.

   (c) It is not possible to define what is meant by the term "detriment to good administration", even by example. Mere inconvenience is not enough. There must be foreseeable positive harm to good administration. There must also be affirmative evidence of detriment or at least evidence from which detriment may be inferred.[31]

   (d) In determining whether detriment flows "from the grant of relief" one may examine not only the particular instance but also the effect of the particular instance on other potential applicants, and the consequences if relief is granted in other judicial review applications.

The above guidelines are, currently, all that practitioners have to dictate the basis of advising on the effect of delay at the full hearing stage.[32] The courts have been similarly reticent as to what might constitute substantial hardship or prejudice but these are, perhaps, easier concepts to envisage and likely to depend very much upon the particular facts of the individual case. It should always be borne in mind that the court is entitled to take the issue of delay of its own motion, whether the respondent does so or not.[33]

Different considerations probably apply where there is a continuing breach of a public law duty such as a failure to reach a decision or to exercise a statutory duty at all. In such circumstances it is doubtful whether applicants are constrained by the provisions of Order 53, r. 4. The delay rules cannot be evaded, however, by seeking to elicit a later "decision" when, in truth, the challenge is to an earlier one,[34] or by contending that the validity of an earlier decision is inextricably linked to that of a subsequent decision which is challenged timeously.[35]

---

[31] *cf.* Lord Diplock in *O'Reilly v. Mackman* [1983] 2 A.C. 237 at pp. 280H–281A. In *Caswell* itself Lord Goff (see n. 21 above at pp. 749F–750A) considered that certainty was relevant to the question of "detriment to good administration" together with the effect of the decision and the impact if it were to be re-opened.

[32] For an attempt to list discretionary factors as to how undue delay should be dealt with under s.31(6), see the judgment of Popplewell J. in *Caswell, The Times,* December 7, 1988.

[33] *R. v. Dairy Produce Quotas Tribunal, ex p. Wynne-Jones* (1987) 283 E.G. 643.

[34] See, *e.g. R. v. Westminster City Council, ex p. Hilditch* [1990] C.O.D. 434.

[35] *R. v. Lloyd's of London, ex p. Briggs,* n. 77 above. Presumably, though, the fact of interdependent validity may provide a good reason to extend time under R.S.C., Ord. 53,

Alternative remedy

2–033   The existence of an alternative remedy[36] is not, by itself, a ground for refusing relief. Such remedy may not be designed to achieve the same ends as judicial review. The right of appeal, for example, frequently relates to merits rather than legality.[37] There are numerous instances where Order 53 relief will be appropriate even if there is an independent remedy.[38]

Where, however, it is considered legally more convenient to pursue an existing remedy, judicial review may be refused.[39] Convenience is dictated not only for the parties but also in the public interest.[40] Order 53, r. 3(8) reflects this reasoning by providing that an application for leave may be adjourned if a right of appeal lies against an order, etc. which is sought to be quashed by certiorari until the appeal is determined or the time limit for appeal has expired.

It is hard to detect consistency in the court's approach to alternative remedy as a basis for refusing substantive relief on judicial review. In *Ex p. Waldron*[41] Glidewell L.J. observed that the choice of remedy ought to depend upon whether an alternative statutory remedy would resolve the question fully, whether it would be quicker and whether it demanded special knowledge. Other cases have emphasised that where there is an alternative remedy judicial review will only be granted exceptionally.[42]

In reality, however, it has been observed that "when genuine grounds for judicial review are alleged, it is the refusal rather than the grant of relief which is the exceptional course."[43] Where an alternative remedy is in the course of being pursued, judicial review is sometimes refused.[44] The fact

---

r. 4. *cf.* the approach taken in *Webb v. Minister of Housing and Local Government* [1965] 1 W.L.R. 755 (*held*: timeous challenge to subsequent decision was not precluded by fact that earlier decision on whose validity later decision depended had not been challenged within the six weeks permitted by statute).

[36] For a useful analysis of the alternative remedy doctrine, see Neil Collar, "Judicial Review and Alternative Remedies: An analysis of recent English decisions", (1991) 10 C.J.Q. pp. 138 *et seq.*

[37] See para. 6–012.

[38] *R. v. Huntingdon D.C., ex p. Cowan* [1984] 1 W.L.R. 501 (licensing appeal); *R. v. Hillingdon L.B.C., ex p. Royco Homes Ltd* [1974] Q.B. 720 (planning appeal); *R. v. Paddington Valuation Officers, ex p. Peachey Property Corp.* [1966] 1 Q.B. 380 (rating appeal); *R. v. Leeds City Council, ex p. Hendry, The Times,* January 20, 1994 (appeal to justices); *R. v. Bristol Magistrates' Court, ex p. Rowles* [1994] C.O.D. 137 (right of appeal to Crown Court); *R. v. Devon C.C., ex p. Baker* [1993] C.O.D. 253 (statutory complaints machinery).

[39] Of the many cases see, *e.g. R. v. Epping Forest D.C., ex p. Green* [1993] C.O.D. 81; *R. v. Westminster City Council, ex p. Hilditch,* n. 34 above; *R. v. Trafford B.C., ex p. Colonel Foods* [1990] C.O.D. 351; *R. v. West Sussex C.C., ex p. Wenman* [1992] C.O.D. 427; *R. v. Birmingham City Council, ex p. Ferrero,* n. 84 above.

[40] *R. v. Huntingdon D.C., ex p. Cowan,* n. 38 above.

[41] [1986] Q.B. 824 at p. 852.

[42] See, *e.g., R. v. Chief Constable of Merseyside Police, ex p. Calveley* [1986] Q.B. 424 at p. 433 (Lord Donaldson of Lymington M.R.), and 435 (May L.J.); *R. v. I.R.C., ex p. Preston* [1985] A.C. 835 at p. 82, *per* Lord Scarman; *R. v. Secretary of State for the Home Department, ex p. Swati* [1986] 1 W.L.R. 477 at p. 485 (Lord Donaldson of Lymington M.R.).

[43] See Wade and Forsyth, *op. cit.,* n. 30 above at p. 725.

[44] *R. v. Civil Service Appeal Board, ex p. Bruce* [1989] 2 All E.R. 907.

that a potential alternative remedy is being pursued should always be drawn to the court's attention on making an application for leave to apply for judicial review,[45] as should the existence of such a remedy.[46]

The court may decide, in a particular case, that a statutory provision curtails the right to make an Order 53 application. Problems relating to preclusive clauses are separately considered.[47]

Apart from this jurisdictional exclusion, however, it is important to note that the alternative remedy bar to judicial review operates as a matter of discretion rather than jurisdiction.[48]

Miscellaneous factors affecting discretion

The court may also refuse relief by exercising its general discretion against an applicant.[49] The most usual bases for denial of relief in this way are because:

    (a) of an applicant's conduct or motives[50];
    (b) of waiver[51];
    (c) relief is futile,[52] or unnecessary[53];
    (d) the outcome is inevitable[54];
    (e) of adverse public consequences[55];
    (f) an application is considered to be premature.[56]

These factors are by no means exhaustive.[57]

2–034

---

[45] *R. v. Mid-Worcestershire JJ., ex p. Hart* [1989] C.O.D. 397.

[46] See D.C. decision in *R. v. Cornwall C.C., ex p. Huntingdon* [1992] 3 All E.R. 566 at p. 576f–g, *per* Brooke J. The case was appealed, unsuccessfully, on a different point to the C.A.; see [1994] 1 All E.R. 694.

[47] See para. 6–011.

[48] *Leech v. Deputy Governor of Parkhurst Prison* [1988] A.C. 533, especially at p. 562D *per* Lord Bridge.

[49] For a helpful summary of the general bases of judicial discretion, see Sir Thomas Bingham M.R.'s "Should Public Law Remedies be Discretionary?" (1991) P.L. 64.

[50] See, *e.g. Fulbrook v. Berkshire Magistrates' Courts Committee* (1970) 69 L.G.R. 75; *Dorot Properties Ltd. v. Brent L.B.C.* [1990] C.O.D. 378; *R. v. Secretary of Education and Science, ex p. Birmingham City Council* (1985) 83 L.G.R. 79. Misconduct, as these cases exemplify, includes behaviour that is undeserving rather than morally blameworthy.

[51] *R. v. Williams, ex p. Phillips* [1914] 1 K.B. 608; *R. v. Governors of Small Heath School, ex p. Birmingham City Council* [1990] C.O.D. 23. Contrast *R. v. Inner London Quarter Sessions, ex p. D'Souza* [1970] 1 W.L.R. 376.

[52] See, *e.g. R. v. Secretary of State for Social Services, ex p. Association of Metropolitan Authorities* [1986] 1 W.L.R. 1.

[53] *R. v. Monopolies and Mergers Commission, ex p. Argyll Group Plc* [1986] 1 W.L.R. 763.

[54] *R. v. Secretary of State for Education and Science, ex p. Lewisham L.B.C.* [1990] C.O.D. 319.

[55] *R. v. Secretary of State for Social Services, ex p. Cotton, The Times*, December 14, 1985.

[56] *R. v. Oxford City JJ., ex p. Berry* [1988] Q.B. 507; *Merrill v. Chief Constable of Merseyside Police* [1990] C.O.D. 61; *R. v. Attendance Allowance Board, ex p. Moran* [1990] C.O.D. 381; *R. v. Association of Futures Brokers and Dealers Ltd., ex p. Mordens* [1991] C.O.D. 40.

[57] Consider, *e.g. R. v. G.L.C., ex p. Blackburn* [1976] 1 W.L.R. 550 (possibility of order being granted at future date in the light of the respondent's reaction to court judgment); *Buchoke v. G.L.C.* [1970] 1 W.L.R. 1092 (respondent likely to behave fairly); *R. v. Panel on Take-Overs and Mergers, ex p. Guinness plc* [1990] 1 Q.B. 146 (impact on third parties).

THE EFFECT OF ILLEGALITY

2–035   Where the court does decide to intervene by way of judicial review and grant relief, it seems clear that the act or decision complained of is regarded as void.[58] Although judges have occasionally flirted with the notion of voidable decisions,[59] there is no necessary contradiction between a decision being acted upon before being challenged, or being capable of being challenged only by certain applicants according to the application of judicial discretion, and yet being void if successfully challenged. As Wade has consistently observed, the concept of a decision being void is a relative one; it does not disturb the nature of the defect complained of.[60]

It is also clear that an act or decision may be partially valid and partially void. For example, conditions attached to a planning permission may be defective, yet the permission itself remain perfectly lawful.[61]

On judicial review the court is prepared, exceptionally, to quash or declare unlawful the defective part of the act or decision. The process is known as severance.

The leading case on severance is *D.P.P. v. Hutchinson*.[62] This concerned delegated legislation in the form of a byelaw that restricted access to a military base taking away rights of commoners outwith the provisions of the enabling Act. The House of Lords held that the byelaw was neither textually nor substantially severable and, therefore, declared it to be completely invalid.

In reaching this conclusion the House held (Lord Lowry dissenting) that there were circumstances in which severance could be effected even though this involved modifying the text of the legislative instrument. In so doing the House has moved away from the former test of textual severability to one of substantial severability. The latter requires consideration of whether, after severance, what remains is essentially unchanged in its legislative purpose. As Lord Bridge observed, in *Hutchinson*[63]:

> "The test of textual severability has the great merit of simplicity and certainty. When it is satisfied the court can readily see whether the omission from the legislative text of so much as exceeds the law-maker's power leaves in place a valid text which is capable of operating and was evidently intended to operate independently of the invalid text. But I have reached the conclusion, though not without hesitation, that a rigid insistence that the test of textual severability must always be satisfied if a provision is to be upheld and enforced as partially valid will in some cases ... have the unreasonable conse-

---

[58] See, *e.g. Hoffmann-La Roche & Co. A.G. v. Secretary of State for Trade and Industry* [1975] A.C. 295, at p. 365, *per* Lord Diplock; *Anisminic v. Foreign Compensation Commission* [1969] 2 A.C. 147 at p. 171 (*per* Lord Reid) and p. 195 (*per* Lord Pearce).

[59] See, *e.g. Durayappah v. Fernando* [1967] 2 A.C. 337.

[60] See Wade and Forsyth, *op. cit.* n. 30 above at pp. 339–340.

[61] See, *e.g. Mixnam's Properties Ltd. v. Chertsey U.D.C.* [1965] A.C. 735.

[62] [1990] 2 A.C. 783. See also *R. v. I.R.C., ex p. Woolwich Equitable Building Society* [1990] 1 W.L.R. 1400 at p. 1418D–E, *per* Lord Goff.

[63] n. 62 above, at p. 811D–F.

quence of defeating subordinate legislation of which the substantial purpose and effect was clearly within the law-maker's power when, by some oversight or misapprehension of the scope of that power, the text, as written, has a range of application which exceeds that scope."

Although *Hutchinson* deals with severance in relation to delegated legislation, there seems no reason to limit its ratio to subordinate legislation. Indeed, the dangers that the House identified with regard to substantial severability, namely the substitution of the judges' view for that of the legislative intent, would seem to apply to most forms of executive decision-making.[64]

---

[64] In *Commissioner of Police v. Davis* [1994] 1 A.C. 283, the Privy Council applied the substantial severability test to primary legislation outwith the Constitution of the Bahamas.

3. REMEDIES AVAILABLE

THE RANGE OF RELIEF

3–001   An applicant seeking judicial review may (as has been seen) claim one or more of the following final forms of relief:

(a) The prerogative orders of certiorari, prohibition or mandamus.
(b) A declaration or injunction.[1]

These remedies may be claimed as an alternative, or in addition, to each other.[2] It is also possible for damages to be awarded, but these are only available where the applicant has included such a claim in the statement in support of his application for judicial review.[3] The court determining the matter must then be satisfied that damages could have been awarded at the time of making the application had the proceedings been commenced by action.[4]

THE PREROGATIVE ORDERS

3–002   The orders of certiorari, prohibition and mandamus stem from three of the old prerogative writs bearing the same name.

These writs were traditionally used by the common law courts to control the use of power by public bodies. Originally the proceedings were between the Crown and the public body concerned.[5] Subsequently, however, private subjects were permitted to apply to the Crown, *ex parte*, and the application became, in all but name, a contest between the applicant subject and the relevant public body.

By the Administration of Justice (Miscellaneous Provisions) Acts 1933 and 1938,[6] the writs were converted into judicial orders obtainable by application to the Queen's Bench Division. The nature and purpose of each order was identical to the corresponding predecessor writ.

---

[1] Ord. 53 r. 1; Supreme Court Act 1981, s.31(1). Note the circumstances in which declarations and injunctions can be sought outside judicial review proceedings: see paras. 6–002—6–006. *cf.* injunctions under the S.C.A. 1981, s.30 which **must** be claimed by way of judicial review. Interim relief obtainable on judicial review is separately considered; see paras. 8–009—8–013.

[2] Ord. 53, r. 2; S.C.A. 1981, s.31(1).

[3] See para. 3–022.

[4] Ord. 53, r. 7(1); S.C.A. 1981, s.31(4).

[5] Except in the case of prohibition, where subjects were involved directly from the beginning.

[6] See ss.3 and 7 (1933 Act) and s.8 (1938 Act).

None of the modern procedural reforms[7] has altered the nature of the prerogative orders. Thus much of the older case law is still of assistance in determining the scope of these remedies.

CERTIORARI

Certiorari originated as a royal demand for information.[8] In its modern form it lies to quash a decision that is made by a public body and is invalid on one of a number of accepted bases in public law.[9] These have already been considered in Chapter 2.

3–003

Subject matter of certiorari

In order to found a claim for certiorari there must be a "decision" capable of being quashed.[10] Certiorari is not available to quash a mere recommendation,[11] although it will lie against a recommendation falling to be considered within a particular statutory context,[12] or against a preliminary decision.[13] The form of the decision is immaterial. It may for example be a report,[14] or even inactivity.[15] What is required in all cases, however, is a decision or determination which has some legal effect and does "affect subjects".[16]

3–004

Error of law on the face of the record: a declining doctrine

Until recently, error of law on the face of the record was an independent basis of review necessary to justify an award of certiorari where there was a material error of law appearing on the face of the decision ("the record") but no excess of jurisdiction (an *intra vires* error of law).[17] Formerly, most errors of law were, unless they appeared on the face of the record, considered to be immune from judicial review on the basis that:

3–005

> "If a magistrate or any other tribunal has jurisdiction to enter on the inquiry and to decide a particular issue, and there is no irregularity in

---

[7] See paras. 1–011—1–018.

[8] See de Smith, "The Prerogative Writs" [1951] 11 C.L.J. 40.

[9] These are separately considered; see paras. 2–005—2–030.

[10] *R. v. St Lawrence's Hospital Statutory Visitors, ex p. Pritchard* [1953] 1 W.L.R. 1158 at 1166, (Parker J.) See, also, *R. v. Leicestershire Education Authority, ex p. Cannon* [1991] C.O.D. 120. Note that a view expressed in correspondence is not a "decision" capable of being quashed by certiorari. It may, however, be susceptible to declaratory relief; see *R. v. Secretary of State for Employment, ex p. Equal Opportunities Commission* (1995) 1 A.C. 1.

[11] *ibid.*

[12] As, *e.g.* in *R. v. Agricultural Dwelling-House Advisory Committee for Bedfordshire, Cambridgeshire and Northamptonshire, ex p. Brough* (1986) 19 H.L.R. 367.

[13] *R. v. Postmaster General, ex p. Carmichael* [1928] 1 K.B. 291.

[14] As in *R. v. London C.C., ex p. Commercial Gas Co.* (1895) 11 T.L.R. 337.

[15] See *e.g. R. v. Hillingdon L.B.C., ex p. Streeting* [1980] 1 W.L.R. 1430.

[16] *R. v. Criminal Injuries Compensation Board, ex p. Lain* [1967] 2 Q.B. 864 at 888 and 892.

[17] For the resurrection of this doctrine by Denning L.J. see *R. v. Northumberland Compensation Appeal Tribunal, ex p. Shaw* [1952] 1 K.B. 338.

the procedure, he does not destroy his jurisdiction by reaching a wrong decision. If he has jurisdiction to go right he has jurisdiction to go wrong. Neither an error in fact nor an error in law will destroy his jurisdiction."[18]

Increasingly, case law chipped away at the notional edifice of the "record" and the potential technical limitations that it could have involved. In *R. v. Northumberland Compensation Appeal Tribunal, ex p. Shaw*[19] Denning L.J. was prepared to accept that the "record" included not merely the formal order but also the documents properly before the court or by legitimate inference therefrom.[20] Other decisions have held that an incomplete record may require to be perfected,[21] that oral reasons contained in the judgment and recorded in the official transcript are part of the record,[22] and even that the court may, on judicial review, look at evidence which enabled it to deal with the issues before it, despite the fact that such evidence could not technically be regarded as forming part of the record.[23]

The death blow, however to the idea of a formal "record" for the purposes of review by certiorari came from another direction. A series of cases, starting with *Anisminic v. Foreign Compensation Commission*,[24] has virtually obliterated the distinction between an error of law made within or outside jurisdiction that necessitated the separated concept of error of law on the face of the record.[25]

It is now clear that almost every error of law will render a decision susceptible to review if such an error materially affects the decision. Despite earlier dicta to the contrary,[26] it seems also to be established that the principle applies to inferior courts as much as to other bodies vulnerable to certiorari.[27]

---

[18] *R. v. Governor of Brixton Prison, ex p. Armah* [1968] A.C. 192, at p. 234 *per* Lord Reid.
[19] n. 17 above.
[20] To the same effect see *Baldwin and Francis Ltd v. Patents Appeal Tribunal* [1959] A.C. 663.
[21] *R. v. Medical Appeal Tribunal, ex p. Gilmore* [1957] 1 Q.B. 574.
[22] *R. v. Knightsbridge Crown Court, ex p. International Sporting Club (London) Ltd* [1982] Q.B. 304.
[23] *R. v. Knightsbridge Crown Court, ex p. The Aspinall Curzon Ltd, The Times,* December 16, 1982.
[24] [1969] 2 A.C. 147. See also *Re Racal Communications Ltd* [1981] A.C. 374; *O'Reilly v. Mackman* [1983] 2 A.C. 237; *R. v. Greater Manchester Coroner, ex p. Tal* [1985] Q.B. 67.
[25] *Pace* a case such as *R. v. Registrar of Companies, ex p. Central Bank of India* [1986] Q.B. 1114. Note, though, that in *R. v. Hull University Visitor, ex p. Page* [1993] A.C. 682, the House of Lords, by a majority, preserved the distinction in the context of the jurisdiction of the university visitor. To similar effect, in a related context, see *R. v. Visitors to the Inns of Court, ex p. Calder & Persaud* [1993] 3 W.L.R. 287.
[26] *Per* Lord Diplock in *Re Racal*, n. 24 above at p. 383.
[27] See *O'Reilly v. Mackman*, n. 24 above, *per* Lord Diplock at p. 278. And now *R. v. Greater Manchester Coroner, ex p. Tal*, n. 24 above at p. 81, *per* Lord Goff.

Locus standi for certiorari

To obtain certiorari (as with all public law remedies under Ord. 53) an **3–006**
applicant must possess "sufficient interest". The meaning of this term is
separately considered.[28] Traditionally, however, *locus standi* for certiorari
has always been relatively wide and it is unlikely that the position has
changed.

Pre-1977 case law went so far as to suggest that the remedy was even
available to a stranger in appropriate circumstances.[29] There has, however,
always been some kind of limit in its availability, even if that limit relates
more to the court's discretion than to strict standing. In *R. v. Liverpool
Corp., ex p. Liverpool Taxi Fleet Operators' Association*[30] it was held that
certiorari did not lie in favour of "a mere busybody who is interfering in
things which do not concern him".[31]

Whatever the effect (if any) of the modernised version of *locus standi* on
pre-existing rules, it does appear that, as far as certiorari is concerned, *locus
standi* will continue to be interpreted generously.[32]

The Atkin dictum

In the past considerable controversy has surrounded the question of the **3–007**
appropriate respondent to an application for certiorari. This is considered
more generally in the whole context of judicial review.[33] The problem has
been bedevilled by the so-called "Atkin dictum". In *R. v. Electricity
Commissioners, ex p. London Electricity Joint Committee Co. (1920) Ltd*,[34]
Atkin L.J. stated in relation to certiorari (and prohibition) that:

> "Whenever any body of persons having legal authority to determine
> questions affecting the rights of subjects, and having the duty to act
> judicially, act in excess of their legal authority, they are subject to the
> controlling jurisdiction of the King's Bench Division exercised in
> these writs."

Against whom does certiorari lie?

On this basis certiorari is, clearly, available to quash decisions of inferior **3–008**
courts.[35] What other public bodies, it may be asked, have a duty to act
judicially?

Fortunately the *Electricity* case dictum has, like so much else in modern

---

[28] See Chap. 4 *passim*.
[29] *R. v. Thames Magistrates' Court, ex p. Greenbaum* (1957) 55 L.G.R. 129. *Sed quaere* whether
the term "stranger" refers merely to a person with a grievance but not a party to the actual
proceedings or decision. See Thio, *Locus Standi and Judicial Review*, pp. 163–166.
[30] [1972] 2 Q.B. 299.
[31] *ibid. per* Lord Denning M.R. at p. 309A.
[32] See, *e.g. Covent Garden Community Association v. G.L.C.* (1981) J.P.L. 183 (*held*:
community association with 20 per cent non-resident membership had standing to seek
certiorari to quash decision of G.L.C. granting itself planning permission).
[33] See paras. 5–001—5–011.
[34] [1924] 1 K.B. 171 at 205.
[35] Though the meaning of this term is not without difficulty; see paras. 5–003—5–004.

administrative law, been subject to judicial erosion. Although the literal construction is that there is an additional requirement to act judicially,[36] it seems to be accepted that this is a misreading of what Atkin L.J. actually meant.[37] The "judicial" element is to be inferred from the nature of the power exercised and extends to a broad range of administrative decision making. The widening of the dictum in this way ensures that certiorari has been granted in many different situations.[38]

It appears to be the case, however, that it will not lie against:

(a) the Crown[39];
(b) bodies exercising legislative powers[40];
(c) (at least generally) delegated legislation such as byelaws.[41]

PROHIBITION

3–009   Whereas certiorari lies to quash a decision already made, prohibition is used to prevent the respondent from acting or continuing to act in such a way as to abuse jurisdiction or offend against natural justice.[42] it may also be useful in restraining implementation of an unlawful decision[43] or policy.[44]

The jurisdictional rules relating to prohibition are, broadly, co-extensive with those in respect of certiorari. In particular, the grounds for obtaining the remedies and the bodies against whom such order can be made are virtually identical.

Prohibition is, therefore, available to prevent any public body (whether or not an inferior court) from acting outside its powers.[45] The remedy is not, however, available against a public body that has already completed the acts complained of,[46] although if there is something left to act upon an

---

[36] See *e.g. R. v. Legislative Committee of the Church Assembly, ex p. Haynes-Smith* [1928] 1 K.B. 411.

[37] See especially *Ridge v. Baldwin* [1964] A.C. 40 at 74–78, *per* Lord Reid.

[38] As *e.g.* to a Patents Appeal Tribunal, Ministers of the Crown, licensing justices, legal aid committees, local authorities, the Criminal Injuries Compensation Board, etc. For further examples, see Part 3.

[39] But it does lie against persons exercising power on behalf of the Crown. See para. 3–020.

[40] *Ridge v. Baldwin*, n. 37 above; the *Church Assembly* case, n. 36 above.

[41] See Wade and Forsyth, *Administrative Law*, (7th ed., 1994) at p. 638. *cf.*, though, *R. v. Secretary of State for Health, ex p. United States Tobacco International Inc.* [1992] Q.B. 353, where regulations made by the Secretary of State for Health were quashed.

[42] Of the many cases, consider, *e.g.*: *R. v. Horseferry Road JJ., ex p. Independent Broadcasting Authority* [1987] Q.B. 54 (prohibition lay to prevent magistrates dealing with summons disclosing no offence); *R. v. Kent Police Authority, ex p. Godden* [1971] 2 Q.B. 662 (prohibition to prevent doctor acting outwith natural justice). Its scope in relation to abuse of discretion, as opposed to excess of jurisdiction, is obviously limited since it is difficult to detect such abuse until a decision is made.

[43] *R. v. North, ex p. Oakey* [1927] 1 K.B. 491.

[44] *R. v. Greater London Council, ex p. Blackburn* [1976] 1 W.L.R. 550.

[45] See, *e.g. R. v. G.L.C.*, n. 44 above; *R. v. Newcastle-upon-Tyne JJ., ex p. Hindle* [1984] 1 All E.R. 770; *R. v. Liverpool Corp., ex p. Liverpool Taxi Fleet Operators' Association* [1972] 2 Q.B. 299.

[46] *Yates v. Palmer* (1849) 6 Dow. & L. 283.

order may still be made.[47] Nor will prohibition lie to review a finding of fact made by an inferior court for the purpose of assuming jurisdiction.[48]

The remedy may be granted on a contingent basis so as to prevent the exercise of powers until a particular condition is satisfied permitting such powers to be performed lawfully.[49]

Locus standi for prohibition

It is probable that *locus standi* is the same for both certiorari and prohibition. Special difficulties have, in the past, been created where the respondent has alleged waiver on the part of an applicant. In this respect prohibition and certiorari have not developed *pari passu*.

3–010

In relation to prohibition the courts have, for reasons that are not entirely logical,[50] elaborated a distinction between defects that are apparent on the face of the record and those that are not. It has been held, in several cases, that apparent defects cannot be waived and that an applicant may, in such instances, obtain prohibition as of right.[51] Where the error is concealed, however, the applicant's conduct becomes relevant in determining whether the remedy should be granted.[52]

It is unsatisfactory that different rules as to waiver should affect discretion or *locus standi*, according to whether it is certiorari or prohibition that is being asked for. It may well be that the conception of *locus standi* embodied in Order 53 and section 31 of the Supreme Court Act 1981 will govern the way in which the court approaches this problem, since many of the older cases on waiver are clearly influenced by earlier decisions which laid down very wide rules of standing in relation to prohibition.[53]

In *R. v. G.L.C., ex p. Blackburn*,[54] an authority which clearly presages the 1977 judicial review reforms, Lord Denning M.R. linked discretion and standing in a way that suggests that the court will adopt a broad view of both but will not necessarily grant prohibition merely because there is an apparent defect.

---

[47] *Estate and Trust Agencies (1927) Ltd. v. Singapore Improvement Trust* [1937] A.C. 898 at p. 918.

[48] *Joseph v. Henry* (1850) 19 L.J.Q.B. 369.

[49] See, *e.g. R. v. Liverpool Corp., ex p. Liverpool Taxi Fleet Operators' Association*, n. 45 above, (prohibition granted to prevent the exercise of a local authority's licensing powers pending prior consultation).

[50] Since, as to certiorari, there are no fetters on the court's discretion to refuse the remedy where there is error on the face of the record.

[51] See, *e.g. Farquharson v. Morgan* [1894] 1 Q.B. 552; *Parke, Davis & Co. v. Comptroller-General of Patents, Designs and Trade Marks* [1954] A.C. 321.

[52] See *Parke, Davis & Co.*, n. 51 above.

[53] See, *e.g. De Haber v. Queen of Portugal* (1851) 17 Q.B. 171; *Worthington v. Jeffries* (1875) L.R. 10 C.P. 379.

[54] [1976] 1 W.L.R. 550.

Prohibition in the County Court

3–011 In the County Court special rules still apply to prohibition, notwithstanding the passing of the Supreme Court Act.[55]

Section 84 of the County Courts 1984 provides that on an application for prohibition the Judge of the court shall not be served with notice thereof nor (unless ordered to do so) shall he be required to appear or be heard on the application or be liable for costs.

Thus far the section is unexceptionable. However, it also provides that "the application shall be proceeded with and heard in the same manner in all respects as an appeal duly brought from a decision of the judge". This is hard to reconcile with judicial review which is wholly distinct from the process of appeal.[56] Whilst it is no longer clear what meaning can be attached to the cited portion of section 84, that section does not override the provisions of Order 53.[57]

ORDER 53 IN RELATION TO CERTIORARI AND PROHIBITION

3–012 Certain parts of Order 53 have specific application to certiorari and/or prohibition. Thus:

(a) Where leave is sought to apply for judicial review for certiorari against "any judgment, order, conviction or other proceedings" which is subject to appeal, the court may adjourn the application until the appeal is heard or the time limited for appealing has expired (Ord. 53, r. 3(8)).

(b) If the relief sought is certiorari or prohibition, the grant of leave to apply for judicial review operates (if the court so directs) as a stay of the proceedings to which the application relates until either the determination of the substantive application or the court otherwise orders (Ord. 53, r. 3(10)(a)). In *R. v. Secretary of State for Education and Science ex p. Avon C.C.*,[58] the Court of Appeal has held that, under Ord. 53, r. 3(10), the courts are empowered to order a stay of the implementation of a decision by a minister under the Education Reform Act 1988 pending the outcome of the challenge to such decision within the framework of proceedings for judicial review and that a stay is not limited to judicial or quasi-judicial proceedings. Whilst this authority clearly is bind-

---

[55] *cf.* ss.115, 118 and 119 of the former County Courts Act 1959 dealing with other prerogative orders. These sections were repealed by S.C.A. 1981, Sched. 7.

[56] See para. 6–012.

[57] Indeed, all the remedies available under Order 53, including prohibition, have been granted on normal principles in respect of County Court decisions. As to prohibition, see *e.g. Ward v. Nield* [1917] 2 K.B. 832.

[58] [1991] 1 Q.B. 558.

ing,[59] the Privy Council has held (without Avon being cited to it) that a stay of proceedings is limited to "an order which puts a stop to the further proceedings in court or before a tribunal".[60]

(c) The material date for assessing when the grounds for an application for certiorari arise is the date of any relevant "judgment, order conviction or proceedings" (Ord. 53, r. 4(2)).

(d) Where a claim is made for certiorari the applicant must lodge the relevant order, etc., complained of in the Crown Office before the application is heard, or account for his failure to do so by affidavit. Without so doing he may not question the validity of such order (Ord. 53, r. 9(2)).

(e) In addition to granting certiorari the court may, on a successful application, remit the matter to the body concerned with a direction to reconsider it and reach a decision in accordance with the court's findings (Ord. 53, r. 9(4)).

MANDAMUS

Mandamus is a peremptory order requiring the respondent to perform a specified duty in public law. It does not, therefore, lie for breach of a private law obligation, albeit that such obligation is owed by a statutory body with other public law duties to an applicant.[61] Nor will it lie in respect of a discretion that has been exercised against the applicant.[62] The position is, however, otherwise where a discretion or power is coupled with a duty so as to give rise to an obligation in public law.[63] or where a discretion is exercised unlawfully thereby creating a public law duty to reconsider the matter.[64]

3–013

It is a useful adjunct. Often, indeed, mandamus is the most appropriate remedy.[65] It is not (even theoretically) limited to "judicial" acts (*cf.* certiorari and prohibition). There are, moreover, specific procedures for enforcement.[66]

Mandamus is especially useful in compelling adjudication by inferior courts[67]; in requiring such courts to state a case[68]; and in enforcing

---

[59] See dicta of the Court of Appeal in *R. v. Secretary of State for the Home Department, ex p. Muboyayi* [1992] Q.B. 244.

[60] *Minister of Foreign Affairs, Trade and Industry v. Vehicles and Supplies Ltd.* [1991] 1 W.L.R. 550, *per* Oliver L.J. at p. 556.

[61] *R. v. Industrial Court, ex p. A.S.S.E.T.* [1965] 1 Q.B. 377.

[62] See, *e.g. Ex p. Kinally* [1958] Crim.L.R. 474; *Re Fletcher's Application* [1970] 2 All E.R. 527n.

[63] As, *e.g.* in *William Leech (Midlands) Ltd v. Severn-Trent Water Authority* (1982) 80 L.G.R. 102.

[64] See, *e.g. R. v. Tower Hamlets L.B.C., ex p. Chetnik Developments* [1988] A.C. 858.

[65] See *Re Harrington* [1984] 1 A.C. 743.

[66] See, *e.g.* R.S.C., Ord. 45, r. 5; Ord. 52, r. 1.

[67] *R. v. Judge Lailey, ex p.* Hoffman [1932] 1 K.B. 568; *R. v. Judge Pugh, ex p. Graham* [1951] 2 K.B. 623; *Re Harrington*, n. 65 above.

[68] There are statutory provisions facilitating this. See, *e.g.*: Magistrates' Courts Act 1980, s.111(6); Supreme Court Act 1981, s.29(4).

decision-making by public bodies within a reasonable time.[69] It has application, however, to a much wider range of public duties.[70]

Locus standi for mandamus

3–014   The rules on standing are probably now similar to those relating to the other prerogative orders.[71] Whether a particular duty is enforceable by mandamus depends upon whether the definition thereof (statutory or otherwise) gives the applicant, expressly or impliedly, the right to complain.[72]

On that basis, ratepayers have been held to be entitled to seek mandamus to challenge assessments on other ratepayers.[73] It has also been suggested that if the chief officer of police laid down a policy that no housebreaker was to be prosecuted then every householder in the area affected could seek mandamus to have the policy revoked.[74]

In *Inland Revenue Commissioners v. National Federation of Self-Employed and Small Businesses Ltd*,[75] however, the total confidentiality of assessment for income tax and negotiations between individuals and the Revenue were held not to give rise to a general interest on the part of other taxpayers to obtain mandamus directing the Revenue to assess and collect tax on the "Fleet Street casuals". It was emphasised, though, that there might be extreme circumstances in which mandamus would lie against the Revenue. Clearly there are difficult "grey areas" which will need to be considered carefully.

The danger is that courts will interpret duties restrictively so as to make *locus standi* for mandamus more stringent. This was hinted at in *I.R.C.* by Lord Wilberforce.[76] Other cases have suggested that mandamus may be more difficult to obtain than certiorari or prohibition.[77] It should be understood that the court has a very wide discretion to refuse to make an order of mandamus.[78] This discretion may be wider than in the case of the other remedies on judicial review.

---

[69] See, especially: *R. v. Secretary of State for the Home Department, ex p. Phansopkar* [1976] Q.B. 606; *R. v. Thamesdown B.C., ex p. Pritchard* [1989] C.O.D. 377. *cf.*: *R. v. I.R.C., ex p. Opman International U.K.* [1986] 1 W.L.R. 568; *R. v. Secretary of State for the Home Department, ex p. Rofathullah* [1989] Q.B. 219.

[70] As, *e.g.* enforcing police duties, compelling production of local authority accounts, requiring the Minister to consider a complaint, etc. See, generally, Part 3.

[71] See, especially, *R. v. G.L.C., ex p. Blackburn*, n. 54 above at p. 559.

[72] *I.R.C. v. National Federation of Self-Employed and Small Businesses Ltd* [1982] A.C. 617.

[73] *Arsenal Football Club Ltd v. Smith* [1979] A.C. 1.

[74] *R. v. Metropolitan Police Commissioner, ex p. Blackburn* [1968] 2 Q.B. 118, *per* Salmon L.J.

[75] See n. 72 above.

[76] *ibid.* at p. 631. See, also: P.P. Craig *Administrative Law* (3rd ed., 1994) p. 491; Sir Konrad Schiemann "Locus Standi" (1990) P.L. 342 at p. 343.

[77] See, *e.g. R. v. Russell, ex p. Beaverbrook Newspapers Ltd* [1969] 1 Q.B. 342; *R. v. Commissioners of Customs and Excise, ex p. Cook* [1970] 1 W.L.R. 450.

[78] See, *e.g. R. v. Secretary of State for Wales, ex p. South Glamorgan C.C.* [1988] C.O.D. 104.

Crown servants and mandamus

Older cases suggested that mandamus did not lie against the Crown or a **3–015** servant of the Crown *per se*.[79] The position was different where an officer of the Crown owed a duty independently to the applicant under a particular statute.[80] In practice, however, most statutory duties imposed on Ministers of the Crown were normally construed as duties owed to the public and mandamus was, therefore, ordinarily available to enforce them.[81]

The older case law falls to be reassessed in the light of the landmark decision of the House of Lords in *M. v. Home Office*[82] (see also para. 3–020 below). There it was held that an officer of the Crown, acting in his official capacity, was susceptible to both interim and final injunctive relief. The obvious affinity between mandamus on the one hand and mandatory injunctive relief on the other suggests that mandamus now lies against an officer of the Crown without the need to identify a separate duty owed by him to the public.

Order 53, rule 10

This provides that no action or proceeding shall be begun or prosecuted **3–016** against any person in respect of anything done in obedience to an order of mandamus.

DECLARATION

This remedy plays an unusual role in public law. Originally, the **3–017** declaration was principally linked to the enforcement of private law rights. This followed from the courts' general reluctance to "declare" existing rights without granting consequential relief.[83] Scope for public law supervisory use of the declaration came as the result of new rules of court[84] enabling declaratory judgments to be made regardless of whether consequential relief was being, or could be, claimed.

Since *Dyson v. Attorney-General*,[85] declarations have been awarded in an increasing number of public law cases (albeit not, until recently, under the revised judicial review procedure).[86] The 1977 reforms to Order 53 have

---

[79] *R. v. Powell* (1841) 1 Q.B. 352; *R. v. Secretary of State for War* [1891] 2 Q.B. 326.

[80] As in *Padfield v. Minister of Agriculture, Fisheries and Food* [1968] A.C. 997.

[81] The point is well made by Clive Lewis in *Judicial Remedies in Public Law* (1992) at pp. 169–171.

[82] [1994] 1 A.C. 377.

[83] See, *e.g. Barraclough v. Brown* [1897] A.C. 615 at 623; *Jackson v. Turnley* (1853) 1 Dr. 617, 628. For detailed analysis see Zamir and Woolf *The Declaratory Judgment* (2nd ed., 1993) especially Chapter 2.

[84] Now R.S.C., Ord. 15, r. 16 but originally contained in a different Order introduced in 1883. In *R. v. Secretary of State for the Environment, ex p. Lee*, (1987) 54 P. & C.R. 311, Mann J. emphasised that a declaration could be sought under Ord. 53 without the assertion of a private right.

[85] [1911] 1 K.B. 410.

[86] See, generally, Part 3.

resulted in an appreciation of the public law role performed by the declaration but, at the same time, some confusion as to when the public law declaration may be sought outside the judicial review procedure. This is separately considered at paras. 6–002––6–006.

Declarations are particularly useful, in conjunction with certiorari, for challenging the legality of decisions taken,[87] or policies adopted,[88] by public bodies. Additionally, they may be used (for example) to challenge delegated legislation[89]; to determine the ambit of public law obligations[90]; and to pronounce upon questions of law.[91] A growing use for the declaration is likely to lie in determining whether European Community directives have been transposed into domestic law.[92]

Different standing rules for declarations

3–018   Until the 1977 amendments to Order 53 (see Chapter 1), the declaration could be sought only to remedy misuse of public power by means either of a relator action with the fiat of the Attorney-General or in an ordinary action, provided that there was special damage or infringement of some legal right. Efforts by Lord Denning M.R. to broaden the standing rules[93] were disapproved by the House of Lords in *Gouriet v. Union of Post Office Workers.*[94]

Now that the declaration is a remedy obtainable on judicial review, the question arises as to whether the standing rules are the same, whether the applicant proceeds under Order 53 or (as he is entitled to in certain circumstances)[95] by action.

In most instances, the judicial review machinery will be employed. The reasons for this have been separately considered (see paras. 1–019––1–020). The *I.R.C.* case[96] appears to imply that the principle of "sufficient interest" under Order 53 is less strict than the pre-1978 standing rules in respect of declarations. There, the decision in *Gouriet* was distinguished as being an authority concerned with remedies in private law (albeit for redress of a public wrong). On judicial review (according to *I.R.C.*), the *locus standi* necessary to obtain a declaration appears to lie (as for mandamus) in consideration of the duty owed by the respondent to the applicant and, in particular, whether an *ex hypothesi* breach of such duty gives rise to a right to complain.

Where, however, it is appropriate to seek a declaration by action then it is probable that infringement of a private right or some special damage must

---

[87] *R. v. Inner London Education Authority, ex p. Westminster City Council* [1986] 1 W.L.R. 28.
[88] *R. v. Felixstowe JJ., ex p. Leigh* [1987] Q.B. 582.
[89] *R. v. H.M. Treasury, ex p. Smedley* [1985] Q.B. 657.
[90] *R. v. Secretary of State for the Home Department, ex p. Doody* [1994] 1 A.C. 531.
[91] *R. v. West London Coroners' Court, ex p. Gray* [1988] Q.B. 467.
[92] *R. v. Secretary of State for Employment, ex p. Equal Opportunities Commission* [1995] 1 A.C. 1.
[93] *Att.-Gen. v. I.B.A.* [1973] Q.B. 629.
[94] [1978] A.C. 435.
[95] See paras. 6–002––6–004.
[96] n. 2 above.

still be shown. In *Barrs v. Bethell*,[97] Warner J. refused to allow an action to proceed where the plaintiff, seeking a declaration, failed to establish *locus* in the above sense. Although an earlier decision had held that standing was the same in whatever form a declaration was claimed.[98] this preceded *I.R.C.* and it is, therefore, unlikely to represent current law.

The limits of declaratory relief

The ambit of the declaration is particularly wide. In *Barnard v. National Dock Labour Board*[99] Lord Denning M.R. went so far as to observe that "I know of no limit to the power of the Court to grant a declaration except such limit as it may in its discretion impose upon itself".

This form of relief is not affected by artificial rules of the kind that have obfuscated other orders (*cf.* certiorari and prohibition). It is also unique among the other available remedies in that a declaration may be obtained against the Crown.[1]

There are, however, limitations on the scope of the remedy. In particular:

    (a) It is not possible to obtain interim relief by declaration.[2] This flows from the essence of the remedy which is designed to determine parties' rights and obligations. In relation to Crown proceedings it has been stated that the State's decisions are prima facie valid unless and until shown to be wrong and that interim declarations are, therefore, inappropriate.[3] However, in *M. v. Home Office*[4] Lord Woolf of Barnes thought that there might be advantages in the courts being permitted to grant interim declarations.[5]

    (b) Declaratory relief does not lie in respect of claims that are legally unenforceable.[6]

3–019

---

[97] [1982] Ch. 294.

[98] *Steeples v. Derbyshire C.C.* [1985] 1 W.L.R. 256.

[99] [1953] 2 Q.B. 18, at p. 41.

[1] See, especially, *Dyson v. Att.-Gen.* (n. 85 above). *cf.*, too, Crown Proceedings Act 1947, s.21. However, given the effect of *M. v. Home Office*, n. 82 above and para 3–020, it seems unlikely that this any longer represents a difference of substance as between declaratory relief and the relief obtainable under R.S.C., Order 53.

[2] See, especially, *per* Romer J. in *Underhill v. Ministry of Food* [1950] 1 All E.R. 519 at 523; *International General Electric Co. of New York v. Customs and Excise Commissioners* [1962] Ch. 784 at 789; *I.R.C. v. Rossminster* [1980] A.C. 952, *per* Lord Wilberforce at p. 1079; *Riverside Mental Health NHS Trust v. Fox, The Times*, October 28, 1993. *cf.* the Israeli Supreme Court decision in *Yotvin Engineers and Construction Limited v. State of Israel C.A.* 144/79344 1980 P.D. (2) 344 in which, reviewing the English authorities, that Court concluded that there was power to grant interim declaratory relief. *Quaere*, though, whether there might be jurisdiction to grant interim declaratory relief in a case with a European element. See para. 2–030.

[3] *Per* Lord Scarman in *I.R.C. v. Rossminster Ltd* [1980] A.C. 952. *cf.* the judgments of Lords Wilberforce and Dilhorne.

[4] n. 82 above at p. 423A.

[5] In Zamir and Woolf, *loc cit.* n. 83 above, at p. 86, Lord Woolf considered that legislative changes would probably be needed before interim declaratory relief could be awarded.

[6] See, *e.g. Mutasa v. Att.-Gen.* [1980] Q.B. 114. *cf. R. v. Secretary of State for Foreign and Commonwealth Office, ex p. Indian Association of Alberta* [1982] Q.B. 892.

(c) Declarations will not be granted in respect of *intra vires* errors of law appearing on the face of the record.[7]

(d) Declarations are not, as a matter of discretion, granted in respect of matters that are academic or hypothetical.[8] However, the court will, apparently, consider granting a declaration as to whether a respondent would be in breach of a specific order made against it.[9]

(e) In principle, public law declaratory relief is not available as a means of securing a private law entitlement.[10]

INJUNCTIONS

3–020   Injunctions have a similar history to declarations. They originated in equity but were extended to the public law sphere when the prerogative orders were becoming restricted by technical limitations.

On the public law level injunctions lie to restrain unlawful acts about to be, or in the process of being, committed. They have particular application to the prevention of *ultra vires* acts by public bodies.[11] Mandatory injunctions have, however, not been used before the judicial review reforms of 1977 to enforce duties in public law. Since then they have rarely been sought as a final form of relief.[12]

It is difficult to see that injunctive relief does more than duplicate that available, in the public law context, by means of prohibition and mandamus save, materially, that injunctions may be obtained on an interim basis whereas none of the prerogative orders can.[13] The factors affecting

---

[7] *Punton v. Minister of Pensions and National Insurance (No. 2)* [1964] 1 W.L.R. 226. In reality this limitation is no longer of importance since, for all practical purposes the distinction between *intra vires* and *ultra vires* error of law is not significant, (see para. 3–005).

[8] To this rule there are, however, several cases where the courts have been prepared to consider granting declaratory relief because of a public interest element even where the matter is no longer of importance to the parties concerned. See, *e.g. Vince v. Chief Constable of Dorset Police* [1993] 1 W.L.R. 415 and *cf.* McCowan L.J. at p. 426F with Steyn L.J. at p. 432E; *Don Pasquale (A Firm) v. Customs and Excise Commissioners, Practice Note* [1990] 1 W.L.R. 1108; *R. v. Board of Visitors of Dartmoor Prison, ex p. Smith* [1987] Q.B. 106. See also, *R. v. Secretary of State for the Home Department, ex p. Mehari* [1994] 2 W.L.R. 349 at p. 366 *per* Laws J.

[9] *R. v. British Coal Corp. and Secretary of State for the Department of Trade and Industry, ex p. Price* [1993] C.O.D. 482.

[10] See: *Roy v. Kensington & Chelsea & Westminster Family Practitioner Committee* [1992] 1 A.C. 624 at pp. 654C and 650D, *per* Lord Lowry; *Woolwich Equitable Building Society v. Inland Revenue Commissioners* [1993] A.C. 70 at p. 170H–171D, *per* Lord Goff; p. 200F–G, *per* Slynn L.J.; *R. v. Gloucestershire C.C., ex p. P* [1993] C.O.D. 303. *cf.* though, *R. v. Northavon D.C., ex p. Palmer* (1994) 6 Admin. L.R. 145, (leave granted to seek "academics" declaration on which to follow a parasitic damages claim).

[11] See, *e.g. Att.-Gen. v. Aspinall* (1837) 2 My & Cr 613; *Bradbury v. Enfield L.B.C.* [1967] 1 W.L.R. 1311.

[12] For a rare exception see *R. v. Kent C.C., ex p. Bruce, The Times,* February 8, 1986, where, however, the application failed. The position is otherwise at the interlocutory stage where interim mandatory injunctions have been granted especially in homelessness cases (see para. 8–012).

[13] See S.C.A. 1981, s.29.

the grant of interlocutory injunctions in public law cases are separately considered.[14]

The decision of the House of Lords in *M. v. Home Office*,[15] overruling its decision only four years earlier in *Factortame v. Secretary of State for Transport*[16] establishes that the High Court has jurisdiction in judicial review proceedings to grant both interim and final injunctions against government departments and other officers of the Crown. This jurisdiction exists, apparently, even prior to the grant of leave to apply for judicial review. The jurisdiction complements the jurisdiction that the High Court already had to grant such relief in respect of directly enforceable Community law rights.[17]

It seems, nonetheless, that, in proceedings outside Order 53, injunctive relief does not lie against the Crown (including Ministers acting in their official capacity) because of the clear wording of the Crown Proceedings Act 1947.[18]

M was an asylum seeker whom the Home Office proposed to deport to Zaire. On an application for leave to apply for judicial review, a mandatory *ex parte* order was granted in M's favour requiring the Home Secretary to procure M's return to the United Kingdom. Acting on advice that there was no jurisdiction to make the order,[19] the Home Secretary failed to comply with it. An application was made to commit the Secretary of State for contempt of court.

In the Divisional Court Simon Brown J. rejected the argument that either the Crown or the Home Secretary could be held liable in contempt.[20] The Court of Appeal, by a majority, held that the Home Secretary personally was in contempt of court for breach of the judge's order, even though neither the Crown itself nor a Minister acting in his official capacity could be guilty of a contempt.[21]

In the House of Lords, Lord Woolf of Barnes said this:

"[T]he language of s.31 [SCA] being unqualified in its terms, there is no warrant for restricting its application so that in respect of ministers and other officers of the Crown alone the remedy of an injunction, including an interim injunction, is not available. In my view the history of prerogative proceedings against officers of the Crown supports such a conclusion. So far as interim relief is concerned, which is the practical change which has been made, there is no justification for adopting a different approach to officers of the Crown from that adopted in relation to other respondents in the absence of clear language such as that contained in s.21(2) of the 1947 Act. The

[14] See para. 8–012.
[15] See n. 82 above. For an illuminating analysis of the decision, see Mark Gould, "M v. Home Office: Government and the Judge" (1993) P.L. 568.
[16] [1990] 2 A.C. 85.
[17] See: *R. v. Secretary of State for Transport, ex p. Factortame (No. 2)* [1991] A.C. 603.
[18] See ss.21 and 38.
[19] Based on the House of Lords' reasoning in *Factortame*, see n. 16 above.
[20] *The Times*, August 5, 1991.
[21] [1992] Q.B. 270.

fact that in any event a stay could be granted against the Crown under Ord. 53, r. 3(10)[22] emphasizes the limits of the change in the situation which is involved. It would be most regrettable if an approach which is inconsistent with that which exists in Community law should be allowed to persist if this is not strictly necessary. The restriction provided for in s.21(2) of the 1947 Act does, however, remain in relation to civil proceedings."[23]

The standing rules for injunctions are, essentially, the same as for declarations. Thus, outside Order 53 and the relator action a plaintiff seeking an injunction in a public law case (where this is permitted) will have to show either infringement of some private right[24] or the suffering of special damage.[25] The *locus standi* required is probably greater than that contained in the "sufficient interest" test on judicial review.[26]

INJUNCTIVE AND DECLARATORY RELIEF UNDER ORDER 53

3–021   On an application under Order 53 the court may grant injunctive or declaratory relief only where it considers that it would be just and convenient to make such award by way of judicial review having regard to:

(a) the nature of the matters in respect of which relief may be granted by a prerogative order;

(b) the nature of the respondent; and

(c) all the circumstances of the case.[27]

The above provision seems to contain all the elements of the court's discretion in relation to injunctive and declaratory relief. Where discretion is exercised against the applicant there is power, under Order 53, r. 9(5), to order the proceedings to continue as if they had been begun by writ.[28]

Despite earlier dicta to the contrary,[29] the House of Lords has held in *R. v. Secretary of State for Employment, ex p. Equal Opportunities Commission*,[30] that declaratory (and injunctive) relief is obtainable under Order 53 even where none of the prerogative orders is capable of being granted. In Lord Browne-Wilkinson's view:

"under Order 53 any declaration as to public rights which could formerly be obtained in civil proceedings in the High Court can now also be obtained in judicial review proceedings. If this were not so . . .

---

[22] See para. 3–012.

[23] See n. 82 at p. 422F–H.

[24] *Boyce v. Paddington B.C.* [1903] 1 Ch. 109.

[25] *Benjamin v. Storr* (1874) L.R. 9 C.P. 400.

[26] See paras. 4–003—4–005. There seems no reason, in principle, why the rules should be different as between declarations and injunctions.

[27] Ord. 53, r. 1(2); S.C.A. 1981, s.31(2).

[28] But possibly no power to order a writ action to continue as judicial review proceedings; see para. 9–020.

[29] See: *Inland Revenue Commissioners v. National Federation of Self-Employed and Small Businesses Ltd* [1982] A.C. 617 at p. 648, *per* Lord Scarman; *Davy v. Spelthorne B.C.* [1984] A.C. 262 at p. 278E, *per* Lord Wilberforce.

[30] [1995] 1 A.C. 1.

the purely procedural decision in O'Reilly v. Mackman, requiring all public law cases to be brought by way of judicial review, would have had the effect of thenceforward preventing a plaintiff who previously had locus standi to bring civil proceedings for a declaration as to public rights (even though there was no decision which could be the subject of a prerogative order) from bringing any proceedings for such a declaration."[31]

Finally, Order 53, r. 1(1) prescribes that applications for injunctions under section 30 of the Supreme Court Act, seeking to restrain a person from acting in any office in which he is not entitled to act, must be made in judicial review proceedings.[32] Whilst an award may be refused on discretionary grounds,[33] it would seem that there is no power to order the proceedings to continue as a writ action.

THE RIGHT TO DAMAGES ON JUDICIAL REVIEW

This is not an independent remedy. It is available on judicial review only where there is a right to damages in private law.[34] This result is ensured by the phraseology of Order 53 which provides that before damages can be awarded, the court must be satisfied that "if the claim had been made in an action begun by the applicant at the time of making his application, he could have been awarded damages."[35] The applicant must include the claim in his statement in support of the application for leave.[36] In view, however, of the court's wide powers of amendment,[37] the omission of a claim for damages would not appear to be fatal provided that such right existed at the time the application was made.

Where damages are sought they must be pleaded with the same particularity as in an ordinary action.[38] The inclusion of such a remedy is a concession to procedural convenience. Nonetheless the following consequences ought to follow from the fact of a private law remedy being available in public law proceedings:

3–022

(a) If the applicant fails to persuade the court that he has a remedy in public law he should not be awarded damages. This is implicit in the requirement that damages cannot be claimed unless subordinate to a claim for one or more of the principal orders available.[39] In R. v. Northavon D.C., ex p. Palmer[40] Sedley J. was prepared to

---

[31] See n. 30 at p. 36C–E. For a contrary analysis (leading to the same conclusion) see Gordon, "Judicial Review and Equal Opportunities" (1994) P.L. 217.

[32] See also S.C.A. 1981, s.31(1).

[33] As, e.g. in Everett v. Griffiths [1924] 1 K.B. 941, 958.

[34] The distinction between private and public law is, in this context, less important where a breach of Community law is alleged; see para. 2–030.

[35] Ord. 53, r. 7(1)(b). cf. S.C.A. 1981, s.31(4)(b) which uses "would" rather than "could". Is this material?

[36] Ord. 53, r. 7(1)(a); S.C.A. 1981, s.31(4)(a).

[37] Under Ord. 53, r. 3(6) and 6(2). See Chap. 8.

[38] Ord. 53, r. 7(2).

[39] See Davy v. Spelthorne, n. 29 above at p. 274, per Lord Fraser.

[40] n. 10, above.

grant to move for judicial review in order to facilitate a claim for damages, dependent upon established breach of a public law obligation, even where the respondent authority had conceded the application.

(b) Even if a right to damages is made out, the court, in judicial review proceedings, presumably has a discretion to refuse the order.[41]

(c) Since, *ex hypothesi*, the remedy lies for infringement of a private law right, it cannot be an abuse of process to initiate a claim for damages by action rather than proceeding under Order 53 (*cf.* declarations and injunctions).

(d) Interest on the amount of damages should be capable of being recovered.[42]

SELECTING A REMEDY

3–023   The scope of the various orders is not always distinct and it is sometimes difficult to predict the court's determination of the appropriateness of particular remedies. There are many instances, on judicial review, of one remedy being preferred to another, even if that other is technically available.[43]

Whilst an applicant may apply to amend by adding new relief it is safer, if there is any doubt, to claim all possible orders cumulatively or alternatively. This is permitted under Order 53, r. 2.

No further remedies under Order 53

3–024   In *R. v. Secretary of State for Education and Science, ex p. M.G.*,[44] the respondent consented to all the orders sought, save for discovery which the appellant wanted for the purpose of his remitted appeal. It was argued on his behalf that Order 24, r. 3 and Order 53, r. 9(4) gave the court an implied power to make such an order. The order was refused, Neil L.J. saying that:

"It seems to me that this application for discovery is based on a fundamental misconception of the powers of the court on an application for judicial review. The relief that can be given on such an application by way of final order really falls under six headings. These are certiorari, prohibition, mandamus, declarations, injunctions and generally, in certain cases, damages. An order for discovery can certainly be made for the purpose and in the course of judicial review proceedings so that the case can be disposed of. But in my judgment

---

[41] Both Ord. 53, r. 7(1) and S.C.A. 1981, s.31(4) state that the court "may" award damages.

[42] See: *R. v. Liverpool City Council, ex p. Coade, The Times*, October 10, 1986.

[43] *cf., e.g.: R. v. Boundary Commission for England, ex p. Foot* [1983] Q.B. 600, (declaration would be preferred to prohibition where the ambit of what was sought to be prohibited was uncertain); *R. v. Home Secretary, ex p. Anderson* [1984] Q.B. 778, (mandamus refused since unnecessary; declaration preferred); *Re Harrington*, (n. 65 above) (mandamus preferred to certiorari where decision was a nullity).

[44] [1990] C.O.D. 65.

the court cannot make an order by way of judicial review for discovery of documents to be used in some subsequent, though maybe related proceedings."

Once the court has made a final order in judicial review proceedings, there is no jurisdiction to vary such order since the court is *functus officio*.[45]

---

[45] *R. v. British Coal Corp., ex p. Price (No. 2), The Times*, February 23, 1993.

4. THE APPLICANT

RULES OF ATTRIBUTION

4–001   Proceedings in judicial review occur on the level of public law. That does not, however, connote that any member of the public may apply for the remedy. Unlike the *actio popularis* in Roman law, where any citizen could maintain an action for breach of a public wrong,[1] English law has always sought to restrict the availability of the remedies now included within Order 53.

Prior to the reforms to Order 53 introduced in 1977,[2] there were separate rules governing standing not merely for declarations and injunctions—then outside the reformed procedure—but also as between the individual prerogative remedies.[3] The terminology of Order 53 suggests, however, that there may now be a uniform test of standing for applicants seeking judicial review whatever the particular remedy being sought. This question is considered below. The treatment here proceeds on the assumption that the revised procedure contains a single test for an applicant's standing. Insofar as any separate test may still prevail, reference should be made to the analysis of specific remedies where the former standing rules are outlined.

An applicant will have his standing examined both on the preliminary application for leave[4] and on the substantive hearing. It is now clearly established that the test for determination of standing differs according to when it is being considered. The court's approach at the *ex parte* stage is, whilst not wholly cursory, much less searching than on the *inter partes* hearing.[5]

Order 53, referring specifically to *locus standi*, requires "sufficient interest" to be made out.[6] There is consensus that judicial review will not be

---

[1] The closest proceedings to the *actio popularis* in English law are private prosecutions where no standing is required to be established.

[2] For an outline see paras. 1–011—1–018.

[3] These may have been more apparent than real; see below at para. 4–006.

[4] Ord. 53, r. 3(7); S.C.A. 1981, s.31(3).

[5] See *I.R.C. v. National Federation of Self-Employed and Small Businesses Ltd* [1982] A.C. 617. See also para. 4–002.

[6] Ord. 53, r. 3(7). It must be a sufficient interest "in the matter to which the application relates." See also S.C.A. 1981, s.31(3). Equally relevant, but less often a problem, is an applicant's *capacity* to institute proceedings. For example, an unincorporated association has no capacity to seek judicial review; see: *R. v. Darlington B.C., ex p. Association of Darlington Taxi Owners, The Times,* January 21, 1994. So, too, a statutory body may have no capacity to

available to a mere busybody interfering in things that do not concern him.[7] By contrast a direct financial or legal interest is, of itself, not required.[8] The minimum *locus standi* necessary lies somewhere between these extremes but attribution of status depends in each case, upon the context.

The attempt to develop detailed principles involves consideration of the decision in *Inland Revenue Commissioners v. National Federation of Self-Employed and Small Businesses Ltd*[9] ("the *I.R.C.* case"). Analysis of the term "sufficient interest", as approached in *I.R.C.*, discloses the following particular problems:

(a) What is the appropriate test at the *ex parte* stage?
(b) What is the test on the full hearing?
(c) What is the nature of the relationship between standing and discretion?
(d) What is the nature of the relationship between standing and legality?
(e) Is there now a uniform *locus standi* for all remedies on judicial review?
(f) What is the court's general approach?

These will now be examined.

SUFFICIENT INTEREST AT THE PRELIMINARY STAGE

Some caution is needed here. The words of Order 53 stipulate that it is at **4–002** the *ex parte* stage that determination of sufficient interest becomes relevant. Order 53, r. 3(7) states that "The court shall not grant leave unless it considers that the applicant has a sufficient interest in the matter to which the application relates."

In *I.R.C.*, discussion of the standing rules was undoubtedly based on the premise that the above rule provided a starting point for the full hearing/second-stage test.[10] The House of Lords went on to develop a fact-based method of assessing *locus standi*, at that second stage, necessitating close attention to evidence and merits.

Whatever the attraction of this approach, which is separately considered, *I.R.C.* is also authority for the proposition that this is not the way the court deals with *locus* on the application for leave. Here logic appears to fall away, since the only mention of sufficient interest in Order 53 is in relation to that first stage.

---

seek review as, where, it acts outwith its statutory powers (see: *R. v. Secretary of State for Employment, ex p. Equal Opportunities Commission* [1995] 1 A.C. 1 where this issue was in play).

[7] See n. 5 above at p. 646, *per* Lord Fraser of Tullybelton. So, too, "quixotic" applications will not be entertained; see: *R. v. Legal Aid Board, ex p. Bateman* [1992] 1 W.L.R. 711, at p. 718C, *per* Nolan L.J.

[8] See n. 7 above, *per* Lord Fraser. Note, also, *R. v. Secretary of State for the Environment, ex p. Rose Theatre Trust Co.* [1990] 1 Q.B. 504 at p. 520D, *per* Schiemann J.; *R. v. Legal Aid Board, ex p. Bateman* n. 7 above at p. 721D, *per* Jowitt J.

[9] See n. 5 above.

[10] See para. 4–003.

It was recognised, in the *I.R.C.* case, that a court might be justified in granting leave to apply for judicial review even if, at the later stage, it was held that the applicant did not possess requisite standing. On that basis, there was material whereby the Divisional Court could grant leave to the National Federation of Self-Employed and Small Businesses to pursue its substantive application, albeit that when all the evidence was heard there was an absence of *locus*.[11]

The correct approach to standing, on the preliminary application, was succinctly set out in the speech of Lord Diplock. He stated as follows:

> "So this is a 'threshold' question in the sense that the court must direct its mind to it and form a *prima facie* view about it on the material that is available at the first stage. The *prima facie* view so formed, if favourable to the applicant, may alter on further consideration in the light of further evidence that may be before the court at the second stage, the hearing of the application for judicial review itself."[12]

The point was put, in similar fashion, by Lord Fraser of Tullybelton who referred to the grant of leave as "a provisional finding of sufficient interest, subject to revisal later on."[13] Lord Scarman, also, spoke of the applicant being obliged to make out a "prima facie case" to obtain leave.[14]

It would appear, however, that the prima facie view or provisional finding is not based on any real analysis of merit. If there is clearly no case, the threshold requirement of leave will operate to "prevent abuse by busybodies, cranks and other mischief-makers."[15] Otherwise (again from Lord Diplock):

> "If, on a quick perusal of the material then available, the court thinks that it discloses what might on further consideration turn out to be an arguable case in favour of granting to the applicant the relief claimed, it ought, in the exercise of a judicial discretion, to give him leave to apply for that relief. The discretion that the court is exercising at this stage is not the same as that which it is called upon to exercise when all the evidence is in and the matter has been fully argued at the hearing of the application."[16]

---

[11] See n. 5 above. See especially at pp. 635–636 (Lord Wilberforce); pp. 643–644 (Lord Diplock); pp. 653–654 (Lord Scarman).

[12] *ibid.* at p. 642F–H.

[13] *ibid.* at p. 645F.

[14] *ibid.* at p. 653G. This was, though, in the context of the grant of leave generally and not merely in respect of sufficient interest.

[15] See n. 5 above at p. 653G, *per* Lord Scarman.

[16] *ibid.* at pp. 644 A–B. Note, though, Lord Donaldson of Lymington M.R.'s observation in *R. v. Legal Aid Board, ex p. Hughes* (1993) 5 Admin.L.R. 623 that the test appropriate at the leave stage has "moved on" since Diplock L.J. made his comments in *I.R.C.* and that the test though not "in depth" amounts to more than a "quick perusal".

THE TEST ON THE FULL HEARING

Taken literally, Order 53[17] gives no guidance as to the appropriate **4–003** standing requirements on the substantive hearing. Indeed it might once have been open to argument that the granting of leave was itself determinative of an applicant having sufficient interest.

That this position is untenable is no longer open to doubt.[18] In *I.R.C.* the House of Lords evolved a detailed approach to *locus standi* apposite to the final hearing for judicial review. By accepting Order 53[19] as the *fons et origo* of sufficient interest for this purpose, it is submitted that unnecessary confusion was introduced into the first- and second-stage tests.[20] Nonetheless these stages were unequivocally demarcated in fact (if not in logic) in most of the speeches.

In *I.R.C.* the respondent Federation sought, against the Inland Revenue Commissioners:

(a) a declaration invalidating an arrangement in the nature of an amnesty[21] concluded with the so-called "Fleet Street Casuals";

(b) mandamus directing the Revenue to assess and collect past tax on the newspaper employees.

In the Divisional Court, leave to apply for judicial review was refused on the ground that the Federation lacked standing. Their appeal was allowed by the Court of Appeal which held that, as a preliminary issue, there was sufficient interest within the meaning of Order 53.[22]

Both lower courts treated *locus standi* as an abstract question severable from the merits of the case.[23] Indeed in the Court of Appeal it was conceded, for the purpose of argument, that the Revenue had acted unlawfully.

By the time of the appeal (by the I.R.C.) to the House of Lords this concession had been withdrawn and the case was argued in a different way by linking standing to merits. This alternative presentation and the procedural history had a material effect on the formulation of the test applicable to standing on the final hearing.

So, too, did the content of Order 53. Lords Wilberforce and Scarman emphasised that sufficient interest must be assessed in the light of "the

---

[17] And to the same effect *cf.* S.C.A. 1981, s.31(3).

[18] See, *e.g.* the Supreme Court Practice 1995, para. 53/1–14/11.

[19] *I.R.C.* was decided before the passing of the S.C.A. 1981. Since s.31(3) thereof is couched in almost identical terms, however, presumably it would similarly have been taken as the appropriate starting point.

[20] See paras. 4–006–4–009. *cf.* also Wade and Forsyth, *Administrative Law* (7th ed., 1994) at pp. 710 *et seq.*

[21] In essence, the taxpayers were to fill in detailed returns for the past two years and earlier periods would be quietly forgotten.

[22] *Semble* on the basis that the Federation had a genuine grievance and was not a mere busybody. Note that the relevant rule was then r. 3(5) but is now r. 3(7).

[23] *cf. Scottish Old People's Welfare Council Petitioners* [1987] S.L.T. 179 (*held*: "the matter of *locus standi* is logically prior to and conceptually distinct from the merits of the case").

matter to which the application relates."[24] It would, therefore, be wrong in law for the court to attempt such evaluation without regard to the matter of the complaint.[25]

Most of the Law Lords in *I.R.C.* were heavily critical of the parties' agreement to treat standing as a preliminary issue. Only Lord Fraser considered that sufficient interest should be logically anterior to discussion of the merits.[26] Lord Diplock would have preferred to defer examination of *locus standi* altogether since, on the merits, the Federation's case failed *in limine*.[27]

The majority view, however, was that merits were inextricably linked to standing. The implications of this approach are considered below.[28] In theory at least the test is simply stated. Except in straightforward cases where *locus*—or its absence—is easily discernible the court must proceed to investigate the applicant's claim in detail. Lord Wilberforce put it thus:

> "it will be necessary to consider the powers or the duties in law of those against whom the relief is asked, the position of the applicant in relation to those powers or duties, and the breach of those said to have been committed. In other words the question of sufficient interest cannot, in such cases, be considered in the abstract, or as an isolated point: it must be taken together with the legal and factual context."[29]

Inevitably the above reasoning is easier to express than to apply. In the *I.R.C.* case it was by no means obvious, at the outset, that the Federation lacked sufficient interest. The "legal and factual context" required consideration of the Inland Revenue's duties towards taxpayers in general and of the particular breaches or failure of duties complained of. In other cases the approach would not necessarily be similar. Examination of a respondent's duty and the scope thereof in relation to the applicant was described by Lord Wilberforce as "a good working rule though perhaps not an exhaustive one."[30]

Essentially *I.R.C.* prescribes flexibility. In itself this is a good thing. No one wants the law on standing to revert to a self-enclosed system of "outdated technical rules".[31] On the other hand the cession of rules to facts in this area is potentially dangerous. It has led some commentators to doubt whether standing still exists, after *I.R.C.*, as a restrictive principle of public law.[32] We must now examine why.

---

[24] See n. 5 above at p. 630E (Lord Wilberforce); p. 653F (Lord Scarman).

[25] *ibid.* at p. 653F (Lord Scarman).

[26] *ibid.* at p. 645C.

[27] *ibid.* at p. 637D.

[28] See paras. 4–004 and 4–005.

[29] See n. 5 above at p. 630C–E.

[30] *ibid.* at p. 631F.

[31] *ibid.* at p. 644, *per* Lord Diplock.

[32] See especially Wade and Forsyth, *op cit.* n. 20 above, p. 711. *cf.* Peter Cane, "Standing, Legality and the Limits of Public Law" [1981] P.L. 322–339.

STANDING AND DISCRETION

Judicial review is a discretionary remedy. The general ambit of that **4–004** discretion is considered separately.[33] That is not to say that the question of standing is subject to the court's discretion. The judgments in *I.R.C.*, however, come suspiciously close to such assertion.

In *I.R.C.*, Lord Scarman regarded it as the unanimous view of the House of Lords that sufficient interest was a mixed question of law and fact.[34] This was not in fact so, though the law/fact conception of *locus* was expressed by (apart from Lord Scarman) Lords Wilberforce and Roskill.[35]

It is as well to analyse the implications of that view. If standing is an amalgam of law and fact it is, presumably, divorced from discretion. The court reaches a finding on the facts and then applies the relevant law. This seems to have been accepted by Lord Wilberforce who stated, in respect of Order 53, that "it does not remove the whole—and vitally important—question of *locus standi* into the realm of pure discretion. The matter is one for decision, a mixed question of fact and law, which the court must decide on legal principle."[36]

Neither Lord Scarman nor Lord Roskill appear to have followed the logic of their own opinion of standing. In their respective judgments both sought to subsume sufficient interest to discretion.

Of the law/fact mixture, Lord Scarman observed: "The legal element in the mixture is less than the matters of fact or degree: but it is important, as setting the limits within which, and the principles by which, the discretion is to be exercised."[37]

It is, with respect, hard to see why the balance should swing in favour of fact or why the element of law should be used to circumscribe discretion rather than (as traditionally) to ascribe or deny status. Lord Scarman's reasoning was, nonetheless, taken up by Lord Roskill who criticised the Court of Appeal for treating sufficient interest as a matter of jurisdiction rather than one of overall discretion.[38]

The remaining speeches did not refer to the law/fact blend but contained different views on the nature of the court's discretion. Lord Diplock believed sufficient interest to be at the "unfettered discretion" of the court.[39] Lord Fraser, more cautiously, did not accept an "uncontrolled discretion".[40] He did not, though, expand on the nature of such discretion as he thought might exist.

Where, then, does this leave sufficient interest? It is, unfortunately, difficult to find any definitional content in *I.R.C.* Perhaps the decision intended no more than to lay bare the process by which, in doubtful cases,

---

[33] See Chap. 2 at paras. 2–031–2–034.
[34] See n. 5 above at p. 653B.
[35] *ibid.* at p. 631C (Lord Wilberforce); p. 659A–B (Lord Roskill).
[36] *ibid.* at p. 631C.
[37] *ibid.* at p. 653B.
[38] *ibid.* at p. 661H.
[39] *ibid.* at p. 642E.
[40] *ibid.* at p. 646A.

the court attributes *locus standi*. Where an applicant's status is ambiguous there is, undeniably, a policy/discretionary element in the court's approach. Where, however, a category is well established,[41] discretion tends to give way to rules.

It is, in any case, regrettable that such predominance was given to discretion. Clearly if standing is entirely a matter of discretion, as many of the judgments indicate, it disappears as an independent concept. If it remains conceptually distinct its assimilation to discretion makes the formulation of legal principles all the more difficult.

STANDING AND LEGALITY

4–005   A similar problem attaches to the relationship between standing and legality. In the *I.R.C.* case it was unanimously held that the Revenue possessed extensive managerial powers enabling it to conclude "special arrangements" with taxpayers. Although there was a general duty of fairness to other taxpayers that duty was, in the present context, fulfilled unless it could be shown that the Revenue had abused its discretion.[42]

This analysis is uncontroversial. Unhappily, however, some of the judgments appear to link the legality of a respondent's actions with the applicant's standing in such a way that the independent existence of the latter is threatened.

Thus, having stated the general principle, Lord Wilberforce went on to say:

> "That a case can never arise in which the acts or abstentions of the revenue can be brought before the court I am certainly not prepared to assert, nor that, in a case of sufficient gravity, the court might not be able to hold that another taxpayer or other taxpayers could challenge them. Whether this situation has been reached or not must depend upon an examination, upon evidence, of what breach of duty or illegality is alleged."[43]

To the same effect Lord Fraser observed (in respect of a hypothetical applicant) that "It may be that, if relying upon some exceptionally grave or widespread illegality, he could succeed in establishing a sufficient interest, but such cases would be very rare indeed and this is not one of them."[44]

It is not easy to understand these statements. If they merely refer to the fact that serious illegality would itself be a breach of the general duty of fairness, it would have been simpler to put it in that way. What seems to be being posited, however, is a direct correlation between legality and *locus*. Not only must an applicant prove breach of some duty, he must also establish a particular kind of illegality. The court, as part of its investigation into standing, will examine the quality of the illegality alleged.

That, with respect, is an entirely novel approach to standing and one that

---

[41] As, *e.g.*; ratepayers. See especially *Arsenal Football Club Ltd v. Smith* [1979] A.C. 1.
[42] See n. 5 above. See especially the formulation of Lord Scarman at p. 651E–G.
[43] *ibid.* at p. 633D.
[44] *ibid.* at p. 647B.

threatens to extinguish it altogether. Whereas before *I.R.C.* there was a clear separation between *locus standi* and merits, that may no longer be so. If the court in every case is to conduct an enquiry into the seriousness or otherwise of the respondent's actions before attributing status, then discretion, merits and standing all fuse and the reasoning process becomes indistinct. The amorphism that would be created has led one commentator to conclude that, in *I.R.C.*, "the House of Lords may well have sown the seeds of the eventual death of standing."[45]

IS *locus standi* NOW UNIFORM?

Even before the revised Order 53 made its appearance, the standing rules in respect of the prerogative orders were drawing together and it was generally recognised that similar, if not identical, principles prevailed.[46] The same was not true in relation to declarations and injunctions which, for historical reasons, were subject to the more stringent requirement that an applicant, to acquire *locus standi*, had to establish infringement of a private right or the suffering of special damage.[47]

4–006

Order 53 itself makes no reference to the possibility of a uniform test for *locus standi*. The term "sufficient interest" neither negates nor confirms its existence.[48] The Law Commission (in 1976) was, apparently, anxious not to lay down specific rules for fear of "imposing an undesirable rigidity".[49]

With the inclusion, for the first time, of declarations and injunctions in the same procedure, it was open to the House of Lords in the *I.R.C.* case to consider the question of uniformity. It must be remembered, however, that the case was decided prior to the passing of the Supreme Court Act 1981. Unless, therefore, rules relating to standing were procedural rather than substantive,[50] there was a limit to what Order 53 could achieve in this respect.

In the event, *I.R.C.* goes a long way towards recognising that principles of *locus standi* are the same for all the remedies obtainable on judicial review. Lords Diplock, Scarman and Roskill strongly implied that this was so.[51] Only Lord Diplock, however, went so far as to say: "the main purpose of the new Order 53 was to sweep away ... procedural differences including, in particular, differences as to *locus standi*."[52]

Given Lord Diplock's view that standing rules were, essentially, rules of

---

[45] See Cane, n. 32 above at p. 336.
[46] See, *e.g. R. v. G.L.C., ex p. Blackburn* [1976] 1 W.L.R. 550.
[47] See Chap. 3 and *Gouriet v. Union of Post Office Workers* [1978] A.C. 435.
[48] The term "sufficient interest" is itself intended to be less restrictively interpreted than the former expression "person aggrieved" (see *Cook v. Southend B.C.* [1990] 2 Q.B. 1 at p. 8B–C, *per* Woolf L.J.).
[49] See Law Comm. No. 73 Cmnd. 6407 (1976) *Report on Remedies in Administrative Law*.
[50] This was indeed the view of Lord Diplock. See *I.R.C.* n. 5 above at p. 638B. It was not, however, generally shared.
[51] See n. 5 above at pp. 638 and 640 (Lord Diplock); pp. 649–653 (Lord Scarman); pp. 656–658 (Lord Roskill).
[52] *ibid.* at p. 638E.

practice[53] it was easy for him to interpret the effect of Order 53 liberally. Others were more cautious. Lord Fraser was unwilling to find that all the older law had been overthrown.[54] Lord Wilberforce underlined this by observing that "the fact that the same words are used to cover all the forms of remedy allowed by the rule does not mean that the test is the same in all cases."[55]

Anything said in *I.R.C.* about uniformity in relation to the standing principles is *obiter* (albeit persuasive *obiter*), since the decision was, specifically, on the requisite *locus standi* for mandamus and declarations in a particular factual situation.

It is, nonetheless, submitted that the case supports the proposition that there is now a broadly uniform test for *locus standi* for all the remedies under Order 53. The fact that particular relief may not be granted to a particular applicant is, analytically, relevant to the question of appropriateness, or grant, of remedy rather than to standing.[56]

Certainly in relation to mandamus the majority view, in *I.R.C.*, was that the standing test was, despite earlier contrary dicta,[57] no stricter than for certiorari.[58] Moreover, since *I.R.C.*, the House of Lords has held, in *R. v. Secretary of State for Employment, ex p. Equal Opportunities Commission*,[59] that declaratory relief is obtainable, in judicial review proceedings, even where the prerogative orders are unavailable. This suggests, potentially at least, that standing in relation to the declaration is, within Order 53, not intended to be more stringent than for those orders.

It should be emphasised that outside Order 53, in respect of declarations and injunctions, more restrictive standing rules probably still apply.[60]

THE COURT'S GENERAL APPROACH TO STANDING SINCE I.R.C.

4–007   One detects in the *I.R.C.* case a genuine desire to escape the technicality that has dogged *locus standi* in the past. A broader, more liberal approach was preferred to the old conceptual categories such as "person aggrieved", "specific legal right", etc.[61]

This very flexibility, as has been seen, creates its own problems and, in

---

[53] See n. 49 above.

[54] See n. 5 above at p. 646A.

[55] *ibid.* at p. 631C. He also suggested that the test of standing for mandamus was more strict than for certiorari or prohibition. Later cases, such as *R. v. Felixstowe JJ., ex p. Leigh* [1987] Q.B. 582 at p. 597B also suggest that standing may depend on the remedy being sought. To similar effect see Sir Konrad Schiemann 'Locus Standi' in (1990) P.L. 342.

[56] Consider Purchas L.J.'s insight in *R. v. Department of Transport, ex p. Presvac Engineering Ltd* (1992) 4 Admin. L.R. 121 at pp. 145G–146B that standing is, more appropriately, to be described as a threshold test, with (if apposite) discretion operating to refuse relief in the light of all the merits.

[57] *cf. R. v. Russell, ex p. Beaverbrook Newspapers Ltd* [1969] 1 Q.B. 342; *R. v. Commissioners for Customs and Excise, ex p. Cook* [1970] 1 W.L.R. 450.

[58] See n. 5 above at p. 640D (Lord Diplock); p. 653C (Lord Scarman); p. 656G (Lord Roskill). *cf.* though, *per* Lord Wilberforce at p. 631D.

[59] n. 6 above. See, especially, *per* Lord Browne-Wilkinson at pp. 34F–37C.

[60] See, *e.g. Barrs v. Bethell* [1982] Ch. 294. See also paras. 3–018—3–020.

[61] See n. 5 above at p. 630F (Lord Wilberforce).

particular, the danger of applications being refused under a residual, enlarged discretion. It does seem clear, however, that the intention at least was to accord standing more freely.

Case law since *I.R.C.* suggests that, in general, this approach will be followed. The following authorities are illustrative of the way in which the High Court now tends to approach the issue of standing on an application for judicial review.

In *R. v. Secretary of State for the Environment, ex p. Ward*[62] the respondent argued that a gypsy had no standing to challenge the Secretary of State's decision not to exercise his powers under section 9 of the Caravan Sites Act 1968 directing local authorities to provide caravan sites for gypsies. Woolf J. determined that there was, in the absence of contrary authority, a sufficient interest for judicial review. It would have been open to him to take a restrictive view of *locus standi*, having regard to earlier decisions which held that duties under the 1968 Act were not owed to gypsies as a class or individually. He distinguished these authorities as deriving from private law and, therefore, having no relevance to Order 53.

In *R. v. Secretary of State for Social Services, ex p. Child Poverty Action Group*[63] standing was accorded, both at first instance and on appeal, to C.P.A.G. to challenge the manner in which the Secretary of State was administering the law to the alleged detriment of social benefits claimants.

In *R. v. Her Majesty's Treasury, ex p. Smedley*[64] a taxpayer sought to establish that a government undertaking to pay a contribution to the European Community, laid before Parliament in the form of a draft Order in Council, was *ultra vires*. Although the challenge failed on the merits, Slade L.J. dealt with the argument that the applicant lacked standing by observing that: "I do not feel much doubt that Mr. Smedley, if only in his capacity as a taxpayer, has sufficient *locus standi* to raise this question by way of an application for judicial review; on the present state of the authorities, I cannot think that any such right of challenge belongs to the Attorney-General alone."

In *R. v. Attorney-General, ex p. I.C.I.*[65] a taxpayer, as a trade competitor whose interests would be prejudiced, was permitted to challenge a decision of the Inland Revenue on the method of valuation of a rival company's profits.

---

[62] [1984] 1 W.L.R. 834. See also: *R. v. Avon C.C., ex p. Rexworthy* (1989) 21 H.L.R. 544.

[63] *The Times*, August 16, 1984 (Woolf J.); *The Times*, August 8, 1985 (C.A.). *cf.* also: *R. v. Secretary of State for Social Services, ex p. C.P.A.G.* [1990] 2 Q.B. 540; *R. v. Shropshire Health Authority, ex p. Duffus* [1990] C.O.D. 131; *R. v. Westminster City Council, ex p. Monahan* [1990] 1 Q.B. 87; *R. v. Hammersmith and Fulham L.B.C., ex p. People before Profit* (1983) 45 P. & C.R. 364. Contrast: *Scottish Old People's Welfare Council, Petitioner* [1987] S.L.T. 179 where standing was denied to a welfare organisation disputing the legality of a circular on social security payments for severe weather.

[64] [1985] 1 Q.B. 657.

[65] [1987] 1 C.M.L.R. 72. For analagous situations see also *R. v. Department of Transport, ex p. Presvac Engineering Ltd*, n. 56 above; *R. v. St. Edmundsbury B.C., ex p. Investors in Industry Commercial Properties* [1985] 1 W.L.R. 1168; *R. v. Monopolies and Mergers Commission, ex p. Argyll Group* [1986] 1 W.L.R. 763.

In *R. v. Felixstowe JJ.*, ex p. Leigh[66] a journalist succeeded in obtaining a declaration that justices had erred in law in concealing their identity as a matter of policy. On the same facts, however, mandamus in respect of a particular decision was refused since no sufficient interest had, in the court's view, been established. In delivering judgment Watkins L.J. made it clear that he was not deciding whether or not a stricter test of sufficient interest still applied for the issue of mandamus, although he was inclined to think that it did not.

In *R. v. Secretary of State for Employment, ex p. Equal Opportunities Commission*,[67] the House of Lords held that the Equal Opportunities Commission had standing (derived from its statutory responsibilities) to monitor the transposition of a European directive into domestic law.

In *R. v. H.M. Inspectorate of Pollution and Ministry of Agriculture, Fisheries and Food, ex p. Greenpeace Ltd*,[68] Otton J. held that Greenpeace had sufficient interest to seek judicial review of the Inspectorate's decision to vary authorisations for the discharge of radioactive waste from Sellafield. Although the application failed on its merits, one of the principal factors affecting the judge's approach to standing was that, if denied, those persons whom Greenpeace represented might not have an effective way to bring issues before the court.

To similar effect is the *Maastricht* case: *R. v. Secretary of State for Foreign and Commonwealth Affairs, ex p. Rees-Mogg*,[69] where Lloyd L.J., delivering the judgment at the Divisional Court, asserted that the applicant had. standing "because of his sincere concern for the constitutional issues".[70]

The same stance is exemplified in *R. v. Secretary of State for Foreign and Commonwealth Affairs, ex p. The World Development Movement Ltd*[71] in which the applicant company sought to challenge decisions of the Foreign Secretary in relation to and to fund the Pergau Dam in Malaysia. For the Secretary of State it was argued that because neither the applicant nor its individual members had any direct personal interest in funding, the mere desire of the pressure group to seek to act in the interests of potential recipients of aid overseas was too remote and L.J. rejected this argument. He saw that "the authorities referred to seemed to me to indicate an increasingly liberal approach to standing on the part of the courts during the last 12 years".[72]

In according standing to the applicants in Pergau Dam the Court considered the following to be significant:

    (a) the importance of vindicating the rule of law;
    (b) the importance of the issue raised;
    (c) the likely absence of any other responsible challenger;

---

[66] n. 55 above.
[67] n. 6 above, at p. 25H–26E, *per* Lord Keith.
[68] [1994] 4 All E.R. 321, see, especially, p. 350C–H; r.351B–D.
[69] [1994] 2 W.L.R. 115.
[70] n. 69 above at p. 119D.
[71] [1995] 1 W.L.R. 386.
[72] n. 71 above, at p. 395F.

(d) the nature of the breach of duty against which relief was sought;

(e) the prominent role of the applicant in giving advice, guidance and assistance with regard to aid.

One authority distinctively contrary to this trend is *R. v. Secretary of State for the Environment, ex p. Rose Theatre Trust Company*[73] the applicant company consisted of a number of persons of undoubted expertise and distinction in the fields of archaeology, the theatre, literature and other fields who had joined together to mount a campaign to preserve the remains of the ancient Rose Theatre. The challenge was to a decision of the Secretary of State not to schedule the remains as a monument of national importance under the Ancient Monuments and Archaeological Areas Act 1979. Schiemann J. denied *locus standi* to the applicant on the basis that the decision not to schedule was one of a class of governmental decisions in respect of which the ordinary citizen, even when represented by a substantial pressure group, lacks standing.

The *Rose Theatre* case is potentially disturbing in its implications if it marks a change of emphasis in the judicial approach to standing. In effect it introduces the concept of the unchallengeable decision and, by applying standing rules restrictively, restricts the court's power to intervene in cases of public importance sought to be raised by applicants who are, clearly, not mere busybodies with no legitimate complaint in the sense contemplated in *I.R.C.*

It is submitted that *Rose Theatre* is inconsistent with the modern approach to standing which, in summary, is that provided that the applicant has an arguable case, he will probably be given leave to apply for judicial review. At the full hearing, if he has a meritorious claim, the court will strive to accord *locus standi* so long as he falls outside the category of "mere busybody". In *Rose Theatre* it was held, before standing was considered, that the applicant's claim was unmeritorious. That may be the all-important distinguishing feature of an authority which, albeit only at first instance, is otherwise difficult to reconcile with the trend of recent cases.[74]

---

[73] n. 8 above.

[74] But see also: *R. v. Tower Hamlets L.B.C., ex p. Thrasyvoulou* [1991] C.O.D. 123. (*held*: hotelier used by local authority to provide bed and breakfast accommodation for the homeless had no standing to complain about a policy decision by the authority not to use low-grade hotels); *R. v. Poole B.C., ex p. Beebee* [1991] J.P.L. 643. (*held*: British Herpetological Society had standing to challenge planning decision on S.S.S.I. Nature Conservancy Council would have had standing. By itself, Worldwide Fund for Nature did not); *R. v. Director of the Serious Fraud Office, ex p. Johnson* [1993] C.O.D. 58. (*held*: husband did not have standing to challenge notice served under C.J.A. 1987, s.80 on his wife seeking information from her in respect of fraud charges against him); *R. v. Secretary of State for Defence, ex p. Sancto* [1993] C.O.D. 144. (*held*: parents of a serviceman lacked sufficient interest to challenge an executive decision not to disclose a Board of Inquiry Report supplied to the coroner following the death of their son whilst on non-operational duties in the Falklands.) For an outline of his views on standing, see Sir Konrad Schiemann "Locus Standi" n. 55 above.

5. THE RESPONDENT

SELECTING A RESPONDENT FOR JUDICIAL REVIEW

5–001   In recent years the test for determining an appropriate respondent for the purpose of judicial review has broadened considerably.

In *Council of Civil Service Unions v. Minister for the Civil Service*[1] Lord Diplock laid down the following general principles:

> "to qualify as a subject for judicial review the decision must have consequences which affect some person (or body of persons) other than the decision-maker, although it may affect him too. It must affect such other person either:
>
> (a) by altering rights or obligations of that person which are enforceable by or against him in private law; or
>
> (b) by depriving him of some benefit or advantage which either:
>
>> (i) he had in the past been permitted by the decision-maker to enjoy and which he can legitimately expect to be permitted to continue to do until there has been communicated to him some rational grounds for withdrawing it on which he has been given an opportunity to comment; or
>>
>> (ii) he has received assurance from the decision-maker will not be withdrawn without giving him first an opportunity of advancing reasons for contending that they should not be withdrawn . . . .
>
> For a decision to be susceptible to judicial review the decision-maker must be empowered by public law (and not merely, as in arbitration, by agreement between private parties) to make decisions that, if validly made, will lead to administrative action or abstention from action by an authority endowed by law with executive powers, which have one or other of the consequences mentioned."

The above formulation contemplates two prerequisites for determining a respondent under Order 53. These are that:

(a) the decision is made by a public body;

(b) such body is acting in a public law rather than a private law capacity.

The following bodies are, potentially, amenable to judicial review:

(a) bodies deriving authority from statute;

(b) certain non-statutory bodies set up to undertake public functions.

---

[1] [1985] A.C. 374 at pp. 408–409.

BODIES DERIVING AUTHORITY FROM STATUTE

Usually the remedies available on judicial review are obtainable against **5–002** bodies that derive their authority from an Act of Parliament.[2] It is not hard to see why this is so. Statute provides the foundation of administrative control. Powers exercised on a contractual basis generally relate to private rather than to public law.

In *R. v. National Joint Council for the Craft of Dental Technicians (Disputes Committee), ex p. Neate*[3] Lord Goddard C.J. stated expressly (in respect of certiorari and prohibition) that:

> "the bodies to which in modern times the remedies of these prerogative writs have been applied have all been statutory bodies on whom Parliament has conferred statutory powers and duties which, when exercised, may lead to the detriment of subjects who may have to submit to their jurisdiction."

As will be seen below, it is not sufficient for a body to be created by statute to be an appropriate respondent to judicial review proceedings. It must perform public law functions.[4] On this basis certain statutory bodies do not (or are not considered to) fulfil such functions at all.[5]

Conversely, although a respondent's power may be derived from statute, it does not follow that only express statutory powers or duties exercisable by such respondent are susceptible to judicial review.[6] Further, the fact that a statutory body has a contractual relationship with the applicant does not necessarily prevent an application for judicial review in relation to the contract where there is a "public" element involved.[7] Parliamentary

---

[2] See, *e.g. Council of Civil Service Unions v. Minister for the Civil Service*, n. 1 above at p. 409C–D, *per* Lord Diplock.

[3] [1953] 1 Q.B. 704 at p. 707.

[4] See, *e.g. Vidyodaya University Council v. Silva* [1965] 1 W.L.R. 77; *R. v. Post Office, ex p. Byrne* [1975] I.C.R. 221.

[5] As, *e.g.* some Agricultural Marketing Boards. *cf. Marshall v. Scottish Milk Marketing Board* [1956] S.C. (H.L.) 37, with *R. v. Milk Marketing Board, ex p. North* (1934) 50 T.L.R. 559. Note, also, that the Att.-Gen. when performing statutory functions under s.13 of the Coroners Act 1988 is immune from judicial review; see: *R. v. Att.-Gen., ex p. Ferrante,* [1995] C.O.D. 18. The C.A. when dismissing the applicant's appeal did not deal with jurisdiction; see *The Independent,* April 13, 1995.

[6] For example, rules of practice adopted in the exercise of statutory duties may be challenged on judicial review; see *R. v. Derby JJ., ex p. Kooner* [1971] 1 Q.B. 147. See, also: *R. v. Life Assurance and Unit Trust Regulatory Organisation, ex p. Ross* [1993] Q.B. 17, (fairness to third parties); *R. v. Norfolk C.C., ex p. M.* [1989] Q.B. 619; *R. v. Harrow L.B.C., ex p. D* [1989] 3 W.L.R. 1239; *R. v. Lewisham L.B.C., ex p. P* [1991] 1 W.L.R. 308, (child abuse registers maintained by local authorities under non-statutory power); *R. v. Commissioner of Police of the Metropolis, ex p. Blackburn* [1968] 2 Q.B. 118, (non-statutory exercise of police powers).

[7] See, *e.g. R. v. Basildon D.C., ex p. Brown* (1981) 79 L.G.R. 655; *R. v. Wear Valley D.C., ex p. Binks* [1985] 2 All E.R. 699; *R. v. Cleveland CC., ex p. Cleveland Care Homes* [1994] C.O.D. 221; *R. v. Hammersmith and Fulham L.B.C., ex p. Beddowes* [1987] Q.B. 1050; *R. v. Midlands Electricity Board, ex p. Busby, The Times,* October 28, 1987.

accountability does not operate to prevent a statutory body from being susceptible to review.[8]

There is, on any view, a bewildering array of statutory bodies subject to the supervisory jurisdiction of judicial review. They include, where appropriate, the Executive, inferior courts, local authorities, statutory tribunals and inquiries,[9] and a variety of miscellaneous entities that have been variously designated as quangos or "fringe" bodies.[10]

Certain statutory bodies merit special consideration because the test of whether their statutory status renders them amenable to judicial review is not immediately obvious.

Inferior courts

5–003   It is well established that judicial review does not lie against any superior court.[11] Determination of what constitutes an inferior court or tribunal[12] so as to found amenability to review can, however, cause particular problems.

Superior courts include the House of Lords and the Supreme Court. The Supreme Court comprises the Court of Appeal, the High Court and the Crown Court.[13] Masters of the High Court are also part of the Supreme Court and immune from judicial review,[14] as is the Registrar of Criminal Appeals.[15] There is, however, no necessary bar to judicial review where a High Court judge or other member of the Supreme Court is not acting in such capacity.[16]

In respect of the Crown Court there is an important exception[17] permitting judicial review of many Crown Court decisions. Section 29(3) of the Supreme Court Act 1981 enables the High Court to make prerogative orders[18] against the Crown Court to the same extent as it may

---

[8] R. v. Parliamentary Commissioner for Administration, ex p. Dyer [1994] 1 W.L.R. 621.

[9] Such tribunals have proliferated in recent years extending to social security, pensions, health education, etc. Many have their own systems of appeal but this does not preclude the possibility of review.

[10] For an interesting treatment of fringe organisations see Craig, Administrative Law (3rd ed., 1994) at pp. 86 et seq.

[11] The Rioters' Case [1683] 1 Vern. 175; R. v. Oxenden [1691] 1 Show. 217; Re Racal Communications [1981] A.C. 374.

[12] It is now recognised that there is no distinction to be drawn between inferior courts and tribunals so far as the application of judicial review is concerned; see para. 3–005.

[13] S.C.A. 1981, s.1(1).

[14] Murrell v. British Leyland Trustees [1989] C.O.D. 389; R. v. Shemilt (A Taxing Officer) ex p. Buckley [1988] C.O.D. 40.

[15] R. v. Registrar of Criminal Appeals, ex p. Pegg [1993] C.O.D. 192.

[16] See, e.g. R. v. Visitors to the Inns of Court, ex p. Calder and Persaud [1994] Q.B. 1; R. v. Master of the Rolls, ex p. McKinnell [1993] 1 W.L.R. 88. So, too, a taxing master acting under statutory powers is susceptible to judicial review; see R. v. Supreme Court Taxing Office, ex p. John Singh, The Times, May 3, 1995.

[17] Within the statutory exception there is no additional or alternative inherent supervisory jurisdiction over the Crown Court so as to enable declaratory relief to be granted; see R. v. Chelmsford Crown Court, ex p. Chief Constable of the Essex Police [1994] 1 W.L.R. 359.

[18] This would seem to entail the proposition that declaratory relief cannot be granted against the Crown Court under any circumstances, a proposition supported by the fact that

against an inferior court other than in relation to the Crown Court's jurisdiction "in matters relating to trial on indictment".

This expression requires some clarification. In *Re Smalley*[19] the House of Lords held that the section 29(3) exception did not admit of a precise test but that it extended to (and, therefore, excluded judicial review of) decisions:

(a) "affecting the conduct of a trial on indictment, whether given in the course of the trial or by way of pre-trial directions"[20]; and

(b) "certain orders made at the conclusion of a trial on indictment . . . [which] are themselves an integral part of the trial process".[21]

In *R. v. Manchester Crown Court, ex p. Director of Public Prosecutions*,[22] the House of Lords further observed that where the decision sought to be reviewed is one that arises in the issue formulated by the indictment then it is probably excluded from review under section 29(3); where, however, the decision does not so arise then it is probably collateral to the indictment and amenable to judicial review.

Decisions of the Crown Court falling within section 29(3) and, therefore, outside the scope of judicial review on the above basis include (apart, self-evidently, from verdict and sentence):

(a) the making of a legal aid contribution order after trial[23];

(b) an order vetting a jury panel prior to trial[24];

(c) the refusal of legal aid for trial on indictment[25];

(d) an order prohibiting publication of a witness's name[26];

(e) a costs order following trial[27];

(f) a refusal to direct a verdict of not guilty[28];

(g) an order for a witness summons for trial[29];

(h) an order that charges lie on the court file and may not be proceeded with except by leave of the court[30];

---

declaratory relief may issue irrespective of whether a prerogative order is available, (*R. v. Secretary of State for Employment, ex p. Equal Opportunities Commission* [1995] 1 A.C. 1). See also: *R. v. Chelmsford Crown Court, ex p. Chief Constable of Essex*, n. 17 above.

[19] [1985] A.C. 622. See also *Re Ashton* [1994] 1 A.C. 9. For a useful analysis see: Ward "Judicial Review and Trials on Indictment: s.29(3) of the Supreme Court Act 1981" (1990) P.L. 50.

[20] n. 19 above at p. 642G.

[21] See *Re Sampson* [1987] 1 W.L.R. 194 at p. 196F. A matter is integral to the trial process if it engages a decision in the light of what the Court has learned of the nature of the case during the trial and in the light of the conduct and outcome of the trial; *ibid.*

[22] [1993] 1 W.L.R. 1524, at p. 1530E–F, *per* Lord Browne-Wilkinson.

[23] *R. v. Cardiff Crown Court, ex p. Jones* [1974] Q.B. 113. Doubted in *Smalley*, n. 19 above at p. 644, but approved in *Re Sampson*, n. 21 above.

[24] *R. v. Sheffield Crown Court, ex p. Brownlow* [1980] Q.B. 530. The result of this case, but not its reasoning, was approved in *Re Smalley*, n. 19 above.

[25] *R. v. Chichester Crown Court, ex p. Abodunrin* (1984) 79 Cr.App.R. 293.

[26] *R. v. Central Criminal Court, ex p. Crook* (1985) 82 L.S.Gaz. 1408, D.C.

[27] *Ex p. Meredith* [1973] 1 W.L.R. 435.

[28] *R. v. Preston Crown Court, ex p. Fraser* [1984] Crim.L.R. 624.

[29] *Ex p. Rees, The Times*, May 7, 1986.

[30] *R. v. Central Criminal Court, ex p. Raymond* [1986] 1 W.L.R. 710.

    (i)   decision to give leave to prefer a voluntary bill of indictment[31];

    (j)   decision to revoke order discharging a legal aid certificate[32];

    (k) decision staying trial for abuse of process[33];

    (l)   decision whether indictment should be quashed.[34]

Apart from the prohibition contained in section 29(3) of the Supreme Court Act 1981, the Crown Court is susceptible to the making of prerogative orders by way of judicial review.[35] In practice this susceptibility usually lies in respect of its appellate jurisdiction over magistrates' courts.[36]

Additionally, however, certain decisions may be sufficiently remote from the trial process to permit judicial review. Such decisions include:

    (a) the estreatment of a recognizance[37];

    (b) the binding over of a witness at trial[38];

    (c) an order lifting ban on identification of a juvenile defendant[39];

    (d) an order relating to forfeiture of property against a person who is not the accused.[40]

Conceptually, the borderline separating matters that relate to trial on indictment from those that do not may not be easy to draw in particular cases.[41]

Where there is doubt over the High Court's jurisdiction in respect of a particular Crown Court decision it is suggested that judicial review is usually preferable to case stated as a means of challenge. The leave stage under Order 53 enables early judicial appraisal of the jurisdictional position and ensures that those cases where jurisdiction is lacking are disposed of with minimum delay and expense.

Usually there should be little difficulty in ascertaining the identity of inferior courts or tribunals for the purpose of determining their liability to judicial review. This is, however, not always so. Certainly magistrates' and coroners' courts are included. So too, it would seem, is a local election

---

[31] *R. v. Manchester Crown Court, ex p. Williams and Simpson* [1990] Crim.L.R. 654.

[32] *R. v. Isleworth Crown Court, ex p. Willington* [1993] 1 W.L.R. 713.

[33] *Re Ashton*, n. 19 above, overruling *R. v. Central Criminal Court, ex p. Randle* [1991] 1 W.L.R. 1087.

[34] *R. v. Knightsbridge Crown Court, ex p. O'Grady and Gallagher* [1993] C.O.D. 456.

[35] But not, *semble*, to declaratory relief; see n. 18 above.

[36] Including the refusal of leave to appeal out of time; see *R. v. Birmingham Crown Court, ex p. Sharma* [1988] C.O.D. 12. *Quaere* whether this case, brought on judicial review, ought not to have proceeded under the case stated procedure; see *R. v. Clerkenwell Metropolitan Stipendiary Magistrate, ex p. D.P.P.* [1984] Q.B. 821.

[37] *Re Smalley*, n. 19 above. See also *R. v. Southampton JJ., ex p. Green* [1976] 1 Q.B. 11.

[38] *R. v. Swindon Crown Court, ex p. Singh (Pawittar)* [1984] 1 W.L.R. 449.

[39] *R. v. Leicester Crown Court, ex p. S* [1993] 1 W.L.R. 111.

[40] *R. v. Maidstone Crown Court, ex p. Gill* [1986] 1 W.L.R. 1405.

[41] *Quaere, e.g.* whether a solicitor's costs order may be reviewed. See *R. v. Smith (Martin)* [1975] 1 Q.B. 531, 540–541, *per* Lord Denning M.R.; 546, *per* Sir Eric Sachs. (*cf. ibid.* pp. 544–545, *per* Megaw L.J.; *Re Smalley*, n. 19 above at p. 644, *per* Lord Bridge of Harwich. So, too, following the House of Lords' decision in *Re Ashton*, n. 19 above, it is questionable whether dismissal of charges under s.6 C.J.A. 1987 would be held to be subject to judicial review as it was in *R. v. Central Criminal Court, ex p. Director of Serious Fraud Office* [1993] 1 W.L.R. 949.

court,[42] and a Patents Appeal Tribunal even though a High Court Judge sits on it.[43] For most purposes the county court is an inferior court[44] but there are occasions when it performs functions resulting in its being treated as a superior court.[45] It has also been held that an ecclesiastical court is not amenable to certiorari, based, as it is, on a different system of law to the common law.[46]

Statutory tribunals as inferior courts

The question of whether a statutory tribunal is an inferior court of record **5–004** and, therefore, subject to judicial review, depends in every case on the precise nature and powers of the tribunal.[47] One factor of importance (as tending to preclude Order 53) is whether the tribunal is presided over by a High Court judge. This is, though, by no means conclusive. Just as relevant are the tribunal's powers and its relationship with the High Court which are to be inferred from the enabling statute.[48]

In *R. v. Cripps, ex p. Muldoon*[49] Robert Goff L.J., at first instance, having set out the above principles stated that:

> "there is an underlying policy in the case of tribunals of limited jurisdiction, whether limited by area, subject matter or otherwise, that unless the tribunal in question should properly be regarded in all the circumstances as having a status so closely equivalent to the High Court that the exercise of the power of judicial review by the High Court is for that reason inappropriate, it is in the public interest that remedies by way of judicial review by the High Court should be available to persons aggrieved; though in some cases there may be special reasons why such remedy should be available only to curb an excess of jurisdiction but not to review and correct an error of law committed within the jurisdiction."[50]

---

[42] See the judgment of Robert Goff L.J. in a Divisional Court in *R. v. Cripps, ex p. Muldoon* [1984] Q.B. 68. The point was, however, left undecided by the Court of Appeal [1984] Q.B. 686 at 698.

[43] *Baldwin & Francis Ltd v. Patents Appeal Tribunal* [1959] A.C. 663.

[44] See, *e.g.: R. v. Hurst, ex p. Smith* [1960] 2 Q.B. 133; *R. v. Bloomsbury & Marylebone County Court, ex p. Blackburne* (1985) 275 E.G. 1273. Note, also, ss.83 and 84 of the County Courts Act 1984.

[45] See, *e.g. Skinner v. Northallerton County Court Judge* (1899) A.C. 439.

[46] *R. v. Edmundsbury and Ipswich Diocese (Chancellor), ex p. White* [1948] 1 K.B. 195. But *semble* such court is subject to prohibition. *cf. R. v. North, ex p. Oakey* [1927] 1 K.B. 491.

[47] See Divisional Court judgment of Robert Goff L.J. in *R. v. Cripps, ex p. Muldoon*, n. 42 above. The appeal did not turn on these dicta.

[48] See n. 42 above.

[49] *ibid.*

[50] *ibid.*

NON-STATUTORY BODIES

5–005   There are an increasing number of situations where a public body exercises power without any statutory basis. In several cases the courts have been prepared to apply judicial review, and the general principle appears now to be that such a body is potentially amenable to remedies under Order 53 (at least) where it "has been authorised by the State to perform public functions, that is the carrying out of duties and the exercise of powers on behalf of the public, in the interests of the community".[51] Once that condition is satisfied the source of such powers and duties is, save as set out below, irrelevant.

Although the different types of non-statutory body excluded from, or susceptible to, judicial review are not limited to finite classes, the categories set out below may be helpful in analysing the court's general approach, and the manner in which it has developed.

Non-statutory bodies established by consent

5–006   Non-statutory bodies whose authority to make a decision, or exercise functions, derives solely from contract, or the parties' consent, fall outside the scope of judicial review.

The starting point for this proposition is the decision in *R. v. Criminal Injuries Compensation Board, ex p. Lain.*[52] There Lord Parker C.J. stated expressly that "Private or domestic tribunals have always been outside the scope of certiorari since their authority is derived solely from contract, that is, from the agreement of the parties concerned."

This was taken up in *R. v. British Broadcasting Corporation, ex p. Lavelle.*[53] In that case the B.B.C. had employed the applicant as a tape examiner. As a result of a number of tapes being found at her home she was interviewed and dismissed. She appealed to a disciplinary tribunal set up by the employer which confirmed the original dismissal.

The application for judicial review clearly assumed that the disciplinary tribunal in question was exercising functions of a public nature. Woolf J. thought differently, holding that the appeal procedure set up by the B.B.C. depended purely upon the contract of employment between the applicant and the Corporation and was, therefore, a procedure of a merely private or domestic character. The precedent in *Lain* was referred to and approved.

In *Law v. National Greyhound Racing Club,*[54] the Court of Appeal held, similarly, that the Club's decision to suspend the applicant trainer's licence was not amenable to judicial review because its authority to take the decision derived wholly from contract.

---

[51] David Pannick "What is a Public Authority for the Purposes of Judicial Review?" in *New Directions in Judicial Review* (1988) at p. 29.

[52] [1967] 2 Q.B. 864 at 882. See also the earlier decision in *R. v. National Joint Council for the Craft of Dental Technicians (Disputes Committee), ex p. Neate,* n. 3 above, where it was held that judicial review will not lie against an arbitrator acting by consent of the parties.

[53] [1983] 1 W.L.R. 23.

[54] [1983] 1 W.L.R. 1302.

Finally, there is Lord Diplock's statement in the *G.C.H.Q.* case, cited above,[55] to the effect that a decision will not be susceptible to judicial review if the decision-maker's authority is *merely* derived from agreement between the parties, and the Court of Appeal judgments, to identical effect, in *R. v. Panel on Take-overs and Mergers, ex p. Datafin*,[56] discussed below at para. 5–008.

On this basis a wide range of domestic or private tribunals whose sole source of authority over individuals to make a particular decision is contractual are excluded from the judicial review jurisdiction.[57]

Less clear is the extent to which a body will be classed as immune from judicial review in circumstances where the decision complained of is not founded on a subsisting contract even though the general authority of such body is solely dependent upon a contract with individual persons.[58]

In part, of course, this depends upon an examination of the functions performed by the decision-maker and whether they are sufficiently "public" to attract the supervisory jurisdiction of the High Court (see para. 5–008 below). Assuming the existence of public law functions, however, the courts have, so far, not decided whether the absence of a private law contractual remedy in respect of a particular decision or action may afford the basis for Order 53 proceedings against what would otherwise be categorised as a domestic tribunal.

A Divisional Court, in *R. v. Disciplinary Committee of the Jockey Club, ex p. Massingberd-Mundy*,[59] considered itself to be bound by *Law* to hold that all decisions of the Jockey Club were immune from judicial review. In the event it held that there was a subsisting contractual relationship in any event. However, given that the Club was a body created under the royal prerogative by royal charter, and that it held a position of major national importance with near monopolistic power in an area in which the public generally had an interest, Roch J. would have concluded that at least some of its decisions, not deriving from contract, were amenable to review. In *R. v. Jockey Club, ex p. RAM Racecourses*[60] a differently constituted Divisional Court found it unnecessary to confront the jurisdictional issue because the claim failed *in limine*. However, Simon Brown J. thought that there might be sufficiently public decisions of the Jockey Club to merit judicial review.

The Court of Appeal in *R. v. Disciplinary Committee of the Jockey Club, ex*

---

[55] See n. 1, above.

[56] [1987] Q.B. 815; see, especially, *per* Sir John Donaldson M.R. at p. 838E.

[57] Of the many cases, see, especially: *Law v. National Greyhound Racing Club*, n. 54 above; *R. v. Football Association of Wales, ex p. Flint Town United Football Club* [1991] C.O.D. 44; *R. v. Football Association Ltd, ex p. Football League Ltd* [1993] 2 All E.R. 833; *R. v. Lloyd's of London, ex p. Briggs* (1993) 5 Admin. L.R. 698; *R. v. Disciplinary Committee of the Jockey Club, ex p. Aga Khan* [1993] 1 W.L.R. 909.

[58] This question is analytically distinct from whether public law powers may be exercised through a contract which is discussed below at para. 5–008.

[59] [1993] 2 All E.R. 207.

[60] [1993] 2 All E.R. 225. Note that this Divisional Court (it is submitted rightly) concluded that, in fact, there was no contractual relationship in *Massingberd-Mundy*; see, *ibid.* at pp. 287C and 292F–293A.

p. Aga Khan[61] was dealing with a decision of the Jockey Club founded (so it concluded) wholly on contract. It dismissed the application on that basis. The court, therefore, held that it was unnecessary to decide whether decisions of the Jockey Club could ever be open to review. Sir Thomas Bingham M.R. observed that "cases where the applicant or plaintiff has no contract on which to rely may raise different considerations and the existence or non-existence of alternative remedies may then be material".[62] Farquharson L.J. suggested that if the Jockey Club breached its royal charter obligations by, for example, making discriminatory rules, then "it may be that those affected would have a remedy in public law".[63]

Non-statutory bodies exercising prerogative powers

5–007 It is now, undoubtedly, established that a person or body exercising powers delegated by prerogative power[64] may, depending upon the subject matter of the power, be amenable to judicial review.[65]

The point arose directly for consideration in *Council for Civil Service Unions v. Minister for the Civil Service.*[66]

In that case the Prime Minister issued an instruction to ban union membership by staff at G.C.H.Q. The instruction was made pursuant to article 4 of the Civil Service Order in Council 1982. This Order had been issued by the Sovereign by virtue of her prerogative (albeit on the advice of Government). Arguing from the premise that direct exercise of the prerogative was not reviewable by the courts, the respondent contended that the instruction was, similarly, immune from challenge under Order 53 as being a delegated power conferred by the Sovereign under the prerogative.

The House of Lords rejected this argument. Most of the speeches commented on the absence of any difference in logic between the exercise of powers derived from a statutory source and one derived ultimately from the prerogative.[67]

For example, Lord Fraser observed that:

> "Whatever their source, powers which are defined, either by reference to their object or by reference to procedure for their exercise, or in some other way, and whether the definition is expressed or implied, are ... normally subject to judicial control to ensure that they are not exceeded."[68]

Lord Diplock made the same point in a different way, stating that there

---

[61] n. 57 above.

[62] n. 57 above at p. 924D.

[63] n. 57 above at p. 930F.

[64] Used, in this sense, as denoting all non-statutory acts of executive government; see Dicey *Introduction to the Study of the Law of the Constitution* (10th ed., 1959) at p. 25.

[65] *R. v. Criminal Injuries Compensation Board, ex p. Lain* [1967] 2 Q.B. 864.

[66] See n. 1 above. The case failed on the merits.

[67] See the speeches of Lord's Fraser, Scarman, Diplock and Roskill at, respectively, pp. 399, 407, 409, 417.

[68] See n. 1 above at p. 399.

was "no reason why simply because a decision-making power is derived from a common law and not a statutory source it should for that reason only be immune from judicial review".[69]

It was suggested in *G.C.H.Q.* that there were a number of exercises of prerogative power which were not reviewable. Lord Roskill considered that they probably included the following[70]:

(a) treaty-making;
(b) defence of the realm;
(c) prerogative of mercy;
(d) grant of honours;
(e) dissolution of Parliament;
(f) appointment of ministers.

Notwithstanding Lord Roskill's reservations, the prerogative of mercy has, since *G.C.H.Q.*, been held to be susceptible to judicial review.[71] Further, although some prerogative powers such as treaty-making appear to be inherently unsusceptible to review,[72] the High Court will always consider whether an asserted prerogative power exists,[73] or has been limited or extinguished by statute.[74] It has, therefore, with some force been suggested that "[i]t may be that the subject-matter of each individual exercise of power needs to be considered rather than whether a particular prerogative power is or is not amenable to review".[75]

The High Court has, following *G.C.H.Q.*, also been prepared to apply its supervisory jurisdiction to other exercises of prerogative power including:

(a) a decision of the Civil Service Appeal Board, a non-statutory body having the power to consider appeals against dismissal of Crown servants[76];
(b) a decision of the Secretary of State refusing a passport[77];
(c) the residual power of the Home Secretary to depart from the immigration rules.[78]

---

[69] *ibid.* at pp. 410–411.

[70] n. 1 above at p. 418B–C. See also *per* Lord Fraser at p. 398F.

[71] *R. v. Secretary of State for the Home Department, ex p. Bentley* [1994] Q.B. 349 (refusal to grant posthumous pardon subject to judicial review).

[72] See, *e.g. Blackburn v. Att.-Gen.* [1971] 1 W.L.R. 1037; *J. H. Rayner (Mincing Lane) Ltd. v. Department of Trade and Industry* [1990] 2 A.C. 418.

[73] See, *e.g.: R. v. Secretary of State for the Home Department, ex p. Northumbria Police Authority* [1989] Q.B. 26.

[74] Consider, *e.g.: Att.-Gen. v. De Keyser's Royal Hotel Ltd.* [1920] A.C. 508; *R. v. Secretary of State for the Home Department, ex p. Rees-Mogg* [1994] Q.B. 552.

[75] Clive Lewis *Judicial Remedies in Public Law* (1992) at p. 16.

[76] *R. v. Civil Service Appeal Board, ex p. Bruce* [1987] 2 All E.R. 907. *Quaere* whether this is truly a decision on the exercise of prerogative powers by a non-statutory power. See Wade and Forsyth, *Administrative Law* (7th ed., 1994), at p. 383. See also *R. v. Civil Service Appeal Board, ex p. Cunningham* [1991] 4 All E.R. 310, (*held*: Board required to give reasons for low award to officer).

[77] *R. v. Secretary of State for Foreign and Commonwealth Affairs, ex p. Everett* [1989] Q.B. 811.

[78] *R. v. Secretary of State for the Home Department, ex p. Beedassee* [1989] C.O.D. 525.

The fact that a body may be created by Royal Charter under the prerogative does not mean that its powers are to be regarded as derived from the prerogative.[79] The question of susceptibility to judicial review will depend, rather, upon whether the particular body is exercising governmental powers (see para. 5–008 below).

Non-statutory bodies exercising governmental powers

5–008   Until the end of 1986 the law appeared to be clear that, despite the extension of judicial review to cover the exercise of most prerogative powers, the public law supervisory jurisdiction of the High Court did not extend to reviewing the activities of non-statutory bodies generally.[80]

In December 1986, however, the Court of Appeal in *R. v. Panel on Take-overs and Mergers, ex p. Datafin plc*[81] held that the High Court had jurisdiction to review decisions of the Panel on Take-overs and Mergers which is a wholly non-statutory body forming part of a system of self-regulation in the City of London.

The Take-overs Panel was, in the view of the Court of Appeal, exercising "immense power *de facto*" because its decisions, based neither on contract nor statute, had enormous impact on those persons doing business in the City. Infringement of the Panel's code could, in particular, lead to expulsion from the Stock Exchange or comparable serious sanctions.

Underpinning *Datafin* was the reasoning that susceptibility to public law remedies should be governed by reference to the nature of the functions being exercised by a decision-maker rather than (as before) solely by reference to the source of its power.

As Sir John Donaldson M.R. observed:

> "In all the reports it is possible to find enumerations of factors giving rise to jurisdiction, but it is a fatal error to regard the presence of all those factors as essential or as being exclusive of other factors. Possibly the only essential elements are what can be described as a public element, which can take many different forms, and the exclusion from the jurisdiction of bodies whose sole source of power is consensual submission to its jurisdiction."[82]

Lloyd L.J. remarked that "the source of power will often, perhaps usually, be decisive" but that if the decision-maker was "exercising public law functions, or if the exercise of its functions has public law consequences

---

[79] See, *e.g.*: *R. v. Jockey Club, ex p. Massingberd-Mundy*, n. 59 above.

[80] Though some governmental non-statutory bodies had been subject to the remedy. See, *e.g. R. v. Home Secretary, ex p. Hosenball* [1977] 1 W.L.R. 766 at 781, (*held*: judicial review applied to non-statutory body of advisers to the Home Secretary on deportation decisions). See also *R. v. Chief Immigration Officer, Gatwick Airport, ex p. Kharrazi* [1980] 1 W.L.R. 1396 on status of non-statutory immigration rules.

[81] n. 56 above. The application failed on the merits. See also *R. v. Panel on Take-overs and Mergers, ex p. Guinness plc.* [1990] Q.B. 146, where, again, the application failed. For commentary see [1987] 103 L.Q.R. 323; [1987] P.L. 356, by C. F. Forsyth.

[82] n. 56 above at p. 838E.

then that may . . . be sufficient to bring that body within the reach of judicial review".[83]

Materially, Nicholls L.J. rejected, *sub silentio*, the notion that a contractual source of power necessarily affected the issue of public law functions or consequences. He said that:

> "whether or not there is a legally binding contract, there is an understanding between the bodies whose representatives are members of the panel that they will take all such steps, by way of disciplinary proceedings against their members or otherwise, as are reasonably and properly open to them to ensure that the code and the rulings of the panel are observed. Similarly with the Bank of England: its weighty influence in the City of London is directed to the same end. Indeed, the leading part played by the Bank of England in setting up and running the panel is one of the matters which must be kept in mind if the true role of the panel is to be evaluated."[84]

Notwithstanding the quasi-governmental status of the Take-overs Panel,[85] the decision in *Datafin* is a broad one and appears, in the light of the above dicta, to subject a body to judicial review if the following criteria are satisfied, namely that:

(a) There is an essential public element, as where such body—
   (i) performs or operates as an integral part of a regulatory system which performs public law duties; or
   (ii) is non-statutory by Government decision; or
   (iii) is supported by a periphery of statutory powers and penalties.
(b) The source of power does not derive exclusively from the consent of those over whom it exercises such power.

Implicit in *Datafin* is the proposition that public functions may be exercised just as much through the medium of consensual submission as through a statutory source of power. This is because the reality of monopolistic power cannot, sensibly, be said to be dependent upon its source. As Lloyd L.J. clarified: "Nor is it any answer that a company coming to the market must take it as he finds it. The City is not a club which one can join or not at will."[86]

Notwithstanding this, the courts have found themselves, post *Datafin*,

---

[83] n. 56 above at p. 847A–B.
[84] n. 56 above at p. 850G–H. Sir John Donaldson M.R. said (at p. 838B) that a *solely* contractual source of power was fatal to judicial review. But, in context, (and given the agreement of Lloyd and Nicholls L.JJ.), this can mean no more than that private law functions plainly fall outside the ambit of a public law remedy.
[85] The Secretary of State used the Panel "as the centrepiece of his regulation of [the financial market]".
[86] n. 56 above at p. 846A. See also: Nicholls L.J. at p. 850E; Sir John Donaldson M.R. at p. 826B–D.

veering uneasily between a functions and a source test of jurisdiction. In *R. v. Chief Rabbi, ex p. Wachmann*,[87] for example, Simon Brown J. said:

> "To attract the court's supervisory jurisdiction there must be not merely a public but potentially a governmental interest in the decision-making power in question ... where non-governmental bodies have hitherto been held reviewable, they have generally been operating as an integral part of a regulatory system which, although itself non-statutory, is nevertheless supported by statutory powers and penalties clearly indicative of government concern."[88]

Although the functions test was ostensibly applied, it is apparent that the source of a decision-maker's powers was treated as important in that, but for the establishment of the body in question, the government would have created a statutory regime. This appears to narrow the ratio of *Datafin* to one requiring potential governmental interest rather than, as suggested above, to the less stringent requirement of exercise of functions with a "public" element.

Datafin has ostensibly been narrowed even further by the Court of Appeal's ruling in *R. v. Disciplinary Committee of the Jockey Club, ex p. Aga Khan*,[89] referred to above in connection with domestic tribunals. There, the applicant sought judicial review of a decision of the Jockey Club's Disciplinary Committee to disqualify the applicant's filly from the 1989 Oaks and to fine the horse's trainer for a breach of the Rules of Racing. Although the Aga Khan had a contract with the Jockey Club it was argued that the Club was the effective controller of a significant national activity and that its decisions were amenable to judicial review.

Jurisdiction was dealt with as a preliminary issue. The application for judicial review was, on that footing, dismissed. The applicant appealed to the Court of Appeal, which dismissed his appeal on the basis of lack of jurisdiction.

In *Aga Khan*, the Court seems to lay down additional requirements for amenability to review, namely the existence of "governmental"[90] as opposed to simply "public" functions, and possibly (*per* Sir Thomas Bingham M.R.) actual (as opposed to potential) governmental intervention.[91] Given that the Jockey Club was not exercising governmental functions, because it had not been woven into any system of governmental control, it was held to fall outside the court's supervisory jurisdiction.

The Court was manifestly influenced by the fact that the Club's source of

---

[87] [1992] 1 W.L.R. 1036.

[88] n. 57 above at p. 1041D–E. To similar effect see Rose J. in *R. v. Football Association Ltd., ex p. Football League Ltd.*, n. 57 above, (*held*: Football Association *not* amenable to judicial review because of absence of governmental underpinning).

[89] n. 57 above. For further analysis of this decision see: Richard Gordon and Craig Barlow, "Falling at the last fence" (1993) 143 N.L.J. at pp. 158–169; Nicholas Bamforth "The scope of judicial review: still uncertain" (1993) P.L. 239 *et seq.*

[90] n. 57 above at p. 923H (*per* Sir Thomas Bingham M.R.); p. 930B (*per* Lord Farquharson); p. 932F, (*per* Lord Hoffmann).

[91] Sir Thomas Bingham M.R. expressed himself as being "willing to accept that if the Jockey Club did not regulate this activity the government would probably be driven to create a

98

power was contractual, and that there was a remedy in private law available to the applicant.[92] This was material even though there was no effective alternative but to contract with the Jockey Club for those who wished to participate in racing.[93] Farquharson L.J. observed that "nobody is obliged to race his horses in this country and it does not destroy the element of consensuality".[94]

However, as Hoffmann L.J. alone recognised: "a body ... which exercises governmental powers is not any the less amenable to public law because it has contractual relations with its members".[95]

So far as the decision in *Law* was concerned, Hoffmann L.J. stated that:

"The case was decided before [*Datafin*] and did not consider whether, notwithstanding the lack of any public source for its powers, the Club might *de facto* be a surrogate organ of government. I would accept that if this were the case, there might be a conflict between the principle laid down in [*Datafin*] and the actual decision in [*Law*]."[96]

It is submitted that Hoffmann L.J.'s approach is right and that the mere existence of a contract cannot be decisive of whether a body is exercising functions of a kind sufficient to attract susceptibility to judicial review. Following *Aga Khan*, however, it seems clear that the functions required to be exercised by a decision-maker to achieve this consequence must, at least, be specifically "governmental" in nature.

However, it has been held that a contractual source of power may preclude judicial review even where a body is woven into a governmental system.

In *R. v. Insurance Ombudsman Bureau, ex p. Aegon Life Assurance Ltd*,[97] a Divisional Court refused Aegon's application for judicial review of compensatory awards made against it by the Insurance Ombudsman Bureau ("I.O.B.") because of lack of jurisdiction even though the I.O.B. was a body performing functions that, although contractual in source, may be thought to have been governmental in nature, at least in the sense used by the Court of Appeal in *Aga Khan*, being a body woven into a system of governmental control. Aegon was a member of the I.O.B. and in a contractual relationship with it. Although the awards were made in respect of matters prior to the coming into force of the Financial Services Act 1986, and were not directly regulated by the Act, the I.O.B. was recognised by LAUTRO under the complaints machinery established thereunder.

---

public body to do so."; *ibid.* at p. 923G. As to this need for actual governmental involvement, see also: *R. v. Lloyd's of London, ex p. Briggs*, n. 57 above.

[92] Analytically, the presence or absence of a private law remedy ought not to affect the issue of jurisdiction. See, *e.g. R. v. Lord Chancellor's Department, ex p. Nangle* [1992] 1 All E.R. 897 (non-availability of private law remedy could not of itself afford ground for amenability to judicial review); *Leech v. Deputy Governor of Parkhurst Prison* [1988] A.C. 533 (question of alternative remedy goes to discretion not jurisdiction).

[93] n. 57 above at p. 924B, *per* Sir Thomas Bingham M.R.

[94] n. 57 above at p. 928H.

[95] See n. 57 above at p. 932C–E.

[96] n. 57 above at p. 932D–E.

[97] *The Times*, January 7, 1994.

Rose L.J., who delivered the court's judgment, considered that the expression "governmental functions" could be defined so that even if a body had been woven into a system of governmental control it would not be exercising governmental functions if the source of its power was consensual.

He said[98]:

> "when Sir Thomas Bingham M.R. spoke of the Jockey Club not being 'woven into any system of governmental control' I do not accept that he was thereby indicating that such interweaving was in itself determinative ... I do not accept that their judgments or that of Lord Justice Hoffmann, or those of the members of the court in *Ex parte Datafin* can be construed as contemplating that such a body as the I.O.B., even if it became interwoven into a governmental system, would be susceptible to judicial review."

Second, Rose L.J. treated the fact of a contractual source of power as determinative in any event. He said[99]:

> "The I.O.B.'s power over its members is ... despite the [Financial Services] Act, solely derived from contract and it simply cannot be said that it exercises government functions. In a nut shell, even if it can be said that it has now been woven into a governmental system, the source of its power is still contractual."

It can be seen that, in Rose L.J.'s view, the second proposition subsumes the first. If, by reason of a contractual source of power, the function being exercised cannot be categorised as "governmental" it follows, inevitably, that the fact of a public body being woven into a system of government control is not determinative of whether governmental functions are being exercised. But to express the matter thus disguises (if Rose L.J.'s reasoning is correct) that the Court is thereby reverting to an entirely source-based test of jurisdiction thought to have been swept away by *Datafin*.

In the light of *Datafin* it had been suggested that there "may be virtually no limit" to the scope of Order 53.[1] The case law since then appears, however, to mark something of a retreat from the literal logic of the judgments of the Court of Appeal in that decision. Even so, there is still a wide range of non-statutory public bodies now amenable to judicial review that would have been excluded prior to *Datafin*.[2]

Non-statutory bodies exercising non-governmental functions

5-009   Many non-statutory bodies are immune from judicial review, even where their source of authority is neither, necessarily, solely contractual nor consensual, because they are not considered to be exercising governmental powers, (see para. 5-008 above).

---

[98] See transcript at pp. 13–14.

[99] See transcript at pp. 14–15.

[1] See Wade, *Administrative Law* (6th ed. 1988) at 640, 52n.

[2] See, *e.g.*: *R. v. General Council of the Bar, ex p. Percival* [1991] 1 Q.B. 212; *R. v. Ethical Committee of St. Mary's Hospital (Manchester), ex p. Harriott* [1988] 1 F.L.R. 512; *R. v. Code*

In *R. v. Royal Life Saving Society, ex p. Howe*,[3] for example, the Court of Appeal refused a renewed application for leave to move for judicial review of a decision of the Society, whose source of authority was incorporation by royal charter, to hold an inquiry into a local authority's complaints about the applicant. The basis of refusal was that, although the Society performed a useful function in the public domain, the function complained of had no public law element.

R. v. Chief Rabbi, ex p. Wachmann[4] was a case where jurisdiction was argued as a threshold issue at the leave stage. Refusing leave, Simon Brown J. held that a decision of the Chief Rabbi declaring the applicant no longer fit to hold rabbinical office was not susceptible to judicial review because the function exercised was "essentially a religious function" in respect of which "Parliament would never contemplate legislating".

To similar effect is the decision of the Court of Appeal in *R. v. Imam of Bury Park, ex p. Sulaiman*.[5] In that case the Imam had refused certain Muslims the right to vote in the election of a mosque committee. The dissatisfied applicants sought judicial review of the decision. The Court of Appeal upheld Auld J.'s refusal of judicial review on the basis, *inter alia*, that the Imam's functions affected the applicants' rights in a way which was peculiar only to a limited class of persons and was not governmental in nature.

It should also be borne in mind that many of the cases on private or domestic tribunals exercising contractual powers involved the submission, rejected by the court, that the decision-maker's authority did not derive solely from contract but depended upon a parallel public law source. In those cases the courts have held, as part of the reason for declining jurisdiction, that there was, on analysis, no exercise of governmental powers.

In *R. v. Lloyd's of London, ex p. Briggs*,[6] for example, the Divisional Court held, as its primary reason for treating Lloyd's as immune from judicial review, that it was not exercising governmental powers in that its powers were derived from a private Act which did not extend to any persons other than those who wished to operate in one section of the insurance market, and that the government had not involved itself in the self-regulatory activities performed by Lloyd's. As demonstrated above, a similar approach was adopted by the Court of Appeal in *R. v. Disciplinary Committee of the Jockey Club, ex p. Aga Khan*,[7] and by the Divisional Court in *R. v. Insurance Ombudsman Bureau, ex p. Aegon Life Assurance Ltd.*[8]

---

of Practice Committee of the British Pharmaceutical Industry, ex p. Professional Counselling (Aids) Ltd [1991] C.O.D. 228; *R. v. Advertising Standards Authority Ltd, ex p. The Insurance Service Plc* [1990] C.O.D. 42; *R. v. Independent Committee for the Supervision of Telephone Information Services, ex p. Firstcode Limited* [1993] C.O.D. 325.

[3] [1990] C.O.D. 440.

[4] n. 87 above.

[5] [1994] C.O.D. 142.

[6] n. 57 above.

[7] n. 57 above. Indeed, all the Jockey Club cases (see nn. 59, 60) may be viewed in this light.

[8] n. 97 above.

Non-statutory bodies subject to limited review

5–010   Very few non-statutory bodies, most notably university visitors (who derive their powers from the common law),[9] may be held to exercise governmental power but only to be amenable to judicial review in the sense used by the courts prior to the landmark decision in *Anisminic Ltd. v. Foreign Compensation Commission*,[10] before which an error of law was immune from judicial review if made "within jurisdiction" (for the meaning of this term, see para. 3–005).

In relation to students and, in many cases, academic staff,[11] the visitor has exclusive jurisdiction over the application and interpretation of a university or college's internal rules including its charter, statutes and regulations, whether or not involving matters of contract and irrespective of whether the complainant is a member of the institution in question.[12]

In *R. v. Hull University Visitor, ex p. Page*[13] the applicant petitioned the university visitor contending that he had been wrongfully dismissed contrary to the statutes of the university. The visitor dismissed his petition.

The House of Lords refused an application for judicial review of the decision, holding (by a majority) that the visitor was only susceptible to judicial review if he acted outside his jurisdiction or abused his powers or offended against the rules of natural justice. He was not amenable to review for an error of law made within his jurisdiction.[14]

Various reasons were given for what might be thought to be an anomalous exception to the principle, espoused in *Anisminic*, that any error of law material to the decision was an error which a decision-maker has no power to make. In particular Lord Browne-Wilkinson thought that there was no essential difference between an ouster clause precluding review and the achievement of the same result by the common law, and that finality would be lost by permitting judicial review against visitors on any wider basis.[15] This approach, however, ignores the fact that the common law in question was developed before *Anisminic* and on the premise that errors of law could be made within jurisdiction.[16] Indeed, at an earlier point in his

---

[9] Not all universities have visitors. For example, the *universities* (as opposed to the colleges) of Oxford and Cambridge are statutory bodies; as, now, are many former polytechnics incorporated under the Education Reform Act 1988: the rules of such bodies may, of course, appoint a visitor.

[10] [1969] 2 A.C. 147.

[11] See, especially, the Education Reform Act 1988 ss. 203–206. For analysis of visitatorial jurisdiction in relation to academic staff, see Clive Lewis *Judicial Remedies in Public Law* (1992) at pp. 44 *et seq.*

[12] *Thomas v. University of Bradford (No. 1)* [1987] A.C. 795; *Thomas v. University of Bradford (No. 2)* [1992] 1 All E.R. 964; *R. v. University of London, ex p. Vijayatunga* [1988] Q.B. 322.

[13] [1993] A.C. 682.

[14] n. 13 above at p. 740F, *per* Lord Browne-Wilkinson.

[15] n. 13 above at pp. 703G–H and 704E–F. *cf.* the dissenting speech of Lord Slynn at *ibid.* p. 709C–E. Ironically, perhaps, *Anisminic*, the case that widened the concept of error of law, was directed towards the rejection of a statutory ouster provision.

[16] See para. 2–003.

speech, Lord Browne-Wilkinson clearly set out the effect of *Anisminic* on administrative law generally.[17]

In *R. v. Visitors to the Inns of Court, ex p. Calder and Persaud*,[18] decisions of the Visitors to Lincoln's Inn upholding the disciplining of two barristers were held, by the Court of Appeal, to be susceptible to judicial review but only on the *Page* basis. In Calder's case it was held that the visitors had acted in excess of jurisdiction (in the *Page* sense) by conducting an appeal as opposed to a rehearing.

Crown servants

As a result of the landmark decision in *M. v. Home Office*[19] (for which see para. 3–020). Ministers acting on behalf of the Crown are in no different position, in judicial review proceedings, to other respondents. Problems may still arise, however, where the Crown, through its representative, is a defendant in private law proceedings but where public law issues are engaged, because in such proceedings injunctive relief does not lie against the Crown or persons acting on behalf of the Crown, (see para. 3–020). This factor may be an important consideration in determining whether to proceed by way of judicial review if that is possible.

5–011

CAPACITY IN WHICH THE DECISION-MAKER IS ACTING

Although, *prima facie*, susceptible to review it is perfectly possible for a public body to act in a capacity affording relief (if at all) only in private as opposed to public law. For example, such a body may enter into contracts and commit torts in exactly the same way as a private individual. The appropriate remedy for breach of contract or misfeasance then lies in private rather than public law.

5–012

The question in each case is whether or not there is an act or decision with a public law element sufficient to justify judicial review. Even where such element exists it is, at least since the House of Lords' ruling in *Roy v. Kensington and Chelsea and Westminster Family Practitioner Committee*,[20] clear that public law issues in aid of private law rights may be ventilated in a private law forum (see para. 6–003).

Many of the cases involve employment situations. Thus, for example, in *R. v. East Berkshire Health Authority, ex p. Walsh*[21] the Court of Appeal

---

[17] n. 13 above at p. 701F–702B.
[18] [1993] Q.B. 1.
[19] [1994] A.C. 377. See also *Mercury Communications Ltd v. Director General of Telecommunications, The Times*, February 10, 1995.
[20] [1992] 1 A.C. 624.
[21] [1985] Q.B. 152. See also *R. v. Secretary of State for the Home Department, ex p. Moore* [1994] C.O.D. 67, (judicial review refused of confirmation of decision to dismiss prison officer: said to be indistinguishable from *Walsh*).

held that an application for judicial review by a senior nursing officer of a decision by his employer health authority, to dismiss him for misconduct, raised only private law issues based on the applicant's contract of employment.

There is one obvious dividing-line in this area. Cases depending solely upon the construction of contractual terms and conditions of employment are manifestly outside the scope of review.[22]

More difficult are similar cases where a power is exercised which is not wholly contract-based. In *R. v. Derbyshire C.C., ex p. Noble*[23] judicial review of the Derbyshire Police Force's decision not to enter into a formal contract with the applicant was refused by a Divisional Court without the court deciding whether there was a subsisting contract of service between the parties. It was held that there was, in any event, an insufficient public law element in circumstances where there was no relevant statutory provision or code relating to employment. A similar approach was adopted by the Divisional Court in *R. v. Lord Chancellor's Department, ex p. Nangle*[24] where, irrespective of whether a contract existed, disciplinary decisions in relation to a civil servant working for the Lord Chancellor's Department were held to have an insufficient public law element to attract review.

In other, subtly different, instances the courts have perceived a statutory context and been prepared to allow the judicial review jurisdiction to intrude. For example, in *R. v. Secretary of State for the Home Department, ex p. Attard*.[25] the Court of Appeal granted judicial review of a decision suspending the applicant in breach of the Code of Discipline for Prison Officers; the Code having statutory force. So, too, in *R. v. Secretary of State for the Home Department, ex p. Benwell*[26] a Divisional Court held that, in the absence of a contract of employment, the applicant prison officer's conditions of employment were underpinned by statute and a dismissal decision was amenable to judicial review. Other cases have held that the employment conditions of police constables are underpinned by statute and, accordingly, subject to remedies under Order 53,[27] and that the manner in which a public body employer exercises its contractual powers may be susceptible to judicial review.[28]

---

[22] Apart from *Walsh* itself, see, *e.g. McClaren v. Home Office* [1990] I.C.R. 808, (judicial review not appropriate where declarations sought as to terms of employment and sums due for services rendered); *Doyle v. Northumbria Probation Committee* [1991] 1 W.L.R. 1340, (decision to phase out contractual entitlement to mileage allowance gave rise to private law claim not judicial review). See also: *R. v. Independent Broadcasting Authority, ex p. Rank Organisation Plc, The Times*, March 14, 1986, (decision-making power exercised under Company's articles of association as opposed to statute and, hence, not amenable to judicial review).

[23] [1990] I.C.R. 808. See also *R. v. Trent Regional Health Authority, ex p. Jones, The Times*, June 19, 1986.

[24] n. 92 above.

[25] [1990] C.O.D. 261.

[26] [1985] Q.B. 554.

[27] *Chief Constable of North Wales Police, ex p. Evans* [1982] 1 W.L.R. 1155; *R. v. S. Yorkshire Police, ex p. Middup, The Times*, May 1, 1989.

[28] As, *e.g.* in *R. v. Liverpool City Council, ex p. Ferguson and Ferguson* [1985] I.R.L.R. 501.

Apart from the employment context, there are several "borderline" areas where the capacity in which a public body acts may be considered to lack the necessary public law character. Again, the absence of any statutory or governmental context seems to dictate whether judicial review will be permitted.

For example, in *Davy v. Spelthorne B.C.*[29] the House of Lords held that advice given in relation to an enforcement notice raised, if negligent, only private law issues. Macpherson J. held, in *R. v. National Coal Board, ex p. National Union of Mineworkers*[30] that the Coal Board's decision to close a colliery was a management decision not susceptible to review. A challenge by a firm of shorthand writers to the tendering procedure for court reporting services was refused, in *R. v. The Lord Chancellor, ex p. Hibbit and Saunders (a firm)*,[31] as being non-reviewable. Rose J., in *R. v. Secretary of State for Defence, ex p. Sancto*,[32] refused judicial review of a Home Office executive decision to withhold the report of an Army Board of Inquiry into the applicant's son's death in the Falklands as being immune from review.

None of the above situations involved the exercise of powers, even indirectly, in a statutory or governmental context. By contrast, the courts have allowed judicial review to operate in areas where there is, albeit indirectly, a perceived statutory or governmental connection with the function under challenge.

Thus, in *R. v. Port Talbot B.C., ex p. Jones*,[33] the allocation of a council house to a councillor for the purpose of providing a presence before a municipal election was held to be amenable to judicial review. The unfair suspension of a contractor from a local authority's tender list,[34] decisions of authorities refusing, on policy grounds, not to contract,[35] or deciding to contract,[36] or deciding to contract on particular terms,[37] or deciding to terminate a contract,[38] have all been held to be susceptible to review.

---

[29] [1984] A.C. 262.

[30] [1986] I.C.R. 791. Contrast *R. v. Secretary of State for Trade, ex p. Vardy* [1993] I.C.R. 720 (*held*: pit closure decisions by Coal Board and Minister without application of statutory consultation procedure were amenable to judicial review).

[31] [1993] C.O.D. 326. *cf. R. v. Walsall M.B.C., ex p. Yapp, The Times*, August 6, 1993 (*held*: judicial review refused in respect of Council's invitation for new tenders after accepting in-house tender); *R. v. Avon C.C., ex p. Terry Adams Ltd* [1994] Env. L.R. 442 (*held*: undue discrimination by Council as against unsuccessful tenderer: judicial review granted).

[32] [1993] C.O.D. 144.

[33] [1988] 2 All E.R. 207.

[34] *R. v. Enfield L.B.C., ex p. T. F. Unwin (Roydon) Ltd* [1989] C.O.D. 466.

[35] *R. v. Lewisham L.B.C., ex p. Shell U.K.* [1988] 1 All E.R. 938, (decision to boycott Shell products); *R. v. Derbyshire C.C., ex p. The Times Supplements Ltd* [1991] C.O.D. 129, (decision not to advertise in Times Group newspapers).

[36] *R. v. Lancashire C.C., ex p. Telegraph Service Stations, The Times*, June 25, 1988.

[37] *R. v. Cleveland C.C., ex p. Cleveland Care Homes*, n. 7 above.

[38] *R. v. Basildon D.C., ex p. Brown*, n. 7 above; *R v. Wear Valley D.C., ex p. Binks*, n. 7 above.

Most of the relevant decisions in this area demonstrate the difficulty of defining the true ambit of public law in circumstances where governmental power is exercised through the medium of contractual relations. This difficulty is likely to increase in the years ahead with the development of privatisation, contracting out, and compulsory competitive tendering.[39]

---

[39] For an outline of the problems see Mark Freedland "Government by Contract and Private Law" (1994) P.L. 86; Sandra Fredman and Gillian Morris "The Costs of Exclusivity" (1994) P.L. 69.

PART 2

PROCEDURE

6. THE RELATIONSHIP BETWEEN JUDICIAL REVIEW AND OTHER FORMS OF PROCESS

INTRODUCTORY

During Part I of this book, it will have become apparent that an important **6–001** aspect of the growing development of public law is concerned with identifying the type of cases with a sufficient public law element for judicial review.

The problem of differentiating the subject matter of an Order 53 application is, however, only partially related to successful categorisation of a factual situation as one involving issues of public or private law. Questions of public law may intrude into other procedures as well. In order to understand why, in a given case, judicial review is appropriate the nature and purpose of these related forms of process should be clearly recognised.

Before embarking on consideration of the Order 53 procedure, therefore, it is proposed to examine some processes with which judicial review may easily become confused.

The proceedings described between paras. 6–007 to 6–011 are all proceedings that fall within the ambit of the Crown Office List and are all affected by a number of relevant Practice Directions in relation to Crown Office proceedings generally.[1]

PRIVATE LAW ACTION: PROCEDURAL EXCLUSIVITY IS THE GENERAL RULE

The effect of *O'Reilly v. Mackman*[2] and *Cocks v. Thanet D.C.*[3] (see para. **6–002** 1–019) has been to delimit, much more strictly, the procedures whereby declarations and injunctions may be sought. In principle, an action is appropriate for the enforcement of rights in private law whereas if a dispute sounds in public law then the procedure is by way of an application for

---

[1] See Appendix C.
[2] [1983] 2 A.C. 237.
[3] [1983] 2 A.C. 286.

judicial review (or other appropriate public law procedure).[4] It may, indeed, be necessary to establish a public default in order to establish the basis of a private law right.[5]

There are now important qualifications to this general principle but the courts have sometimes found difficulty in formulating them with logical precision. As stated by Lord Diplock in *O'Reilly v. Mackman*[6] they amount (in the context of judicial review) to permitting a public law issue to be resolved by action rather than judicial review where either:

(a) all parties consent; or
(b) the invalidity of a particular decision arises as a collateral issue in a claim for infringement of a right of the plaintiff existing in private law.

Lord Diplock went on to suggest that further exceptions might arise on a "case to case" basis. Whatever this may mean[7] it is now clear that, after the 1977 reforms, declarations and injunctions have lost their former effectiveness as public law remedies outside Order 53. However, the case law suggests a number of situations in which the court may not insist on the utilisation of judicial review. In view of Lord Diplock's pragmatic "case to case" qualification, and subsequent case law, the categories set out at paras. 6–003–6–006 below are not intended to be exhaustive.

Lord Diplock's collateral issue exception

6–003   Lord Diplock's express exception to the general rule is "where the invalidity of the decision arises as a collateral issue in a claim for infringement of a right of the Plaintiffs arising under private law".[8]

There are, however, obvious difficulties in applying the exception accurately. In a typical case, where the problem arises, public and private law elements are not easy to separate. The exercise of determining which element is "collateral" to another is, self-evidently, fraught with conjecture.

Davy v. Spelthorne B.C.[9] was the first time that the problem arose following *O'Reilly*, and there the court found no difficulty. The plaintiff had commenced an action for damages against the local planning authority for negligence. He alleged that he had refrained from appealing against an enforcement notice in reliance upon negligent advice given to him by the

---

[4] See, *e.g.*: *Ali (Mohram) v. Tower Hamlets L.B.C.* [1993] Q.B. 407 (*held*: sole avenue for challenge to housing authority's offer of accommodation was judicial review; private law claim struck out).

[5] This was the ratio of *Cocks v. Thanet D.C.*, n. 3 above. See, also, *R. v. Northavon D.C., ex p. Palmer* (1994) 6 Admin. L.R. 195 (leave to move granted so as to allow claim for declaratory relief to proceed to lay the basis for a private law damages claim); *Cato v. Minister of Agriculture, Fisheries and Food* [1989] 3 C.M.L.R. 513 (discretionary decision as to payment of decommissioning grant a precondition to establishment of private law right to payment).

[6] n. 2 above, at p. 285.

[7] Its possible scope is canvassed at para. 6–003.

[8] n. 2 above at p. 285.

[9] [1984] A.C. 262.

authority. As well as seeking damages he also claimed an injunction ordering the defendants not to implement the notice, together with an order setting it aside.

The defendants applied to have the writ and statement of claim struck out as an abuse of process under the principles in *O'Reilly v. Mackman.*

At first instance Sir Robert Megarry V.-C. made no order on the defendant's motion. They appealed. In the Court of Appeal the claims for injunctions and setting aside of the enforcement notice were struck out on the ground that they involved questions of public law which could be raised only on an application for judicial review. The action for damages was, however, allowed to proceed and the Council appealed to the House of Lords for this to be struck out as well. There was (strangely perhaps) no cross-appeal seeking the continuation, by action, of the plaintiff's other claims.

The House of Lords unanimously held, dismissing the appeal, that the claim for damages raised no question of public law but was merely a tortious action. In the words of Lord Wilberforce[10]:

> "The only 'public law' element involved in the present claim is that which may require the court, after it has decided the issue of duty of care and of negligence, in assessing damages to estimate, as best it can, the value of the chance which the plaintiff lost of resisting enforcement of the council's notice. The presence of this element is in my opinion quite insufficient to justify the court, on public policy grounds, in preventing the plaintiff from proceeding by action in the ordinary way in the court of his choice, particularly when one has regard to the serious procedural obstacles[11] which he would find if compelled to seek judicial review."

A similar result obtained in *Roy v. Kensington and Westminster Family Practitioner Committee,*[12] though, in that case, the public and private law elements were more closely fused. There, the committee, pursuant to a statutory power, decided to reduce by 20 per cent the basic practice allowance payable to Dr Roy (a general practitioner) who issued a writ alleging breach of contract and seeking payment of the 20 per cent reduction together with a declaration of illegality.

The House of Lords held that although it was doubtful whether a contract for services existed between Dr Roy and the committee,[13] the presence or absence of such contract was not decisive in determining whether Dr Roy was able to challenge the committee's action in private law was opposed to being required, as the committee contended, to pursue proceedings in judicial review given that: "he has ... a bundle of rights

---

[10] n. 9 at p. 278G–H. For similar observations see pp. 273E and 274E–F (*per* Lord Fraser of Tullybelton).

[11] These presumably being the provisions as to delay and the uncertainty of obtaining damages on judicial review. See n. 9 above at p. 274G–H (*per* Lord Fraser).

[12] [1992] 1 A.C. 624.

[13] Thereby differing from the Court of Appeal which had held that the relationship between Dr Roy and the committee was purely contractual; see (1990) 2 Admin. L.R. 669.

which should be regarded as his individual private law rights against the committee, arising from the statute and regulations and including the very important private law right to be paid for the work that he has done."[14]

In *Roy*, Lord Lowry (with whose speech there was unanimous agreement) declined to choose between what he termed the broad and narrow approaches to Lord Diplock's collateral issue exception in *O'Reilly*. Lord Lowry said this[15]:

> "The 'broad approach' was that the rule in *O'Reilly v. Mackman* did not apply generally against bringing actions to vindicate private rights in all circumstances in which those actions involved a challenge to a public law act or decision, but that it merely required the aggrieved person to proceed by judicial review only when private law rights were not at stake. The 'narrow approach' assumed that the rule applied generally to *all* proceedings in which public law acts or decisions were challenged, subject to some exceptions when private law rights were involved. For my part, I much prefer the broad approach which is both traditionally orthodox and consistent with the *Pyx Granite* principle [1960] A.C. 260, 268, as applied in *Davy v. Spelthorne Borough Council* [1984] A.C. 461, 510. It would also, if adopted, have the practical merit of getting rid of a procedural minefield. I shall, however, be content for the purpose of this appeal to adopt the narrow approach, which avoids the need to discuss the proper scope of the rule, a point which has not been argued before your Lordships and has hitherto been seriously discussed only by the academic writers."[16]

Lord Lowry's preference for a broad approach is, thus, not part of the ratio decidendi of *Roy*. It remains arguable, therefore, that actions commenced[17] which involve a mixture of public and private law issues will still be required to be litigated under Order 53 where it cannot, sensibly, be said that private rights are the predominant issue and public law issues are being used to support, and are collateral to, such rights.

In practice, however, it is likely that the broad approach will be adopted. In *An Bord Bainne Cooperative Ltd. (Irish Dairy Board) v. Milk Marketing Board*,[18] the plaintiffs brought an action seeking, *inter alia*, an injunction to restrain the defendants from differentiating between the prices at which they sold milk in alleged contravention of their obligations under European law. There was also a damages claim. It was contended by the defendants

---

[14] n. 12 above, *per* Lord Lowry at p. 649H.

[15] n. 12 above at p. 653E–H.

[16] See, also, Lord Lowry's indication in *R. v. Secretary of State for the Environment, ex p. Equal Opportunities Commission* [1995] 1 A.C. 1 at p. 34C, that the collateral issue exception needs reformulating. In *Mercury Communications v. Director General of Telecommunications, The Times*, February 10, 1995, the House of Lords observed that the collateral issue exception should be applied flexibly in view of the impressive overlap between public and private law.

[17] Different criteria apply in relation to defendants as opposed to plaintiffs. See para. 6–004 below.

[18] [1984] 2 C.M.L.R. 584.

that these claims were an abuse of process applying the *O'Reilly* test because the issues raised were primarily in public law.

On the defendants' appeal against Neill J.'s refusal to strike out the plaintiff's points of claim[19] the Court of Appeal had no difficultly in rejecting that argument.

Sir John Donaldson M.R. subtly inverted the collateral issue exception by deciding that the relevant test was whether, even though the principal issue was one of public law, private rights were involved and it could cause the citizen injustice to be required to use the judicial review procedure. It was reiterated that exceptions were to be decided on a "case to case" basis and that public policy must be applied in the light of the guidance given in *O'Reilly v. Mackman*. On the particular facts the issues of private and public law were inextricably mixed and it was not, therefore, an abuse of process to proceed by way of an ordinary action.

The decision in *An Borde Bainne* involved the assertion of Community law rights and it may be, therefore, that different considerations were involved because national procedural rules may not prevent the enforcement of such rights.[20] Notwithstanding this, however, it is certainly the case that the procedure exclusivity introduced by *O'Reilly* is a discretionary, rather than jurisdictional, principle.[21] As Lord Wilberforce emphasised in *Davy*, before a proceeding at common law can be said to be an abuse of process, the onus is on the party challenging such proceeding to establish not merely that the claim in question *could* have been brought by judicial review, but that it *should* have been so commenced.[22]

The scope of the collateral issue exception is, nonetheless, still unclear. If a narrow view if the exception is adopted, the attempt to evaluate whether one issue is sufficiently collateral to another is an uncertain process since the court may reach a different conclusion and separate particular claims (as in *Davy v. Spelthorne B.C.* or decide in the light of public policy that collaterality is unimportant (as in *An Bord Bainne*). Equally disturbing is the prospect that the courts may fail to treat essentially similar situations consistently by adopting a broad view of the collateral issue exception in some cases, and a narrow view in others.[23]

Despite the support for beginning a private law claim by action that the above mentioned cases appear to give to the intending plaintiff, even where public law issues are involved, there is tactical sense in starting by way of judicial review proceedings[24] if there is any real doubt as to the correct procedure, having regard to the fact that the court can order such

---

[19] In fact only parts of the points of claim were sought to be struck out.

[20] See para. 2–030 where the effect of Community law is analysed further.

[21] See n. 2 above at p. 274H, *per* Lord Diplock.

[22] See n. 9 above at p. 277A.

[23] Consider, *e.g.*: *Guevara v. Hounslow L.B.C., The Times*, April 17, 1987. (Judicial review required where substantial element of public law even if damages are claimed.)

[24] Perhaps, in conjunction with a private law action; see *R. v. Football Association Ltd, ex p. Football League Ltd* [1993] 3 All E.R. 833.

proceedings to continue as if begun by writ,[25] but has no express power to convert an action to a claim for judicial review.

Collateral challenge exception

6–004   Generally, a defendant in civil proceedings and an accused person in criminal proceedings is entitled to raise a defence by way of collateral challenge on the merits, even if such defence involves issues of public law. This may be merely a limb of Lord Diplock's collateral issue exception[26] but, if so, it has been interpreted in the "broad" rather than "narrow" sense in civil proceedings and rather differently in criminal proceedings.

The principle, in civil cases, was shown to effect in *Wandsworth L.B.C. v. Winder*.[27] In that case the defendant was permitted to raise, by way of defence to possession proceedings brought by the Council for non-payment of rent, the argument that he was not liable for arrears because certain resolutions and notices of increase were *ultra vires* for unreasonableness. The Council challenged his right to do so and applied to strike out the defence and counterclaim.

When the matter eventually reached the House of Lords[28] the unanimous view was that the Order 53 procedure was not intended to curtail or remove a citizen's actionable rights and that it could not, therefore, be an abuse of process to raise issues relating to such rights even where that resulted in a challenge to the validity of the decision of a public authority.

This was so (*per* Lord Fraser), even where the principal issue was one of public law. The essential differences between the *O'Reilly* and *Cocks* decisions and the present case were, according to the House of Lords, that here:

(a) there was an infringement of private law rights as opposed to public law "rights";
(b) the defendant had not initiated the proceedings.

A different result ensued, however, in two cases virtually indistinguishable from *Winder*. In both *Tower Hamlets L.B.C. v. Abdi*[29] and *Hackney L.B.C. v. Lambourne*,[30] defences to possession actions to remove the defendants from temporary accommodation were struck out on the basis that the contention that permanent accommodation offered by the Councils was unsuitable was a matter solely of public rather than private law and, accordingly, raised no actionable defence in private law.

In *Winder*, however, Mr Winder was able to argue that the contractual rate of his rent would be affected by an invalid rent rise resolution. Winder

---

[25] Ord. 53, r. 9(5).
[26] See, *e.g.*: *R. v. Reading Crown Court, ex p. Hutchinson* [1988] Q.B. 384 at p. 392, *per* Lloyd L.J.
[27] [1985] A.C. 461.
[28] The Registrar dismissed the Council's application to strike out; the county court judge allowed it on appeal. The defendant thereupon appealed to the Court of Appeal, which allowed the appeal (Ackner L.J. dissenting).
[29] *The Times*, October 26, 1992.
[30] [1993] C.O.D. 231.

was seeking to prevent the Council, despite its contractual powers, from increasing his rent. *Mutatis mutandis* the same was true of *Abdi* and *Lambourne*. They had contracts which by their terms entitled the Council to terminate the agreements after giving notice. They, too, challenged the validity of the Councils' decision to exercise that right. Therefore, on analysis, *Abdi* and *Lambourne* are identical to *Winder*.[31]

It appears that the Court failed to identify correctly the private law right which was the right to have the contract for the temporary accommodation continued. This does not, however, disturb the *Winder* principle which is that public law issues may be ventilated in circumstances where private law rights are at stake.[32]

There is, nonetheless, a material distinction to be drawn between a defence on the merits involving issues of public law and a defence which is restricted to challenging, on a public law basis, the decision to commence the particular proceedings.

In the latter instance two decisions have prevented such defence being raised, holding instead that separate proceedings in judicial review ought to have been commenced.

Waverley D.C. v. Hilden[33] was a case involving the use of land as a gypsy site. The local authority eventually resolved to bring proceedings for an injunction to prevent such use. Scott J. refused to permit the defendants to challenge, by way of defence to such proceedings, the authority's resolution, considering instead whether to stay the claim in order to allow the defendants to seek judicial review. On the facts he decided that a stay was inappropriate because of the slender prospects of an Order 53 application succeeding.

The same issue arose in *Avon C.C. v. Buscott*.[34] There a local authority sought an order for summary possession under Order 113 of the R.S.C. The defendants, who were gypsies, did not raise a defence on the merits but attacked, instead, the basis of the decision to institute the proceedings. Upholding in the Court of Appeal the judge's refusal to allow such challenge by way of defence, Lord Donaldson of Lymington M.R. approved the decision in *Waverley* and contrasted the ratio of *Winder* by observing as follows:

> "Mr Winder was seeking to raise a true defence. He was saying that he had a valid tenancy, that he did not owe any rent and, accordingly, was not liable to eviction. It was a defence on the merits. In the present case the defendants do not allege any right to occupy the land and, accordingly, do not deny that they are liable to be evicted. They do not suggest that they have any defence on the merits. What they say is quite different, namely that the council is not entitled to enforce its

---

[31] See Anthony Tanney "Procedural Exclusivity in Administrative Law" (1994) P.L. 51 at p. 58, n. 38.

[32] *i.e.*, the "broad" view of Lord Diplock's collateral issue exception as interpreted by Lord Lowry in *Roy*; see para. 6–003 above.

[33] [1988] 1 W.L.R. 246.

[34] [1988] Q.B. 656.

rights . . . . When a defendant is seeking, in effect, to strike out an action on the basis of a public law right, he should in my judgment proceed by way of an application for judicial review, thus ensuring that the matter is dealt with speedily as a preliminary point and in a manner which gives the public authority and the public which it serves the protections enshrined in the judicial review procedure."[35]

In *criminal* cases the position as to collateral challenge is more complicated.

There are, in relation to byelaws, conflicting decisions of Divisional Courts as to whether: (i) a criminal court has jurisdiction to investigate the validity of byelaws or orders which form the basis of a criminal prosecution, and (ii) the scope of the jurisdiction.

In *Plymouth City Council v. Quietlynn*[36] it was held that, unless a decision was invalid on its face, criminal courts must presume that decisions of licensing authorities relating to the grant or refusal of licences to use premises as a sex establishment were valid and that, accordingly, no defence could be raised to the charge of operating such premises without a licence on the ground that such licence had been unlawfully refused.

The decision in *Quietlynn* was criticised in *R. v. Reading Crown Court, ex p. Hutchinson*[37] which held that the invalidity of a byelaw may be challenged by way of defence to a criminal prosecution without recourse to separate judicial review proceedings. Lloyd L.J. considered that "justices have always had jurisdiction to inquire into the validity of a byelaw. They are not only entitled, but bound to do so when the defendant relies on the invalidity of the byelaw by way of defence."[38]

However, in *Bugg v. D.P.P.*,[39] the Divisional Court opted for a compromise between the two positions advocated above.

In *Bugg* the defendants, in summary trials before magistrates, challenged the validity of two sets of byelaws restricting access to protected military areas without authority or permission. In determining that the byelaws were unlawful because they had failed to define the protected areas, Woolf L.J. considered the more general issue of the ability of defendants charged with offences under subordinate legislation to challenge the validity of that legislation in the course of criminal proceedings.

The court held that challenges to an order or byelaw on the ground that it is "substantively invalid" (as in the instant case) may be raised before criminal courts by way of defence to proceedings founded on the order or byelaw. Substantive invalidity, in this sense, means cases where the instrument in question is said to be outside the powers of the decision-maker, or irrational as producing consequences which (for example):

---

[35] *ibid.* at p. 663.

[36] [1988] Q.B. 114.

[37] n. 26 above. See, also, *R. v. Oxford Crown Court, ex p. Smith* [1990] C.O.D. 211 (*held*: it was not an abuse of process to challenge the validity of an enforcement notice by means of statutory appeal).

[38] n. 26 above at p. 391E.

[39] [1993] Q.B. 473.

"were found to be partial and unequal in their operation as between different classes; . . . were manifestly unjust; . . . disclosed bad faith; . . . involved such oppressive or gratuitous interference with the rights of those subjects to them as could find no justification in the minds of reasonable men."[40]

However, in cases where an order or byelaw is contended to be procedurally invalid, it is not for a criminal court to investigate. Procedural invalidity connotes non-compliance with a procedural requirement with regard to the making of the byelaw as, for example, a failure to consult.

Woolf L.J. considered that the disadvantages of permitting such challenges to be ventilated in the criminal courts included requiring evidence which might differ as between different courts in the same issue; it would also involve the person upholding the byelaws to be a party to the criminal proceedings. Further, although Woolf L.J. accepted that he was bound by authority to hold that a defendant could raise substantive invalidity as a defence, the same consideration did not apply to procedural invalidity. As to this he said:

"You cannot in respect of non-compliance with the public law duties of public bodies treat individual members of the public in the same way whether or not their private rights or interests have been infringed. They have no private right which entitles them to complain of procedural defects in delegated legislation unless they have been prejudiced by default."[41]

It is, at first sight, difficult to understand why a person should be subject to jeopardy in criminal proceedings if a public body has behaved in a procedurally unfair manner any more than if it has behaved substantively unfairly. Moreover, it has been observed that "[t]he proposition that, as a general rule, a person challenging a byelaw in judicial review proceedings needs to be able to point to a private right or interest, is contrary to the principles underlying the application for judicial review procedure."[42]

Currently, however, the decision in *Bugg* represents the approach that a criminal court must adopt where public law collateral challenges are sought to be mounted to orders or byelaws relied on as providing the authority for prosecution.[43] The reasoning in earlier authorities which have allowed, in criminal proceedings, public law defences to challenge prosecutions

---

[40] See *Kruse v. Johnson* [1898] 2 Q.B. 91 at pp. 99–100, *per* Lord Russell C.J.

[41] n. 39 above, at p. 500C.

[42] See Feldman "Collateral challenge and judicial review: the boundary dispute continues" (1993) P.L. pp. 37 *et seq.* See also Wade and Forsyth, *Administrative Law* (7th ed. 1994) at p. 323.

[43] The C.A. declined the opportunity of resolving the conflicting Divisional Court decisions in *R. v. Ettrick Trout Co. Ltd* [1995] C.O.D. 53.

alleging contravention of, respectively, enforcement notices[44] and stop notices[45] must, presumably, be revisited in the light of *Bugg* so as to exclude defences founded on an assertion of procedural invalidity.[46]

Consensual exception

6–005   It is possible, albeit unusual, for parties to agree that a matter otherwise solely justiciable under Order 53 may be dealt with in an action by writ or originating summons.

Clearly, such consent would be unusual, especially where proceedings have been commenced by mistake in the wrong forum. An instance of late consent did, however, occur in *Gillick v. West Norfolk and Wisbech Health Authority and the D.H.S.S.*[47] where proceedings were begun outside Order 53 before the law had been clarified by the decision in *O'Reilly v. Mackman*. Parties may not, however, confer public law jurisdiction by consent.[48]

Exception where case is unsuitable for judicial review

6–006   Judicial review is designed to be expeditious. There have been dicta indicating that where a case is unsuitable for the Order 53 machinery as, for example, where unwieldy discovery[49] or complicated issues of fact or law[50] are involved, or where the remedy sought is inappropriate,[51] judicial review will not be required.

THE RELATOR ACTION AND SIMILAR PROCEEDINGS

6–007   The status of the relator action would seem to be unaffected by judicial review.[52] Nothing was said about it in *O'Reilly v. Mackman* and there would seem to be no strong public policy arguments against its use as an alternative to judicial review where appropriate. The consent of the Attorney-General operates as a "filter" to frivolous or delayed applications

---

[44] *Scarborough B.C. v. Adams and Adams* (1983) 147 J.P. 449.
[45] *R. v. Jenner* [1983] 1 W.L.R. 873.
[46] Yet, procedural invalidity could, applying *Winder*, n. 27, be raised as a collateral challenge in *civil* proceedings in which the enforcement or stop notices were in issue.
[47] [1986] A.C. 112.
[48] *R. v. Durham City Council, ex p. Robinson, The Times*, January 31, 1992.
[49] See *Air Canada v. Secretary of State for Trade (No. 2)* [1983] 2 A.C. 394; Lord Denning M.R. in the C.A. in *O'Reilly v. Mackman*, n. 2 above, at pp. 258–259.
[50] *R. v. I.R.C., ex p. Rossminster* [1980] A.C. 952, *per* Lord Scarman; *R. v. Jenner*, n. 45 above at, *per* Watkins L.J.
[51] See, *e.g.*: *Roy v. Kensington and Chelsea and Westminster Family Practitioner Committee*, n. 12 above at p. 654C *per* Lord Lowry; *Woolwich Equitable Building Society v. Inland Revenue Commissioners* [1993] A.C. 70, at p. 200F *per* Lord Slynn.
[52] See Susan Nott, "The Use of the Relator Action in Present-Day Administrative Law" (1984) P.L. 22. *cf.*, though, the recommendations of the JUSTICE-All Souls Review that the relator action should be abolished.

in much the same way as the requirement of preliminary leave in Order 53.[53]

Proceedings analagous to the relator action exist by virtue of section 13 of the Coroners Act 1988. The High Court is, thereby, empowered to quash an inquest verdict upon application made by or under the Attorney-General's authority and to order an inquest (or, as appropriate, a new inquest) where satisfied that the coroner has refused or neglected to hold an inquest which should be held, or that it is necessary or desirable in the interests of justice that another inquest be held.

In most circumstances judicial review will be wider than section 13 proceedings because of the range of decisions, outside the inquest verdict or in relation to the holding of an inquest, made by a coroner that are susceptible to Order 53 relief. However, there will be cases where the section 13 remedy is solely appropriate.[54] Frequently, judicial review and section 13 applications are made together. Where this happens the fiat of the Attorney must still be obtained, as well as the leave of the court for the making of an application for judicial review.[55] As a matter of practice, section 13 applications and applications for judicial review of coroners' decisions are listed for hearing before the Divisional Court.

A refusal by the Attorney-General to give authority for proceedings under section 13 is immune from judicial review.[56]

HABEAS CORPUS (R.S.C., ORD. 54)

The prerogative writ of habeas corpus impinges on public law by providing a method whereby a variety of administrative orders resulting in an applicant's detention may be supervised by the High Court. Once obtained it undermines the validity of the original order for detention by requiring the release of the detainee. The procedural regime is contained in R.S.C., Order 54. The most significant practical difference between habeas corpus and judicial review is that habeas issues as of right.[57] **6–008**

In practice the remedy is used sparingly, and often in conjunction with an application for judicial review.[58] Those areas in which habeas corpus is most employed involve the challenging of detentions in relation to:

    (a) extradition proceedings;

---

[53] In the sense that the Attorney-General's decision is final and is immune from judicial review (see *Gouriet v. Union of Post Office Workers* [1978] A.C. 435) it is even more difficult to bring a relator action.

[54] See Simon Brown J. in *R. v. H.M. Coroner for the County of Central Cleveland, ex p. Dent* (1986) 150 J.P. 251, (s.13 procedure relevant to verdicts contended to be "unsafe and unsatisfactory" where no material error of law could be established to found relief under Order 53).

[55] *Re Rapier dec'd* [1988] Q.B. 26.

[56] See: *R. v. Attorney-General, ex p. Ferrante*, [1995] C.O.D. 18. The C.A. decision (which did not address this issue) is at *The Independent*, April 3, 1995.

[57] For a detailed exposition of the remedy see Sharpe, *The Law of Habeas Corpus* (2nd ed., 1989); Gordon *Crown Office* Proceedings (1990) at section D.

[58] As, *e.g.*, in *Att.-Gen. of Hong Kong v. Ng Yuen Shiu* [1983] 2 A.C. 629; *R. v. Governor of Brixton Prison, ex p. Walsh* [1985] A.C. 154.

    (b) deportation cases;

    (c) illegal immigration cases;

    (d) under the Mental Health Act 1983.

With the advent of modern judicial review the importance of habeas corpus has diminished in recent years as a separate substantive remedy.[59] Perhaps its most significant limitation is that it is usually a sufficient response to an application for habeas corpus to satisfy the court that there is, *ex facie*, a statutory authority for the detention without the detaining authority being required, as in judicial review, to defend the legal or factual merits of the underlying decision-making process leading to the detention.[60]

The tendency is to view habeas corpus as a specific application of principles of common law judicial review to cases affecting the liberty of the subject. In *R. v. Secretary of State for the Home Department, ex p. Khawaja*,[61] Lord Scarman made this clear when he observed that:

> "There are, of course, procedural differences between habeas corpus and the modern statutory judicial review ... in the instant cases the effective relief sought is certiorari to quash the immigration officer's decision. But the nature of the remedy sought cannot affect the principle of the law. In both cases liberty is in issue. 'Judicial review' under R.S.C. Ord. 53 and the Supreme Court Act 1981 is available only by leave of the court. The writ of habeas corpus issues as of right. But the difference arises not in the law's substance but from the nature of the remedy appropriate to the case."[62]

There are, nonetheless, occasions where habeas corpus offers distinct advantages over judicial review. Thus:

    (a) In certain circumstances habeas corpus may operate more expeditiously than judicial review so as (for example) to prevent an applicant's removal from the jurisdiction.[63]

    (b) Habeas corpus may not be refused (as judicial review may) because of the existence of an alternative remedy.[64]

---

[59] See Wade and Forsyth, *op. cit.* n. 42 above, at pp. 615 *et seq.*, especially p. 619.

[60] *R. v. Managers of South Western Hospital, ex p. M* [1993] Q.B. 683. See, also, *R. v. Secretary of State for the Home Department, ex p. Cheblak* [1991] 1 W.L.R. 890, *per* Lord Donaldson M.R.; *R. v. Same, ex p. Muboyayi* [1992] Q.B. 244.

[61] [1984] A.C. 74.

[62] n. 61 above at p. 111B–C.

[63] See *R. v. Secretary of State for the Home Department, ex p. Muboyayi*, n. 60 above.

[64] See, *e.g.: R. v. Governor of Durham Prison, ex p. Singh Hardial* [1984] 1 W.L.R. 704. See, also, *R. v. Secretary of State for the Home Department, ex p. Mighal* [1973] 1 W.L.R. 1113 at p. 1116. *Cf.* the inroads to this fundamental principle suggested *obiter* in *R. v. Governor of Pentonville Prison, ex p. Osman (No. 3)* [1990] 1 W.L.R. 878 (court could refuse habeas corpus for a technical flaw in the process leading to detention).

STATUTORY APPEALS (R.S.C., ORD. 55)

Many statutes lay down a form of appeal from various ministers and **6–009** tribunals to the High Court. These appeals, which are determined (as appropriate) by a Divisional Court or single judge, are procedurally distinct from appeals heard under the case stated regime (see below) and from judicial review itself.[65]

A general procedure for this form of appeal is contained in R.S.C., Order 55. This general procedure applies to an appeal "subject to any provision made in relation to that appeal by any other provision of these rules or by or under any enactment."[66] It is, therefore, always important to examine other Rules of the Supreme Court as well as the statutory source to see whether Order 55 has been modified or replaced in relation to a particular appeal. In practice a great many statutory appeals are restricted to points of law, whereas Order 55, r. 7(2) contemplates a limited form of rehearing.[67]

In *R. v. Inland Revenue Commissioners, ex p. Preston*[68] Lord Templeman indicated, *obiter*, that all errors of law are susceptible, where such provision exists, to statutory appeal.[69] Apart from issues involving breach of natural justice, where judicial review may be thought to be more appropriate, the existence of an alternative remedy in the form of a statutory appeal will preclude judicial review in all but the most exceptional circumstances.[70]

CASE STATED (R.S.C., ORD. 56)

Case stated is a species of appeal on a point of law to the High Court from **6–010** magistrates' courts, the Crown Court, and, less commonly, decisions or actions of government ministers and certain tribunals. It is an entirely distinct procedure from judicial review[71] and a specific type of statutory appeal requiring the decision-maker to set out his findings of fact and law and to specify questions for the opinion of the High Court. Leave of the High Court is not required to bring such proceedings. Case stated is, principally, governed by Order 56 of the Rules of the Supreme Court.[72]

---

[65] The time limits vary but the general time permitted is usually 28 days from the decision, etc., complained of. Leave of the High Court is generally not required for statutory appeals, although it is for some appeals as, *e.g.* under s.289 of the Town and Country Planning Act 1990.

[66] Ord. 55, r. 1(4).

[67] For a detailed exposition of statutory appeals, see Gordon, *op cit.* n. 57 above, at s. E.

[68] [1985] A.C. 835 at p. 862.

[69] Contrast *Henry Moss of London Ltd v. Customs and Excise Commissioners* [1981] 2 All E.R. 86 where the C.A. suggested that the proper method of challenging the validity of regulations and administrative directions made under the authority of statute was by way of an application under Ord. 53.

[70] See, generally, para. 2–033.

[71] There are different (and varying) time limits for the bringing of a case stated appeal. Leave of the High Court is not required.

[72] Many appeals from ministers and tribunals are also regulated by other R.S.C.s in addition to Ord. 56. Consider, *e.g.*, Ord. 94 which modifies the Ord. 56 regime for some tribunals such

Usually appeal is to a Divisional Court but is, sometimes, to a single judge of the Queen's Bench Division.[73]

Practitioners frequently experience difficulty in deciding whether to proceed by way of case stated or judicial review.[74] The remedy of case stated is available where a particular court or tribunal has erred in exercising jurisdiction. The following general principles should be applied:

(a) Case stated is especially valuable where the facts are involved and in dispute.[75]

(b) It should be used where the ground of attack is that there is no legally sufficient evidence before the decision-maker to found the conclusions which he reached on the facts.[76]

(c) It should, in any event, be used in preference to judicial review unless clearly inappropriate so that the High Court knows what facts were found by the court or tribunal and the relevant points of law for the High Court's decision.[77] Where the facts found are unclear, an application for judicial review is likely to be refused in the court's discretion on the basis that case stated should have been deployed.[78]

(d) Where jurisdiction is unlawfully declined, either judicial review or case stated may be used but case stated is the better remedy.[79]

(e) Case stated is generally unsuitable where a breach of natural justice is contended.[80]

(f) Judicial review is usually more appropriate than case stated where there is alleged to be a misunderstanding by the tribunal of its functions,[81] or the decision is manifestly irrational or otherwise wrong in law.[82]

(g) So, too, in respect of criminal matters, judicial review, subject to exercise of the court's discretion to refuse relief on the ground of

---

as the Mental Health Review Tribunal. For a detailed exposition of the Case Stated procedure, see Gordon, *op. cit.* n. 57 above, at s. F.

[73] *cf.* Ord. 56, r. 7 with Ord. 56, r. 1 and 5.

[74] Exceptionally, the applications are brought together. See, *e.g.*: *R. v. Metropolitan Stipendiary Magistrate, ex p. London Waste Regulation Authority* [1993] 3 All E.R. 113.

[75] See: *R. v. Ipswich Crown Court, ex p. Baldwin* [1981] 1 All E.R. 596; *R. v. Epping and Harlow General Commissioners, ex p. Goldstraw* [1983] 3 All E.R. 257; *R. v. Morpeth Ward JJ., ex p. Ward* (1992) 95 Cr.App.R. 215.

[76] *R. v. Central Criminal Court, ex p. Behbehani* [1994] C.O.D. 193.

[77] *R. v. Morpeth JJ., ex p. Joseland, The Times,* March 4, 1992; *R. v. Brent JJ., ex p. Liles* [1992] C.O.D. 269; *D.P.P. v. Connors* [1992] C.O.D. 81. See, also, *Benham v. Poole B.C.* (1991) 135 S.J. (L.B.) 173, (judicial review should be reserved for when there is no true alternative remedy).

[78] *R. v. Beaconsfield JJ., ex p. Stubbings* (1988) 152 J.P. 17.

[79] *R. v. Clerkenwell Metropolitan Stipendiary Magistrate, ex p. D.P.P.* [1984] Q.B. 821.

[80] *R. v. Wandsworth JJ., ex p. Read* [1942] 1 K.B. 281; *Rigby v. Woodward* [1957] 1 W.L.R. 50.

[81] *R. v. Chief Commons Commissioners, ex p. Winnington, The Times,* November 26, 1982.

[82] *R. v. Clerkenwell Stipendiary Magistrate, ex p. Director of the Serious Fraud Office* (unrep, June 23 1994); see transcript at p. 7.

prematurity,[83] is the sole remedy for unlawful interlocutory decisions made by the Crown Court[84] and magistrates' courts.[85] There is a discretion to grant case stated for unlawful interlocutory decisions made by the Crown Court and magistrates' courts in relation to civil matters.[86] It is, however, a discretion to be exercised sparingly and exceptionally.[87] Judicial review is probably preferable.

(h) Refusal to state a case is enforceable by judicial review.[88]

STATUTORY JUDICIAL REVIEW (R.S.C., ORD. 94)

Many facets of administrative decision-making require greater certainty and immunity from delayed challenge than are conventionally afforded by the supervisory remedy of judicial review. Accordingly, Parliament has (since 1930)[89] consistently legislated a distinct scheme of review whereby particular statutes lay down the criteria for challenging the validity of a variety of decisions.[90] Additionally, R.S.C., Order 94, rr. 1–3 prescribe a uniform procedural regime for the disposal of such cases in the Crown Office List.[91]

6–011

The standard statutory formula operates as a preclusive clause restricting challenge to decisions to certain classes of person,[92] within a strict time limit which cannot be extended,[93] and on specified grounds.[94] On the remedial level statutory review is, thus, somewhat narrower than judicial review, although the court's leave is not required for the making of such application.

By a more or less uniform formula, statutory review clauses operate to prevent challenge to the validity of a particular order or decision outside the

---

[83] See para. 2–034.

[84] *Loade v. D.P.P.* [1990] 1 Q.B. 1052.

[85] *Streames v. Copping* [1985] Q.B. 920.

[86] See: *Kavanagh v. Chief Constable of Devon and Cornwall* [1974] Q.B. 624, (Crown Court decisions); *R. v. Chesterfield JJ., ex p. Kovacs* [1990] C.O.D. 367.

[87] *Loade v. D.P.P.*, n. 84 above; *R. v. Chesterfield JJ., ex p. Kovacs*, n. 86 above.

[88] In the case of (*e.g.*) justices there is statutory provision for an application for mandamus; see M.C.A. 1980, s.111(6).

[89] Housing Act 1930 s.11.

[90] There are a great number of these provisions occurring, predominantly, in the areas of compulsory acquisition and control of land but also, now, as part of the mechanism for control and planning of industry.

[91] For a detailed exposition of the procedure see Gordon, *op cit.* n. 57 above, at section G.

[92] The most common formula is "any person aggrieved". *cf.*, *e.g.*: "airport operator ... aggrieved" (Airports Act 1986, s.49(1)).

[93] The usual time limit is "six weeks" or "42 days". Occasionally, different time limits prevail as, *e.g.*, three months under the Medicines Act 1968, s.107.

[94] The essential basis of challenge under a statutory review clause is either: (i) that the order, etc., is "not within the powers of this Act", or (ii) "that any requirement of this Act has not been complied with".

specified time limit and grounds. The most usual expression is that, apart from the specified mode of challenge, such order or decision "shall not be questioned in any legal proceedings whatever".

It is important to distinguish between this form of time clause which appears in statutory review provisions, and ouster clauses that could have the effect of precluding judicial review altogether.

Typical expressions used in "total" ouster clauses are that a particular decision "shall be final" (finality clauses), "shall have effect as if enacted in this Act" (as if enacted clauses), and "shall not be questioned" (shall not be questioned clauses).

Most of these clauses are now in disuse and have been judicially disapproved.[95] In relation to each type of clause, judicial review has been held to be available in respect of jurisdictional error. Since jurisdictional error has now been held to encompass every material error of law (see para. 2–004), there ought to be little prospect of variants on the above being successful.[96]

In *Anisminic Ltd. v. Foreign Compensation Commission*[97] the House of Lords struck down an ouster clause of the "shall not be questioned" variety. As Lord Wilberforce observed,[98] "What would be the purpose of defining by statute the limit of a tribunal's powers, if by means of a clause inserted in the instrument of definition, those limits could safely be passed?"

Many total ouster clauses passed prior to August 1, 1958 are, in any event, invalidated under the 1958, 1971 and 1992 Tribunals and Inquiries Acts.[99] Professor Wade has suggested that clauses which constitute a substantial re-enactment of a pre-1958 clause would be treated as also being invalid.[1] Certainly, a total ouster clause is likely to be regarded as contrary to Community law.[2]

The courts have, however, adopted a different approach to the "time" clauses that appear in statutory review provisions. The validity of these form of clauses has been upheld in decisions pre- and post-*Anisminic*.

In *Smith v. East Elloe R.D.C.*[3] and *R. v. Secretary of State for the*

---

[95] A colourful account of the history is set out by Lord Denning in *The Discipline of Law* (1979) Chap. 2. For a possible judicial review proof exception, see *R. v. Registrar of Companies, ex p. Central Bank of India* [1986] Q.B. 1114.

[96] See, though, *South East Asia Fire Bricks Sdn. Bhd. v. Non Metallic Mineral Products Manufacturing Employees Union* [1981] A.C. 363, (ouster clause prevented review of error of law on the face of the record). See the critique of this case as resurrecting pre-*Anisminic* distinction between errors of law that went to jurisdiction and those that did not, by Wade and Forsyth, *op cit.* n. 42 above, at pp. 303, 305. See, also: *Re Racal Communications Ltd.* [1981] A.C. 374 where Lord Diplock clarified that the distinction was, for practical purposes, abolished.

[97] [1969] 2 A.C. 147.

[98] *ibid.* at p. 208.

[99] See, now, s.12 of the Tribunals Inquiries Act 1992 (formerly s.12 of the 1971 Act).

[1] See Wade and Forsyth, *op cit.* n. 42 above, at p. 740. See, also: *R. v. Preston Supplementary Benefits Appeal Tribunal, ex p. Moore* [1975] 1 W.L.R. 624.

[2] See *Johnston v. Chief Constable of the Royal Ulster Constabulary* (Case 222/84) [1987] Q.B. 129m (conclusive evidence clause protecting Ministerial certificate from review held by ECJ to be contrary to E.C. law).

[3] [1956] A.C. 736.

Environment, ex p. Ostler,[4] compulsory purchase orders were challenged outside the six week period on the basis *inter alia,* of bad faith. The time clause was, in each case, held effective to exclude review. In *Ostler* the Court of Appeal held that nothing in *Anisminic* had overruled *East Elloe.*

Time clauses have also been upheld in other statutory contexts; the court considering itself to be bound by *Ostler.*[5] Ironically, perhaps, the strict terminology of a statutory review clause may have the effect of preventing a challenge before the decision, act or order in question (and, therefore, the six-week time period) takes effect.[6] In *R. v. Warwickshire C.C., ex p. Boyden*[7] the court left open the question of whether decisions to make traffic regulation orders could be challenged by judicial review, when the orders themselves could be challenged only by the statutory review procedure in Part VI of Schedule 9 to the Road Traffic Regulations Act 1984.

In some exceptional cases the High Court has considered judicial review to be appropriate, notwithstanding the existence of a statutory review clause. This has occurred where:

(a) the challenge is to the reasoning underpinning the decision and not to the decision itself[8];

(b) the challenge is not to a decision to which the statutory review clause applies but to decisions or steps antecedent thereto[9];

(c) the challenge is to the declining of jurisdiction by a decision-maker in relation to a matter which would otherwise be solely justiciable under a statutory review clause[10];

(d) the challenge is to a decision which would ordinarily lead to a further decision to which a statutory review clause would apply but where the applicant is, for some reason, not obliged to pursue a route leading to statutory review.[11]

Despite a more stringent time limit it is probable that the type of review available in statutory review proceedings is the same as in conventional judicial review proceedings.

In the *East Elloe* decision the House of Lords found it necessary to

---

[4] [1977] Q.B. 122.

[5] See, *e.g.*: *R. v. Secretary of State for the Environment ex p. Kent* (1990) J.P.L. 124; *Khan v. Newport B.C.* [1991] C.O.D. 157; *R. v. Camden L.B.C., ex p. Woolf* [1992] C.O.D. 456; *R. v. Cornwall C.C., ex p. Huntington* [1994] 1 All E.R. 694.

[6] See: *R. v. Cornwall C.C., ex p. Huntington,* n. 5 above; *R. v. Test Valley B.C., ex p. Peel Estates Ltd* [1990] C.O.D. 215.

[7] [1991] C.O.D. 31.

[8] *G.L.C. v. Secretary of State for the Environment and Harrow L.B.C.* (1985) J.P.L. 868, (*held:* reasoning of decision of planning inspector favourable to applicants could be challenged to obtain declaration to prevent repetition of reasoning in other cases).

[9] *R. v. Camden L.B.C., ex p. Comyn Ching and Co. (London) Ltd* (1984) 47 P. & C.R. 1417, (resolution to make compulsory purchase order but no order made justified judicial review; judicial review was precluded once order made even though not confirmed). See, also, *Islington L.B.C. v. Secretary of State for the Environment* (1982) 43 P. & C.R. 300.

[10] *Etheridge v. Secretary of State for the Environment* (1984) 48 P. & C.R. 35; *Lenlyn v. Secretary of State for the Environment* (1984) 50 P. & C.R. 129.

[11] See, *e.g.*: *R. v. Hillingdon B.C., ex p. Royco Homes* [1974] Q.B. 720.

examine the nature of the review process both within and outside the six-week period. There was an unfortunate division of opinion as to whether such clauses should be treated restrictively, so as to allow review only where there was an express violation of statute, or (at the other extreme) whether review on the ground of fraud or bad faith was permissible, even after the statutory period for review had expired, as being outside the scheme of the Act altogether.[12] The majority of the House of Lords held, without really addressing the problem, that, in any event, the clause was intended to prohibit any kind of review after the specified period.

The case law since *East Elloe*, however, has clarified that all the heads of challenge under the modern judicial review procedure (see Chapter 2) are also available to an applicant for statutory review.[13]

APPEAL VERSUS REVIEW

6–012 The conceptual difference between appeal and review is well established, yet is often overlooked. Essentially, review is concerned with validity rather than merits; with the reasoning process rather than the correctness of the decision that has been reached.

Two modern authorities have pointed to the fallacy of equating review with some kind of evaluation of the fairness or correctness of a decision on the merits.

In *Chief Constable of the North Wales Police v. Evans*[14] it was emphasised that were the court to ignore its function, on judicial review, of confining its attention to the decision-making process it would, under the guise of preventing abuse of power, be guilty of usurping power.[15] Lord Brightman showed how the Court of Appeal had fallen into that very trap when he said:

> "With profound respect to the Court of Appeal, I dissent from the view that 'Not only must [the probationer constable] be given a fair hearing but the decision itself must be fair and reasonable.' If that statement of the law passed into authority without comment, it would in my opinion transform, and wrongly transform, the remedy of judicial review. Judicial review, as the words imply, is not an appeal

---

[12] *cf.* the judgment of Lord Morton (restrictive) at n. 3 p. 755, with those of Lord Reid and Lord Somervell (liberal) at *ibid.* pp. 763, 772.

[13] For statements of principle, see: *Ashbridge Investments Ltd v. Minister of Housing and Local Government* [1965] 1 W.L.R. 1320 at p. 1326, *per* Lord Denning M.R.; *Webb v. Minister of Housing and Local Government* [1965] 1 W.L.R. 755 at p. 770, *per* Lord Denning M.R. For instances see: *Peak Park Joint Planning Board v. Secretary for State for the Environment* [1979] J.P.L. 618 (illegality); *Westminster City Council v. Same* [1984] J.P.L. 27 (irrationality); *Fairmount Investments v. Same* [1976] 1 W.L.R. 1255 (procedural impropriety); *Coleen Properties Ltd v. Minister of Housing and Local Government* [1971] 1 W.L.R. 433 (no evidence).

[14] [1982] 1 W.L.R. 1155.

[15] *ibid.* at p. 1160.

from a decision but a review of the manner in which the decision was made. The statement of law which I have quoted implies that the court sits in judgment not only on the correctness of the decision-making process but also on the correctness of the decision itself."[16]

A similar view was expressed in *R. v. Entry Clearance Officer, Bombay, ex p. Amin*,[17] where the above case was referred to and approved. Lord Fraser of Tullybelton observed that:

"Judicial review is concerned not with the merits of a decision but with the manner in which the decision was made .... Judicial review is entirely different from an ordinary appeal. It is made effective by the court quashing an administrative decision without substituting its own decision, and it is to be contrasted with an appeal where the appellate tribunal substitutes its own decision on the merits for that of the administrative officer."[18]

EUROPEAN ECONOMIC COMMUNITY LAW

The role played by Community law in judicial review has already been discussed (see para. 2–030).   **6–013**

Article 177 of the EEC Treaty contains a preliminary ruling procedure enabling the European Court of Justice to give a ruling on questions of Community law referred to it by the national court. Article 177 will be potentially relevant to any judicial review case with a Community law element. Unlike the other procedures contained in this chapter, the preliminary ruling procedure is not separate from judicial review and to be distinguished from it. It is, rather, a part of the judicial review proceedings themselves.

The purpose of the preliminary ruling procedure is to ensure that Community law is applied uniformly by national courts. Divergent national judgments on the validity and interpretation of Community acts or on the exercise of Community rights are liable to jeopardise the unity of the Community legal order. The ECJ is best placed to ensure this uniformity. As Bingham J. stated in *Customs and Excise Commissioners v. ApS Samex*[19]:

"It has a panoramic view of the Community and its institutions, a detailed knowledge of the treaties and of much subordinate legislation made under them, and an intimate familiarity with the functioning of the Community market which no national judge denied the collective experience of the Court of Justice could hope to achieve."

---

[16] *ibid.* at p. 1174.

[17] [1983] 2 A.C. 818.

[18] *ibid.* at p. 263. See also: *Tsai v. Woolworth, The Times,* November 30, (*held: Evans v. Bartlam* [1937] A.C. 473 and not *Associated Provincial Picture Houses Ltd v. Wednesbury Corp.* [1948] K.B. 223 is the appropriate test for reviewing appellate discretion); *G v. G* [1985] 1 W.L.R. 647 (to similar effect).

[19] [1983] 1 All E.R. 1042 at p. 1055h.

From that case it is apparent that the Court, in considering whether to make a reference must ask itself:

(a) Is a decision on the question of Community law necessary to enable the court to give judgment?
(b) If so, should the court in the exercise of its discretion order that a reference be made?[20]

Four points are relevant to the question of whether a decision is necessary from the ECJ. These are:

(a) the point must be conclusive;
(b) there must be an absence of existing ruling;
(c) the point must not be *acte claire*[21];
(d) the facts must have been decided.[22]

As to the guidelines governing discretion, Sir Thomas Bingham M.R. summarised them as follows:

(a) the time to obtain a ruling;
(b) the undesirability of overloading the ECJ;
(c) the need to formulate the question;
(d) the difficulty and importance of the point;
(e) expense;
(f) wishes of the parties.[23]

In practice, the parties should agree the terms of a draft reference and invite the High Court to approve it prior to any hearing of the substantive application for judicial review. The detailed procedure for references under Article 177 is set out in R.S.C. 114. The Court frequently refers cases to the European Court in the course of Order 53 proceedings, most notably in *R. v. Secretary of State for Transport, ex p. Factortame Limited (No. 2)*[24] where the ECJ held that the national court did have jurisdiction to grant interim relief to disapply a national law so as to protect putative rights in Community law.

---

[20] See *ibid.* at p. 1054f. The question of discretion does not arise if the case reaches the House of Lords.
[21] Note Lord Diplock's warning in *R. v. Henn and Darby* [1981] A.C. 850 at p. 906 that English judges should "not . . . be too ready to hold that because the meaning of the English text . . . seems plain to them no question of interpretation can be involved". For the relevant criteria in determining whether the matter is *acte claire* see, also: Case 283/81 *Srl C.I.L.F.I.T. v. Ministry of Health* [1982] E.C.R. 3415, paras. 16–20.
[22] n. 19 above, at pp. 1054g–1055c.
[23] *ibid.* at p. 1055d–g.
[24] [1990] E.C.R. 1–2433; [1991] 1 A.C. 603. For cases where references were refused by the House of Lords despite reversing C.A. rulings, see, *e.g. R. v. London Boroughs Transport Committee, ex p. Freight Transport Association Limited* [1992] 1 C.M.L.R. 5; *Kirklees B.C. v. Wickes Building Supplies Ltd* [1993] A.C. 227.

7. OBTAINING LEAVE TO APPLY FOR JUDICIAL REVIEW

Learning Resources
Centre

WHERE TO APPLY

As has been seen, the application for judicial review is conducted in two separate stages. Leave to apply must be obtained before the substantive application can be determined.[1]

7–001

The application for leave should be filed in the Crown Office (Room C315, Royal Courts of Justice). A fee is payable on lodging it.[2] All enquiries in relation to procedural matters should be directed to the Crown Office itself (tel. 0171 936 6205).

Applications outside London

Wherever practicable, applications should be commenced in London. Where urgency dictates, an application may be made outside London but the Crown Office should be informed beforehand (by telephone if necessary). The application should be conducted in accordance with such arrangements as the Crown Office may make.

7–002

Even if it is necessary to make the initial application outside London, the proceedings should continue in London. The hearing should be confined to those matters that have to be dealt with urgently.[3]

FORM OF APPLICATION

The applicant is required to seek leave to move for judicial review by applying, *ex parte*, to a High Court Judge by filing in the Crown Office:

7–003

   (a) a notice of application in Form 86A[4];
   (b) a supporting affidavit verifying the facts relied on.[5]

Prior to filing any application in the Crown Office, practitioners should heed the important warning given by Brooke J. in *R. v. Horsham D.C., ex p.*

---

[1] Ord. 53, r. 3(1).
[2] Currently this is £20. Further fees are payable if and when it becomes necessary to file other documents. See Chap. 8.
[3] See *Practice Note* [1983] 1 W.L.R. 925.
[4] Contained in R.S.C. Appendix A. See para. **D–01** for a specimen notice of application.
[5] Ord. 53, r. 3(2). And see para. **D–02** for a specimen affidavit.

Wenman[6] to the effect that a letter before action should invariably, be written prior to embarking on an application for leave to apply for judicial review, and that the belief that the inevitable reply to such a letter would be a denial of the claim ought not to be regarded as rendering a preliminary letter unnecessary.

Determination of the initial application

7–004   In both civil and criminal matters the applicant has a choice at the preliminary stage.

Under Order 53, r. 3(3) he may request an immediate oral hearing in his notice of application. Unless he so specifies, however, the papers in the case will be placed before a judge who may deal with the application for leave without hearing oral submissions. The judge has power to order an immediate oral hearing.[7] The judge's decision will be formally communicated in writing,[8] although in the case of an oral hearing his decision is also announced in court.[9]

Paper or oral hearing?

7–005   The rationale of the "paper" application is, essentially, to save costs. There are other advantages from an applicant's point of view. If the judge refuses the paper application it is possible to make a renewed oral application.[10] Moreover, where a paper application is refused the single judge will often given brief reasons for his refusal. Any obvious defects may, therefore, be eliminated before the renewed hearing. Tactically, a paper application (subject to the judge ordering an oral hearing) obviates the prospect of the respondent appearing.[11]

In certain instances it may be preferable to proceed directly to an oral hearing.[12] This will be so, predominantly, where there is an urgent need for determination. Where a stay of proceedings or interim relief is sought at the leave stage such relief will rarely lie on the papers alone. An oral application is almost always required. This was underlined by the decision in *R. v.*

---

[6] [1995] 1 W.L.R. 680.

[7] Ord. 53, r. 3(3). In practice an oral hearing is now frequently ordered where the judge considers that the respondent should appear at the leave stage (see below).

[8] *i.e.* on Form JRJ.

[9] Where leave is granted it is unusual for the judge to deliver a judgment. Where leave is refused a short judgment is invariably given explaining the basis of refusal.

[10] Whereas it is not possible to renew (except to the Court of Appeal) after an oral hearing in a civil case. Renewal to the Court of Appeal is also available to "paper" applicants, in a civil case, after they have made a renewed application for an oral hearing. Given that judges vary enormously in their propensity to grant leave (as to which, see by Sunkin, Bridges and Meszaros, "Trends in Judicial Review" (1993) P.L. 443), the "two bites at the cherry" rationale may be a consideration of the utmost practical importance.

[11] Though it is open to the respondent to write to the Crown Office and request an oral hearing.

[12] In *R. v. Northamptonshire C.C. and Secretary of State for Education, ex p. K* [1994] C.O.D. 28 Hutchinson J. observed that those advising applicants in cases involving school closures or analogous issues should give the most careful consideration to whether it would not be more appropriate to apply for leave orally and on notice.

Kensington and Chelsea Royal L.B.C., ex p. Hammell[13] where Parker L.J. observed as follows:

> " . . . where an application for interim relief is intended to be made, the applicant would be well advised to give notice to the other party that such an application is being made in order that the other party may, if he so wishes, attend and assist the court by filling in any gaps in the information which may be available and thereby enable the matter to be dealt with properly at the first hearing and dispense with the necessity of having a second hearing. I can therefore say no more than that notice that an *ex parte* application for interim relief is going to be made would be an advisable step in all cases."[14]

Generally, oral argument seems more likely to result in leave being granted than a paper application.[15] The process of renewing inevitably takes time. If, in the meantime, an allegedly defective decision may have serious effects, an immediate oral hearing is desirable since interim relief rarely lies until the grant of leave.[16] If there are genuine reasons for requesting an expedited hearing (see paras. 7–012 and 7–029 below) an oral hearing should also, generally, be sought because, having regard to the heavy case load in the Crown Office List, expedition is rarely granted on the papers.

THE NOTICE OF APPLICATION

This will be in exactly the same form whether the matter is civil or criminal. It must contain, pursuant to Ord. 53, r. 3(2), a statement of the following: **7–006**

(a) the name and description of the applicant;
(b) the relief sought and the grounds upon which it is sought;
(c) (if appropriate) the name and address of the applicant's solicitors; and
(d) the applicant's address for service.

Particular care is necessary in setting out the relief and grounds.

---

[13] [1989] Q.B. 518.

[14] *ibid.* at p. 539.

[15] See Maurice Sunkin, "What is happening to applications for Judicial Review?" (1987) 50 M.L.R. 432.

[16] Ord. 53, r. 3(10) suggests that interim relief may *only* be made following the grant of leave. However, in *M. v. Home Office* [1994] 1 A.C. 377 at p. 423C–E Lord Woolf clarified that, exceptionally, injunctions may be granted before leave issues. Note that an injunction or stay should be requested at the leave stage, rather than being left to a later date (*R. v. London Boroughs Transport Committee, ex p. Freight Transport Association* [1990] R.T.R. 109; [1989] C.O.D. 572).

Claiming relief

7–007   The range of relief available by way of judicial review has already been discussed (see Chapter 3). Although there is, clearly, no point in including a claim for an obviously inappropriate remedy[17] it is, generally, safer to add relief which may, in the event, prove to be inappropriate in order to avoid having to apply to amend later.

The application should specify whether each form of relief is being claimed cumulatively or in the alternative.[18]

If, at the outset, an applicant is unsure of the interrelationship between the remedies that he is seeking, the blanket phrase "further or in the alternative" might usefully be employed.

Apart from the prerogative orders, declarations and injunctions it is, as has been seen, possible for the court to award damages on judicial review provided that the applicant has included such claim in his notice of application and that the court is satisfied that had the claim been made in an action, he could have been awarded damages.[19]

In formulating a claim for damages, the usual rules of pleading apply.[20] Thus, full particulars must be given of any alleged special damage or of any damage (whether special or general) where it is contended that the loss suffered was other than a necessary or immediate consequence of the specified default. Claims for exemplary damages must be specifically itemised together with a statement of full supporting facts.

When drafting the claim for relief, sufficient detail should be given so as to identify the order or proceeding in respect of which relief is sought and the purpose of the relief.

Establishing grounds

7–008   Even at the preliminary stage it is necessary to establish prima facie grounds for relief. Moreover, Form 86A will form the basis of the applicant's case of the substantive hearing if leave is granted.

It is important, therefore, that the notice of application should set out a concise and coherent statement of the essential points of fact and law so that the basis of the argument is shown.[21]

In general terms the statement of grounds should be directed towards satisfying the court that:

(a) there has been a failure of duty, abuse of discretion, etc., in public law, and

(b) the applicant has a "sufficient interest".[22]

---

[17] As, *e.g.*, for prohibition where the respondent has completed the acts complained of. See, further, paras. 3–002 *et seq.*

[18] Ord. 53, r. 2.

[19] See Ord. 53, r. 7(1); S.C.A. 1981, s.31(4).

[20] See Ord. 53, r. 7(2) which incorporates into judicial review proceedings the provisions of Ord. 18, r. 12.

[21] *cf.* notes to *The Supreme Court Practice 1995*, Vol. 1, para. 53/1–14/30.

[22] As to the appropriate test both on the initial and substantive application see, paras. 4–002 *et seq.*

Intelligent anticipation may avoid premature and unnecessary rejection. If, for example, it is questionable whether the applicant has *locus standi*, as full a statement as possible should be included on that issue.

In *R. v. Cornwall C.C., ex p. Huntington*[23] Brooke J., in the Divisional Court, observed that Counsel were under a duty to include the existence of a possible ouster clause or other jurisdictional difficulties when drafting the notice of application.

Delay

Applications for leave to apply for judicial review must be made promptly and, in any event, within three months from the date when grounds for the application first arose, unless the court considers that there is good reason for extending the period within which the application shall be made.[24] This does not mean that any such application made within the three month period will, necessarily, be regarded as having been made promptly.[25]

7–009

The provisions as to delay are not entirely straightforward and are separately considered.[26] Procedurally, however, the position is clear. Where there is, or might be, delay in the above sense the notice of application should set out the reasons for it. If the respondent's consent to an extension of time has been obtained, such consent should be submitted with the application.[27]

It is submitted that there is no obligation on an applicant guilty of delay in applying for leave to move for judicial review to serve notice of his *ex parte* application on the respondent or to seek an oral *ex parte* hearing.[28]

Interim relief etc.

Although there is no express requirement in Order 53 that claims for interim relief or a stay of proceedings[29] must be made in Form 86A, the practice is to include such claims therein if sought at the leave stage.[30]

7–010

---

[23] [1992] 3 All E.R. 566 at p. 576f–g. The case went to the Court of Appeal and is reported at [1994] 1 All E.R. 694. The C.A. did not, however, deal with this point.
[24] Ord. 53, r. 4(1).
[25] See, *e.g.*: *R. v. Greenwich L.B.C., ex p. Cedar Transport Group Ltd* [1983] R.A. 173. See, also, the cases at para. 2–032.
[26] See para. 2–032.
[27] See *Practice Note*, n. 3 above.
[28] In *R. v. Ashford (Kent) Justices, ex p. Richley* [1955] 2 All E.R. 327 Lord Goddard C.J. held that an applicant for extension of the time limited by the former R.S.C., Order 59, r. 4(2) must give notice of an intended application under the former Order 64, r. 7 to the proposed respondent in order that he might be heard on the question of whether or not it is a fit case in which to extend time. It seems unlikely that this requirement still subsists, given that extension of time is a matter which, under Ord. 53, r. 4(1), the court must consider on an *ex parte* application for leave to apply for judicial review and where there is no independent requirement (as formerly) for the applicant to apply for such extension.
[29] *i.e.* under Ord. 53, r. 3(10) if leave is granted. See below.
[30] See, also, n. 12 above.

Request for oral hearing

7–011   If an applicant desires an immediate oral hearing he is entitled to it, but this must be requested in Form 86A.[31] The circumstances in which such oral hearing is desirable have been considered above.[32] Oral hearings are listed on the footing that the applicant will take no more than 20 minutes, and that any reply by a respondent who attends will take no more than 10 minutes. A written time estimate must be supplied by counsel if it is considered that the hearing is likely to be longer.[32a]

Request for expedited hearing

7–012   The popularity of judicial review is such that, unless an expedited hearing is ordered, there is likely to be a long delay before the matter is listed for hearing. In an urgent case, therefore, requests for expedition and an order abridging time for service of the respondent's affidavit evidence[33] should be included in Form 86A.

Case suitable for other Divisions of the High Court

7–013   In *R. v. Dover Magistrates Court, ex p. Kidner*,[34] Woolf J. stated that where applications are made for leave to apply for judicial review of matrimonial and family orders, it is desirable that the notice of application should include a request that, if leave is granted, the matter be dealt with by a Judge of the Family Division.[35] In practice it is probably also desirable that an applicant should insert a similar request if a particular application raises issues more suited to adjudication by a judge of a different Division to that of the Queen's Bench.[36]

THE AFFIDAVIT IN SUPPORT

7–014   There is no prescribed content for the affidavit required to be filed in support of the application for leave to apply for judicial review. It must, however, set out and verify all relevant facts upon which the applicant intends to rely.[37] Being an affidavit filed in interlocutory proceedings, it may contain hearsay, provided that the deponent's sources and grounds of belief are stated.[38]

---

[31] Ord. 53, r. 3(3).

[32] See para. 7–005.

[32a] See *Practice Direction (Crown Office List) (No. 2)* [1991] 1 W.L.R. 280, which is reproduced at **C–10**.

[33] See *Practice Note (Q.B.D.) (Judicial Review : Affidavit in Reply)* [1989] 1 W.L.R. 358, reproduced at para. **C–08**.

[34] [1983] 1 All E.R. 475 at p. 477.

[35] In Family cases the Crown Office will, in practice, now submit the case to the President of the Family Division.

[36] Albeit sitting as a judge of the Queen's Bench Division.

[37] Ord. 53, r. 3(2). For a specimen form of affidavit, see para. **D–02**.

[38] See Ord. 41, r. 5(2). Note, however, that at the full hearing Ord. 41, r. 5(1) applies and, in principle, an affidavit may then only contain such facts as the deponent is able of his own knowledge to prove; see: *R. v. Sandhutton P.C., ex p. Todd and Fox* [1992] C.O.D. 409.

It is fairly common for deponents merely to refer to and verify their statement of grounds in Form 86A. However, care should always be taken to ensure that all the evidence which the applicant wishes to use, or which is relevant, is included in a supporting affidavit, whether or not it is included in Form 86A itself. Failure to do so could restrict an applicant from adducing such evidence at a later stage.[39]

As with all *ex parte* applications, it is incumbent on an applicant to make full disclosure to the court of all material facts of which he is aware, even though disadvantageous to his cause.[40] Failure to make such disclosure in the affidavit may, of itself, constitute ground for setting aside leave either on or before the full hearing, or for refusing relief that would otherwise have been granted.[41]

Where certiorari is sought to remove any proceedings for the purpose of quashing them, Order 53, r. 9(2) stipulates that the applicant must, prior to the full hearing, lodge in the Crown Office a copy of the relevant order, etc.,[42] or account for his failure to do so before he may question the validity of such an order.

In practice it is usual to exhibit the order complained of in the affidavit in support of the application for leave and failure to do so has, on occasion, been taken into consideration by the single judge when refusing a "paper" application.

THE NEED FOR CAREFUL DRAFTING

A decision on whether or not to grant leave to apply for judicial review   7–015
will, in most cases, be made by perusal of the filed documents. It is, therefore, of the utmost importance that they provide a clear statement of the applicant's case. In particular, failure to do so may result in:

(a) refusal of the initial application thereby necessitating a renewed *ex parte* hearing;

(b) unnecessary applications to amend the notice of application on the hearing of the *inter partes* application or at an earlier interlocutory stage;

(c) the need to file further affidavit evidence which may not be permitted.[43]

It is emphasised that the relief and grounds contained in Form 86A are those that the applicant is confined to arguing on the full hearing.[44]

---

[39] Since the introduction of further affidavits is discretionary. See, especially, Ord. 53, r. 6(2).

[40] For the consequences of non-disclosure see *R. v. British Coal Corp., ex p. Whittaker* [1989] C.O.D. 528. See, also: *R. v. Jockey Club Licensing Committee, ex p. Wright* [1991] C.O.D. 306, applying the principles laid down in *Brink's Mat Ltd v. Elcombe* [1988] 1 W.L.R. 1350; *R. v. Bromsgrove D.C., ex p. Kennedy,* [1992] C.O.D. 129.

[41] See: *R. v. Lloyd's of London, ex p. Briggs* (1993) 5 Admin. L.R.

[42] The full expression is "order, warrant, commitment, conviction, inquisition or record".

[43] See Ord. 53, r. 6(2), which leaves the matter at the discretion of the court.

[44] Ord. 53, r. 6(1).

INDEX OF DOCUMENTS

7–016   Documents filed in support of an application for leave to move for judicial review should be properly paginated and, if more than 10 pages, supplied with an index. They should conform with the requirements of *Practice Direction (Evidence: Documents)* [1983] 1 W.L.R. 922 relating to all bundles of documents filed for use before the Court of Appeal and every Division of the High Court.[45] The original and two copies of any documents should be provided.[46] In addition, a list must be provided of the pages essential for reading by the court.[46a]

CRIMINAL AND CIVIL MATTERS

7–017   Until first consideration of the application for leave the procedure is the same whether the matter is "criminal" or "civil". It is after this point that an applicant's procedural options will diverge. Particular attention must be directed to the different rules relating to renewal and appeal in criminal and civil cases where the original application for leave to move for judicial review is unsuccessful.[47]

The expression "criminal cause or matter" which is used in Order 53[48] is the same as that employed in section 18(1) of the Supreme Court Act 1981 and earlier legislation and appears, therefore, to mean any proceedings "the direct outcome of which may be trial of the applicant and his possible punishment for an alleged offence by a Court claiming jurisdiction to do so".[49]

From this general terminology, however, it is not always easy to categorise particular proceedings as obviously "criminal" or "civil" in nature. Although the case law is not wholly consistent the following further principles may assist in making the distinction more precise:

(a)   In judicial review proceedings the test for determining the nature of the proceedings does not depend upon the nature of the order granting or refusing judicial review but, rather, upon the order or decision sought to be challenged under Order 53.[50]

---

[45] Certainly failure to do so at the full hearing stage renders the application liable to be struck out with costs against the applicant or his solicitor. See *R. v. Home Secretary, ex p. Meyer-Wulff* [1986] Imm. A.R. 258.

[46] Exceptionally, three copies should be filed for a three-judge Divisional Court.

[46a] See *Practice Direction (Crown Office List: Preparation for Hearing)* which is reproduced at para. 17–019.

[47] See below.

[48] Ord. 53, r. 3(4)(a) and 5(1).

[49] *Amand v. Secretary of State for Home Affairs* [1943] A.C. 147 at 156, *per* Viscount Simon L.C.

[50] *Carr v. Atkins* [1987] Q.B. 963. See also: *R. v. Blandford JJ., ex p. Pamment* [1990] 1 W.L.R. 1490. (*held*: A question determined by a Divisional Court in respect of criminal proceedings after the proceedings had been concluded was still a criminal cause or matter); *R. v. Secretary of State for the Home Department, ex p. G, The Times,* June 26, 1990. (*held*:

(b) Decisions made as a result of disciplinary proceedings for offences against the Prison Rules,[51] and orders of the Court striking off a solicitor for misconduct[52] are classified as civil matters.

(c) Where, otherwise, the direct outcome of an order or decision sought to be challenged by judicial review may be the trial and possible punishment of the applicant for an alleged offence by a Court claiming the necessary jurisdiction, such proceedings will be "criminal" in nature. On this basis, for example, extradition proceedings, cases under the Fugitive Offenders Act 1967, and breaches of certain regulations under the Immigration Acts have been classified as constituting a criminal cause or matter.[53]

(d) However, an order or decision which is wholly collateral to criminal proceedings, such as estreatment of a recognizance, does not constitute a criminal cause or matter.[54]

RENEWING THE APPLICATION FOR LEAVE

Where the first application for leave to apply for judicial review is unsuccessful, it is possible to renew it. This involves a fresh presentation of the same application.[55] In all cases there is an oral hearing, *de novo*, and the court is not concerned with the way in which the matter was approached previously.[56] In this respect it differs from an appeal.

7–018

In order to renew an application for leave under Order 53 the applicant must, pursuant to rule 3(5), lodge notice of his intention to do so in the Crown Office within 10 days of being served with notice of refusal. The prescribed form is Form 86B.[57]

The following points should be noted in relation to Form 86B:

(a) The same form is used whether the application is civil or criminal in nature.

(b) Form 86B is designed solely for use under Order 53. It should not be used where a renewed application is made to the Court of Appeal as it may be in civil cases.

Where an applicant wishes to continue to rely on grounds contained in

---

The Home Secretary's power to refer a case to the Court of Appeal under the Criminal Appeal Act 1968, s.17, was an extension of the right of appeal against conviction or sentence and was, accordingly, a criminal cause or matter.)

[51] *R. v. Board of Visitors of Hull Prison, ex p. St Germain* [1979] Q.B. 425.
[52] *Re Hardwick* [1883] 12 Q.B.D. 148.
[53] See, *e.g.: ex p. Woodhall (Alice)* (1888) 20 Q.B.D. 832; *R. v. Governor of Brixton Prison, ex p. Savarkar* [1910] 2 K.B. 1056.
[54] See *Carr v. Atkins*, n. 50 above, applying the reasoning in *Re Smalley* [1985] A.C. 622 to justify the result in *R. v. Southampton J., ex p. Green* [1976] Q.B. 11.
[55] With such modifications as may be thought necessary in the light of the prior refusal.
[56] In practice, though, the court on a renewed oral hearing will be fully aware of the previous reasons for refusal.
[57] See para. **D–05**.

his Form 86A in respect of which leave to move for judicial review has been refused, but where leave to move has been granted on other grounds, the correct procedure is not to renew but, rather, to give notice of those other grounds to the respondent within 21 days of service of the notice of motion.[58]

Renewing civil applications for leave

7–019   In civil cases the applicant is allowed only one oral hearing in the High Court.[59] Thus, if he has requested an oral hearing in his Form 86A[60] his only recourse, if leave is refused, is to make a further application to the Court of Appeal (see below).

If, however, the initial refusal was made on a "paper" application there is provision for renewing the application, under Order 53, r. 3(4), to a single judge sitting in open court or, if there has been a direction to that effect, to a Divisional Court.

Renewing criminal applications for leave

7–020   Where the application is in respect of a criminal cause or matter, the applicant may renew by applying to a Divisional Court.[61]

If he has originally requested an oral hearing before the single judge and this is unsuccessful, there remains the option of a further oral hearing.

On a "paper" refusal, by contrast, there is no hearing before the single judge. The matter is renewed direct to a Divisional Court.

Renewing to the Court of Appeal

7–021   There is the possibility of a further renewal to the Court of Appeal, in civil cases,[62] under Order 59, r. 14(3). This provides that where an *ex parte* application has been refused by the court below[63] a similar application may be made to the Court of Appeal within seven days after the refusal. The application should be made by notice of *ex parte* application.[64]

Where the Court of Appeal grants leave it will usually remit the matter to

---

[58] *R. v. Bow Street Metropolitan Stipendiary Magistrate, ex p. Roberts* [1990] 1 W.L.R. 1317.

[59] Ord. 53, r. 3(4).

[60] Or, if an oral hearing occurs through direction or by agreement between the parties.

[61] Ord. 53, r. 3(4)(a).

[62] *cf. R. v. Tottenham JJ., ex p. Ewing* (July 30, 1986, unrep.) where it was held that the Court of Appeal had no jurisdiction to determine a leave application in a *criminal* cause or matter. In the civil context, though, renewal to the Court of Appeal has been described as an important avenue of relief. See *R. v. Beverley County Court, ex p. Brown, The Times,* January 25, 1985. In re *Thirugnanasampauther The Times,* April 28, 1995, The C.A. stressed that legal aid should not be granted when renewal to the C.A. was almost certain to fail.

[63] *Quaere* whether direct renewal to the Court of Appeal is possible after an unsuccessful "paper" application. Certainly, it is not precluded by Ord. 53, r. 13 which is concerned with *appeal* rather than *renewal.* Note, also, that if leave to move for judicial review is subsequently set aside, the correct process is probably to renew an application for leave rather than to appeal: see *R. v. Secretary of State for the Home Department, ex p. Soon Ok Ryoo* [1992] C.O.D. 134. See para. 7–035 below.

[64] For a form, see *The Supreme Court Practice 1995,* Vol. 1, para. 59/14/21.

the appropriate court[65] except where the court below is bound by authority or there is some other reason why an appeal is inevitable.[66]

Extending time for renewal

If for any reason the applicant fails to renew within the prescribed time he may apply to the court having jurisdiction to determine a renewed application, for an extension of time.[67] Ordinarily this is done by filing additional grounds in the notice of renewal or notice of *ex parte* application (as appropriate) together with an affidavit in support explaining the need for an extension. An application for extension of time may be made after the time for compliance has expired.[68]

7–022

CRITERIA ON *EX PARTE* APPLICATIONS FOR LEAVE

The determination of the application for leave to apply for judicial review is usually relatively cursory. Oral hearings usually precede the list of substantive *inter partes* applications for the day.

7–023

Apart from being satisfied that there is an arguable case for review, the court is required at the leave stage to consider whether the applicant has a "sufficient interest" and whether there has been "undue delay".[69]

Order 53, r. 3(7) stipulates that leave to apply for judicial review shall not be granted unless the court considers that the applicant has a sufficient interest in the matter to which the application relates. Although this might be thought to imply that the granting of leave is determinative of that question, it is now clearly established that the court hearing the full application is free to reconsider the applicant's *locus standi*.[70] Indeed it has been stated that the substantive hearing is the appropriate forum for this where the court will have the benefit of argument on both sides and more detailed evidence than on the application for leave.[71]

In relation to delay the court may refuse leave where it considers that there has been undue delay in making the application.[72]

---

[65] The application should be set down before a single judge unless a nominated judge directs a hearing before a Divisional Court; see *Practice Direction (Judicial Review) Appeals* [1990] 1 W.L.R. 51, reproduced at para. **C–01**.

[66] See *Practice Direction (Judicial Review) Appeals* [1982] 1 W.L.R. 1375, reproduced at para. **C–01**, and *Practice Direction (Judicial Review) Appeals* [1990] 1 W.L.R. 51, reproduced at para. **C–09**.

[67] Under Ord. 3, r. 5.

[68] *ibid.*

[69] These matters are separately considered at paras. 14–001 *et seq.* and 2–032 respectively.

[70] *Inland Revenue Commissioners v. National Federation of Self-Employed and Small Businesses Ltd* [1982] A.C. 617.

[71] *ibid.*

[72] Undue delay means either a failure to act promptly or within three months at the latest; see *R. v. Dairy Produce Quotas Tribunal, ex p. Caswell* [1990] 2 A.C. 738. See generally Ord. 53, r. 4.

Where delay is relevant, the principal consideration, at the leave stage, is whether there is good reason to extend time for the making of the application for leave.[73] As with the case of *locus standi*, however, it is frequently considered to be more appropriate and satisfactory for the issue of delay to be deferred until the full application, especially where the applicant has an arguable case on the merits.[74]

The court's general approach to applications for leave was summarised by Lord Diplock in *Inland Revenue Commissioners v. National Federation of Self-Employed and Small Businesses Ltd.*,[75] where he indicated that it would defeat the whole purpose of requiring preliminary leave if the court had to go into the matter in any depth at that stage. What was required was a "quick perusal" of the available material to see if it disclosed an arguable case on the various criteria that had to be considered.[76]

Arguability may, of course, embrace quite complicated considerations and so result in fairly lengthy judgments.[77] Whilst this is not itself inconsistent with the summary nature of the process, care is obviously necessary to ensure that what should be merely a preliminary sifting to discourage hopeless applications does not become a decision on the merits.[78]

THE RESPONDENT

7–024   Ordinarily the respondent will not appear at the leave stage. There are, however (and increasingly), circumstances in which this may occur. The most important instances are as follows:

(a) Where an application for interim relief is sought the applicant should give notice to the proposed respondent so that he may, if desired, attend and assist the court by filling in any gaps in the available information.[79]

(b) In a complicated case the Crown Office may, at the instigation of the court, invite the respondent to be represented at the leave stage so as to assist the court.

---

[73] See Ord. 53, r. 4.

[74] *R. v. Stratford on Avon D.C., ex p. Jackson,* [1985] 1 W.L.R. 1319; *R. v. Dairy Produce Quotas Tribunal, ex p. Caswell,* n. 72 above.

[75] See n. 70 above.

[76] *ibid.* at pp. 643H–644B. Note, though, that in *R. v. Legal Aid Board, ex p. Hughes* (1993) 5 Admin. L.R. 623, Lord Donaldson of Lymington M.R. observed that the approach of the court had moved on since the *I.R.C.* case and that although in-depth examination was inappropriate at the leave stage the court would often give more than a "quick perusal" to the case. *cf.* Lord Donaldson's interpretation of Lord Diplock's comments in *I.R.C.* in *Winch v. Jones* [1986] Q.B. 296.

[77] For a case in point see *R. v. Inspector of Taxes, ex p. Kissane* [1986] 2 All E.R. 37.

[78] The distinction between arguability and merits was emphasised in *R. v. Secretary of State for the Home Department, ex p. Sivakumaran* [1988] A.C. 958.

[79] See para. 7–005 above.

    (c) Although there is no express provision in the Rules of the Supreme Court it is, undoubtedly, the case that the court may adjourn an *ex parte* application for the proposed respondent to be present.[80]

In *R. v. Secretary of State for the Home Department, ex p. Doorga*[81] and *R. v. Secretary of State for the Home Department, ex p. Begum*[82] Lord Donaldson of Lymington M.R. has outlined cases appropriate for adjournment so that the respondent may appear whilst emphasising that his categories are not intended to be comprehensive. Essentially:

    (a) if the judge is satisfied that there is no arguable case, he should dismiss the application;

    (b) if the judge is satisfied that the case is arguable, he should grant the application;

    (c) if the judge is uncertain or thinks it possible that the application might have some "totally mock-out point", he should adjourn for an *inter partes* leave hearing.

Similarly, *Ex p. Oral*[83] the Court of Appeal indicated that where there may be doubts about the evidence, the *ex parte* application should be adjourned to be dealt with *inter partes*. Where a respondent is required to attend, counsel should be fully instructed, although the court will not normally expect evidence to be filed or discovery provided in advance of the adjourned hearing.[84]

Exceptionally, the parties may agree, subject to the court's leave, to conduct an opposed *ex parte* application for leave or even to waive the leave stage and treat the first application as the substantive hearing.[85]

Both these courses are designed to save unnecessary time and costs, yet they have their dangers.

Opposed *ex parte* hearings are usually agreed for the purpose of taking preliminary points. Conceptually, however, it is inconsistent with the court's function at the leave stage to hear full argument. Moreover, the isolation of law from merits is rarely a satisfactory method of dealing with questions such as delay or *locus standi*.[86]

Similar difficulties attach to waiver of the leave stage. This may be appropriate as, for example, where the facts are clear and the dispute is solely one of law. However, there may be considerable prejudice in embarking on a full hearing before the whole factual picture has been ascertained.

---

[80] *I.R.C. v. National Federation of Self-Employed and Small Businesses Ltd*, n. 70 above at p. 642F (*per* Lord Diplock).

[81] [1990] Imm. A.R. 98; [1990] C.O.D. 109.

[82] [1990] Imm. A.R. 1.

[83] [1990] Imm. A.R. 208.

[84] See n. 75 above. In practice, though, respondents often do put in evidence.

[85] For an example of the latter see *R. v. Secretary of State for the Environment, ex p. Brent L.B.C.* [1982] Q.B. 593 at p. 642.

[86] See especially *Inland Revenue Commissioners v. National Federation of Self-Employed and Small Businesses Ltd*, n. 70 above at p. 630C–E.

COSTS AT THE *EX PARTE* STAGE

7–025   (a) Usually there is no provision for costs at this stage unless the respondent has appeared.

(b) If, on an opposed *ex parte* hearing, the applicant is unsuccessful in obtaining leave he may be ordered to pay the costs of such hearing.[87] Where leave is granted the usual order will be either "costs reserved" or "costs in the cause", since the merits of the substantive application have yet to be determined. It should, however, be observed that the court may as a condition of granting leave "impose such terms as to costs and as to giving security as it thinks fit".[88]

(c) Where, after leave has been granted, a respondent performs the act in respect of which an order was sought, the applicant may seek to obtain the costs of the application for leave. An application should be made to the court on two clear days' notice of motion supported by affidavit.[89]

ON GRANTING LEAVE

7–026   Certain consequences follow the grant of leave to apply for judicial review and there are, additionally, a number of orders that the court may make. These are outlined below at paras. 7–027 to 7–032.

Stay of proceedings

7–027   Order 53, r. 3(10)(a) provides that, where prohibition or certiorari is sought, and the court so directs, leave shall operate as a stay of the proceedings to which the application relates until the full hearing or further order.

---

[87] *Quaere* though, whether costs can or should in any event be awarded where the respondent appears at the court's request. In principle it is submitted that an adverse award of costs at the leave stage should be rare given the applicant's right under the R.S.C. to an *ex parte* hearing.

[88] Ord. 53, r. 3(9).

[89] See *The Supreme Court Practice 1995*, Vol. 1, para. 53/1–14/37. *Quaere*, though, whether costs can be awarded *before* leave is granted if, *e.g.* the respondent concedes. This practically important issue would seem to depend on whether an application for leave is a "proceeding" so as to justify costs under S.C.A. s.51. Probably it is; see: *R. v. Islington L.B.C., ex p. Ewing* [1992] 1 W.L.R. 388. *cf.*, though, *R. v. Test Valley B.C., ex p. Goodman* [1992] C.O.D. 101 (*per* Hodgson J.: costs prior to the grant of leave to move for judicial review cannot be recovered if leave is not granted because the application for leave is not a "proceeding"); *R. v. Commissioners of Inland Revenue, ex p. Mead and Cook* [1993] C.O.D. 324 (*per* Popplewell J., disagreeing with Hodgson J.: costs incurred prior to the grant of leave *can* be recovered because the leave application is a "proceeding"). In neither of the above cases was *Ewing* drawn to the court's attention. See, also *Rozhon v. Secretary of State for Wales*, 91 L.G.R. 667: (*held*: leave to appeal against an enforcement notice was a "proceeding" under S.C.A. s.1).

A stay is available against all respondents, including the Crown.[90] However, its precise scope depends upon the meaning to be ascribed to the word "proceedings". In *R. v. Secretary of State for Education and Science, ex p. Avon C.C.*,[91] the Court of Appeal held that it had jurisdiction, under Ord. 53, r. 3(10)(a), to stay decisions of the Secretary of State and that the rule was not limited to judicial proceedings.

However, in the later Privy Council decision in *Minister of Foreign Affairs Trade and Industry v. Vehicles and Supplies Ltd,*[92] (where similarly worded provisions were under consideration) Lord Oliver of Aylmerton observed that:

"A stay of proceedings is an order which puts a stop to the further conduct of proceedings in court or before a tribunal at the stage which they have reached, the object being to avoid the hearing or trial taking place."[93]

The decision in *Avon* was not cited to the Privy Council and it is not referred to in the judgments. Moreover, *Avon*, being a Court of Appeal decision, is still binding on the Court of Appeal and the High Court. Lord Donaldson of Lymington M.R. pointed this out in *R. v. Secretary of State for the Home Department, ex p. Muboyayi*,[94] expressing no view as to whether *Avon* would be likely to survive an appeal to the House of Lords. The cogent reasoning of the Privy Council suggests, however, that it may not.

The basis upon which a stay will be granted is, essentially, the same as for interlocutory injunctions (see para. 8–012). The court will take into account the effect on third parties and may, applying balance of convenience considerations, refuse a stay notwithstanding granting leave to move.[95]

Interim relief

Where the relief sought is other than prohibition or certiorari the court may, at any time after granting leave, grant such interim relief as could be granted in an action commenced by writ. Special rules used to, but no longer, apply in relation to interim injunctive relief against the Crown.[96] The bases on which the most important forms of interim relief are granted are considered between paras. 8–010 and 8–013.

7–028

[90] See *R. v. Secretary of State for Education and Science, ex p. Avon C.C.*, [1991] Q.B. 558. Interim (and final) injunctive relief is also now potentially available against the Crown as a result of the House of Lords' decision in *M v. Home Office*, n. 16 above.
[91] *ibid.*
[92] [1991] 1 W.L.R. 550.
[93] *ibid.* at p. 556E–F.
[94] [1992] Q.B. 244.
[95] See, *e.g.: R. v. Her Majesty's Inspectorate of Pollution, ex p. Greenpeace Ltd* [1994] C.O.D. 56.
[96] See n. 90 above.

Expedited hearing

7–029   When giving leave to move, the court may direct that the case be expedited by inclusion in Part D of the Crown Office List.[97] Where an expedited hearing is ordered the judge should be invited, by the applicant, to order that time for service of the respondent's affidavit be abridged where the circumstances so require.[98]

Other directions

7–030   The court is empowered to grant leave on terms, including such terms as to costs and as to giving security as it thinks fit.[99] Apart from the express directions permitted by Order 53 itself[1] it may, presumably, make such further directions as it considers reasonable.

This power appears to be flexible and to extend, for example, to the making of a recommendation that parallel proceedings, such as wardship, should be instituted where thought proper,[2] or that a particular application be determined by a judge of another Division of the High Court, sitting as an additional Queen's Bench judge.[3]

Bail

7–031   Although there has been some confusion in the past, the High Court has consistently viewed itself as possessing an inherent discretion to grant bail pending the *inter partes* application for judicial review.[4]

The question of bail under Order 53 has been clarified by the Court of Appeal in *R. v. Secretary of State for the Home Department, ex p. Turkoglu*.[5] There, Lord Donaldson of Lymington M.R. laid down the following general points as to the jurisdiction of the High Court and the Court of Appeal in relation to the grant of bail at the leave and full hearing stage. It was held that:

(a)   There was jurisdiction in the High Court to allow bail where an application for judicial review or leave to apply was pending.

(b)   If the application for leave was adjourned the High Court was still seised of the application and jurisdiction to grant bail continued.

---

[97] See *The Supreme Court Practice 1995*, Vol. 1, para. 53/1–14/37.

[98] *Practice Note (Q.B.D.) (Judicial Review: Affidavit in Reply)* [1989] 1 W.L.R. 358, reproduced at para. **C–08**.

[99] Ord. 53, r. 3(4). For the approach of the court to a security for costs application, see *R. v. Westminster City Council, ex p. Residents Association of Mayfair* [1991] C.O.D. 182.

[1] As in Ord. 53, r. 5(2), 5(4), 6(4) and 8(1).

[2] *R. v. Newham L.B.C., ex p. McL* (1988) 18 Fam. Law 125.

[3] *R. v. Dover Magistrates Court, ex p. Kidner*, n. 34 above.

[4] See, *e.g.*: *R. v. Spilsbury* [1898] 2 Q.B. 615; *Amand v. Home Secretary and Minister of Defence of Royal Netherlands Govt.* [1943] A.C. 147. On this aspect see [1941] 2 K.B. 439, subsequently affirmed by the House of Lords.

[5] [1988] Q.B. 398. *cf. Re Vilvarajah, The Times,* October 31, 1987.

(c) If the application for leave was refused then, at that point, there was no jurisdiction to grant bail because the court was *functus officio*, the order refusing leave being unappealable.[6]

(d) If the substantive application was refused there was jurisdiction to grant bail pending appeal.

(e) The Court of Appeal may entertain a direct appeal in relation to any refusal of bail by the High Court in whatever proceedings it has been made.[7]

(f) There is also an inherent jurisdiction in the Court of Appeal to grant bail on a renewed application for leave to apply for judicial review.[8]

(g) The general principle is that jurisdiction to grant bail arises only (whether in criminal or civil proceedings) as ancillary to some other proceedings. In particular it is not possible to apply to any court for bail *in vacuo*.

Unhappily, the *Turkoglu* decision leaves certain residual procedural questions unresolved. The procedure for seeking bail is not illuminated. In a criminal cause or matter bail applications are regulated by Order 79. In civil cases, however, there is no specified procedure. There seems to be no logical reason for distinguishing between a procedural regime for criminal or civil proceedings in this respect and it is submitted that the Order 79 procedure ought to be followed in civil cases.[9]

Amendment of Form 86A

Order 53, r. 3(6) provides that on the application for leave.[10] the court may allow Form 86A to be amended, whether by specifying different or additional grounds or relief or otherwise on such terms, if any, as it thinks fit. **7–032**

APPEALING THE REFUSAL OF LEAVE IN A CIVIL CASE

(a) Order 53, r. 13 precludes any appeal against refusal of leave where renewal lies under rule 3(4). **7–033**

(b) After a renewal under Order 53, r. 3(4) a further renewal of an unsuccessful civil application lies to the Court of Appeal (see above).

(c) It seems clear that instead of renewing to the Court of Appeal in a civil case, an applicant may, with leave, appeal to the Court of

---

[6] *Quaere* whether this is always so. See para. 7–033 and text.

[7] *i.e.* not following Sir John Donaldson M.R.'s dicta in *Dhillon v. Secretary of State for the Home Department* (1987) 86 Cr.App.R. 14., which had overlooked S.C.A. 1981, s.16. *Quaere*, though, whether there can be a direct appeal in a criminal cause or matter where bail is refused. See below.

[8] For the procedure of renewal see paras. 7–018 *et seq.*

[9] In practice, applications for bail are determined in open court at the appropriate stage of the judicial review proceedings.

[10] For the other stages at which amendment is possible see paras. 8–013 *et seq.* below.

Appeal.[11] It is only very rarely that an appeal should be necessary, given the fact that the matter will come before the Court of Appeal on a renewal in any event.[12]

(d) Where the Court of Appeal refuses to grant leave there is no further appeal to the House of Lords.[13]

APPEALING THE REFUSAL OF LEAVE IN A CRIMINAL CASE

7–034
(a) As with civil cases there is, by virtue of Order 53, r. 13, no appeal against an order refusing leave to apply for judicial review, where renewal to a Divisional Court lies under Order 53, r. 3(4).

(b) Where leave to move is refused by a Divisional Court in a criminal cause or matter it is doubtful whether any further appeal lies therefrom.[14] It has already been observed that no further renewal lies to the Court of Appeal as it would in a civil case.[15]

SETTING ASIDE THE GRANT OF LEAVE: CRIMINAL/CIVIL

7–035
(a) Where leave to apply for judicial review has been granted *ex parte* (and whether the matter is civil or criminal) it appears to be open to the respondent to apply to the court to set aside the order granting leave.[16]

(b) Such application must be made timeously. If it is not made before the substantive hearing it has been held that there is no point in making the application at all, since it saves no costs and is to no one's advantage.[17]

(c) A setting aside application ought only to be made in the most exceptional circumstances and should, if possible, be made to the judge who granted it.[18] In *R. v. Westminster City Council, ex p. Zestfair Ltd*[19] Otton J. observed that the jurisdiction to set aside an order granting leave to apply for judicial review

"should be exercised only in very special circumstances such as

---

[11] See *R. v. Governor of Pentonville Prison, ex p. Herbage (No. 2)* [1987] Q.B. 1077.

[12] Note, though, that the time limits for appeal (28 days) are longer than for renewal (seven days). Consider, too, whether an "opposed *ex parte*" application for leave to move may, properly, be renewed as opposed to appealed to the Court of Appeal; see, *e.g.*: *Hunter and Partners v. Wellings and Partners* (1987) 131 S.J. 75.

[13] *Re Poh* [1983] 1 W.L.R. 2 – though the reasoning adopted in this case is opaque.

[14] Following the reasoning in *Re Poh*, n. 13 above. If appeal does lie it is to the House of Lords under the A.J.A. 1960, s.1(2) with leave.

[15] See n. 62 above.

[16] *i.e.* under Ord. 32, r. 6. The grounds alleged to support such application must be specified with particularity; see: *R. v. Lloyd's of London, ex p. Briggs* (1993) 5 Admin. L.R. 698.

[17] *R. v. Derbyshire C.C., ex p. Noble* [1989] C.O.D. 285. Nor should a discovery application be used to challenge the grant of leave; see *R. v. Secretary of State for the Home Department, ex p. Herbage (No. 2)* [1987] Q.B. 1077 at pp. 1093E–G and 1095E–G.

[18] *R. v. District Auditor, ex p. Judge* [1989] C.O.D. 390. See, also: *R. v. Bromsgrove D.C., ex p. Kennedy* [1992] C.O.D. 129.

[19] Unrep., March 11, 1987.

fundamentally misconceived proceedings,[20] or where leave has been granted where there has been either fraud on the part of the applicant . . . or non-disclosure of a material fact or facts, or where there is any misconception of law".

(d) On an application to set aside the court is constrained by the same need as on the original leave application to try not to defeat the purpose of the Order 53 procedure by going into the case in more depth than is necessary to consider the arguability of the substantive claim for judicial review.[21] On the other hand if the judge is satisfied, after hearing argument, that the substantive motion for judicial review must fail, the jurisdiction to set aside should be exercised.[22]

(e) In *W.E.A. Records Ltd v. Visions Channel 4 Ltd*[23] Lord Donaldson of Lymington M.R. emphasised that it was difficult if not impossible to envisage circumstances in which it would be appropriate to appeal against an order made *ex parte* without first applying to have the order set aside.

(f) There are different judicial views about the correct procedure to adopt after leave to apply for judicial review (in a civil case) being granted *ex parte*, such leave is then set aside by the judge on the respondent's application. Should the applicant bring the matter before the Court of Appeal by way of a renewed application for leave or by appealing against the judge's revocation of the leave originally granted? In *R. v. Secretary of State for the Home Department, ex p. Begum*[24] the point was left open. In *R. v. Same, ex p. K. Al-Nafeesi*[25] Lord Donaldson of Lymington M.R. expressed the view that, of the two routes, it is very much preferable that leave to appeal the decision to set aside should be sought. However, in *R. v. Same, ex p. Ok Ryoo*[26] the Court of Appeal (*per* Russell L.J.) inclined to the view that it was more appropriate that the applicant should bring the case before the Court of Appeal by way of a renewed application.

---

[20] As, *e.g.*, where the court has no jurisdiction; see: *R. v. Cornwall C.C., ex p. Huntington* [1994] 1 All E.R. 694.

[21] *R. v. Arthur Young (a firm), ex p. Thamesdown B.C.* [1989] C.O.D. 392.

[22] *R. v. Secretary of State for the Home Department, ex p. Begum* [1989] Imm.A.R. 302.

[23] [1983] 1 W.L.R. 721.

[24] [1990] Imm.A.R. 1.

[25] [1990] C.O.D. 262.

[26] [1992] C.O.D. 134.

8. THE INTERLOCUTORY STAGE

SERVICE

8–001 Service must be effected within 14 days of leave being granted.[1] The documents that should be served are:

  (a) the notice of motion or summons[2];
  (b) a copy of the affidavit in support[3];
  (c) a copy of Form 86A.[4]

Order 53, r. 5(3) requires service on "all persons directly affected". The meaning of this phrase is not entirely clear.[5] Because of the possible scope for ambiguity the court has power to direct service upon persons who have not been served but who, in the court's view, ought to have been served.[6] In addition, directions may be given as to proper service.[7] The applicant should, in cases of difficulty,[8] seek such directions at an early stage including, possibly, directions as to substituted service where the number of possibly "directly affected" persons is numerous.[9]

Where the application relates to any court proceedings and the object of the application is to compel the court to do any act in relation to the proceedings or to quash them or any order made therein, then the motion or summons must also be served on the clerk or registrar of the court.[10] If objection is made to the conduct of the judge he is, additionally, required to be served.[11] An application should, in respect of cases involving court proceedings, name as respondent any other party to those proceedings.[12]

---

[1] This is implicit in the requirement as to filing the affidavit of service; see below.

[2] Ord. 53, r. 5(3).

[3] This is not expressly required but, in practice, the supporting affidavit is invariably served with the notice of motion. See specimen notice of motion at para. **D–07**.

[4] Ord. 53, r. 6(1).

[5] It was construed restrictively by Turner J. in *R. v. Legal Aid Board, ex p. Megarry* [1994] C.O.D. 468. See, also, C.A. in *R. v. Liverpool City Council, ex p. Muldoon, The Times*, April 18, 1995 (*held*: r. 5(3) should be given a restrictive construction).

[6] Ord. 53, r. 5(7).

[7] *ibid.*

[8] See, *e.g.*: *R. v. General Commissioners of Income Tax, ex p. Hood-Barrs* (1947) 27 T.C. 506.

[9] Consider, *e.g.* a judicial review challenge, by a defendant, to the award of legal aid to thousands of plaintiffs.

[10] Ord. 53, r. 5(3).

[11] *ibid. cf.* County Courts Act 1984, s.84.

[12] Including, *semble*, a landlord (or tenant) in proceedings before a rent tribunal. See *R. v. St Helens Rent Tribunal, ex p. Pickavance* (unrep. February 12, 1952).

ENTERING A MOTION FOR HEARING

If leave is granted to apply for judicial review, the applicant or his **8–002** solicitors must enter a motion for hearing within 14 days of the grant of leave.[13] This is done by filing a copy of the notice of motion or summons in the Crown Office within that period.[14] There cannot be an effective entry of motion prior to filing the affidavit of service.[15]

In a criminal cause or matter the application for judicial review is required to be made by originating motion to a Divisional Court.[16] In civil cases the application must be made by originating motion to a judge sitting in open court, unless the court has directed that it be made by originating motion to a Divisional Court, or by originating summons to a judge in chambers.[17] The latter form of application is expressed to be subject to the judge's power under Order 32, r. 13 to direct or adjourn the summons for hearing in open court if he wishes.[18]

THE AFFIDAVIT OF SERVICE

Order 53, r. 5(6) provided that, before a motion or summons is entered **8–003** for hearing, an affidavit of service must be filed. In practice the affidavit and motion/summons are filed together.[19]

The affidavit of service should contain the following information[20]:

(a) the names and addresses of all persons who have been served with the motion/summons;
(b) the places and dates of service upon such persons;
(c) whether any person required to be served has not been served;
(d) the reason for non-service upon any such person.

OTHER PROCEDURAL CONSIDERATIONS

The following mandatory provisions of Order 53 should be considered **8–004** at this stage:

(a) There must, unless the court has otherwise directed, be at least 10 days between service on a respondent and the full hearing.[21]
(b) A copy of any "order, warrant, commitment, conviction, inquisition or record" must – where certiorari is sought – be lodged in

---

[13] Ord. 53, r. 5(5). Delay in complying with this time limit may result in an application for an extension of time being refused; see *R. v. Haringey LBC., ex p. Haringey Letting Association* [1993] C.O.D. 489.

[14] Ord. 57, r. 2. Copies of the proceedings should also be lodged for the judges' use.

[15] Ord. 53, r. 5(6). See above.

[16] Ord. 53, r. 5(1).

[17] Ord. 53, r. 5(2).

[18] *ibid.*

[19] Form 86A and supporting affidavit will already be filed.

[20] Ord. 53, r. 5(6).

[21] Ord. 53, r. 5(4).

the Crown Office, together with a verifying affidavit, prior to the hearing.[22]

THE RESPONDENT'S AFFIDAVIT

8–005   A respondent who intends to use an affidavit is required to file it in the Crown Office as soon as is practicable and in any event, subject to the court otherwise ordering, within 56 days after service of the motion or summons.[23] The respondent should inform the Crown of his intention to serve such evidence within 10 days of being served with notice of the grant of leave.

The former time limit for filing a respondent's evidence was 21 days after such service. In practice this was rarely adhered to and was widely regarded as unrealistic. The new time limit is, however, enforced with the utmost strictness. For all practical purposes respondents should treat the 56-day stipulation as absolute. Any application for an extension of time must be made before such period expires. Extension will only be granted in wholly exceptional circumstances.[24] In practice the Crown Office will refuse to accept late affidavits filed by a respondent without extension being granted, although the court would appear to have jurisdiction to allow such affidavits to be used at the full hearing.[25] Such jurisdiction is unlikely to be experienced unless the affidavit (whether coming from applicant or respondent) is permitted to the other side at least five clear working days before the hearing.[25a]

In most cases it will certainly be prudent for a respondent to file an affidavit. It should set out the facts upon which he intends to rely. It should also deal fully with the issues raised by the applicant in his statement and supporting affidavit, as well as making clear any factual conflict that there is likely to be.[26]

CROWN OFFICE LISTING

8–006   Applications for judicial review are included within the ambit of the Crown Office list. The list consists of five parts (A–E) (see *Practice Direction* 1989 1 W.L.R. 232 (reproduced at para. **C–05**)).

Part B of the Crown Office list operates, effectively, as a "warned list" of cases which may be listed for hearing at short notice. Applications will be entered in Part B – unless specific application to stand out is made – when

---

[22] Ord. 53, r. 9(2). In practice this will usually be done on the application for leave; see above. If the applicant is unable to lodge the relevant order, etc., he must, under r. 9(2), still file an affidavit accounting for his failure to do so.

[23] See *Practice Note (Judicial Review: Affidavit in Reply)* [1989] 1 W.L.R. 358, reproduced at para. **C–08**.

[24] *ibid.* For the procedure in seeking extension, see para. 8–009.

[25] *i.e.* under Ord. 53, r. 6(2); see below.

[25a] See *Practice Direction (Crown Office List): Preparation for Hearing* reproduced at para. **C–11**.

[26] It should, of course, also exhibit all relevant documentation.

all relevant time limits have expired. In the present context this will usually be after the 56-day period allowed for service of the respondent's affidavit. Particular attention should be paid to whether there is any need to apply for the application to be stood out in Part C of the list.[27]

USING FURTHER AFFIDAVITS

Order 53, r. 6(2) enables the court, on the full hearing, to permit further affidavits to be used.[28] **8–007**

An applicant intending to seek the court's permission to use further affidavits must give notice of his intention to every other party.[29] Strangely there is no similar requirement upon the respondent. The different may, however, be semantic. All parties are, by Order 53, r. 6(5), required to supply to every other party on demand and on payment of the proper charges, copies of every affidavit proposed to be used at the hearing.[30]

SERVING AFFIDAVITS

Affidavits are, almost invariably, served on the other side as well as being filed in the Crown Office. The express requirement is, however, to file rather than to serve.[31] Unless, therefore, each side makes formal demand (together with payment of the appropriate charges) there is, technically, no entitlement to service. This difficulty can be circumvented by sensible liaison and, in any event, by a formal request at an early stage for service of all affidavits intended to be used on the full hearing. **8–008**

INTERLOCUTORY PROCEDURE

Most forms of interlocutory relief are now available in proceedings for judicial review. Certain of these, such as bail, have already been outlined. **8–009**

Order 53, r. 8(1) provides that an interlocutory application "includes" applications for the following forms of relief:

(a) leave to cross-examine the deponent of any affidavit under Order 38, r. 2(3);
(b) discovery and inspection under Order 24;
(c) discovery by interrogatories under Order 26;
(d) an order dismissing the judicial review application by consent.

---

[27] For the procedure, see below.
[28] Formerly, there was a restriction, under Ord. 53, r. 6(2), that any further affidavits must deal with new matters arising out of the affidavit of another party. However, following the decision of Popplewell J. in *R. v. Secretary of State for the Environment, ex p. ARC Properties, The Times*, December 5, 1991, that there was no additional inherent discretion in the court to admit further affidavits, the terminology of Ord. 53, r. 6(2) was amended to include a much wider discretion. The wording of the new r. 6(2), however, appears to be limited to applicants' affidavits.
[29] Ord. 53, r. 6(3).
[30] Including the affidavit in support of the leave application.
[31] Ord. 57, r. 1(1) and r. 4(1).

The general way in which the rules have been formulated makes it difficult to set out a comprehensive range of relief. Order 53, r. 8(1) refers to "any interlocutory applications". Order 53, r. 3(10) permits the granting of "such interim relief as could be granted in an action begun by writ" where the relief sought is other than prohibition or certiorari.

It remains unclear whether the rules relating to pleadings in writ actions have been incorporated, *mutatis mutandis*, into judicial review proceedings. It is, for example, by no means obvious that a respondent is entitled to seek an order for further and better particulars of an incomplete Form 86A under Order 18, r. 12(3) since this is a prescribed form rather than a pleading.[32]

Nonetheless, including the relief already considered or expressly incorporated into Order 53, the principal types of interlocutory applications capable of being made on or after the grant of leave and prior to the full hearing are for:

(a) leave to cross-examine under Order 38, r. 2(3);

(b) discovery and inspection under Order 24;

(c) discovery by interrogatories under Order 26;

(d) amendment under Order 20, rr. 7 and 8;

(e) interlocutory injunctive relief under Order 29[33];

(f) setting aside leave under Order 32, r. 6;

(g) an order striking out proceedings under Order 18, r. 19[34] or under the court's inherent powers[35];

(h) unless/or orders and related relief under Order 2, r. 1(2);

(i) extension of time under Order 3, r. 5;

(j) consolidation under Order 4, r. 10[36];

(k) an order relating to the misjoinder or non-joinder of a party to the proceedings under Order 15, r. 6;

(l) an order requiring further and better particulars of the applicant's Form 86A in so far as it relates to a claim for special damages under Order 18, r. 12[37];

(m) security for costs under Order 53, r. 3(9)[38];

(n) expedited hearing;

---

[32] Otherwise, perhaps, if particulars are required of a special damages claim since Ord. 53, r. 7(2) expressly incorporates the requirements of Ord. 18, r. 12 into such claims.

[33] Where the relief sought is certiorari or prohibition, a stay of proceedings under Ord. 53, r. 3(10)(a) will have the same effect (see para. 7–027).

[34] *R. v. Governor of Pentonville Prison, ex p. Herbage (No. 2)* [1987] Q.B. 1077. In *R. v. Humberside CC., ex p. Bogdal* [1991] C.O.D. 66, Pill J. refused to strike out, under Order 18, r. 19, a number of documents, exhibited to the respondent's affidavit, alleged to be "scandalous, irrelevant or otherwise oppressive", holding that the applicant cannot pick and choose amongst issues and that once he sought to quash a decision the court should not be excluded from having before it the relevant background documents.

[35] *R. v. Secretary of State for the Home Department, ex p. Dew,* [1987] 1 W.L.R. 881.

[36] *cf.* Ord. 53, r. 12 (express provision for consolidation of applications under S.C.A. 1981, s.30 and L.G.A. 1972, s.92).

[37] Ord. 53, r. 7(2).

[38] For the approach of the court to a security for costs application, see *R. v. Westminster City Council, ex p. Residents Association of Mayfair* [1991] C.O.D. 182.

(o) standing case out of Part B, D or E of the Crown Office List.[39]

All interlocutory applications, save for those relating to movement of cases within the Crown Office List,[40] should be made to a Divisional Court or single judge as appropriate.[41] A motion supported by affidavit should be served on the other side at least two clear days before the hearing.[42] The hearing takes place in open court.

Appeals from interlocutory orders are considered in Chapter 9.

Particular aspects of interlocutory relief are considered below between paras. 8–010 and 8–013.

Cross-examination

Formerly it was exceptionally rare for applications to be made, or leave to be granted, for cross-examination in judicial review proceedings. In *O'Reilly v. Mackman*,[43] however, Lord Diplock took the opportunity to emphasise that:

    8–010

> "whatever may have been the position before the rule was altered in 1977 in all proceedings for judicial review that have been started since that date the grant of leave to cross-examine deponents upon applications for judicial review is governed by the same principles as it is in actions begun by originating summons; it should be allowed whenever the justice of the particular case so requires."[44]

Notwithstanding the generality of this statement there have been indications (both pre- and post-*O'Reilly v. Mackman*) that the court will be slow to permit cross-examination under Order 53.[45]

In *George v. Secretary of State for the Environment*[46] Lord Denning M.R. observed that it would only be upon rare occasions that the interests of justice would require that leave to cross-examine be given. There were similar dicta in *R. v. Inland Revenue Commissioners, ex p. Rossminster Ltd*,[47] and *R. v. Board of Visitors of Albany Prison, ex p. Fell*.[48] In *R. v. Home Secretary, ex p. Khawaja*[49] it was said that the interests of justice would rarely require the attendance of an overseas deponent for cross-examination.

---

[39] See para. 8–006.

[40] These applications should be made to the Master of the Crown Office by summons supported by affidavit.

[41] *i.e.* the application should be made to the court having jurisdiction over the full hearing.

[42] The affidavit should set out the basis for the interlocutory relict sought.

[43] [1983] 2 A.C. 237.

[44] *ibid.* at pp. 282–283, correcting the statement of Geoffrey Lane J. in *R. v. Board of Visitors of Hull Prison, ex p. St Germain (No. 2)* [1979] 1 W.L.R. 1401 at 1410.

[45] A good instance is afforded by *R. v. Jenner* [1983] 1 W.L.R. 873 where Watkins L.J. observed that judicial review was unsuited to trying questions of fact. For cases where cross-examination has been allowed, see *R. v. Waltham Forest L.B.C., ex p. Baxter* [1988] Q.B. 419; *R. v. Derbyshire CC, ex p. The Times Supplements* [1991] C.O.D. 129.

[46] (1979) 77 L.G.R. 689.

[47] [1980] A.C. 952, 1027.

[48] (unrep.; July 8, 1981).

[49] [1984] A.C. 74. See also *R. v. Home Secretary, ex p. Patel* [1986] Imm.A.R. 208 where Webster J. deprecated the use of cross-examination of witnesses who needed an interpreter

Even in *O'Reilly v. Mackman* Lord Diplock qualified the effect of his observations by indicating that the nature of the issues that normally arise on judicial review rarely requires cross-examination. The only expressly recognised exceptions to this were alleged procedural unfairness or a breach of natural justice.[50] He warned that:

> "the tribunal or authority's findings of fact, as distinguished from the legal consequences of the facts that they have found, are not open to review by the court in the exercise of its supervisory powers except on the principles laid down in *Edwards v. Bairstow* [1956] A.C. 14, 36; and to allow cross-examination presents the court with a temptation, not always easily resisted, to substitute its own view of the facts for that of the decision-making body upon whom the exclusive jurisdiction to determine facts has been conferred by Parliament".[51]

These dicta, whilst rightly underlining the essence of the review process, appear to posit a somewhat narrow test for the exercise of the court's discretion to allow cross-examination. It is possible to envisage other situations where, applying Lord Diplock's test, the justice of a particular case may require cross-examination. In particular, a conflict of evidence on the affidavits before the court may need to be resolved in order to investigate the factors affecting a decision and whether there has been an abuse of discretion.[52]

Practitioners should apply for an order permitting cross-examination in an appropriate case since failure to make such application may be commented upon by the court as a reason for accepting the deponent's evidence.[53]

Orders for discovery and inspection

8–011   Parties seeking discovery and inspection of documents may experience more difficulty than in an ordinary action, notwithstanding the incorporation of Order 24 into judicial review proceedings.

Whereas in most actions discovery occurs automatically under Order 24, rr. 1 and 2,[54] there is no inherent right, in applications for judicial review, to orders for discovery or inspection.

The retention of control by the court may indicate that such orders will

---

or whose first language was not English; (decision upheld at [1986] Imm.A.R. 515); *Richard Read Transport v. Secretary of State for the Environment and Forest of Dean District Council* [1994] C.O.D. 361 (*held*: cross-examinator at decision-maker performing quasi judicia function was undeniable).

[50] See n. 43 above at p. 282.

[51] *ibid.*

[52] See, *e.g.* the observations of Woolf J. in *R. v. Home Secretary, ex p. Rouse and Shrimpton*, November 13, 1985 (unrep.) *cf.*, though, *R. v. Reigate JJ., ex p. Curl* [1991] C.O.D. 66. (*held*: Dispute as to events in magistrates' courts did not generally make cross-examination appropriate.)

[53] See, *e.g.*: *R. v. Secretary of State for the Home Department, ex p. Oladehinde* [1991] 1 A.C. 254, *per* Lord Griffiths at p. 302B–C; *R. v. Inland Revenue Commissioners, ex p. T. C. Coombs & Co.* [1991] 2 A.C. 283, *per* Lord Lowry at p. 303F.

[54] Though applications for specific discovery must be made under Ord. 24, r. 7.

be more difficult to obtain in cases under Order 53. Certainly this was the view of the Court of Appeal in *R. v. Secretary of State for the Home Office, ex p. Harrison*[55] where it was stated that on an application for judicial review discovery would be appropriate in fewer cases and was likely to be more circumscribed.

In general, the following principles appear to govern the grant or refusal of discovery under Order 53;

(a) Discovery will not be ordered so as to make good defects in the applicant's evidence.[56]

(b) One will seldom obtain full private law type discovery in a *Wednesbury* challenge.[57]

(c) By contrast, discovery will be ordered under Order 53 where it is required so that the justice of the case may be advanced and where it is necessary for disposing fairly of the matter[58] (within the meaning of Order 24, r. 8).

(d) Discovery will also be ordered to go behind the contents of affidavits if there was some matter before the Court which suggested that the contents of the affidavits were not accurate.[59]

The most authoritative pronouncement remains that of Lord Scarman in *Inland Revenue Commissioners v. National Federation of Self-Employed and Small Businesses Ltd.*[60] In relation to discovery under Order 53 he indicated that:

"Upon general principles, discovery should not be ordered unless and until the court is satisfied that the evidence reveals reasonable grounds for believing that there has been a breach of public duty; and it should be limited strictly to documents relevant to the issue which emerges from the affidavits."

The second limb of this statement is unexceptionable. It is a guiding rule that discovery and inspection must be restricted to matters relevant to an existing dispute.[61]

---

[55] Unrep., December 10, 1987. Applied in *R. v. Secretary of State for the Environment, ex p. Doncaster B.C.* [1990] C.O.D. 441. See, also: *R. v. Secretary of State for the Environment, ex p. Islington L.B.C.* [1992] C.O.D. 67. (*held*: where the issue on an application for judicial review was whether the decision-maker had power to make his decision, and there was no reason to doubt the bona fides or accuracy of the reasons given, it was unnecessary to order discovery of documents relating to the reasons for the decision.) See, also, to similar effect C.A. in *R. v. Secretary of State for Health, ex p. L.B. of Hackney*, unrep. July 29, 1994.

[56] *R. v. Inland Revenue Commissioners, ex p. Taylor* [1988] C.O.D. 61. See, also: *R. v. Secretary of State for Education, ex p. J* [1993] C.O.D. 146; *R. v. Inland Revenue Commissioners, ex p. National Federation of Self-Employed and Small Businesses Ltd* [1982] A.C. 617 at p. 635H *per* Lord Wilberforce.

[57] *R. v. Secretary of State for the Environment, ex p. Smith* [1988] C.O.D. 3.

[58] *R. v. Inland Revenue Commissioners, ex p. J. Rothschild Holdings plc.* [1987] S.T.C. 163; *R. v. Governor of Pentonville Prison, ex p. Herbage (No. 2)* [1987] Q.B. 1077.

[59] See *Re H, The Guardian*, May 17, 1990.

[60] [1982] A.C. 617 at 654.

[61] In judicial review, however, discovery must also be central to the application; *R. v. Secretary of State for the Home Department, ex p. Benson* [1989] C.O.D. 329.

It is, however, questionable whether, as a preliminary requirement, the court must attempt an evaluation of merits. Interlocutory relief will be granted only after leave has been granted to apply for judicial review.[62] In that sense, therefore, an applicant seeking discovery has, *ex hypothesi*, an arguable case for asserting a breach of public duty. In the circumstances it is difficult to see what else the court can do when considering discovery/ inspection, beyond determining whether potentially discoverable documents are relevant to the issues between the parties.[63]

Given the two-stage procedure under Order 53 it may be that Lord Scarman was merely emphasising the overall hurdles to be surmounted before discovery could become available. Even if these hurdles are surmounted, the doctrine of public interest immunity would appear to have more scope, having regard to the nature of judicial review,[64] as a means of opposing an order for discovery in Order 53 proceedings.

Interlocutory injunctions

8–012   In practice, injunctions are the main substantive type of relief awarded by way of interlocutory application under Order 53.[65] A stay of proceedings, under Order 53, r. 3(10)(a) is, in all but name, a class of prohibitory injunction. It operates in exactly the same way as interim prohibitory injunctive relief, although it may have more limited effect.[66] It is governed by the same criteria (see para. 7–027).

The circumstances affecting the grant of an interlocutory injunction are, in a public law case, slightly different to those prevailing in private law, although the essential principles are as set out in *American Cyanamid Co. v. Ethicon Ltd.*[67]

Generally, as in *Cyanamid*, the applicant must establish: (a) that damages are an inadequate remedy,[68] and (b) that the balance of

---

[62] See Ord. 53, r. 3(10) and 8(1). Discovery is not available as a final relief; *R. v. Secretary of State for Education and Science, ex p. M.G.* [1990] C.O.D. 65.

[63] See: *R. v. Secretary of State for Transport, ex p. APH Road Safety Limited* [1993] C.O.D. 150, where Schiemann J. left open the possibility that, in an appropriate case, the grant of leave in judicial review may sometimes be taken to establish a prima facie ground of irrationality, thereby justifying an order for discovery.

[64] *i.e.* being more than a *lis inter partes*. As to the doctrine of public interest immunity see, generally, *Supreme Court Practice* (1995) at 24/5/15. For a modern example of its application, see *Taylor v. Anderton* [1995] 1 W.L.R. 447.

[65] The reason for this is unclear. Ord. 53 provides no basis for seeking an interim prerogative order. Declaratory relief has never been awarded on an interim basis. *Quaere*, though, whether this might, exceptionally, be possible. See *Meade v. Haringey L.B.C.* [1979] 1 W.L.R. 637, 648–649, 657. Note, too, the observations of Lord Woolf in *M. v. Home Office* [1994] 1 A.C. 377 at p. 423A.

[66] It is only a stay of *proceedings*. See para. 7–027.

[67] [1975] A.C. 396.

[68] This consideration will rarely apply in relation to law enforcement in the public interest as where the Crown is seeking to enforce the law. Here, the Court will, almost always, find itself engaged in the balance of convenience issue. See *per* Lord Goff in *R. v. Secretary of State for Transport, ex p. Factortame Ltd (No. 2)* [1991] 1 A.C. 603 at pp. 672G–673B.

convenience[69] favours the making of an interim order. However, in the context of judicial review, the following principles are especially important:

(a) Where public bodies are concerned, the balance of convenience may be more difficult to make out.[70] In particular, ordinary financial considerations which arise when applying the *Cyanamid* test are liable to be qualified under Order 53 by a recognition of the interests of the general public.[71]

(b) Judicial review is more than a *lis inter partes*, so that the balance of convenience test should not be applied merely as between the parties.[72]

(c) The mere fact that leave is granted to apply for judicial review does not mean that interim relief should follow as a matter of course. It is perfectly possible to have an arguable case which is not sufficiently strong to justify the grant of an interlocutory injunction in the applicant's favour.[73] Certainly, in the case of a mandatory injunction, it is necessary to show a strong prima facie case of breach of duty at the interlocutory stage before such interim relief will be granted.[74]

(d) If an interim injunction is granted, cross-undertakings as to damages will usually be required.[75]

(e) Where a public authority applies for an interlocutory injunction to enforce a public law duty which can be enforced by other means, such authority may be required to give a cross-undertaking in

---

[69] Of the many attempts to define this term, perhaps the most helpful is the suggestion of Hoffmann J. in *Films Rover International Ltd v. Cannon Film Sales Ltd* [1987] 1 W.L.R. 670 as taking whatever course appeared to carry the lower risk of injustice if it should turn out to have been wrong to grant the injunction. See, also, *Scotia Pharmaceuticals International Limited v. Secretary of State for Health and Norgine Limited* [1994] C.O.D. 241 (which followed Hoffmann J.'s approach); *R. v. Secretary of State for Transport, ex p. Factortame (No. 2)* [1991] A.C. 603 at pp. 659, 674, 679 *per* (respectively) Lords Bridge, Goff and Jauncey.

[70] *Smith v. I.L.E.A.* [1978] 1 All E.R. 411, *per* Browne L.J. at p. 422h; *R. v. Secretary of State for Transport, ex p. Factortame Ltd (No. 2)* [1991] 1 A.C. 603 at p. 673C.

[71] *Sierbein v. Westminster City Council* (1988) 86 L.G.R. 431. See also *R. v. Secretary of State for the National Heritage, ex p. Continental Television BV (Red Hot Dutch)* [1993] 2 C.M.L.R. 333 at p. 348 *per* Leggatt L.J.: "when the moral welfare of minors is weighed against the applicants' profits there can only be one side upon which the scales can come down" and upheld by the C.A. at [1994] C.O.D. 121.

[72] *R. v. Epping Forest D.C., ex p. Strandmill*, April 14, 1989 (unrep.).

[73] As to this, see the observations of Lord Donaldson of Lymington M.R. in *R. v. Secretary of State for the Home Department, ex p. Doorga* [1990] C.O.D. 109.

[74] *R. v. Kensington and Chelsea Royal L.B.C., ex p. Hammell* [1989] Q.B. 518; *R. v. Westminster City Council, ex p. Augustin* [1993] 1 W.L.R. 730. Contrast *R. v. Cardiff City Council, ex p. Barry* [1990] 22 H.L.R. 261. (*held*: in a homeless person's case an applicant ought, as a usual concomitant of granting leave, to be enabled to stay in temporary accommodation pending the final outcome by the grant of an interim injunction.)

[75] Certainly the court has jurisdiction not to order a cross-undertaking (*R. v. Lambeth L.B.C. and Caballito Properties Ltd, ex p. Sibyll Walter*, February 2, 1989 (unrep.)). It will, though, be slow not to require it (*R. v. Secretary of State for the Environment, ex p. Rose Theatre Trust Company Ltd* [1990] C.O.D. 47).

damages.[76] However, no undertaking is usually required where the Crown or another public authority seeks such relief as the only method of enforcing the law.[77]

(f) In a community law case interim injunctive relief may be granted to disapply a domestic provision asserted to be contrary to community law. For this to occur, however:

"the court should not restrain a public authority by interim injunction from enforcing an apparently authentic law unless, it is satisfied, having regard to all the circumstances, that the challenge to the validity of the law is, *prima facie*, so firmly based as to justify so exceptional a course being taken".[78]

(g) It seems, also, that interim injunctive relief may be granted to suspend a domestic law that is based on a putatively invalid Community regulation provided that there are serious doubts as to the validity of the Community measure, threats of serious and irreparable damage to the applicant and due account taken of the Community's interests.[79]

(h) Finally, in *M v. Home Office*[80] the House of Lords has confirmed that (whether in a Community law context or not) interim (and final) injunctive relief is available against Ministers of the Crown. The earlier decision of the House in *Factortame v. Secretary of State for Transport (No. 1)*[81] was overruled, and earlier decisions of the High Court,[82] and Court of Appeal,[83] reinstated. *M* is also authority for the proposition that, exceptionally, interim injunctive relief may be awarded prior to the grant of leave.[84]

Rules of amendment

8–013   The need for careful drafting of Form 86A has already been observed. Unless prior leave to amend is given, the applicant is bound by that document. Order 53, r. 6(1) provides, *inter alia*, that "no grounds shall be relied upon or any relief sought at the hearing except the grounds and relief set out in the statement."

On a separate interlocutory application, amendment of Form 86A is

---

[76] *Rochdale B.C. v. Anders* [1988] 3 All E.R. 490.

[77] *Hoffman-La Roche (F.) & Co. A-G v. Secretary of State for Trade and Industry* [1975] A.C. 295; *Director-General of Fair Trading v. Tobyward Ltd* [1989] 1 W.L.R. 517; *R. v. Secretary of State for Transport, ex p. Factortame Ltd (No. 2)* [1991] A.C. 603 *per* Lord Goff at pp. 672G–673B; *Kirklees M.B.C. v. Wickes Building Supplies Ltd* [1993] A.C. 227.

[78] *per* Lord Goff in *R. v. Secretary of State for Transport, ex p. Factortame (No. 2)* [1991] 1 A.C. 603 at p. 673C.

[79] See: *Joined Cases 143/88, C–92/89 Zuckerfabrik Suderdithmarschen AG v. Hauptzollamt Itzehoe and Zuckerfabrik Soest GmbH v. Hauptzollamt Paderborn* [1991] E.C.R. 1–415.

[80] n. 65 above.

[81] [1990] 2 A.C. 85.

[82] *R. v. Secretary of State for the Home Department, ex p. Herbage (No. 1)* [1987] Q.B. 872.

[83] *R. v. Licensing Authority, ex p. Smith Kline and French Laboratories Ltd (No. 2)* [1990] 1 Q.B. 574.

[84] n. 65 above at p. 423D–E.

governed by Order 20, r. 8(1). This stipulates that the court may at any stage, on application or of its own motion, permit amendment "on such terms as to costs or otherwise as may be just and in such manner (if any) as it may direct" for the purpose of "determining the real question in controversy between the parties . . . , or of correcting any defect or error".

Ordinarily a proposed amendment will be allowed if it can be made without injustice. There is usually no injustice if the other side can be compensated by an award of costs.[85] Any notice of intention to seek leave to amend the grounds or relief must be given to the other party or parties and the known office, together with the proposed amendments, no later than five clear working days before the hearing date. Unless this is done, the Court will, save exceptionally, be prepared to allow the amendment.[85a]

The principles affecting amendment are probably the same whenever the application is made. It may, nonetheless, be helpful to bear in mind that there are, in fact, three stages at which an applicant may seek to amend his statement. They are:

(a) on the application for leave (Order 53, r. 3(6));
(b) as a separate interlocutory application (as above);
(c) on the hearing of the substantive application for judicial review (Order 53, r. 6(2)).

There may be rare occasions where it is necessary to amend a notice of motion or summons. In such circumstances an interlocutory application should be made for that purpose. Similar considerations will apply as on applications to amend the statement.[86]

---

[85] See, *e.g. Clarapede v. Commercial Union Association* (1883) 32 W.R. 236 (*per* Brett M.R.).
[85a] See *Practice Direction*, n. 25a, above.
[86] *cf.* Ord. 20, r. 5 and 7.

9. THE FULL HEARING

WAITING PERIOD

9–001   In judicial review proceedings there is no equivalent to setting the case down for hearing or filing certificates of readiness. Once the application has been entered for hearing[1] it takes its place in the Crown Office List.

The practitioner should be aware of the timetable operating in the Crown Office for expeditious disposal of cases in the Crown Office List (see Appendix C, where the relevant *Practice Direction* [1981] 1 W.L.R. 1296 is reproduced). Immediately prior to the case being entered in Part E of the List a date for hearing will be fixed. At this stage the applicant or his solicitor (as appropriate) will be informed and given as much notice as possible.

REPRESENTATION

9–002   It is desirable, in most cases, for counsel to be instructed because of the specialised nature of this form of proceedings.

The Crown Office sometimes lists cases at short notice and there is no certainty that an applicant will be able to be represented by counsel of his first choice.[2] It is, therefore, sensible for solicitors to liaise with the Head Clerk well in advance, especially if there are particular dates to be avoided.

REVIEW OF MERITS

9–003   It has been observed that counsel and solicitors instructed by an applicant for judicial review should give further careful consideration to the merits of the application once they have received notice of the respondent's evidence, even though leave to move for judicial review has been obtained.[3]

UNCONTESTED PROCEEDINGS

9–004   There is provision, in uncontested civil or criminal cases, for judicial review proceedings to be listed in open court without the necessity of the parties or their representatives having to attend. The procedure is set out in two Practice Directions.[4]

---

[1] As it must be within 14 days of the grant of leave. See Ord. 53, r. 5(5).

[2] See the *Notes for Guidance* [1994 update] published by the Crown Office, (set out at paras. **D–09** *et seq*).

[3] See *R. v. Horsham D.C., ex p. Wenman* [1995] 1 W.L.R. 680; *R. v. Secretary of State for the Home Department, ex p. Brown, The Times*, February 6, 1984. See also the terminology of Form JRJ, which is reproduced at para. **D–04**.

[4] *i.e. Practice Direction (Crown Office List: Uncontested Proceedings)* [1982] 1 W.L.R. 979 (civil); *Practice Direction (Uncontested Proceedings: Crown Office List)* [1983] 1 W.L.R. 925 (criminal). These are reproduced in Appendix C.

Where parties are agreed as to the order to be made they should hand into the Crown Office a document (together with two copies) signed by them and setting out the terms of the proposed agreed order. They should also supply a short statement of the matters relied on as justifying the making of the order, quoting any relevant authorities and statutory provisions. Where practicable, copies of any appropriate statutory instruments should be annexed to the document.

The Crown Office will then pass the document and statement to a judge who will, if satisfied that the order can be made, cause the proceedings to be listed for hearing in open court without the parties' attendance.

Sometimes the information provided may be insufficient for a decision to be made. If so, the Crown Office will request further details. Where the judge is not satisfied that the proposed order should be made he will simply cause the proceedings to be listed for hearing in the normal way. It will then be up to the parties to satisfy the court determining the application that the order should be made.

Adherence to the above procedure saves both time and costs. It should be resorted to whenever it is proposed that there should be a consensual order. If there is a possibility that the proceedings will be uncontested but no final agreement has been reached, the correct procedure appears to be for either party to apply by summons to the Master of the Crown Office to have the case stood out into Part C of the Crown Office List.

BUNDLES OF DOCUMENTS

Applicants are required to have sufficient copies of properly prepared bundles of documents before the court.[5] *Practice Direction (Evidence: Documents)* [1983] lays down requirements to which such bundles must conform.[6] Failure to comply renders the application liable to be struck out with costs against the applicant or his solicitors.[7] The bundles should, in particular, be: **9–005**

   (a) firmly secured together;
   (b) arranged in chronological order;
   (c) paged consecutively at centre bottom;
   (d) fully and easily legible.

On applications for judicial review the bundles should, generally, contain:

   (a) Form 86A;
   (b) the affidavit in support;
   (c) forms relating to the grant of leave;
   (d) notice of motion;
   (e) the decision complained of if not separately exhibited;
   (f) any further affidavit evidence;

---

[5] Three copies should be provided.
[6] *Practice Direction (Evidence: Documents)* [1983] 1 W.L.R. 922. This is reproduced in Appendix C.
[7] See *R. v. Secretary of State for the Home Department, ex p. Meyer-Wulff* [1986] Imm.A.R. 258.

(g) any relevant correspondence between the parties;

(h) any order made in the course of the proceedings.

All bundles should be properly indexed, and lodged in the Crown at least five clear working days before the hearing.[7a] *Practice Direction (Crown Office List: Preparation for Hearings)* which is reproduced at para. **C–11**.

ESTIMATING LENGTH OF HEARING

9–006   As with any case in the Crown Office List, great care must be taken by counsel to provide a well-judged and realistic estimate of time for hearing. This duty was emphasised in a Practice Note during 1987.[8]

Time estimates will be required from each party once the application has been entered in Part B of the List. Any variation of the original estimate should be notified to the Crown Office immediately.

COMPLIANCE WITH ACTIVE CASE LETTER

9–007   On receipt of what is sometimes referred to as the active case letter[9] from the Crown Office the applicant's solicitor must, within two weeks of receipt thereof, confirm that the application is still active. Failure to do so will result in the case being listed before the court to show cause as to why the matter should not be struck out for want of prosecution.[9a]

Where the application is still active the following must be lodged with the Crown Office at least five clear working days prior to the hearing:

(a) a time estimate including delivery at judgment;

(b) a list of issues;

(c) a list of propositions of law to be advanced with supporting authorities and page references to passages relied on;

(d) a chronology by reference to the bundle of documents;

(e) a list of the essential documents for advance reading by the court with page references to passages relied upon; and

(f) (if appropriate) a list of "*dramatis personae*".[10]

Failure to submit a proper summary of the argument in advance may result in the hearing of an application for judicial review being adjourned with possible penalty in costs.

PARTIES

9–008   All persons who are "directly affected" are required to be served with notice of the proceedings,[11] and are thereby afforded the opportunity of

---

[7a] See *Practice Direction (Crown Office List: Preparation for Hearings)* which is reproduced at para. **C–11**.

[8] *Practice Note (Q.B.D.) (Crown Office List)* [1987] 1 All E.R. 1184. This is reproduced in Appendix C.

[9] For the form of letter, see para. **D–08.**

[9a] See *Practice Direction (Crown Office List) (No. 2)* reproduced at para. **C–10**.

[10] See n. 7a, above.

[11] Ord. 53, r. 5(3). The meaning of this phrase is considered at para. 8.001.

appearing. If, on the full hearing, the court takes the view that a person ought to have been served it may adjourn the hearing, pursuant to Order 53, r. 5(7), on such terms as it thinks fit for service to be effected.

OTHER INTERESTED PERSONS

Apart from the applicant and all relevant respondents there is provision in the rules for other persons to appear at the full hearing. Order 53, r. 9(1) states that:

> "any person who desires to be heard in opposition to the motion or summons, and appears to the court to be a proper person to be heard, shall be heard, notwithstanding that he has not been served with notice of the motion or the summons".

9–009

Presumably this is a broader category than those persons required to be served and enables the court to admit a wide variety of interested parties to make representations at the hearing.[12] This is not entirely clear, however, and it may be that this rule is merely intended to be an alternative to adjourning the application for proper service under Order 53, r. 5(7).

At best, r. 9(1) would seem to alow only *opposition* to an application for judicial review.[13] Presumably, though, the court has an inherent discretion to allow interested parties to intervene to support the grant of judicial review.[14]

APPEARANCE BY JUSTICES

In a case involving a challenge to a decision of justices it is not usually considered appropriate for the justices or their clerk to appear personally or by counsel, unless their character or bona fides have been questioned or other special circumstances prevail.[15] If they do appear they are at risk as to costs.[16]

9–010

Where justices decline to consent to relief being granted, they may in appropriate cases be ordered to pay the costs of the hearing occasioned by their default.[16a] Justices may, without appearing file an affidavit with the Head Clerk to the Crown Office. It should be sent by the clerk directly to the Crown Office.

Occasionally, the court may require the justices to appear or may invite

---

[12] Probably such representations may be made by affidavit.

[13] See, *e.g.*: *R. v. Licensing Authority, ex p. Smith, Kline & French Laboratories Ltd* [1990] 1 A.C. 64 (rival licence applicants intervened throughout the proceedings to oppose the application for review).

[14] Consider, *e.g.*: *R. v. Central Criminal Court, ex p. Francis & Francis* [1989] A.C. 346, where the law Society intervened to support the application.

[15] *R. v. Camborne JJ., ex p. Pearce* [1955] 1 Q.B. 41; *R. v. Thornton etc. JJ.* (1898) 67 L.J.Q.B. 249. *R. v. Newcastle under Lyme JJ., ex p. Massey* [1994], 1 W.L.R. 1684.

[16] *R. v. Marlow (Bucks) JJ., ex p. Schiller* [1957] 2 Q.B. 508; *R. v. Llanidloes Licensing JJ., ex p. Davies* [1957] 1 W.L.R. 809n. Exceptionally, justices may be liable in costs even if they do not appear; see *R. v. Wareham JJ., ex p. Seldon*, October 29, 1987 (unrep.) CO/143/86. *R. v. Newcastle under Lyme JJ., ex p. Massey*, n. 15 above.

[16a] *See R. v. Newcastle under Lyme JJ., ex p. Massey*, n. 15 above.

the appointment of an *amicus*.[17] In the latter case, the Crown Office, at the court's direction, invites the Treasury Solicitor to appoint counsel to appear on for the assistance of the court.

THE COURT

9–011 Applications in a criminal cause or matter are, invariably, heard by a Divisional Court of the Queen's Bench Division.[18] Usually this consists, nowadays, of two judges. In complex cases three judges may sit and parties should be alert to the need to inform the Crown Office of those cases where an uneven number of judges is desirable so as to avoid the possibility of "deadlocked" judgments.[19]

Civil cases are usually determined by a single judge sitting in open court.[20] There remain, however, the following possibilities:

   (a) A Divisional Court.[21]
   (b) A hearing before a judge in chambers.[22]
   (c) In exceptional cases the Court of Appeal will, where it deals with a renewed application, itself hear the substantive application for judicial review.[23]

It is the practice to list *inter partes* hearings after *ex parte* applications for leave. There is, however, no necessary connection between the court that originally granted leave and that which finally determines the application.[24]

PROCEDURE

9–012 The hearing is conducted in the form of legal argument based upon Form 86A and the affidavit evidence. The court will hear the applicant's counsel and, thereafter, counsel for the respondent.[25] There is a right of reply in favour of the applicant.

In conducting the hearing the following points should be borne in mind:

---

[17] This will, most typically, be where a point of law of difficulty is involved and/or where there is no other respondent appearing.

[18] Ord. 53, r. 5(1). Proceedings which require to be immediately or promptly heard may now, in vacation, be brought before a single judge rather than a Divisional Court.

[19] *cf. Practice Note (Court of Appeal: New Procedure)* [1982] 1 W.L.R. 1312 at 1318. In the Divisional Court in *Re Findlay* [1985] A.C. 318 (see p. 325H), *e.g.* Parker L.J. and Forbes J. were unable to agree. "The applicants chose, very sensibly, to treat the result as a dismissal", *ibid. per* Lord Scarman.

[20] Ord. 53, r. 5(2).

[21] *ibid.* This is usually reserved for complex cases.

[22] In practice this is rare.

[23] See *Practice Direction (Judicial Review: Appeals)* [1982] 1 W.L.R. 1375 clarifying that it is an exceptional course to take. For cases where the Court of Appeal did hear the full application, see *British Airways Board v. Laker Airways Ltd* [1984] Q.B. 142 (subsequently reversed: [1985] A.C. 58); *R. v. Panel on Take-Overs and Mergers, ex p. Datafin Plc.* [1987] Q.B. 815. See also *Practice Direction (Judicial Review: Appeals)* [1990] 1 W.L.R. 51.

[24] Usually the substantive hearing is determined by a different judge or court from that which granted leave.

[25] If oral evidence is allowed it will usually take place after the applicant's counsel has opened.

(a) It is not open to the applicant to argue any ground or seek any relief that does not appear in his Form 86A.[26]
(b) The parties should not seek to attack or defend a decision or order on the merits. This follows from the general nature of the remedy of judicial review.

FRESH EVIDENCE AT THE HEARING

On the substantive hearing the court will admit new evidence in the following circumstances:

9–013

(a) to show the nature of the material before the decision-making body;
(b) to determine a fact upon which jurisdiction depended or whether essential procedural requirements were observed;
(c) to prove alleged misconduct as, for example, bias on the part of the decision-maker or fraud or perjury by a party.[27]

ORDERS THAT MAY BE MADE

The court has a wide range of powers on the full hearing. Clearly, it retains all the interlocutory powers already considered. In addition, two further powers are expressly referred to in Order 53:

9–014

(a) If, on the full hearing, the court takes the view that a person ought to have been served it may adjourn the hearing, pursuant to Order 53, r. 5(7), on such terms as it thinks fit for service to be effected.
(b) The court also has power to allow amendment of an applicant's statement "whether by specifying different or additional grounds or relief or otherwise, on such terms, if any, as it thinks fit".[28] However, amendments will not usually be permitted unless notice of the proposed amendment has been served on the respondent at least five clear working days prior to the hearing.[28a]

By way of final resolution of an application under Order 53, the range of possible orders are set out below at paras. 9–015 to 9–022.

Mandamus, prohibition, certiorari

These remedies may be granted either singly or in combination.[29] By virtue of section 29(1) of the Supreme Court Act 1981, the court has jurisdiction to make the orders "in those classes of cases in which it had power to do immediately before the commencement of this Act."

9–015

---

[26] Ord. 53, r. 6(1).
[27] See *R. v. Secretary of State for the Environment, ex p. Powis* [1981] 1 W.L.R. 584 (*per* Dunn L.J.).
[28] Ord. 53, r. 6(2).
[28a] See n. 7a, above.
[29] Ord. 53, r. 1(1)(a) and 2; S.C.A. 1981, s.31.

Remission

9–016   Where the court awards certiorari and quashes the decision to which the application relates it may, in addition, remit the matter to the court, tribunal or authority concerned with a direction to reconsider it and reach a decision in accordance with the findings of the court.[30]

Remission would seem to be solely appropriate for those cases where the decision-making body has made a clear error of law and where a complete rehearing with new evidence is unnecessary in the light of the legal principles found by the court.[31]

Variation of sentence

9–017   In a criminal case the court may vary a sentence passed in circumstances where it would otherwise have awarded certiorari to quash the conviction.[32]

This occurs where the sentencing court had no power to pass the original sentence.[33] It should be borne in mind that there is no jurisdiction to determine, by judicial review, any application dealing with matters relating to trial on indictment.[34] Thus the above power is restricted to sentences passed by:

(a) a magistrates' court; or

(b) the Crown Court on committal for sentence; or

(c) the Crown Court on appeal against conviction or sentence.[35]

Any sentence so substituted runs from the date of the original proceedings, unless otherwise ordered, but any time during which the applicant was released on bail, pending the application under Order 53, is disregarded.[36]

Whilst the power of variation appears to be exercisable in relation to sentences that are irrational as well as those made without jurisdiction, it has been held that such power should be treated with circumspection.[37] For the power to vary to be applied, an irrational sentence must be "truly astonishing".[38]

---

[30] Ord. 53, r. 9(4); S.C.A. 1981, s.31(5). For an example of the kind of directions that may be given under r. 9(4), see *R. v. Vaccine Damage Tribunal, ex p. Loveday, The Times*, April 20, 1985.

[31] See, generally, Emery and Smythe, *Judicial Review* (1986).

[32] S.C.A. 1981, s.43(1).

[33] Note that the court has power to vary under section 43 even where the magistrates have no power to impose a sentence because the applicant himself was not present; see *R. v. Nuneaton JJ., ex p. Bingham* [1991] C.O.D. 56.

[34] See S.C.A. 1981, s.29(3) and para. 5–003.

[35] S.C.A. 1981, s.43(1).

[36] S.C.A. 1981, s.43(2).

[37] *R. v. Acton Crown Court, ex p. Bewley* [1988] 152 J.P. 327.

[38] *R. v. Croydon Crown Court, ex p. Miller* (1987) 85 Cr.App.R. 152. See also *R. v. Chelmsford Crown Court, ex p. Birchall* [1990] C.O.D. 200; *The Times*, November 10, 1989; *R. v. Burnley Magistrates' Court, ex p. Halstead* [1991] C.O.D. 156.

Declaration, injunction

Declarations or injunctions may be granted alone or together with one or more of the prerogative orders.[39]   **9–018**

Before making such an award the court must be satisfied[40] that it would be "just and convenient" to grant a declaration or injunction in judicial review proceedings, having regard to:

(a) the nature of the matters in respect of which relief may be granted by way of a prerogative order;

(b) the nature of the persons and bodies against whom relief may be granted by way of an order; and

(c) all the circumstances of the case.[41]

Damages

Such an order can be made only where the applicant has included a claim for damages arising from any matter related to the application.[42] It is not a substantive right in itself although there seems to be no reason why the court, in its discretion, may not refuse to award another relief but still give damages.[43]   **9–019**

The court must be satisfied that, had the claim been made in an action rather than in judicial review proceedings, the applicant could have been awarded damages.[44] If the court grants damages it may determine quantum by hearing evidence or, alternatively, order damages to be assessed.[45]

Conversion into a writ action

Where the relief sought is a declaration, injunction or damages the court may, under Order 53, r. 9(5), order the proceedings to continue as if begun by writ.[46] Order for directions on future conduct of the action may be made under Order 28, r. 8.[47]   **9–020**

It is by no means clear under what circumstances the court should exercise the above power.

---

[39] Ord. 53, r. 1(2); S.C.A. 1981, s.31(1)(b).

[40] Except in relation to injunctions under S.C.A. 1981, s.30 which are granted solely by judicial review.

[41] cf. Ord. 53, r. 1(2) and S.C.A. 1981, s.31(2).

[42] Ord. 53, r. 7(2); S.C.A. 1981, s.31(4).

[43] In practice, though, this is unlikely.

[44] Ord. 53, r. 7(1); S.C.A. 1981, s.31(4). The notional date of such action is the time of making the application for judicial review. For the circumstances in which damages lie against a public authority for the exercise of its statutory powers, see Harding, *Public Duties and Public Law* (1989), especially Chap. 7. Consider, too, *Lonrho v. Tebbitt* [1992] 4 All E.R. 280; *Bradford City Metropolitan Council v. Arora* [1991] 2 Q.B. 507.

[45] i.e. before a Master under Ord. 37, r. 1(1).

[46] In *R. v. Reading JJ., ex p. S.W. Meat Ltd* (1992) 156 J.P. 728, Watkins L.J. stated that it was unheard of and thoroughly improper for a respondent, after leave has been granted for judicial review, to move to have the case proceed as if started by writ a short time before the full hearing was due, in a move designed to prevent the hearing from occurring.

[47] See generally Ord. 25, r. 2

In *R. v. East Berkshire Health Authority, ex p. Walsh*[48] the Court of Appeal refused to make an order where the applicant had claimed only certiorari and prohibition in his Form 86A. As Lord Donaldson of Lymington M.R. observed:

> "This is an anti-technicality rule. It is designed to preserve the position of an applicant for relief who finds that the basis of *that relief* is private law rather than public law. It is not designed to allow him to amend and to claim different relief."[49]

May L.J. made the point, also, that the issues in any subsequent private law action required precise identification which could not be done in the context of extensive documents and affidavits.[50]

In *R. v. Secretary of State for the Home Department, ex p. Dew*[51] McNeill J. held that a misconceived application for judicial review, even where damages are claimed in Form 86A, may not be ordered to proceed as if commenced by writ. In his view the purpose of the "conversion" rule was merely to assist applicants whose allegations of breaches of public law had, as a consequence, given them a right to damages in private law.[52]

If McNeill J. is correct, Order 53, r. 9(5) is of very limited application since, on a successful judicial review application, the court has power to award damages in any event and there is no need for conversion to a writ action at all.[53] It is submitted that the scope of the rule is somewhat wider and this would appear to be confirmed by the decision of the Court of Appeal in *Calveley v. Chief Constable of the Merseyside Police*[54] which considered Order 53, r. 9(5) as extending to the situation where the application for judicial review was unsuccessful but there was an arguable claim for damages.[55]

Whatever the exact position under Order 53 the court may, it is submitted, have power to allow an application wrongly commenced by writ to be converted into an application for judicial review. Order 2, r. 1(3) provides that:

> "The court shall not wholly set aside any proceedings or the writ or other originating process by which they were begun on the ground that the proceedings were required by any of these Rules to be begun by an originating process other than the one employed."[56]

---

[48] [1985] Q.B. 152.

[49] *ibid.* at p. 166.

[50] *ibid.* at p. 173. For a case where the issues were sufficiently identified, see *R. v. B.B.C., ex p. Lavelle* [1983] 1 W.L.R. 23.

[51] [1987] 1 W.L.R. 881.

[52] *ibid.* at p. 895D.

[53] See also Wade and Forsyth, *Administrative Law* (7th ed., 1994) at p. 678, 65n and text.

[54] [1989] A.C. 1228.

[55] See, also, *R. v. London Commodity Exchange (1986) Limited, ex p. Brealey* [1994] C.O.D. 145 (claim which was wholly unsuitable for Order 53 proceedings ordered to proceed as if begun by writ).

[56] The effect of Ord. 2, r. 1(3) has, however, yet to receive consideration in the cases in this context. It could, for example, be argued that conversion to judicial review is objectionable

Dismissal of application

Such order will be appropriate if the applicant fails to establish a ground **9–021** for review, or requisite *locus standi*, or if there is a discretionary reason for the refusal of relief. These matters have all been separately considered in Chapters 2, 4 and 5.

Costs

Usually costs will follow the event.[57] A successful party will (subject to **9–022** the qualifications set out below) generally recover costs against the other (including, as appropriate the costs of the application for leave).[58] Costs are, of course, in the discretion of the court which must be exercised judicially.[59]

Wasted costs orders may, exceptionally be made against legal representatives who, through inadequate expertise or otherwise, incur unnecessary expenditure through (for example) failing: (a) to send a letter before action thereby possibly rendering judicial review unnecessary, or (b) to comply with their disclosure obligations when seeking leave to apply for review, or (c) to appreciate the significance of a possible alternative remedy to judicial review, (d) to understand and apply the principle that judicial review ought not to be invoked to resolve disputed questions of fact.[60]

Restrictions on costs on judicial review

Where the applicant succeeds against a public body the court is unlikely **9–023** to award costs where such body has not appeared and has not been represented, provided that any error of law made is not something that calls for strong disapproval by the court.[61] This principle applies, *inter alia*, to

---

as dispensing with the requirement of leave contained in the procedure; see *Heywood v. Board of Visitors at Hull Prison* [1980] 1 W.L.R. 1386. See, also, the dicta of Lord Diplock in *O'Reilly v. Mackman* [1983] 2 A.C. 237 at p. 283H–284A (no power under R.S.C. to permit writ action to proceed as judicial review application) and, to similar effect, *per* Lord Fraser in *Davy v. Spelthorne B.C.* [1984] A.C. 262 at p. 274G.

[57] But by no means always. Consider, *e.g.*: *R. v. Secretary of State for the Environment, ex p. Greenpeace Ltd* [1994] 4 All E.R. 352 (no costs order against applicants who had brought challenge in the public interest).

[58] Note that where discontinuance of proceedings can safely be equated with defeat or acknowledgement of defeat, costs will be awarded against the applicant; see: *R. v. Liverpool City Council, ex p. Newman* [1993] C.O.D. 65. Late discontinuance of an application for judicial review can also lead to an adverse costs award against the applicant; see: *R. v. Warley JJ., ex p. Callis* [1994] C.O.D. 240. (Three days before hearing.)

[59] See generally Ord. 62 and S.C.A. s.51(1). See also, *R. v. Woodhouse* [1906] 2 K.B. 501. The proper approach to the question of costs where an application for judicial review is premature or is rendered otiose was considered by Farquharson J. in *R. v. Barnet L.B.C., ex p. Field* [1989] 1 P.L.R. 30.

[60] See *R. v. Horsham D.C., ex p. Wenman*, n. 3 above. For the principles applicable to wasted costs orders generally, see: *Ridehalgh v. Horsefield* [1994] Ch. 205.

[61] *R. v. West Yorkshire Coroner, ex p. Kenyon, The Times*, April 11, 1984. *Aliter* if there is bad faith, perversity or oppression; *R. v. Meyer* (1875) 1 Q.B.D. 173.

justices[62] and to coroners.[63] The position is otherwise where there is an appearance and a respondent is not successful.[64]

Parties who have not been served are rarely awarded costs even if the court allows them to be heard under Order 53, r. 9(1) (see above).

Similarly, costs are not usually granted to two or more successful parties with the same interest.[65] The court's general reluctance to award two or more sets of costs may, however, be disturbed for sufficiently good reason[66] as where separate interests are at stake or the issues are complex and require separate argument.[67]

Costs against justices

9–024   If costs are awarded against justices or the clerk to the justices there was formerly provision, under section 54(2) of the Justices of the Peace Act 1979, for the Lord Chancellor to defray all or part of the costs from moneys provided by Parliament, "if he thinks fit".[68] Section 54(2) has been repealed by section 108 of the Courts and Legal Services Act 1990, but there is a saving provision under schedule 19 of the Act "in relation to any matter arising before the coming into force of section 108" (*i.e.* January 1, 1991).

Legal aid

9–025   An applicant seeking judicial review is, subject to financial eligibility and merits,[69] entitled to legal aid. In such cases orders must conform to the requirements of the Legal Aid Act 1988 and the Legal Aid Regulations thereunder.[70]

A successful respondent may be able to seek an order against the Legal Aid Fund under section 18 of the Legal Aid Act 1988, but such order is largely dependent upon the respondent being able to establish "severe financial hardship" unless such order is made. Because of the nature of judicial review proceedings it is unlikely that most public bodies will be able to satisfy this requirement. However, in *R. v. Greenwich L.B.C., ex p. Lovelace*,[71] the court held that there was no reason in principle why a local

---

[62] *R. v. Meyer, ibid.*

[63] *R. v. West Yorkshire Coroner*, n. 61 above. See also, *R. v. Maidstone Coroner, ex p. Johnstone* [1995] C.O.D. 24.

[64] *R. v. Camborne JJ., ex p. Pearce* [1955] 1 Q.B. 41.

[65] *R. v. Industrial Disputes Tribunal, ex p. American Express Co. Inc.* [1954] 1 W.L.R. 1118; *Bolton M.D.C. v. Secretary of State for the Environment (No. 2), The Times*, July 1, 1995.

[66] *R. v. Registrar of Companies, ex p. Central Bank of India* [1986] Q.B. 1114 at 1162; *Bolton B.C. v. Secretary of State for the Environment and the British Coal Corporation* [1989] C.O.D. 352. *Bolton M.D.C. v. Secretary of State for the Environment (No. 2)* n. 65 above.

[67] See, *e.g. R. v. Monopolies & Mergers Commission, ex p. Matthew Brown plc.*, July 17, 1986 (unrep.); *R. v. Panel on Take-Overs and Mergers, ex p. Datafin Ltd* [1987] Q.B. 815.

[68] This option was never available if only declarations or injunctions were sought. See Justices of the Peace Act 1979, s.54(2) which refers only to the prerogative remedies.

[69] As to the appropriate test, see *R. v. Legal Aid Board, ex p. Hughes* (1992) 24 H.L.R. 698 (essentially the same as for the granting of leave to move for judicial review).

[70] See the *Supreme Court Practice 1995*, Vol. 2, paras. 4046–4282.

[71] [1992] 1 Q.B. 155.

authority or any other large public body should not be able to recover costs against the Legal Aid Board under s.18 of the 1988 Act.

Central funds

In criminal cases a Divisional Court has power to order the costs of any **9–026** party to the proceedings to be paid out of central funds to compensate him for expenses properly incurred, either wholly or in a proportion that is considered just and reasonable.[72] Such orders may be made in favour of prosecutors as well as defendants, except that a prosecutors' costs order may not be made where the prosecutor is a "public authority" or a person appointed by, or acting on behalf of, such an authority.[73]

The House of Lords, in *Steel Ford & Newton v. Crown Prosecution Service*,[74] has held that there is no general power, deriving from section 51(1) of the Supreme Court Act 1981 or section 50 of the Solicitors Act 1974, to order parties' costs to be paid out of central funds in civil cases.

Civil appeals

In civil cases there is the prospect of an appeal from whichever court **9–027** determined the substantive application. Leave is, however, required except in immigration cases.[75] Appeal lies to the Court of Appeal.[76]

The time limit for appeal (or, as appropriate for leave to appeal) is four weeks after the date on which the judgment or order was sealed or otherwise perfected.[77] A further appeal lies from the Court of Appeal to the House of Lords on (in practice) a point of law of general public importance, provided that leave is granted by the Court of Appeal or the House of Lords itself.

CRIMINAL APPEALS

In a criminal cause or matter the procedure on judicial review appeals is **9–028** very different. There is no appeal to the Court of Appeal.[78] Instead, section 1 of the Administration of Justice Act 1960 provides for direct appeal from a Divisional Court to the House of Lords.

Leave must first be obtained from the Divisional Court or, if that is refused, from the House of Lords. It is a condition of leave being granted that the Divisional Court certifies that a point of law of general public importance is involved in the decision. The court granting leave must also view the point as one which ought to be considered by the House of Lords.[79]

---

[72] Prosecution of Offences Act 1985, ss.16 and 17.
[73] *ibid.* s.17(2).
[74] [1994] C.O.D. 102.
[75] Ord. 59, r. 1B(c).
[76] S.C.A. 1981, s.16(1).
[77] Ord. 59, r. 4.
[78] S.C.A. 1981, s.18(1)(a).
[79] A.J.A. 1960, s.1(2).

INTERLOCUTORY APPLICATION APPEALS

9–029   Interlocutory applications are subject to the following appellate regime:

(a) (where appropriate) appeals from orders of the Master of the Crown Office lie, without leave, to the judge[80];

(b) in civil cases an appeal lies from orders of the single judge or Divisional Court, usually with leave,[81] to the Court of Appeal;

(c) in criminal cases interlocutory judgments may only be appealed to the House of Lords under the provisions of the Administration of Justice Act 1960.[82]

APPEALING COSTS ORDERS

9–030   A party wishing to appeal an order that relates solely to costs must obtain leave from the court hearing the application for judicial review.[83] Only that court may grant leave. There is no further right of recourse if leave is refused.

FRESH EVIDENCE ON A JUDICIAL REVIEW APPEAL

9–031   Fresh evidence may be received in judicial review proceedings themselves (see above) and also on appeal. On appeal the principles are probably similar to those that prevail generally in civil and criminal appeals, subject to the overriding principle that judicial review is more than a mere *lis inter partes.*

In *R. v. Secretary of State for the Home Department, ex p. Momin Ali*[84] it was held that where an application was made to adduce fresh evidence to the Court of Appeal hearing an appeal from a Divisional Court, the principle of finality in litigation was applicable.[85] This was, however, always subject to the court's discretion to depart from this principle if the wider interests of justice so required.[86]

---

[80] Ord. 58, r. 1. The appeal will, in Crown Office cases, be heard in open court.

[81] S.C.A. 1981, s.18(1)(h), subject to the exceptions therein specified where leave is not required. Such leave must be obtained from the judge or Court of Appeal.

[82] S.C.A. 1981, s.18(1)(a). *Quaere* whether there is any sensible distinction between interlocutory judgments and orders so as to render the latter susceptible to appeal to the Court of Appeal.

[83] S.C.A. 1981, s.18.

[84] [1984] 1 W.L.R. 663.

[85] Presumably this applies to all species of judicial review appeal, *i.e.* from the single judge as well.

[86] See also *R. v. Governor of Pentonville Prison, ex p. Tarling* [1979] 1 W.L.R. 1417 at pp. 1422–1423. And since judicial review is more than a *lis inter partes* there is, arguably, somewhat greater scope for permitting fresh evidence. Moreover, issue estoppel appears not to arise in judicial review proceedings; see: *R. v. Secretary of State for the Environment, ex p. Hackney L.B.C.* [1984] 1 W.L.R. 592 at pp. 602A–B and 606D. Abuse of process is, however, only relevant judicial review as to any other proceeding: see *R. v. Lloyd's of London, ex p. Briggs* (1993) 5 Admin. L.R. 698.

PART 3

JUDICIAL REVIEW IN PRACTICE

10. THE CRIMINAL JURIS-DICTION OF MAGISTRATES

THE SCOPE OF REVIEW

It has become clear, following the Divisional Court's decision in *R. v.*
Greater Manchester Coroner, ex p. Tal,[1] that the Court will review not only
errors of law appearing on the face of the record, but also errors which are
material to the decision. The Court has, for example, reviewed both
unlawful policies[2] and guilty pleas obtained by unreliable prosecution
evidence.[3]

    10–001

In principle it is now apparent that any error of law is subject to the
court's review jurisdiction. This is not to say that every such error will lead
to a remedy.[4] Specifically, it has been clarified that whilst there is no rule
against quashing committal proceedings other than where a court has
declined jurisdiction or acted outside its jurisdiction,[5] such relief should
only be granted in limited circumstances.[6] There is jurisdiction to quash a
committal where the court ought to have held that the prosecution
constituted an abuse of process.[7]

DECLINING JURISDICTION

To decline jurisdiction is, in many cases, to exceed it.[8] In general, a
magistrates' court is required to hear the case and arrive at a decision; if it
fails to do so, mandamus will lie to compel a determination.

    10–002

Thus, in *R. v. Bromley JJ., ex p. Haymills (Contractors) Ltd*[9] magistrates,
faced with conflicting expert evidence relating to a road traffic accident,

---

[1] [1985] Q.B. 67.

[2] See, *e.g. R. v. Felixstowe JJ., ex p. Leigh* [1987] 1 Q.B. 582 and *R. v. Farnham J., ex p. Gibson*
[1991] R.T.R. 309.

[3] *R. v. Bolton JJ., ex p. Scally* [1991] 1 Q.B. 537.

[4] Since judicial review is discretionary. See *ex p. Tal* [1985] Q.B. 67 at p. 83.

[5] *i.e.* in the pre-*Anisminic* sense (see para. 3–005). See *Neill v. North Antrim Magistrates* [1992]
1 W.L.R. 1220. *Semble*, that *R. v. Wells Street Magistrates Court* [1986] 1 W.L.R. 1046 at
p. 1052C is no longer good law.

[6] *R. v. Oxford City Magistrates, ex p. Berry* [1988] 1 Q.B. 507. *cf. R. v. Metropolitan Stipendiary*
Magistrate, ex p. Director of Public Prosecutions (1994) C.O.D. 23.

[7] *R. v. Horseferry Road Magistrates' Court, ex p. Bennett* [1994] 1 A.C. 42. This would seem to
erode the Divisional Court's reasoning in *R. v. Plymouth JJ., ex p. Driver* [1986] 1 Q.B. 95.

[8] *R. v. Marsham* [1892] 1 Q.B. 371.

[9] (1984) 148 J.P. 363.

ordered a rehearing before a different bench because they were unable to reach a decision. Ackner L.J. held that where justices felt unhappy about convicting a defendant, their duty was to acquit.[10] Conversely, where magistrates are equally divided, they are entitled to either adjourn the case to a different bench or dismiss the information.[11] They do not have a discretion to do what is just in all the circumstances of the case. They may, however, permit withdrawal of a summons without adjudication.[12]

An adjournment for a long period can constitute a declining of jurisdiction so as to permit judicial review.[13] So, too, a refusal to issue a distress warrant because the magistrate considers it excessive is susceptible to challenge under Order 53.[14]

In general, the refusal to hear evidence before dismissing an information amounts to a declining of jurisdiction.[15] Difficult problems occur when magistrates dismiss an information without any adjudication on the basis that it is an abuse of process; these are discussed below.

Occasionally, jurisdiction is deliberately and unjustifiably declined. This happened in *R. v. Clerkenwell Green Metropolitan Stipendiary Magistrate, ex p. Ibrahim*[16] where certiorari was granted to quash the refusal of the magistrate so rehear a case, under section 142 of the Magistrates' Courts Act 1980, purely because of the defendant's late arrival at the original hearing. Most often, however, jurisdiction will unwittingly be declined because of a mistaken belief as to the court's powers.

A difficulty has sometimes arisen with regard to the appropriate remedy when a bench of magistrates improperly acquits a defendant. Following *R. v. Hendon JJ., ex p. D.P.P.*[17] it is clear that where magistrates make a decision which can properly be regarded as a nullity, certiorari will lie to quash the acquittal and the defendant can be retried for the offence because the maxim *autrefois acquit* will not apply.[18] Although it follows that where the decision is not a nullity, certiorari may not lie, errors of law that are material to the acquittal will ordinarily, result in the acquittal being treated as a nullity.[19]

---

[10] *i.e.* following the earlier decision in *R. v. Bridgend JJ., ex p. Randall* [1975] Crim.L.R. 287.

[11] *R. v. Redbridge JJ., ex p. Ram* [1992] Q.B. 384.

[12] *R. v. Redbridge JJ., ex p. Sainty* [1981] R.T.R. 13. A summons, unlike an information, does not go to jurisdiction.

[13] *R. v. Southampton JJ., ex p. Lebern* (1907) 41 J.P. 332.

[14] *R. v. Essex JJ.* (1877) 41 J.P. 676.

[15] *R. v. Birmingham JJ., ex p. Lamb* [1983] 1 W.L.R. 339.

[16] (1984) 148 J.P. 400.

[17] [1994] Q.B. 167, following *R. v. Dorking JJ., ex p. Harrington* [1984] A.C. 743. See also: *R. v. Barnet Magistrates' Court, ex p. D.P.P. The Times*, April 8, 1994, (*held*: judicial review lay to quash acquittal where adjournment improperly refused to C.P.S.); *R. v. Metropolitan Stipendiary Magistrate, ex p. Serious Fraud Office, The Independent*, June 24, 1994 (*held*: judicial review lay since justices erred in law to acquit on the basis of the "reasonable excuse" exception in s.2 C.J.A. 1987.) To similar effect is the principle, accepted in *R. v. Portsmouth Crown Court, ex p. D.P.P.* [1994] C.O.D. 13, that certiorari lies to quash the decision of the Crown Court, allowing an appeal against a magistrates' court conviction.

[18] *R. v. Swansea JJ., ex p. D.P.P.* (1990) 154 J.P. 709 and *R. v. Sutton JJ., ex p. D.P.P.* [1992] All E.R. 129, which took a contrary view, are to be doubted.

[19] See: *In re A Company* [1981] A.C. 374, *per* Lord Diplock at p. 383C.

The abuse of process cases

In a sequence of cases it has been held that magistrates may, in limited   **10–003**
circumstances, stop a prosecution on the basis that it is an abuse of
process.[20]

In *R. v. Derby Crown Court, ex p. Brooks*[21] a Divisional Court held that a
prosecution could be an abuse of the process of the Court if either (a) the
prosecution has manipulated or misused the process of the court so as to
either (i) deprive a defendant of some protection afforded to him by the
law; or (ii) take unfair advantage of a technicality[22]; or (b) it is more likely
than not than the defendant has or will be prejudiced in the preparation or
conduct of his defence or unjustifiable delay on the part of the prosecution.

In *R. v. Bow Street Stipendiary Magistrate, ex p. D.P.P.*[23] a Divisional
Court held that, according to the circumstances, a magistrate was entitled
to infer prejudice from the passage of time and particularly when the charge
arose from a single confused event which depended on the recollection of
those involved. In *R. v. Telford JJ., ex p. Badhan*[24] the Court held that, save
where the defendant has concealed his own wrongdoing or his person,
where a defendant could show that on the balance of probabilities a fair trial
was no longer possible, then it mattered not that the delay was not the fault
of the prosecution.

It should, however, be remembered that the High Court will only
interfere with a decision if the *Wednesbury* criteria are satisfied. It will not
substitute its discretion for that of the magistrate.[25]

Reaching a decision: the role of the justices' clerk

One aspect of the declining of jurisdiction is the delegation of decision   **10–004**
making. It is trite law that an inferior body cannot delegate a decision-
making function entrusted to it without express authority to do so.[26] Thus,
magistrates cannot delegate decisions as to either matters of fact or law to
their clerks.[27]

A practice has developed whereby lay magistrates usually accept the
legal advice given to them by their clerks.[28] It is undoubtedly the case that
justices may seek the advice of their clerk on matters of law. There is,

---

[20] What constitutes an abuse of process is not divorced from public policy.

[21] (1984) 80 Cr.App.R. 164.

[22] Consider, *e.g. R. v. Grays JJ., ex p. Low* [1990] 1 Q.B. 54, (*held*: fresh summons issued
repeating charge in withdrawn summons was an abuse of process).

[23] (1989) 91 Cr.App.R. 283.

[24] [1991] 2 Q.B. 78. Contrast the facts of *R. v. Wimbledon JJ., ex p. Doyle* (1994) C.O.D. 191,
(*Held*: 13–16 year delay in bringing charges over a three-year period to trial was not an abuse
of process).

[25] *R. v. Canterbury and St Augustine's JJ., ex p. Turner* (1983) 147 J.P. 193.

[26] *Barnard v. National Dock Labour Board* [1953] 2 Q.B. 18.

[27] See the reasoning in *R. v. Gateshead JJ., ex p. Tesco Stores Ltd* [1981] 1 Q.B. 470 and *Bunston
v. Rawlings* [1982] 1 W.L.R. 473. Note, though, that the actual decision in *Gateshead* has
been overruled by *R. v. Manchester Stipendiary Magistrate, ex p. Hill* [1983] A.C. 328.

[28] See *Jones v. Nicks* [1977] R.T.R. 72.

indeed a Practice Direction[29] which stipulates that it is the duty of the clerk to refresh the memories of the bench as to matters of fact and also to advise them on the law and to discharge this obligation in open court if he is not requested by the magistrates to advise them privately.

The importance of compliance with this Practice Direction is illustrated by the cases. In *R. v. Eccles JJ., ex p. Fitzpatrick*[30] the Court quashed a decision to commit the defendant for sentence where the clerk had retired with the magistrates without being asked to do so. Further: it appears that where the issues are only factual, it is extremely unwise for a clerk to retire with the magistrates, even if they specifically request him to do so.[31] Where, however, the conduct of a clerk to the justices has, plainly, had no effect on the decision, judicial review is unlikely to lie.[32]

ERRORS OF FACT AND LAW COMPARED

10–005   Any error of law that materially affects the decision-making process is, in principle, reviewable. A great many of the judicial review cases that come before the courts, in relation to proceedings in magistrates' courts, involve misapprehension as to the relevant law. Examples of this have already been given in the context of the declining of jurisdiction.

Other instances of *ultra vires* decisions by justices include: a decision that because legal ownership of a car remained vested in a single leasing company the description "one owner" was incapable of being misleading, even though a car had been hired to five different companies[33]; a communication to a defendant that he was not entitled to apply to a criminal legal aid committee for a review of the magistrates' refusal to grant him legal aid[34]; the decision to commit for trial two defendants who had elected summary trial because the third defendant had elected trial on indictment.[35]

Where an error of law is established, few problems will be encountered in obtaining review of a particular decision. Errors of fact present more difficulty.

Traditionally, courts have been reluctant to examine alleged factual errors by way of judicial review.[36] Generally such errors will be reviewed only on a basis analogous to abuse of discretion, namely, that the evidence

---

[29] [1981] 1 W.L.R. 1163.
[30] (1989) 89 Cr.App.R. 324. See also: *R. v. Birmingham Magistrates' Court, ex p. Ahmed* [1994] C.O.D. 461.
[31] *R. v. Barry (Glamorgan) JJ., ex p. Nagi Kashim* [1953] 1 W.L.R. 1320 at p. 1323 *per* Sellers J. *Quaere*, whether the Practice Direction has altered the position.
[32] See, *e.g. R. v. Newbury JJ., ex p. Drake* [1993] C.O.D. 24.
[33] *R. v. South Western JJ., ex p. Wandsworth L.B.C.* (1983) 147 J.P. 212.
[34] *R. v. Bury JJ., ex p. N* [1987] 1 Q.B. 284.
[35] *R. v. Brentwood JJ., ex p. Nicholls* [1992] 1 A.C. 1.
[36] For an unusual exception, see *R. v. Stokesley Yorkshire JJ., ex p. Bartram* [1956] 1 W.L.R. 254.

does not reasonably support the decision or that no reasonable tribunal could have reached the same conclusion.[37]

In all cases it is important to determine the conceptual basis on which the application for judicial review is brought. A purported exercise of discretion may be a conventional error of law if not permitted by statute.[38] Similarly, the disregarding by justices of evidence is an error of law rather than one of fact where, for example, they wrongfully reject admissible evidence.[39] Conversely, it is an error of law to consider inadmissible hearsay evidence.[40] The division between errors of fact and of law is not always easy to discern.

THE JUDICIAL EXERCISE OF DISCRETION

Magistrates by the nature of their office are required to exercise their **10–006** discretion in a judicial manner.[41] Further, as an inferior body their decisions must fall within the constraints of the principles enunciated in *Associated Provincial Picture Houses Ltd v. Wednesbury Corp.*[42]

Thus, for example, in *R. v. Brigg JJ., ex p. Lynch*[43] a refusal of legal aid was quashed because of a failure to take into account a material consideration, namely the effect on the livelihood of the defendant of being convicted of indecent exposure. Similarly, an order forfeiting the entirety of a surety's recognisance was quashed because of a failure to enquire into his means.[44]

An illustration of irrelevant factors affecting the decision occurred in *R. v. Walsall JJ., ex p. W.*[45] It was essential to the prosecution case that the uncorroborated evidence of the victim should be admitted. However, the victim was a minor of insufficient understanding to take the oath. The magistrates decided to adjourn the case so that by the date of the next hearing section 34 of the Criminal Justice Act 1988 would be in force and the evidence would then be admissible. However, the Divisional Court held that this was unlawful because the impending change in the law was an irrelevant consideration.[46]

In an appropriate case, the High Court will infer a misdirection even without specific evidence to that effect.[47] Usually, however, a decision must

---

[37] See Wade and Forsyth, *Administrative Law* (7th ed. 1994), p. 312.
[38] There is, *e.g.* no discretion to hear cross-summonses together. See *R. v. Epsom JJ., ex p. Gibbons* [1984] Q.B. 574.
[39] *Re Racal Communications Ltd* [1981] A.C. 374.
[40] *R. v. Coventry JJ., ex p. Bullard* (1992) T.L.R. 74.
[41] *R. v. Clerkenwell Green Metropolitan Stipendiary Magistrate, ex p. Ibrahim* (1984) 148 J.P. 400.
[42] [1948] 1 K.B. 223. See also *R. v. Mansfield JJ., ex p. Sharkey* [1985] Q.B. 613.
[43] (1984) 148 J.P. 214.
[44] *R. v. Uxbridge JJ., ex p. Heward Mills* [1983] 1 W.L.R. 56. Applied in *R. v. Wood Green Crown Court, ex p. Howe* (1991) 93 Cr.App.R. 213.
[45] [1990] 1 Q.B. 253.
[46] See also *R. v. Redbridge JJ., ex p. Redbridge L.B.C. The Times*, November 4, 1982.
[47] *ibid.*

be manifestly unreasonable before the court will intervene in this way. In particular, even where it is established that justices have failed to take relevant matters into account, judicial review may be declined if the same order would have been made in any event.[48]

A decision may be wholly unreasonable in the *Wednesbury* sense, although there is no breach of relevancy. The residual criterion for review is that the decision may be challenged if no magistrates' court properly directing itself on the relevant law and acting reasonably could have reached it.

Decisions having no reasonable basis in fact are open to review in this way. So, also, are those decisions which stray outside discretionary limits whilst remaining within the technical ambit of statute. Thus, exceptionally, it is possible to challenge excessive sentences or costs orders made by justices by means of an application under Order 53.[49]

Challenging discretion: procedural considerations

10–007
Applicants seeking to attack, under the *Wednesbury* principle, a conviction or sentence should be particularly careful to explore the possibility of an appeal instead of (or before) proceedings for judicial review.

In many instances, case stated may be preferable to Order 53 (see below). Alternatively, an appeal to the Crown Court against conviction may be more desirable where the evidence supporting a conviction is weak but where it cannot be said that there is no basis in fact for the conviction. In the context of sentences, other than those that are "truly astonishing",[50] it has been held that complaint against an excessive sentence should be made to the Crown Court on appeal and, thereafter, to a Divisional Court under Order 53 if the sentence is not reduced on appeal.[51]

PROCEDURAL FAIRNESS IN THE MAGISTRATES' COURT

10–008
It has already been shown that procedural fairness is an aspect of natural justice. As a judicial tribunal, magistrates are required to observe a higher standard of procedural fairness than quasi-judicial bodies like local authorities.

The rule *audi alteram partem* is, perhaps, easier to state than to apply. In the words of Roskill L.J.:

"it is impossible to lay down general rules applicable to every case which may arise but if justices ask themselves, before finally ruling, the

---

[48] *R. v. Mansfield JJ., ex p. Sharkey* [1985] Q.B. 613.

[49] See, *e.g. R. v. Tottenham JJ., ex p. Dwarkados Joshi* [1982] 1 W.L.R. 631 (excessive costs order). On sentencing see, *e.g. R. v. St Albans Crown Court, ex p. Cinnamond* [1981] Q.B. 480; *R. v. Highbury Corner JJ., ex p. Uchendu The Times,* January 28, 1994; *R. v. Tamworth JJ., ex p. Walsh The Times,* March 3, 1994.

[50] See, *e.g. R. v. Croydon Crown Court, ex p. Miller* (1986, unrep.) February 5; *R. v. Chelmsford Crown Court, ex p. Birchall* (1990) C.O.D. 200.

[51] See *R. v. Battle JJ., ex p. Shepherd* (1983) 5 Cr.App.R.(S) 124.

single question what is the fairest thing to do in all the circumstances in the interests of everyone concerned?—they are unlikely to err in their conclusion, for the aim of the judicial process is to secure a fair trial and rules of practice and procedure are designed to that end and not otherwise".[52]

Procedural fairness, in essence, necessitates that both the accused and the prosecution be given a fair opportunity to present their case.[53] This is exemplified under a number of different subject headings considered below.

Notice

A defendant is entitled to notice of allegations. Thus, in one case, defendants who were bound over to be of good behaviour without being informed of the reason, successfully applied to the Divisional Court to have those orders quashed.[54]

10–009

Before the hearing itself, the defendant will be informed of the date, time and place by (usually) service of a summons. Service may be effected personally or by post to the defendant's last known or usual address.[55] Without personal service justices should, with limited exceptions,[56] ensure that a summons has actually come to the accused's notice.

There is a discretion to proceed in the defendant's absence if he does not appear after being properly served.[57] Such discretion must, however, be carefully exercised, or judicial review may lie. Where the defendant informed the court that he intended to plead not guilty, it was held to be incumbent on the magistrates to satisfy themselves that notice of an adjourned hearing had actually been received, as opposed to the mere fact of such notice having been sent.[58]

Notice is also ordinarily required before any judicial order is pronounced against the defendant. This requirement applies (despite earlier incorrect decisions) to a warrant of commitment issued in respect of unpaid fines.[59] In *R. v. Faversham and Sittingbourne JJ., ex p. Ursell*[60] the High Court applied *R. v. Poole JJ., ex p. Fleet*[61] and held that a defendant whom justices

---

[52] *Re Clayton* [1983] 2 A.C. 473, at p. 565.
[53] *R. v. Cook* [1959] 2 Q.B. 340, *per* Devlin J. at p. 348.
[54] *R. v. South Molton JJ., ex p. Ankerson* [1989] 1 W.L.R. 40.
[55] See Family Proceedings Rules 1991, r. 3.1.
[56] It will, however, suffice if—in respect of a summary offence—the summons was sent by registered letter or recorded delivery.
[57] See s.11(1) M.C.A. 1980.
[58] *R. v. Seisdon JJ., ex p. Dougan* [1982] 1 W.L.R. 1476. This case is also of interest because of ' the decision to grant a declaration instead of another remedy because the original decision was a nullity.
[59] See *Re Wilson* [1985] A.C. 750, overruling *R. v. Chichester JJ., ex p. Collins* [1982] 1 W.L.R. 334 and *R. v. Clerkenwell Stipendiary Magistrate, ex p. Mays* [1975] 1 W.L.R. 52.
[60] [1992] T.L.R. 125.
[61] [1983] 1 W.L.R. 974.

intended to commit to prison for non-payment of community charge was entitled to have notice of the subsequent committal hearing itself, notwithstanding that he had had notice of the original hearing but had failed to attend.

During the course of the hearing the defendant or his advisers are entitled to notice of all legal matters which might be decided against him.[62]

Applications for adjournments

10–010   It is a fundamental principle of natural justice that a party must be given a reasonable opportunity to prepare his case.[63] Fairness is owed to both prosecution and defence.[64]

Not infrequently, applications are made for adjournments on the basis that one side is not ready to proceed. In deciding whether to grant an adjournment, the justices must exercise their discretion in a judicial manner. Provided that they do so, it is unlikely that the Divisional Court will intervene.

Justices are not entitled to punish the prosecution for delays or inefficiency by dismissing the information. Thus, in *R. v. Sutton JJ., ex p. D.P.P.*[65] a decision peremptorily to dismiss an information because prosecuting counsel was twenty minutes late arriving, when the Court had been informed that counsel would be late, was declared unlawful.

Different considerations may apply where witnesses are unavailable. In *R. v. Grays JJ., ex p. Ward,*[66] the defendant requested an adjournment to enable an expert witness to attend. His application was refused. The Divisional Court held that the refusal of the application was not, *per se,* a breach of natural justice. The impossibility of calling a witness without adjournment was not strictly relevant. The essential question was whether the justices had allowed the applicant a reasonable opportunity to present his case. If such reasonable opportunity has been provided, a decision not to grant an adjournment will not be disturbed.[67] In determining the reasonableness of the opportunity provided, the justices ought properly to enquire into the readiness of the party's case absent that witness.[68]

In *Re Harrington*[69] the prosecution sought an adjournment because one of their witnesses was on holiday. The magistrates were minded to adjourn the case to a date when the witness could attend, but the defence objected. In the light of those objections, the justices dismissed the case without

[62] *D. Ackerman & Sons Ltd v. North Tyneside Metropolitan B.C.* (1991) T.L.R. 377.
[63] See, *e.g. R. v. Thames M.C., ex p. Polemis* [1974] 1 W.L.R. 1371.
[64] *R. v. Birmingham JJ., ex p. Lamb* [1983] 1 W.L.R. 339.
[65] [1992] 2 All E.R. 129. But see now *R. v. Hendon Justices, ex p. D.P.P.* (1992) T.L.R. 349 as to the appropriate remedy.
[66] *The Times,* May 5, 1982.
[67] See, *e.g. Taylor v. Baird & Watters* [1983] Crim.L.R. 551.
[68] *R. v. Guildhall JJ., ex p. Carson-Selman* (1984) 148 J.P. 392.
[69] [1984] A.C. 743.

giving the prosecution an opportunity to proceed on the available evidence. The House of Lords held that not only was this a violation of natural justice, it also constituted a declining of jurisdiction, thereby rendering the decision a nullity. So, too, where justices depart from an established previous practice, so as to "ambush" the prosecution by refusing an adjournment, such decision will be a nullity.[70]

Where the defendant himself is absent through illness and provides medical evidence to support his application, it will rarely be reasonable for justices to refuse an adjournment.[71]

Difficulties with adjournments have arisen, increasingly, because of the introduction of custody time limits. There is now a substantial body of case law setting out the principles upon which justices (or, as appropriate, the Crown Court), may extend the operation of custody time limits if "good and sufficient cause" is shown.[72]

Legal representation

A defendant has no absolute right to be legally represented. If he wishes to be represented he must pay for such representation himself or seek legal aid. If magistrates refuse legal aid he may usually appeal to the legal aid committee. Ultimately, if there is error of law or unfairness in refusal of legal aid, he will have to utilise the Order 53 procedure.　　**10–011**

The only method by which a refusal to grant legal aid can be challenged is if the decision offends against any of the *Wednesbury* principles, *e.g.* by arriving at a decision which is manifestly unreasonable,[73] or by disregarding material considerations.[74]

It is now clear that a defendant is entitled to either the assistance of the magistrates' clerk, or the help of a *McKenzie* friend. In *R. v. Leicester City JJ., ex p. Barrow*[75] justices refused to allow a defendant, appearing before them for non-payment of community charge, the assistance of a *McKenzie*[76] friend. The Court of Appeal held that this was a breach of natural justice and that justices would only be entitled to exercise their discretion so as to deprive a defendant of the in court assistance of a third party in exceptional circumstances.[77] A fortiori, a refusal to hear a party's advocate will almost inevitably give rise to a breach of natural justice.

Nevertheless, there are occasions where a defendant will, due to the

---

[70] *R. v. Bromley JJ., ex p. D.P.P.* (January 25 1993; unrep.) (CO/1156/92).
[71] See *R. v. Bolton JJ., ex p. Merna* (1991) T.L.R. 210.
[72] Of the many cases see, especially, *R. v. Sheffield JJ., ex p. Turner* [1991] 2 Q.B. 472; *R. v. Southampton Crown Court, ex p. Roddie* [1991] 1 W.L.R. 303; *R. v. Luton Crown Court, ex p. Neaves* (1992) C.O.D. 438; *R. v. Norwich Crown Court, ex p. Stiller* (1992) 4 Admin.L.R. 709; *R. v. Norwich Crown Court, ex p. Cox* (1993) C.O.D. 102; *R. v. Maidstone Crown Court, ex p. Schulz and Another* [1993] C.O.D. 182; *R. v. Leeds Crown Court, ex p. Quirk and Khan* (1994) C.O.D. 287; *R. v. Central Criminal Court, ex p. Behbehani* [1994] C.O.D. 193.
[73] *R. v. Highgate JJ., ex p. Lewis* [1977] Crim.L.R. 611.
[74] As in *R. v. Brigg JJ., ex p. Lynch* (1984) 148 J.P. 214.
[75] [1991] 2 Q.B. 260.
[76] After the decision in *McKenzie v. McKenzie* [1971] P. 33.
[77] *e.g.* where that third party sought to disrupt the proceedings.

pressure of circumstance, be denied the opportunity to seek legal advice. In
R. v. Newbury JJ., ex p. Pont,[78] a serious disturbance in the face of the court
which prevented the court from continuing its proceedings was held to
entitle magistrates to make immediate committal orders against the
offending defendants. However, May L.J. observed that in future cases it
was desirable, if legal advice was immediately to hand, to allow defendants
a brief opportunity to avail themselves of that advice.[79]

The hearing

10–012   Anything that restricts, or appears to restrict, a defendant's ability to
present his case may be held to be a breach of procedural fairness and,
thereby, susceptible to judicial review.

In this context, appearance is as important as reality. In *R. v.
Weston-super-Mare JJ., ex p. Taylor*[80] one of the magistrates closed her eyes
and looked down, giving the defendant's solicitor the impression that she
was unwell. On an application under Order 53, it was held that she ought to
have withdrawn; the decision was quashed. Similarly, failure to comply
with procedure is usually reviewable even though a defendant may not have
been misled by non-compliance.[81] Those cases where the clerk retires with
the justices may, in fact, not result in improper advice being given; they are,
nonetheless, undesirable because of the difficulty in determining precisely
what advice was given.

As a court of law, the justices must usually hear cases in open court unless
they are empowered to hear them *in camera*.[82] They should not take
evidence privately,[83] nor is there any discretion to exclude admissible
evidence.[84] Juvenile court cases demand particular adherence to considerations of natural justice. In *R. v. Southwark Juvenile Court, ex p. J.*[85] judicial
review was obtained where a social worker who might have assisted the
juvenile was kept out of court.

A defendant is generally entitled to notice of evidence that might assist
his case. It is, therefore, a breach of natural justice for the prosecution to
conceal such evidence.[86] The prosecution is also obliged to notify the
defence if there is objection to written evidence such as a medical
certificate, so that the defendant has the opportunity to call supporting oral
evidence.[87]

---

[78] (1984) 78 Cr.App.R. 255.
[79] See also: *R. v. Tamworth Magistrates' Court, ex p. Walsh* [1994] C.O.D. 277, (*held*: solicitor
who criticised listing practice ought to have been given an opportunity to obtain advice and
representation before justices decided issue of contempt).
[80] [1981] Crim.L.R. 179.
[81] See, *e.g. R. v. Kent JJ., ex p. Machin* [1952] 2 Q.B. 355.
[82] Further, as a matter of general policy justices should be slow to impose reporting restrictions
over and above those contained in M.C.A. 1980, s.8.
[83] *R. v. Aberdare JJ., ex p. Hones* [1973] Crim.L.R. 45.
[84] See, *e.g. R. v. Highbury Corner M.C., ex p. Boyce* (1984) 79 Cr.App.R. 132.
[85] [1973] 1 W.L.R. 1300.
[86] *R. v. Leyland JJ., ex p. Hawthorn* [1979] Q.B. 283.
[87] *R. v. King's Lynn JJ., ex p. Whitelam, The Times*, June 23, 1982.

It is impossible to categorise all potential instances of procedural unfairness that may occur in the course of a hearing. Provided that justices observe the correct procedures and behave fairly, it will, in practice, be difficult to challenge their decision. In *Re Clayton*,[88] it was held that even though there was an irregularity in adjudicating on several informations in the absence of consent, judicial review would not lie if it was "fair and just" to try them together.

Natural justice and the adjudicative process

Any order made by the justices is subject to the requirements of natural justice. When, for example, binding over to be of good behaviour, it is a breach of natural justice to make such order for anything other than a trivial sum without looking at the defendant's means and allowing him to make representations as to the amount of the recognisance.[89] It has already been observed that most judicial orders are subject to the proviso that there should be prior notice to the defendant and the opportunity to be heard.

10–013

The determination of applications for bail is an area where judicial review is frequently sought on the basis of alleged disregard of natural justice.

Although justices have an obligation to consider granting an application for bail on each occasion it is made,[90] they need not reconsider matters previously fully argued before a bench of justices unless there has been an intervening change of circumstances.[91] It follows that they must investigate an alleged change of circumstances[92] and it may even be that the defendant is—if committed to the Crown Court for trial—entitled to a full review of his bail conditions.[93]

Justices must not attempt to avoid determining an alleged breach of bail by adjourning the case. Even a single justice must hear the matter and once he has started to do so, he may not adjourn.[94]

Protection against bias

Judicial review is available to protect against the real danger of bias in justices' decision making. This seems now to be the appropriate test, having regard to the House of Lords' decision in *R. v. Gough*.[95]

10–014

Applying that principle, bias can take a great many forms. Certainly any direct pecuniary interest in the result will disqualify a magistrate from hearing the case. In *R. v. Altrincham JJ., ex p. Pennington*[96] Lord Widgery

---

[88] [1983] 2 A.C. 473.
[89] *R. v. Central Criminal Court, ex p. Boulding* [1984] Q.B. 813.
[90] See s.4 Bail Act 1976.
[91] *R. v. Nottingham JJ., ex p. Davies* [1981] 1 Q.B. 38; *R. v. Slough JJ., ex p. Duncan* (1982) 75 Cr.App.R. 84.
[92] See *Re Moles* (1981) Crim.L.R. 170. *cf. R. v. Slough JJ., ex p. Duncan* (1982) 75 Cr.App.R. 84.
[93] *R. v. Slough JJ., ex p. Duncan* (1982) 75 Cr.App.R. 84.
[94] *R. v. Liverpool City JJ., ex p. D.P.P.* [1992] 3 W.L.R. 20.
[95] [1993] A.C. 646. For analysis of this decision, see para. 2–018.
[96] [1975] Q.B. 549, at p. 552.

C.J. observed that "for a justice to adjudicate on a matter in which he has a pecuniary or proprietary interest is often a serious dereliction of duty". It may be that if a pecuniary interest is established it is not even necessary to prove a reasonable suspicion of bias.[97]

Some personal interest in the outcome will also vitiate any decision reached on the above basis. In *R. v. Sussex JJ., ex p. McCarthy*[98] a conviction was quashed where the justices' clerk was a member of the same firm of solicitors who were to represent the plaintiff in a civil claim for damages for personal injuries arising out of an accident in respect of which the defendant had been charged with a motoring offence before the court. Personal interest is evidenced not merely by some form of commercial relationship between adjudicator and other interested party, as in *McCarthy*'s case,[99] but also by other non-profitable types of association such as personal friendship,[1] or membership of an education committee.[2]

Decisions are particularly susceptible to the allegation of potential bias where the decision-maker is, in some way, connected with the prosecution. This occurred in *R. v. Pwlheli JJ., ex p. Soane*,[3] where a member of the board of salmon conservators was prevented from sitting on a prosecution that he had personally authorised. Generally, a justice cannot sit in the Crown Court on appeal from his own decision.[4]

Bias can occur in a quite different way by a case being pre-judged.[5] At the very least this is an unlawful fettering of discretion or bad faith on *Wednesbury* principles. The cause of the pre-judging may, however, also indicate bias. A magistrate can indicate an initial strong view, provided he is seen to keep an open mind.[6]

It is, however, crucial that magistrates are even-handed. Thus, in *R. v. Farnham JJ., ex p. Gibson*[7] a policy of not permitting a defendant to give evidence from the witness box like other witnesses, but instead insisting that he gave evidence from the dock, was held to be unlawful. Similarly the production of a list for the express purpose of revealing all pending matters against a defendant was held to be unlawful.[8] Conversely, in *R. v. Weston-super-Mare JJ., ex p. Shaw*[9] the mere fact that justices had before them the day's list of cases, which revealed that the defendant was to appear

---

[97] See, *e.g. R. v. Rand* [1866] L.R. 1 Q.B. 230.

[98] [1924] 1 K.B. 256.

[99] Of course the clerk did not actually decide the case, but he did retire with the magistrates and this gave rise to the suspicion of bias.

[1] See *Cottle v. Cottle* [1939] 2 All E.R. 535.

[2] As in *R. v. Altrincham JJ., ex p. Pennington* [1975] Q.B. 549.

[3] [1948] 2 All E.R. 815.

[4] See r. 5 of the Crown Court Rules 1982. *R. v. Bristol Crown Court, ex p. Cooper* [1990] 1 W.L.R. 1031, is a very limited exception to this principle.

[5] See, *e.g. R. v. Downham Market Magistrates' Court, ex p. Nudd* [1989] R.T.R. 169.

[6] This is essentially the difference between *ex p. Wilder* (1902) 66 J.P. 761 and *R. v. Halifax JJ., ex p. Robinson* (1912) 76 J.P. 233.

[7] [1991] R.T.R. 309.

[8] *R. v. Liverpool City JJ., ex p. Topping* [1983] 1 W.L.R. 119.

[9] [1987] 1 Q.B. 640.

on several matters throughout the day, was held not to create the impression of bias.

An application under Order 53 may be refused if the applicant knew of the risk of bias and made no objection.[10] When applying for judicial review the applicant should, if the issue is raised, state in his affidavit in support of the application that he was, at the material time, unaware of any disqualification on the part of the justices, or their clerk.[11]

Statutory disqualification

Section 64 of the Justices of the Peace Act 1979 provides that justices who are members of local authorities may not adjudicate in any proceedings brought by or against, or by way of appeal from a decision of, their authority.[12] Other statutory provisions seek to prevent justices from dealing with alleged offences under the Factories Act 1961 where they are connected with the factory concerned,[13] or dealing with the defendant on summary trial if, in the course of determining whether bail ought to be granted, they have been informed that the defendant has one or more previous convictions.[14]

Thus, applicants seeking judicial review should examine statutes with care. Firstly, to determine whether there is a section disqualifying certain justices. Secondly, to establish that there are no provisions excluding the possibility of disqualification,[15] or preserving the validity of the decision notwithstanding disqualification.[16]

10–015

JUDICIAL REVIEW OF ACQUITTALS

Judicial review of an acquittal will not lie where there is a risk of double jeopardy.[17] However, the Divisional Court has held, following *Re Harrington*,[18] that where a magistrate's decision can properly be categorised as a nullity (and, therefore, no decision) not only will certiorari go to quash the acquittal, but, additionally, mandamus will issue to compel a new trial.[19]

10–016

---

[10] *R. v. Nailsworth Licensing JJ., ex p. Bird* [1953] 1 W.L.R. 1046.

[11] *R. v. Swansea JJ.* (1913) 49 L.J.N. 10.

[12] *i.e.* including a committee or officer of the authority. *cf. R. v. Cambourne JJ., ex p. Pearce* [1955] 1 Q.B. 41.

[13] s.164(7) thereof.

[14] See s.42, M.C.A. 1980.

[15] See, *e.g.* s.65 of the Justices of the Peace Act 1979.

[16] *ibid.* s.64(5).

[17] *i.e.* a defendant should not be put in peril of conviction for the same offence twice.

[18] [1984] A.C. 743.

[19] See *R. v. Hendon JJ., ex p. D.P.P.* (1992) T.L.R. 349, not following *R. v. Sutton JJ., ex p. D.P.P.* [1992] 2 All E.R. 129.

The difficulty that this approach causes is that it may, at least in theory, require an analysis of degrees of nullity of the justices' decision.

JUDICIAL REVIEW OF COMMITTAL PROCEEDINGS

10–017   Where there is a clear excess of jurisdiction, judicial review will lie in respect of committal proceedings.[20] In general, however, the High Court is reluctant to interfere where there is merely a technical irregularity and the prejudice thereby caused could be remedied at trial.[21]

This reluctance is particularly marked when the committal proceedings themselves have not been concluded. Thus, in *R v. Wells Street Stipendiary Magistrates, ex p. Seillon*,[22] mandamus was refused where a magistrate had refused to permit a particular line of cross-examination of prosecution witnesses to proceed. Similarly in *R. v. Horsham JJ., ex p. Bukhari*,[23] prohibition, to restrain the admission of allegedly inadmissible evidence during committal proceedings, was refused.

Although natural justice must be adhered to during a committal[24] it appears that such proceedings are not vitiated by the admission of inadmissible evidence,[25] nor by the exclusion of admissible evidence.[26]

Where a previous acquittal is a nullity, there is nothing to prevent justices committing the defendant for trial in respect of the same alleged offence.[27] Similarly, the discharging of a defendant, after hearing committal proceedings as examining magistrates under section 6 of the Magistrates' Courts Act 1980 is not an acquittal so that fresh proceedings may be instituted. Prohibition, however, may issue if there are repeated committals in relation to the same alleged offences.[28]

THE SELECTIVE USE OF ORDER 53

10–018   Order 53 should not be used indiscriminately in seeking to challenge decisions of, or matters arising for decision by, justices. There follows a

---

[20] See, *e.g. R. v. Miall* [1992] Q.B. 836.

[21] This is to be distinguished from: (a) judicial review proceedings to stay committal proceedings on the ground of abuse of process, where judicial review is available on established principles; and (b) judicial review of a committal for sentence, where there is an unfettered discretion to commit for sentence at any moment up to committal; see, *e.g. R. v. Dover Magistrates' Court, ex p. Pamment* [1994] C.O.D. 292; *R. v. Doncaster Magistrates' Court, ex p. Goulding* [1993] 1 All E.R. 435.

[22] [1978] 1 W.L.R. 1002.

[23] (1982) 74 Cr.App.R. 291.

[24] See, *e.g. R. v. Witham JJ., ex p. Beck* (1979) 76 L.S.Gaz. 101; *R. v. Coleshill JJ., ex p. Davies* [1971] 1 W.L.R. 1684.

[25] *R. v. Norfolk Quarter Sessions, ex p. Brunson* [1953] 1 Q.B. 50.

[26] *R. v. Highbury Corner M.C., ex p. Boyce* (1984) 79 Cr.App.R. 132.

[27] *R. v. West* [1964] 1 Q.B. 15.

[28] *R. v. Horsham JJ., ex p. Reeves* [1981] Crim.L.R. 566; *R. v. Manchester City Stipendiary Magistrate, ex p. Snelson* [1977] 1 W.L.R. 911.

summary of various problems that may arise, together with an evaluation of the appropriate remedy in each case.

Excessive sentencing

The proper course is to appeal against the sentence to the Crown Court. Only if the Crown Court upholds the sentence below should an Order 53 application be made.[29] *Likely order:* certiorari.

Conviction in breach of natural justice

An appeal, by way of rehearing, lies to the Crown Court and such an appeal should probably be pursued first as an alternative remedy.[30] Case stated does not appear to lie.[31] *Likely order:* certiorari.[32]

Conviction: alleged error of jurisdiction

There is the possibility of an appeal to the Crown Court or case stated to the Divisional Court. Generally, case stated should be used where there is a dispute as to the facts.[33] Judicial review may, nonetheless, be used and should be used where a misunderstanding of the tribunal's functions is alleged.[34] *Likely order:* certiorari.[35]

Conviction: against the weight of the evidence

An appeal to the Crown Court on merits is usually the only available remedy.

Refusal to exercise jurisdiction

Theoretically, both case stated and judicial review are available, but the Court appears to consider case stated the preferable route.[36] *Likely order:* mandamus.

Prospective or continuing error of jurisdiction

Usually the appropriate remedy will be judicial review. *Likely order:* prohibition.[37]

---

[29] See *R. v. Battle JJ., ex p. Shepherd* (1983) 5 Cr.App.R.(S) 124.

[30] See Lewis *Judicial Remedies in Public Law*, at p. 231.

[31] See, *e.g. R. v. Wandsworth JJ., ex p. Read* [1942] 1 K.B. 281; *Rigby v. Woodward* [1957] 1 All E.R. 391.

[32] See, *e.g. R. v. Marylebone JJ., ex p. Farrag* [1981] Crim.L.R. 182 (certiorari lay to quash the decision of justices reached without hearing the defendant's closing speech).

[33] *R. v. Felixstowe JJ., ex p. Baldwin* (1981) 72 Cr.App.R. 131.

[34] *R. v. Chief Commons Commissioner, ex p. Winnington, The Times,* November 26, 1982.

[35] *R. v. Kent JJ., ex p. Machin* [1952] 2 Q.B. 355.

[36] *R. v. Clerkenwell Metropolitan Stipendiary Magistrate, ex p. Director of Public Prosecutions* [1984] Q.B. 821.

[37] See, *e.g. R. v. Hatfield, JJ., ex p. Castle* [1981] 1 W.L.R. 217.

Committal proceedings

Judicial review is the sole remedy available.[38] Depending on the facts, all the relief available under Order 53 is potentially available.

Dismissal of charges

Case stated is the usual remedy but, exceptionally, judicial review may be used.[39]

COLLATERAL CHALLENGE

10–019   It is, generally, wise to challenge alleged misuse of public powers directly and as soon as possible by judicial review. The extent to which a defendant may protect himself by alleging the invalidity of a public law decision is increasingly uncertain.

In *R. v. Reading Crown Court, ex p. Hutchinson*[40] the Court held that magistrates had jurisdiction to determine the validity of byelaws. However, in *Bugg v. Director of Public Prosecutions*,[41] it was held that an inferior criminal court could only determine substantive as opposed to procedural invalidity, and that Order 53 lay exclusively to determine the latter. Similarly, in *R. v. Bristol City Magistrates' Court, ex p. Willsman*[42] it was held that a failure by a local authority to pay the defendant benefit, did not entitle the defendant to raise that public law failure as a defence in non-payment of community charge proceedings before justices. The Court held that he must proceed by way of Order 53 to mount such a challenge.[43]

Thus, in the interests of avoiding any difficulties, whenever a bona fide public law issue is raised, it will nearly always be preferable for justices to adjourn proceeding to enable an application for judicial review to be made.

---

[38] See, *e.g. Atkinson v. U.S. Government* [1971] A.C. 197.
[39] See *R. v. Stipendiary Magistrates, ex p. Director of the Serious Fraud Office* [1994] C.O.D. 509.
[40] [1988] 1 Q.B. 384.
[41] [1993] Q.B. 473.
[42] (1992) 156 J.P. 409.
[43] For further analysis, see para. 6–004.

11. IMMIGRATION AND DEPORTATION DECISIONS

THE RELATIONSHIP WITH ORDER 53

The precise relationship between immigration law as laid down by statute **11–001** and delegated legislation and applications under Order 53 is based on three factors: first, the statutory context in which immigration decisions are made; secondly, the nature and extent of the appellate system laid down by Parliament; thirdly, the extent to which judicial review lies where an applicant has not exercised all his statutory rights of appeal.

AN OUTLINE OF THE LEGISLATION

Where a person has a right of abode in the United Kingdom, citizenship **11–002** is conferred upon him[1] and immigration controls do not apply. There are further provisions governing citizenship of the E.C. and the Republic of Ireland.[2]

The immigration of a non-British citizen is regulated by four statutes: the Immigration Act 1971, the British Nationality Act 1981, the Immigration Act 1988 and the Asylum and Immigration Appeals Act 1993. Those acts are intended (when read with the Immigration Rules)[3] to form a comprehensive code governing entry into the United Kingdom.[4] However, the Secretary of State possesses a residual discretion to depart from the rules and to authorise an immigration officer to do so.[5] This discretion has particular importance in the context of judicial review.[6]

---

[1] See British Nationality Act 1981, B.N.A. ss.1–14.
[2] E.C. citizens are permitted to enter and leave the U.K. to the extent permitted by Articles 48–52 of the Treaty of Rome; the Republic of Ireland is located within the Common Travel Area and travel within that area is not subject to immigration control: ss.1(3), 11 I.A. 1971.
[3] s.3(2) I.A. 1971 provides for the passing of delegated legislation. The legislation takes the form of House of Commons papers laying out the rules which govern immigration decision. The current rules are set out in House of Commons paper H.C. 395 which has effect to all decisions made after October 1, 1994, save insofar as those decisions relate to applications made prior to October 1, 1994. It replaces H.C. 251, the previous statement of the rules.
[4] *R. v. Secretary of State for the Home Department, ex p. Thrakar* [1974] Q.B. 684.
[5] *R. v. Secretary of State for the Home Department, ex p. Rajinder Kaur* [1987] Imm.A.R. 278 DC.
[6] See below.

IMMIGRATION RULES

11–003   The rules only come into existence pursuant to the 1971 and 1988 Acts. These dictate both content and form.

As to content: the rules must make provision for the admission both of persons coming to study, and those coming to take up employment, as visitors and as dependants.[7] However, any provisions governing the entry of such people need not be consistent.[8]

As to form: any rules passed must be *intra vires* the statute. Therefore, judicial review has been applied to particular rules on the basis that they were unreasonable, since their application depended on the class of persons to which they were being applied and as such were unjust and/or involved oppressive and gratuitous interference with the rights of the subject.[9] The mere fact, though, that the rules envisage that E.C. citizens are to be treated differently from non-E.C. citizens does not make them inconsistent and amenable to judicial review.[10]

In theory judicial review would lie if the rules unlawfully fettered the discretion of immigration officers. That argument has been strengthened by the mandatory wording introduced by H.C. 395, replacing the more permissive language of H.C. 251. In two cases on H.C. 251,[11] however, the contention that rules, which required the immigration officer automatically to refuse leave to entrants who did not possess a visa or entry clearance, were an unlawful fetter on the officer's discretion, failed.

The Rules's status in law is ambiguous. Section 19(1)(a)(i) of the Immigration Act 1971 requires an adjudicator to allow an appeal if the rules have been breached. This suggests a potential status as rules of law or delegated legislation.

Although there are dicta to this effect,[12] it is submitted that this view is incorrect, for two reasons. First, several decisions indicate that the Rules are not to be construed as strictly as statute[13] and are to be given a purposive rather than a strict construction.[14] Secondly, the rules are by no means comprehensive.

There are situations which they do not cover. In such circumstances the appellate body is entitled to substitute its own discretion for that of the decision-maker.[15] Further, the power to make immigration decisions arises

---

[7] s.1(4) I.A.

[8] s.3(2) I.A.

[9] See *Kruse v. Johnson* [1898] 2 Q.B. 91; *R. v. IAT, ex p. Manshoora Begum* [1986] Imm.A.R. 385.

[10] *R. v. IAT, ex p. Sheikh Al-Sabah* [1992] Imm.A.R. 25.

[11] *R. v. Secretary of State for the Home Department, ex p. Rajinder Kaur* [1987] Imm.A.R. 278; *R. v. Secretary of State for the Home Department, ex p. Hassan* [1989] Imm.A.R. 75.

[12] See *R. v. Chief Immigration Officer, Heathrow Airport, ex p. Salamat Bibi* [1976] 1 W.L.R. 979 at 985 *per* Roskill L.J.

[13] See *Pearson v. IAT* [1978] Imm.A.R. 212.

[14] *Singh v. IAT* [1986] 1 W.L.R. 910, [1986] Imm.A.R. 352; *R. v. IAT, ex p. Rahman* 1987 Imm.A.R. 313; *Gurdev Singh v. IAT* [1988] Imm.A.R. 510.

[15] See *ex p. Prajapati* (November 12, 1981, unrep.); *R. v. IAT, ex p. Wirdestedt* [1990] Imm.A.R. 20; *Rahman* [1989] Imm.A.R. 325; *Somasundaram* [1990] Imm.A.R. 16.

from the Act, not the Rules. Therefore a residual statutory discretion will always exist.[16] Finally, in several cases the rules operate merely as guidance under which the decision-maker can exercise his discretion.[17] In such cases, the appellate body can review the exercise of the discretion by the immigration officer and decide whether such discretion should have been exercised differently.[18] All these factors suggest that the Rules are not to be viewed as a strict statutory code.

APPLICATION OF THE LEGISLATION

The non-British citizen ("the entrant") can only enter the United Kingdom with leave.[19] Leave may be granted for either a finite or an indefinite period.[20] The decision whether to grant leave to enter is conferred on the immigration officer concerned.[21] Once leave is granted, the terms of that leave can be varied by adding or removing limitations upon it. The relevant decisions in such cases may only be made by the Secretary of State for the Home Department. A distinction is therefore drawn between leave decisions, which are delegable, and decisions made *after* leave to enter is granted, which are not.

11–004

However, there are three provisos to the delegated decision-making structure. First, an entrant seeking political asylum must, if the application is made at a United Kingdom port, have his case referred to the Home Secretary at the leave to enter stage for consideration. The Home Secretary is then bound to consider the case in the light of the provisions of the United Nations Convention concerning the Status of Refugees.[22] The Home Secretary's decision binds the immigration officer and no steps can be taken until that decision has been reached.[23] The entrant must show that he is a refugee within the meaning of Article 1 of the Geneva Convention of 1951 relating to the status of refugees as amended by the 1967 Protocol.[24] Secondly, although deportation decisions[25] which are made after leave has been granted must be taken by the Home Secretary, a court sentencing a non-British citizen for an offence punishable with imprisonment can make recommendations that the defendant be deported.[26] Thirdly, different considerations apply where it is alleged that the entrant unlawfully entered the United Kingdom.[27]

---

[16] Therefore the Rules do not operate to fetter the exercise of this extra-statutory discretion.
[17] See *R. v. Secretary of State for the Home Department, ex p. Hosenball* [1977] 1 W.L.R. 776 CA.
[18] s.19(1)(a)(ii) I.A.
[19] s.3(1)(a) I.A. 1971, as amended by B.N.A. 1981 Sched. 4, para. 2.
[20] s.3(1)(b) I.A. 1971.
[21] s.4 I.A. 1971.
[22] H.C. 395 paras. 327–352.
[23] Paras. 329–330 H.C. 395.
[24] For a detailed discussion of the scope and application of the test, see Macdonald and Blake *Immigration Law and Practice* (3rd ed., 1991) pp. 290 ff.
[25] See below for an examination of the nature and scope of deportation decisions.
[26] ss.5, 6 I.A. 1971.
[27] s.33(1) I.A. 1971.

APPEALS FROM IMMIGRATION DECISIONS

11–005   The Asylum and Immigration Appeals Act 1993 drastically altered the appellate structure. A distinction was drawn between the "fast track" appeals process applicable to asylum applications, and all other cases.

In non-asylum cases, the right to appeal has been curtailed. There can be no appeal by a visitor, a student intending to study for less than six months or a student who has not been accepted for a course of study and their dependants where entry clearance has not been given, against refusal of leave to enter the United Kingdom.[28] Further, a person cannot appeal against a refusal to grant entry clearance or to vary leave if the refusal is on the grounds that the person does not hold a relevant document (including an entry clearance, passport or work permit) or the person fails to meet a mandatory requirement of the Immigration rules, or the period of time for which the person seeks entry is greater than that permitted under the rules.[29]

Where the above do not apply, the entrant can appeal against: conditions imposed on entry or leave to remain in the United Kingdom,[30] deportation decision (whether to make, or refusing to revoke, a deportation order),[31] removal directions[32] and directions for removal to a particular country.[33]

An appeal will lie at first instance, usually, to an adjudicator appointed by the Lord Chancellor.[34] Appeals from adjudicator's decisions are heard by the Immigration Appeal Tribunal (I.A.T.) also appointed by the Lord Chancellor. Where the I.A.T. has made a final determination[35] in any appeal, an appeal will lie on a matter of law to the Court of Appeal if leave is given. In cases where there is no final determination but the I.A.T.'s decision is open to challenge, judicial review would arguably lie.

In leave to enter cases, provided that the exclusions set out in sections 10 and 11 of the Asylum and Immigration Appeals Act do not apply, three categories of appeal exist, namely those against: (i) refusal of leave to enter, (ii) refusal to grant an entry clearance certificate and (iii) the decision that leave to enter is required.

In the first category, once leave to enter has been refused, it is usual for directions for the entrant's removal to apply.[36] The entrant can only appeal against those directions where he was refused leave to enter at a port whilst holding a current entry clearance or work permit.[37] If that appeal process is

---

[28] s.13 I.A. as amended by s.10 Asylum and Immigration Appeals Act 1993.

[29] s.13 I.A. as amended by s.11 Asylum and Immigration Appeals Act 1993.

[30] s.14 I.A.

[31] s.15 I.A.

[32] s.16 I.A.

[33] s.17 I.A.

[34] s.12(a) Immigration Act 1971, Transfer of Functions (Immigration Appeals) Order S.I. 1987/465.

[35] The meaning of "final determination" is unclear. However, by analogy with the I.A., it appears to refer to any determination which finally disposes of the appeal (s.33(4) I.A.).

[36] s.4(2) and Sched. 2, para. 8(1)(a)–(c) I.A.

[37] s.17(5) I.A., H.C. 395, para. 355.

not open to him, he will be removed. An appeal will, therefore, be lodged from the country to which he is removed. In the second category, the entrant will still be overseas and therefore will appeal from there. It follows that in either of these categories, the appellant will not be present at the appeal.[38]

Where leave to enter is granted, the appellant will have a full right of appeal unless he is being deported for breach of leave conditions within seven years of last entry into the United Kingdom. Then, appeal will be confined to the issue of whether there was a power in law to deport.[39]

EXHAUSTION OF REMEDIES AND JUDICIAL REVIEW

Where an immigration decision is susceptible to appeal, the general rule **11–006** was set out by the Court of Appeal in *R. v. Secretary of State for the Home Department, ex p. Swati*.[40]

According to *Swati*, judicial review of immigration decisions cannot, usually, occur until after any applicable statutory appeal route has been exhausted and only then if the appeal decision is itself reviewable. In this way, immigration law is consistent with the normal rules preventing relief being granted in judicial review, in the court's discretion, where an alternative remedy exists. In this context it is important to note the new appellate mechanism from the IAT introduced by the Asylum and Immigration Appeals Act 1993.[41]

However, the general rule does not apply where there are exceptional circumstances[42] which render an out of country appeal worthless[43] as, for example, where an entrant would be unable to pursue an appeal due to political pressures in the country to which he was returned.[44] Although exceptions to the *Swati* principle will be rare,[45] it does appear that the rule will not apply where there has been a manifest error in applying the criteria for entry.[46]

The decision in *Swati* has particular effect on those who are refused leave to enter and must, therefore, exercise an out of country appeal. Until that

---

[38] s.13(3) I.A. H.C. 395 provides that appeals can *only* be made once the applicant has left the U.K. (see H.C. 395, para. 356) except in cases where the entrant is a U.K. passport holder describing him as a British Citizen and is claiming right of abode (H.C. 395, para. 353) or has entry clearance (H.C. 395, para. 354).

[39] s.15 I.A. as amended s.5 Immigration Act 1988; *Oladehinde and Alexander v. Secretary of State for the Home Department* [1991] 1 A.C. 254; *R. v. Secretary of State for the Home Department, ex p. Malhi* [1991] 1 Q.B. 194.

[40] [1986] 1 W.L.R. 477.

[41] See para. 11–005.

[42] *Doorga v. Secretary of State for the Home Department* [1990] Imm.A.R. 98 C.A.

[43] *Grazales v. Secretary of State for the Home Department* [1990] Imm.A.R. 505.

[44] See *R. v. Chief Immigration Officer, Gatwick Airport, ex p. Kharrazi* [1980] 1 W.L.R. 1396; personal and professional inconvenience will not suffice to bypass *Swati*, *R. v. Secretary of State, ex p. Salamat* [1993] Imm.A.R. 239.

[45] See *R. v. Secretary of State for the Home Department, ex p. Pulgarin* [1992] Imm.A.R. 96.

[46] See *R. v. Secretary of State for the Home Department, ex p. Hindjou* [1989] Imm.A.R. 24.

decision, judicial review had operated to grant such entrants an effective right of in-country appeal.

Notwithstanding *Swati*, judicial review ought, in principle, to be available in circumstances where appeal does not afford a true alternative remedy.[47]

In *Soon Ok Ryoo v. Secretary of State for the Home Department*[48] the applicant argued that the Home Office had to show that a statutory appeal structure provided as effective and efficient remedy as that which was available by way of review in order to justify the refusal of relief on discretionary grounds. The Court of Appeal held,[49] however, that there was no basis in principle for such an onus being placed on the respondent and that, therefore, *Swati* applied. Clearly, this decision narrows the scope for qualifying application of the general rule.

WHERE JUDICIAL REVIEW WILL LIE

Immigration decisions with limited or no appeal

11–007   The *Swati* argument does not apply where there is no right of appeal, or only a limited right of appeal.[50] At present, there are three main areas where judicial review is deployed against the decision maker on this basis, namely where: (i) the entrant is refused political asylum and does not fall within the "fast track" appeal procedure,[51] (ii) the Home Secretary has decided to deport the applicant and (iii) the Home Secretary has decided that the applicant is an illegal entrant.

The Asylum and Immigration Appeals Act will add those who are denied a right of appeal under sections 10 and 11 to the above categories.

In such cases, judicial review will lie if the applicant overcomes the threshold test and shows that there is an arguable case.

Miscellaneous

Judicial review will also lie in other circumstances, such as a criminal court exercising its powers in respect of offences under the Immigration Act 1971,[52] and the exercise of certain prerogative functions as, for example, the decision to issue a passport.[53]

---

[47] See, *e.g.* s.19 I.A.

[48] [1992] Imm.A.R. 59.

[49] *per* Russell L.J. at pp. 66–67.

[50] *e.g.* see ss.13(3) I.A. (as amended s.39(5) British Nationality Act 1981, s.3 Immigration Act 1988); 13(5) I.A.; 15(4) I.A.; 14(3) I.A. 15(3) and 5(1) Immigration Act 1988.

[51] See below.

[52] *R. v. Clerk to Birmingham JJ., ex p. Offei* (November 28, 1985, D.C.; unrep.) but note that a Crown Court exercising an immigration function will only be reviewable where ss.10, 34 and Sched. 1 Courts Act 1971 permit it and the more appropriate remedy might be to proceed by way of case stated (see *R. v. Crown Court at Ipswich, ex p. Baldwin* [1981] 1 All E.R. 596 D.C.; *R. v. Crown Court at St Albans, ex p. Cinnamond* [1981] Q.B. 480; *R. v. Crown Court at Croydon, ex p. Miller* [1985] Cr.App.Rep. 152 D.C.).

[53] *Secretary of State for Foreign and Commonwealth Affairs, ex p. Everett* [1989] Q.B. 811.

GROUNDS FOR JUDICIAL REVIEW

The grounds of reviewing immigration decisions are similar to those **11–008** which apply elsewhere. Thus, predominantly, review will lie in cases where there has been procedural impropriety,[54] an error of law,[55] or where the decision has deprived the applicant of some legitimate expectation.

Generally the court will not, on judicial review, challenge the merits of the decision, but only the procedure by which such decision was reached. It is not, for example, open to a person seeking political asylum to challenge whether the Home Office was correct, on the facts, to decide that the applicant fell outwith the requirements for a successful application for political asylum.[56]

There are particular complications which arise from application of the normal principles of judicial review to immigration law. The first concerns the application of the principle of proportionality into administrative law. The second concerns the extent to which immigration decisions involve human rights issues which do not always arise in other cases. These will be examined prior to more detailed consideration of the general grounds for judicial review in the immigration case law.

Proportionality

In *ex parte Brind*,[57] the Court stated that proportionality as a general rule **11–009** had no place in the substantive law of judicial review. The concept might, however, be applied on a case-by-case basis.[58]

Immigration law usually contains a tension between the State's desire to limit the category of persons entitled to enter and reside and an individual's wish to enter and reside. In some cases the consequences for such individual may be disproportionate to the administrative end sought to be achieved, involving possible removal to a third country where that person may have no connections at all. In such circumstances, it is submitted that the principle of proportionality might well be applied by the High Court in appropriate cases.

The potential for such application is reinforced by the increasing applicability of EU law. United Kingdom immigration restrictions may, in theory, limit the free movement of workers between member states.[59] The

---

[54] See *C.C.S.U. v. Minister for the Civil Service* [1985] A.C. 374 at 411.

[55] For example, where the IAT failed to calculate the appellant's period of absence correctly. *R. v. IAT, ex p. Muhammad Saffiullah* [1986] Imm.A.R. 424. *Wednesbury* irrationality is also embraced under this law; see para. 11–013 below.

[56] *R. v. Secretary of State for the Home Department, ex p. Bugdaycay* [1987] A.C. 514 at 535F–H *per* Lord Templeman; *Munongo v. Secretary of State for the Home Department* [1991] Imm.A.R. 616.

[57] See *R. v. Secretary of State for the Home Department, ex p. Brind* [1991] 1 A.C. 696 at 761.

[58] See Roskill L.J. at p. 750A–E; *C.C.S.U. v. Minister of Civil Service*, n. 54 above, at 410.

[59] See *R. v. I.A.T. and Surinder Singh, ex p. Secretary of State for the Home Department* (at present T.L.R. August 31, 1992) where it was held that Article 52 of the Treaty of Rome required a member state to grant leave to enter and reside to the non-E.C. national spouse of

193

European Court of Justice has ruled that these restrictions cannot override the provisions of the Treaty of Rome. Accordingly, it follows that, in making an immigration decision, the Home Secretary and immigration officer must in some circumstances have regard to E.C. law. Given that in E.C. law, the concept of proportionality applies and must be applied by the United Kingdom's courts, it would be consistent to import proportionality into immigration law in all cases and, arguably, illogical not to do so.

Human Rights

11–010   Many applicants seek to raise issues of human rights law in challenging immigration decisions. However, particular difficulties arise.

As a matter of principle, it is questionable whether judicial review is an appropriate mechanism for the enforcement of such rights. Under Article 13 of the ECHR, States are to provide their subjects with adequate remedies if the subject's rights are violated. The European Court of Human Rights has, on two occasions, examined whether judicial review is an appropriate remedy.[60] In both cases the Court ruled that it was.

In neither case, however, did the majority of the Court examine the extent to which judicial review scrutinises legality as opposed to merits. From this perspective, judicial review might not afford an adequate remedy.[61] Of the two cases examined by the European Court of Human Rights in *Soering* the issue did not arise, the facts being agreed by the parties, and in *Vilvarajah* the Court ruled that the applicants could have challenged the decision on *Wednesbury* grounds but chose not to do so. It is submitted that on different facts, it would be open to the applicant to argue that the court should adopt the approach of Judges Walsh and Russo in their dissenting judgment in *Vilvarajah* and hold that judicial review did not satisfy Article 13.[62]

A second difficulty is the extent to which the United Kingdom's general human rights obligations under international law[63] and the European Convention on Human Rights are enforceable in domestic law. It is to be presumed that United Kingdom legislation complies with these obligations[64] and that such obligations may therefore be used to interpret

---

a national of that state when the non-E.C. national had gone with that spouse to another member state to work there. In doing so, the ECJ impliedly overruled the U.K. immigration rule that to qualify for leave to enter or remain, the non-E.C. national must demonstrate that he or she is a spouse and that the primary purpose of the marriage was not to obtain entry clearance.

[60] See *Vilvarajah v. United Kingdom* (1991) Series A ECHR No. 220; *Soering v. United Kingdom* (1989) Series A ECHR No. 161.

[61] See *Chief Constable for North Wales v. Evans* [1982] 1 W.L.R. 1155 at 1173–4; *C.C.S.U.*, n. 54 above, at 415 A–B *per* Roskill L.J.

[62] At para. 2, p. 42 of the transcript.

[63] It is submitted that there are general obligations on states to observe human rights under international law which are justiciable by the International Court of Justice. See Arts. 55 and 56 of the United Nations Charter, *Legal Consequences for States of the Continued Presence of S Africa in Namibia* (1971) I.C.J. 16 at 57 para. 131; *The Barcelona Traction Case* (1970) I.C.J. 4 at 32.

[64] See *Att.-Gen. v. BBC* [1981] A.C. 303 at 354 *per* Lord Scarman.

ambiguous statutory provisions.[65] Given the House of Lords' decision in *Derbyshire C.C. v. Times Newspapers Ltd*[66] it is now arguable that the principle extends further than being merely an aid to construction and that the English common law incorporates and reflects Article 10 of the ECHR.

PROCEDURAL IMPROPRIETY

The general view is that where fairness or procedural propriety is in issue, the court will not confine its determination of the case to *Wednesbury* issues.[67]   **11–011**

In immigration law, judicial review therefore offers the applicant somewhat greater scope to challenge the decision-maker's conclusions than is available under the statutory appeal regime. Applications on natural justice grounds may be directed both towards the initial decision-maker and/or to any appellate body.

Application to the decision-maker

The general principle is that the decision-maker is required to act fairly and honestly and without bias.[68] Although the test can be simply stated as a "duty to be fair",[69] its application will vary according to the facts of each case. Therefore in *ex parte Mughal* the immigration officer was merely required to allow the entrant an opportunity to state her case and to explain the circumstances which the immigration officer alleged aroused suspicion.[70]

In cases involving political asylum, the procedure which was adopted, prior to the passing of the Asylum and Immigration Appeals Act 1993,[71] was that the decision was subject to "rigorous examination".[72] Such decisions do not lie with individual immigration officers. The decisions are to be referred to the Home Office where the Secretary of State, acting through junior civil servants and immigration officers under the *Carltona*

---

[65] See *ex p. Brind*, n. 57 above, in the Court of Appeal at pp. 717E–718B *per* Lord Donaldson of Lymington and in the House of Lords at p. 747H *per* Lord Bridge.

[66] [1993] A.C. 534; see also *R. v. Advertising Standards Authority, ex p. Vernons* [1992] 1 W.L.R. 1289.

[67] *R. v. Panel on Takeovers and Mergers, ex p. Guinness Plc* [1990] 1 Q.B. 146 at 183–4.

[68] *R. v. Home Secretary, ex p. Mughal* [1974] Q.B. 313.

[69] *R. v. ITC, ex p. TSW, The Times*, March 30, 1992.

[70] n. 68 above, *cf.*, though, *R. v. Secretary of State for the Home Department, ex p. Lateef* [1991] Imm.A.R. 334—where the initial notice served on the entrant was defective and a further notice was served outside the required time limits. Leave to move for judicial review was, however, refused on the basis that the defect was not sufficient to permit the court to exercise its discretion and grant leave.

[71] Judicial review has now been excluded to an extent by the operation of the fast track procedure. However, it is submitted that the cases on political asylum will also be relevant in challenges to the fast track procedure.

[72] *R. v. Secretary of State for the Home Department, ex p. Thirukumar* [1989] Imm.A.R. 270 at 282 D.C.; *Gaima v. Secretary of State for the Home Department* [1989] Imm.A.R. 205 at 208 ff. *per* May L.J.

doctrine, reaches a decision.[73] In doing so the decision-maker must "act fairly and promptly upon the case put to him, while remaining willing to consider any further representations".[74]

There are two elements to this. First, the Home Office is under an obligation to act swiftly. Secondly, it must act fairly.

The latter duty comprises several elements. The decision-maker must allow the entrant the opportunity to make representations and attend an interview. In order for the entrant to benefit from that opportunity, the Home Office is obliged to ensure that the entrant's mind is directed to those factors which might defeat the application. Further, if supplemental answers are sought from the entrant, an opportunity should be given to the entrant to reread the original answers given.[75] Finally, where the Secretary of State has taken new evidence into account, a duty may be imposed upon him to allow the entrant an opportunity to comment on such evidence.[76]

There are limits to the fairness required. First, a finding of procedural impropriety does not automatically entitle the applicant to a remedy. Given the discretionary nature of judicial review, it is always open to the court to exercise its discretion to refuse relief.[77] Discretion may be exercised where the court concludes that even if a fair procedure had been adopted, it would have made no difference to the outcome.[78] Secondly, there is no obligation on the Home Office to re-interview the entrant once a decision has been reached[79] if the decision has been finalised and there are no exceptional circumstances which ought to be brought to the Home Office's attention.[80] It follows that the decision-maker will not reach an unlawful decision if he fails to allow the entrant a further opportunity to explain the facts supporting the application for asylum.[81] Thirdly, there is no obligation on the immigration officer to offer the applicant an opportunity to have access to legal advice if the applicant does not raise the question.[82]

The court will not approach the question of procedural impropriety in the abstract. The practical nature of the considerations involved is demonstrated by *R. v. Secretary of State for the Home Department, ex p.*

---

[73] *Carltona v. Works Commissioners* [1943] 2 All E.R. 560 C.A.; *Oladehinde and Alexander v. Secretary of State for the Home Department* [1991] 1 A.C. 254.

[74] *Helal Ahmed v. Secretary of State for the Home Department* [1992] Imm.A.R. 449 at 451.

[75] *Thirukumar* [1989] Imm.A.R. 402 C.A. at 414. *cf.*, though, *R. v. Secretary of State for the Home Department, ex p. Khakhsar Butt* [1992] Imm.A.R. 534—*held*: there is no obligation to remind the applicant of previous answers where the applicant's credibility is not in doubt.

[76] See *R. v. Secretary of State for the Home Department, ex p. Ayse Oran* [1991] Imm.A.R. 290.

[77] In *R. v. Secretary of State for the Home Department, ex p. Pushpaben Patel* [1993] Imm.A.R. 392: the court refused to exercise its discretion and grant judicial review where the applicant refused to make a visa application to another country when faced with deportation from the United Kingdom.

[78] See Wade and Forsyth *Administrative Law* (7th ed. 1994), pp. 528ff.; *Celik v. Secretary of State for the Home Department* [1991] Imm.A.R. 8.

[79] See *Thirukumar*, n. 75 above, at p. 413.

[80] As, for example, where the entrant seeks political asylum and informs the immigration officer at this last interview that he has a genuine fear of persecution since his family have been murdered for political reasons—see *Thirukumar*, n. 75 above, at p. 407.

[81] *Yurekli v. Secretary of State for the Home Department* [1991] Imm.A.R. 153.

[82] *Sheikh Mutengu v. Secretary of State for the Home Department* [1992] Imm.A.R. 419.

Stephen Range.[83] There the court held that it was permissible for the Secretary of State to delegate interviewing the applicant to the same officer, although the officer had previously interviewed the applicant about an illegal entry claim and appeared to be hostile to the applicant.

Consistent with the decision in C.C.S.U., where an asylum decision relates to the issue of national security, the normal rules of natural justice do not apply.[84] Further, the courts' consideration of the issue will be limited by the fact that national security decisions are "non-justiciable". However, a balance must be drawn between the interests of the applicant and the interests of national security.[85]

Application To Appellate Bodies

Under traditional administrative law principles, the rules of natural justice are paramount where a body is exercising a judicial function.[86] Thus, adjudicators and the IAT are, in theory, subject to the full requirements of procedural propriety in hearing appeals. The difficulty lies in determining what standard of procedural propriety is required.

Both the IAT and adjudicators are "masters of their own procedure". Two consequences follow. First, it is a matter of the IAT's or adjudicator's discretion what procedures are adopted in conducting appeals. Secondly, the method adopted will only be open to challenge if the overall standard of fairness falls below that which is required by the task in hand.[87] It follows that an oral hearing will not be required in every case. Therefore there is no requirement that the appellant be given an oral hearing before the IAT grants leave to appeal from an adjudicator's decision.[88]

Further, absent a failure to consider submissions made by the parties, the IAT or adjudicator are perfectly entitled to decline to hear from particular witnesses, and a decision in those terms is not amenable to challenge on the ground that one of the parties has been deprived of a true hearing.[89]

In the light of the extensive discretion granted to the IAT, it is submitted that there will be few occasions on which the IAT's decision can be challenged as a result of procedural impropriety. Further, since whether or not there has been a breach of procedure will be a question of law material to the decision reached, the IAT's decision in that respect can only be challenged by appeal to the Court of Appeal.[90] The cases cited above would be relevant in such an appeal in ascertaining whether or not the alleged procedural impropriety vitiated the decision.

---

[83] [1991] Imm.A.R. 505.
[84] See *R. v. Secretary of State for the Home Department, ex p. Cheblak* [1991] 1 W.L.R. 890 at pp. 907–908.
[85] *R. v. Secretary of State for the Home Department, ex p. Chahal*, [1994] Imm.A.R. 107.
[86] *R. v. Thames Magistrates' Court, ex p. Polemis* [1974] 1 W.L.R. 1371 at 1378.
[87] See *R. v. Army Board of the Defence Council, ex p. Anderson* [1992] Q.B. 169.
[88] *R. v. IAT, ex p. Rachid Bouchtaoui* [1992] Imm.A.R. 433.
[89] *R. v. IAT, ex p. Bashirul Islam* [1992] Imm.A.R. 452.
[90] s.9(1) Asylum and Immigration Appeals Act 1993.

ILLEGALITY

11–012   A challenge based on illegality will arise in two main circumstances. First, where the decision-maker or appeal body makes an error of jurisdictional fact. Secondly, where the decision-maker or appeal body takes account of irrelevant considerations or fails to consider relevant considerations. The first ground is the usual method of challenge in cases of illegal entry into the United Kingdom when the Home Office has sought to deport the illegal entrant. The second usually arises where an entrant has sought asylum and failed.

Illegal entry and jurisdictional fact

A person is an illegal entrant if he enters or has entered the United Kingdom in breach of the immigration laws or a deportation order.[91] For present purposes, there are two categories of person caught by the definition.

First there are those who enter the United Kingdom innocently, that is without being aware (as is, *ex hypothesi*, the case) that leave is required, or wrongly believing that leave has been granted. These persons are, nonetheless, illegal entrants[92] and their only method of challenging the deportation order is by way of judicial review on the basis that the decision to deport is an irrational exercise of discretion. This, it is submitted, is a difficult test to pass. There are no policy guidelines against which the decision can be compared.[93]

Jurisdictional fact affects the second category of entrant, namely those who (it is contended) have entered illegally by obtaining leave to enter through deception. Obtaining leave to enter by deception is an offence under the I.A.[94] It is also a breach of immigration control rendering the entrant an illegal entrant.[95] It is not clear whether the commission of other criminal offences under the Act will also bring the entrant within the definition.[96]

The determination that there has been deception is, in this context, a fact upon which jurisdiction to deport depends. In *R. v. Home Secretary, ex p. Khawaja*,[97] it was held by the House of Lords that the court's duty goes beyond establishing that an immigration officer may have had reasonable grounds for believing the applicant to be an illegal entrant (the normal test for judicial review) but goes, rather, to ascertaining whether the entrant has, in fact, practised deception.

---

[91] s.33(1) I.A.

[92] See *R. Governor of Ashford Remand Centre, ex p. Bouzagou* [1983] Imm.A.R. 69; *R. v. Secretary of State for the Home Department, ex p. Mohan* [1989] Imm.A.R. 436; *Sultan Hamid v. Secretary of State* [1993] Imm.A.R. 216.

[93] *R. v. Secretary of State for the Home Department, ex p. Mustapha* T.L.R., February 22, 1984.

[94] s.26(1)(c) I.A.

[95] See *R. v. Secretary of State for the Home Department, ex p. Khawaja* [1984] A.C. 74.

[96] See *ex p. Rouse and Shrimpton, The Times*, November 25, 1985; *contra R. v. Secretary of State for the Home Department, ex p. Patel* [1986] Imm.A.R. 208.

[97] See n. 95 above.

The following points emerge from the judgments in *Khawaja*:

(a) An immigrant does not owe a positive duty of candour approximately to *uberrimae fidei*.

(b) An immigration officer may order the detention and removal only of a person who has entered the country by virtue of an *ex facie* valid permission if, in fact, that person is an illegal immigrant.[98]

(c) The onus of proving the fact that the applicant is an illegal immigrant lies on the immigration authority once the applicant has raised a prima facie case.[99]

(d) The standard of proof is that of the balance of probabilities. However, because liberty is involved, a high degree of probability must be established.[1]

(e) If the court is not satisfied with any part of the evidence, it may remit the matter for reconsideration, or itself receive further evidence. It should quash the detention order where the evidence was not such as the authorities should have relied on or where the evidence received does not justify the decision reached or for any serious procedural irregularity.[2]

A person will legitimately be classified as an illegal entrant if leave to enter has been granted because of the deception.[3] It therefore follows that such a person must have attempted to pass or have passed immigration control[4] and that the material date for any deception is the date on which it (not the original application) was made.[5] Further, there must have been some action by the entrant which could constitute deception. Silence, it appears, is not deception.[6] Further, classification depends upon the state of mind of the immigration officer. Thus even where the entrant is innocent of any intent to deceive, he may still have obtained leave to enter through deception.[7]

The problem posed by *Khawaja* is the type of review that courts are, in practice, willing to embark on. The decision has resulted in a large increase of applications, all seeking to establish that, on specific facts, the high onus of proof on the Home Office has not been satisfied.[8]

---

[98] n. 95 above at p. 97E (*per* Lord Fraser); p. 109D (*per* Lord Scarman); p. 123A (*per* Lord Bridge) and p. 128A (*per* Lord Templeman).

[99] n. 95 above at p. 112A (*per* Lord Scarman) and p. 124C (*per* Lord Bridge). See, also: *R. v. Governor of Brixton Prison, ex p. Ahsan* [1969] 2 Q.B. 222.

[1] n. 95 above at p. 97G (*per* Lord Fraser); p. 112C (*per* Lord Scarman) and p. 124D (*per* Lord Bridge).

[2] n. 95 above at p. 105E (*per* Lord Wilberforce).

[3] See *R. v. Secretary of State for the Home Department, ex p. Jayakoody* [1982] 1 W.L.R. 405.

[4] See *R. v. Yabu Naillie* [1993] Imm.A.R. 462 (where an entrant is found in possession of forged documents before passing immigration control, there is no illegal entry).

[5] *R. v. Secretary of State for the Home Department, ex p. Mohammed Salim* [1992] Imm.A.R. 316.

[6] *R. v. Secretary of State for the Home Department, ex p. Annabel Dordas* [1992] Imm.A.R. 99.

[7] Therefore ignorance that the work permit relied upon was forged is no defence: *Kwong Chan v. Secretary of State for the Home Department* [1992] 1 W.L.R. 541, [1992] Imm.A.R. 233.

[8] By 1990 immigration decisions comprised 38 per cent of civil judicial review cases (the highest ever): see John Orton "Applying for judicial review" (1991) 88 L.S.Gaz. 37, p. 20.

Generally, the court simply examines the affidavit material before it, rather than undertaking an extensive factual inquiry or permitting cross-examination.

In *R. v. Home Secretary, ex p. Miah*[9] for example, Woolf J., faced with competing affidavits, quashed a determination that the applicant was an illegal immigrant on the basis that he was in a complete state of uncertainty as to whether there was entry by deception. Similarly the Court of Appeal, in another case, refused to accept fresh evidence from the Home Office designed to establish the fact of illegal entry and emphasised, again, the heavy burden of proof resting on the immigration authority.[10]

Finally, in *R. v. Secretary of State for the Home Department, ex p. Khan*[10a] the Court of Appeal held that there was proven to detain a person whose initial entry was illegal under para. 16(2) of Schedule 2 to the Immigration Act 1971 notwithstanding that he subsequently sought asylum. The Court felt Parliament could not have intended an apprehended illegal applicant to avoid detention by claiming asylum.

Asylum decisions

The essential question is whether the entrant falls within the definition of refugee. If he does, then pursuant to this country's obligations under the Geneva Convention on the Status of Refugees, it is bound to grant asylum or remove the person to a safe third country.

The Secretary of State is entitled to test the entrant's assertion that he is a refugee by an examination of the facts and deciding whether there is a real fear of persecution for a convention reason. *R. v. Home Secretary, ex p. Sivakumaran*[11] renders the Secretary of State's decision amenable to challenge on the grounds that he failed to consider the factual basis of the claim correctly.

Certainly, the Secretary of State is entitled to examine factors such as the position in society which the entrant held,[12] the number and frequency of the events which allegedly lead to the fear of prosecution[13] the area in which the entrant lived in relation to the size of the country and the chance that the entrant would not be persecuted elsewhere in that country.[14] Further the Secretary of State is entitled to consider the nature and status of the judicial system of the country of origin and decide that even unfair prosecution of the entrant under that system is not persecution.[15]

---

[9] [1983] Imm.A.R. 91.

[10] *R. v. Home Secretary, ex p. Momin Ali* [1984] 1 W.L.R. 663. See, also, *R. v. Home Secretary, ex p. Addo, The Times,* April 18, 1985 (*held*: in very few cases was judicial review a satisfactory way to test illegal entry questions).

[10a] *The Times,* February 7, 1995.

[11] [1988] A.C. 958.

[12] *Abdullai Conteh v. Secretary of State for the Home Department* [1992] Imm.A.R. 594.

[13] *R. v. Secretary of State for the Home Department, ex p. Kemal Onay* [1992] Imm.A.R. 320.

[14] *R. v. Secretary of State for the Home Department, ex p. Hidir Gunes* [1991] Imm.A.R. 278. The Secretary of State is therefore permitted to refuse to grant asylum to an entrant who might be persecuted in Anatolia but would be perfectly safe in Istanbul (see *Yurekli,* n. 81 above).

[15] *Elvis Ameyaw v. Secretary of State for the Home Department* [1992] Imm.A.R. 206.

Permissible considerations are widely drawn. For an applicant to succeed in challenging the decision, he must show that the Secretary of State acted unreasonably in taking a particular facet into account.[16]

In relation to factors affecting third country removals, the Secretary of State is potentially better informed than the entrant since he is able to draw on the resources of the Foreign and Commonwealth Office to analyse the situation in the proposed third country.[17] Thus, for example, despite potential concerns about German attitudes to refugees, the Secretary of State is entitled to conclude from government sources of information that Germany is a safe country to remove the entrant to.[18]

WEDNESBURY IRRATIONALITY

There is a clear overlap between challenges based on a failure to consider relevant factors and *Wednesbury* challenges.[19] The issue is whether the decision-maker was obliged (or merely entitled) to take certain factors into account and did not.[20] In the latter case, the applicant must, in order to succeed, demonstrate that the decision was *Wednesbury* unreasonable, in the sense of being a decision that no reasonable decision-maker could have reached.

11–013

Appellate decisions are particularly difficult to challenge on a *Wednesbury* basis. It is for an appellate tribunal to decide questions of credibility or weight, so that absent any statutory provisions requiring particular weight to be attached to certain factors, a decision on appeal will not be open to challenge under this head of review.[21] Further, the IAT's or adjudicator's decision is not to be construed as if it were a statute.[22] Given that no duty is imposed to provide a full exhaustive list of reasons for an appeal decision,[23] it is difficult to argue that such decision is flawed or *Wednesbury* unreasonable merely because such decision omits references to certain facts. Finally, as outlined above, the IAT and adjudicator possess considerable discretion as to how they are to operate.

---

[16] See *Secretary of State for the Home Department v. Bugdaycay Re Musisi* [1987] A.C. 514.

[17] *Ahmed Abdulla v. Secretary of State for the Home Department* [1992] Imm.A.R. 438.

[18] *Abdulla*, n. 17 above; *R. v. Secretary of State for the Home Department, ex p. Mangal Singh* [1992] Imm.A.R. 376.

[19] See *C.C.S.U.*, n. 54 above, at p. 410. Lord Diplock distinguished irrationality and illegality and stated that the *Edwards v. Bairstow* [1956] A.C. 14 heuristic fiction (that a manifestly wrong decision must be deemed to have emanated from a misdirection as to the law) need no longer be used. It follows that irrationality is a ground of challenge *per se* (*i.e.* absent misdirection in law and/or failure to take into account relevant facts). The difficulty faced in such challenges lies in demonstrating whether the decision-maker was acting perversely.

[20] See *Miller v. IAT* [1988] Imm.A.R. 358 C.A.; *Alsawaf v. Secretary of State for the Home Department* [1988] Imm.A.R. 410 C.A.

[21] *R. v. IAT, ex p. Naushad Kandiya* [1989] Imm.A.R. 491.

[22] See in the employment context *U.C.A.T.T. v. Brain* [1981] I.C.R. 542 C.A.

[23] *R. v. IAT, ex p. Aftab Hussain* [1991] Imm.A.R. 212. However, it is desirable that full reasons be given: *R. v. IAT, ex p. Chang Shih Yang* [1987] Imm.A.R. 568; *Kandiya and Khan v. IAT* [1990] Imm.A.R. 377.

LEGITIMATE EXPECTATION

11–014   In immigration law the main issues were in respect of entrants who leave the United Kingdom and then seek to re-enter at a later date.

An entrant receives two sorts of information from the Home Office that may afford a basis for the contention that a legitimate expectation has been created.

First are face-to-face meetings with immigration officers. It seems clear that a representation made at such a meeting will found a legitimate expectation that the representation will not arbitrarily be departed from.[24]

Alternatively, information is provided by two stamps being placed in an entrant's passport: a stamp relating to entry conditions imposed on first entry to the United Kingdom[25] and the visa exempt stamp.[26] Do these stamps constitute a representation creating a legitimate expectation on the part of the entrant that he will be readmitted?

Certainly, it will require a clear representation made by an officer of government to generate such expectation.[27] Thus, where the applicant is aware of the Secretary of State's decision for some time and does nothing, he will not be held to have been deprived of a legitimate expectation, having been given ample time to make representations.[28]

Even then, the mere placing of a visa exempt stamp without further comment in the entrant's passport is merely a representation that the entrant will not need a visa on re-entry, not a representation that the entrant will be allowed to re-enter.[29] Following the Court of Appeal decision in *Secretary of State for the Home Department v. Mowla*,[30] an applicant will only succeed in arguing that he possessed a legitimate expectation if other representations were made than the mere placing of the stamp.

PRACTICE AND PROCEDURE

11–015   The courts have expressed particular concern as to the use of legal aid in immigration cases. In *Marchano Singa v. Secretary of State for the Home*

---

[24] See *Adetutu Oloniluyi v. Secretary of State for the Home Department* [1989] Imm.A.R. 135 at 143 ff. *per* Dillon L.J.

[25] Under s.3(3) I.A.

[26] This is simply a stamp which declares that the entrant will not require a visa stamp if entry occurs before a certain date.

[27] See *R. v. IRC, ex p. Preston* [1985] 1 A.C. 835 at 866G–867C, *R. v. Secretary of State for the Home Department, ex p. Ruddock* [1987] 1 W.L.R. 1482 at 1497; *R. v. IRC, ex p. MFK* [1990] 1 W.L.R. 1545 at 1566B–D, 1596H–1570B.

[28] Therefore a long-term resident of the U.K. is not deprived of a legitimate expectation where he has been aware of the decision to deport him for half of his stay in the U.K.: *Mohammed Hussain v. IAT* [1991] Imm.A.R. 413 C.A.

[29] See *R. v. Secretary of State for the Home Department, ex p. Patel* [1991] Imm.A.R. 14 at 21; *R. v. Secretary of State for the Home Department, ex p. Islam* [1990] Imm.A.R. 220; *Sadiq* [1990] Imm.A.R. 364; but *contra R. v. Secretary of State for the Home Department, ex p. Mowla* [1990] Imm.A.R. 224.

[30] [1992] 1 W.L.R. 70, [1991] Imm.A.R. 210.

Department[31] the Court of Appeal observed that where a renewed application for leave was made to the Court of Appeal, counsel was under a duty to advise making such application only where he was in possession of all information relevant to the case. Further, if the application is wholly without merit, the courts have signalled that they will use their powers and make wasted costs orders against the applicant's legal advisers.[32]

This obligation is particularly onerous in the context of an *ex parte* leave application where *ipso facto* the applicant and his advisers may well not be in possession of all the necessary information. Advice at the leave stage is, in other contexts, often provisional on the information that will emerge in the course of the hearing. The difficulty in immigration cases will occur where the crucial documents are in the possession of the Home Office.[33]

However, it is submitted that the heightened awareness of the courts to legal aid issues in immigration can also benefit the applicant. The courts will, in exceptional circumstances, suspend the order dismissing the application for leave to move pending further consideration of the case by the legal aid director and counsel.[34]

Evidence

Immigration cases are subject to the same rules as other applications before the courts. In *R. v. Home Secretary, ex p. Khawaja*, Lord Bridge affirmed that the difficulties of proof raised in immigration cases did not detract from the application of those rules.[35] Clearly, however, the discretion vested in the court to permit cross-examination of a deponent is of particular relevance in immigration cases.[36] Resort may be had to cross-examination where there is a conflict of evidence[37] or where credibility of a witness is at stake.[38]

Nonetheless, cross-examination will only be permitted in limited circumstances.[39] It follows that the applicant will not be entitled to succeed at the leave stage merely because he can demonstrate that there are inconsistencies of fact which should be explored. The court will examine the facts deposed to on affidavit as they stand at the leave hearing and on those facts reach a conclusion as to whether leave should be granted.[40]

11–016

---

[31] [1992] Imm.A.R. 160.

[32] See *R. v. Secretary of State for the Home Department, ex p. Atrivinder Singh* [1993] Imm.A.R. 450.

[33] Given the potential consequences of removal, it is understandable that an analysis of the "reasonableness" threshold for legal aid would balance the strength of the case against the consequences of the entrant being immediately removed to the country of origin and decide in favour of making the application.

[34] *R. v. Secretary of State for the Home Department, ex p. Tolulope Olokodana* [1992] Imm.A.R. 499.

[35] n. 95 above, at p. 124.

[36] R.S.C., Ord. 38, r. 2(2).

[37] *R. v. Secretary of State for the Home Department, ex p. Rouse and Shrimpton, The Times,* November 25, 1985.

[38] *Khawaja,* n. 95 above, at pp. 124–125.

[39] *Khawaja,* n. 95 above, at p. 124G.

[40] *Abisola Fawehinmi v. Secretary of State for the Home Department* [1991] Imm.A.R. 1.

Doubts have been expressed as to the use of cross-examination where the applicant can only communicate through an interpreter,[41] or where the Home Office attempt to buttress a weak case by resort to cross-examination.[42]

Leave to adduce new evidence in immigration cases will be granted on the same principles as apply in all other cases.[43]

TOWARDS THE FUTURE

M. v. Home Office[44]

11–017   *M.* was a political asylum case where the entrant was returned to Zaire, notwithstanding that the full hearing of his application for leave to move was pending.

At the preliminary hearing, counsel for the Home Office made a representation to the court that M. would not be returned. However the Secretary of State, after taking legal advice, decided to return M. to Zaire and did so. M.'s solicitor sought and obtained a mandatory order directing the Secretary of State to return M. to the United Kingdom. The Secretary of State sought to have that order set aside and was successful. M. by this time was out of the jurisdiction. M.'s solicitors therefore started contempt proceedings against the Home Office and the Secretary of State.

The House of Lords held that the Secretary of State was liable in contempt. That liability rested on two grounds. First, the Court had powers to grant coercive orders against government pursuant to s.31 of the Supreme Court Act, and R.S.C. Ord. 53, r. 3(10) gave the court an additional power to grant interim injunction. Therefore there was no reason in principle why the minister could not be liable in contempt. Secondly, the judge's order had been made by a court of unlimited jurisdiction and was, accordingly, merely irregular. Thus, the order had to be complied with unless and until it was set aside, and the Secretary of State's decision not to comply was contemptuous.

The decision in *M.* parallels the courts' willingness to grant habeas corpus as an interim remedy to prevent immediate removal of an entrant from the United Kingdom.[45]

The case also raises important constitutional difficulties concerning the status of the decision-maker. It is difficult to see where the Secretary of State acts *qua* decision-maker for the Crown and *qua* independent legal entity, thus demonstrating the results of the Crown lacking legal personality. As the Minister is liable in his official capacity, it is difficult to analyse the legal person which is being fixed with liability thereby.

---

[41] *R. v. Secretary of State for the Home Department, ex p. Patel* [1986] Imm.A.R. 515 C.A.
[42] *ex p. Rouse and Shrimpton*, n. 37 above.
[43] See *Saleem Abbassi v. Secretary of State for the Home Department* [1992] Imm.A.R. 349 C.A.
[44] [1994] 1 A.C. 377.
[45] *cf. R. v. Secretary of State for the Home Department, ex p. Muboyayi* [1991] 3 W.L.R. 442 C.A.

The Asylum and Immigration Appeals Act 1993

It can be seen from the above that the Asylum and Immigration Appeals Act ("the Act") replaces judicial review with a statutory appeals mechanism. It follows that the Act will have a considerable impact on the use of judicial review in immigration cases. The removal of the right to appeal in sections 10 and 11 will no doubt lead to an increase in applications from visitors, students and their dependants. The creation of a fast track asylum system and new appellate structures will, however, reduce the numbers of applications under those heads.

Control of the decision-making process

The Act states that the Convention and Protocol relating to the status of refugees have primacy in any asylum decision and that the immigration rules cannot lay down any practice contrary to the Convention and Protocol.[46] That said, the Act also makes provision to increase police powers where asylum-seekers are concerned. The police are now entitled to fingerprint asylum-seekers[47] and to request the asylum-seeker to attend at a police station for fingerprints to be taken.[48] The power to request attendance is enforced by a power of arrest.[49] These provisions have been criticised as unnecessary and oppressive, bearing in mind that the asylum-seeker is often fleeing from excessive police persecution in the country of origin.

Further, the Act alters the position of those who claim asylum having been granted limited leave to enter. Section 7 provides that where a person possessing limited leave seeks asylum and the Secretary of State rejects the application, the Secretary of State can, by notice in writing, curtail the duration of the limited leave, decide to make a deportation order and detain the putative asylum-seeker.[50] There is no right of appeal against such curtailment of leave under s.14 I.A.[51]

Appeals from asylum decisions

Section 8 sets out the circumstances where the applicant will be required to appeal to a "special adjudicator". Whatever the decision, whether it be to deny or vary leave, to deport or remove the asylum-seeker, the appeal will lie to the special adjudicator and not under Part II of the I.A. (as outlined above).[52]

Procedure on appeal is governed by The Asylum Appeals (Procedure) Rules 1993.[53] Those rules are detailed and complex, giving the appellant no

---

[46] ss.1 and 2.
[47] s.3(1).
[48] s.3(1)(b).
[49] s.3(5).
[50] s.7(1) and (4).
[51] s.7(2).
[52] Para. 1 of Sched. 2 to the Act.
[53] Made pursuant to para. 4(3) of Sched. 2 to the Act; s.22 I.A.

more than 10 days in which to present an appeal. Where an applicant falls outwith those provisions (either because of time limits or another cause) judicial review will probably still lie.

There is also a "special procedure" for asylum applications which the Secretary of State deems are "without foundation". A claim will be without foundation if it "does not raise any issue as to the United Kingdom's obligations under the Convention" or is otherwise frivolous and vexatious.[54] The onus is on the Secretary of State to demonstrate that there is no issue as to the United Kingdom's obligations.[55] However, that obligation is considerably reduced if the Secretary of State can safely remove the asylum-seeker to a third country through which the asylum-seeker has passed.[56] If the Secretary of State deems that the claim is without foundation, appeal will lie to the special adjudicator but no further. There is no right of appeal from the special adjudicator to the IAT.[57]

Two points follow. First, the Act envisages that whether a claim is without foundation will primarily be a question of fact (that is, whether there is an issue). That question of fact will then give rise to the power to follow the different procedure (if any). It therefore follows that judicial review will lie against such a determination on *Khawaja* and *Wednesbury* grounds. Secondly, the fact that a claim is "without foundation" does not prevent the special adjudicator from considering the claim and deciding that the Secretary of State has reached a wrong conclusion.[58] If the adjudicator comes to that decision he can allow, dismiss or refer the appeal to the Secretary of State for reconsideration.[59] It follows that judicial review may also lie against the decision of the special adjudicator. However, it appears that there can be no challenge to the special adjudicator's decision on the basis of breaches of natural justice.[60] In so far as there is a discretion to refer the case back to the Secretary of State, that discretion will be reviewable on *Wednesbury* grounds.

The Act also makes changes to the grounds on which an asylum-seeker can be excluded. In the 1971 legislation, the Secretary of State can remove a refugee on the grounds that his presence is "not conducive to the public good". The Act makes the application of that test a national security issue.[61] Two consequences will follow. First, it is submitted that the provision attempts to place certain aspects of asylum decisions within the *C.C.S.U.* rule that national security considerations are not justiciable.[62] Secondly, in line with *ex parte Cheblak*, the natural justice requirements will not apply.

[54] Para. 4(3) of Sched. 2 to the Act.
[55] *R. v. Secretary of State for the Home Department, ex p. Mehari* [1994] Q.B. 474.
[56] *Dursun v. Secretary of State for the Home Department* [1993] Imm.A.R. 169; *R. v. Secretary of State for the Home Department and Ors, ex p. Abdi* [1994] Imm.A.R. 402.
[57] s.8 and para. 5 of Sched. 2 of the Act.
[58] *ex p. Mehari*, n. 55 above.
[59] Para. 5(6) of Sched. 2 to the Act. The special adjudicator will not, however, be presented with the material which was before the Secretary of State (*ex p. Abdi*, n. 56 above).
[60] *ex p. Abdi*, n. 56 above.
[61] Para. 6 of Sched. 2 to the Act.
[62] The provision parallels the decision in *R. v. Secretary of State for the Home Department, ex p. Cheblak*, n. 84 above.

Miscellaneous provisions

The Act makes two other changes. First, local authorities are no longer to be under a duty to house an asylum-seeker provided he has accommodation "however temporary, which it would be reasonable" for him to occupy.[63] Asylum-seekers in that category are now removed from the ambit of the provisions in the homelessness legislation.[64] Further, any accommodation provided to an asylum-seeker will only be temporary.

Secondly, the Act expands the scope of the Immigration (Carriers' Liability) Act 1987[65] to cover transit passengers. The Secretary of State is given powers to require that passengers transiting in the United Kingdom who emanate from certain countries require a transit visa. If they do not possess such a visa, the airline can be made liable to a fine.[66] The practical effect of the expansion will be to make airlines unwilling to carry passengers whom it thinks might seek to claim asylum whilst in transit in the United Kingdom.

---

[63] s.4.

[64] See Chap. 13 for covering the homelessness legislation generally.

[65] The Act makes carriers of prospective entrants who lack the required documentation liable to a fine.

[66] s.12.

12. CONTROL OVER LOCAL AUTHORITIES

ULTRA VIRES IN RELATION TO LOCAL AUTHORITIES

12–001   All local authorities are subject to the *ultra vires* principle and are obliged to justify the exercise of their powers by reference to statute.

At its most straightforward, the doctrine operates to ensure that the authorities concerned do not exceed their powers. Thus, in *Attorney General v. Fulham Corp*[1] it was held that a proposal to undertake a laundry service was outside the council's express power to provide baths and washhouses.

A more recent example occurred in *Hazell v. Hammersmith & Fulham L.B.C.*,[2] where the House of Lords held that it is outside the scope of the council's powers under section 111 of the Local Government Act 1972, to enter into interest rate swap option transactions for the sole purpose of making money.

The scope of *ultra vires* is, however, much wider and enables judicial review on the wider basis already discussed in preceding chapters. It is well established that the courts will only intervene where the local authority has exceeded its express or implied powers.[3] Many statutes are drafted in very wide terms (see, especially, section 111(1) of the Local Government Act 1972).

MANDATORY AND DIRECTORY REQUIREMENTS

12–002   It is often the case that before a power either arises or becomes exercisable, a certain state of affairs may or must exist. The question engaged in categorising a particular requirement as mandatory or directory is whether the existence of such requirement is crucial to the power. Important procedural provisions will usually be mandatory rather than directory.

The traditional significance of the categorisation may have diminished following the decision in *London and Clydeside Estates Ltd. v. Aberdeen.*[4] There Lord Hailsham, referring to the categorisation of requirements into "mandatory" and "directory", said: "It may be that what the courts are

---

[1] [1921] 1 Ch. 440.
[2] [1992] 2 A.C. 1. See also, *R. v. Richmond upon Thames LBC., ex p. McCarthy & Stone (Developments) L & J* [1992] 2 A.C. 48.
[3] *Wenlock (Baroness) v. River Dee Company* (1885) 10 App.Cas. 354 *per* Watkinson L.J.
[4] [1980] 1 W.L.R. 182.

faced with is not so much a stark choice of alternatives but a spectrum of possibilities in which one compartment or description fades into another."

This suggests that, when construing a provision, the proper approach is to determine the purpose of the provision and what the requirements are designed to achieve.[5] Thus, in *Brayhead (Ascot) Ltd v. Berkshire C.C.*[6] Winn J. held that even though a provision was mandatory, non-compliance did not necessarily render the exercise of power a nullity.

It appears that procedural requirements relating to the imposition of financial burdens on ratepayers are likely to be held to require strict compliance.[7] Similarly, a provision requiring the giving of notice of the date of a hearing or the existence of appeal rights must usually be substantially adhered to.[8]

It is occasionally the case that there is a validating clause in a statute which preserves the validity of an exercise of power, notwithstanding a failure to adhere to the correct procedure. The courts will, however, narrowly construe such a saving provision.[9]

DELEGATION

It is a public law principle that when statutory power is conferred upon a body, it cannot, without the authority of statute, delegate that power to another body.[10] A *fortiori*, delegation is unlawful where the statute expressly prohibits it.[11]

12–003

In the context of local government, section 101 of the Local Government Act 1972 provides a very wide power to delegate functions to a council committee or any officer of the authority.

In this context it is, therefore, of interest to note that in *R. v. Secretary of State for the Environment, ex p. Hillingdon L.B.C.*[12] Woolf J. held that a "committee" had to consist of more than one member and that in consequence delegation to the chairman of a committee was unlawful. The position is different if the single person is an "officer" of the council.[13]

Sub-delegation by the delegatee, where delegation is permitted, will usually be unlawful because of the assumption, depending on the nature of the power, that the principal intends the initial delegatee alone to act as the instrument of power.

In *R. v. Preston B.C., ex p. Quietlynn Ltd*[14] the Court of Appeal held that where the power to make licence decisions was in one committee, it was wrong for any other committee or sub-committee to hear the applicants' representations about their licence application. By application of the same

---

[5] See, *e.g. R. v. Lambeth L.B.C., ex p. Sharpe* (1988) 55 P. & C.R. 232.
[6] [1964] 2 Q.B. 303.
[7] *Sheffield City Council v. Graingers Wines Ltd.* [1977] 1 W.L.R. 1119.
[8] *Bradbury v. Enfield L.B.C.* [1967] 1 W.L.R. 1311.
[9] See, *e.g. Noble v. I.L.E.A.* [1984] 82 L.G.R. 291.
[10] *Barnard v. National Dock Labour Board* [1953] 2 Q.B. 18.
[11] See, *e.g.* L.G.A. 1972, s.101(6), (7).
[12] [1986] 1 W.L.R. 192. Affirmed on appeal [1986] 1 W.L.R. 807.
[13] See *Provident Mutual Life Assurance Association v. Derby City Council* [1981] 1 W.L.R. 173.
[14] [1984] 83 L.G.R. 184.

principle, it will usually be unlawful for a committee to abdicate decision-making to its chairman.[15]

Where delegation has occurred, it seems probable that the delegating body may continue to exercise concurrent powers of decision-making.[16] In *Battelley v. Finsbury B.C.*,[17] a local authority was not permitted to disregard an offer of employment made by a committee properly set up for that purpose.

ACTING UNDER ANOTHER'S DICTATION

12–004   It is the local authority which is entrusted with the power, and it is the local authority which must exercise it. Thus, the appearance of acting under the direction of another body will render the exercise of power unlawful. In *R. v. Stepney Corp.*[18] a mandamus was issued to compel reconsideration of the compensation payable to a vestry clerk, where the authority had mistakenly believed that the Treasury practice of making a deduction from compensation where the claimant was employed part-time effectively compelled them to assume the same position. The court held that this was tantamount to a failure to consider exercising its own discretion and unlawful.

In *R. v. Waltham Forest L.B.C., ex p. Baxter*[19] Lord Donaldson of Lymington M.R. suggested that if a councillor slavishly adhered to party policy as opposed to making up his own mind, then his vote would be invalid, because it would not be any exercise of discretion at all.[20] Similarly, an officer having had power lawfully delegated to him, must not act under the dictation of a councillor even if he is the chairman.[21]

Conversely, the Courts have refused to impose any duty on a chairman having a casting vote, other than that he must conduct himself honestly and consider the substantive merits of each motion before him.[22]

THE EFFECT OF PREDETERMINED POLICY

12–005   Where there is a discretion to be exercised, the local authority must not adopt a rigid policy. It must consider each case individually on its merits. Provided the policy itself is lawful, the authority may have regard to it, but it must not blindly bind itself to it.[23] The point was well put by Cooke J. in

---

[15] *R. v. Liverpool City Council, ex p. P.A.T.* (1984) 82 L.G.R. 648.
[16] See L.G.A. 1972, s.101(4) and *Huth v. Clarke* [1890] 25 Q.B.D. 391. *cf. Battelley v. Finsbury B.C.* [1958] 56 L.G.R. 165.
[17] n. 16 above.
[18] [1902] 1 K.B. 317.
[19] [1988] Q.B. 419.
[20] n. 19 above, p. 427A–D.
[21] *R. v. Port Talbot B.C., ex p. Jones* [1988] 2 All E.R. 207.
[22] *R. v. Bradford City Metropolitan Council, ex p. Wilson* [1990] 2 Q.B. 375. See also *R. v. Bradford City Metropolitan Council, ex p. Corris* [1990] 2 Q.B. 363, in which *ex p. Wilson* is considered.
[23] See, *e.g. R. v. Port of London Authority, ex p. Kynoch Ltd* [1919] 1 K.B. 176. See, also, *R. v. Warwickshire County Council, ex p. Lollymore* [1995] C.O.D. 52 (*held*: Council's policy of not making discretionary awards had been applied in an inflexible manner).

Stringer v. Minister of Housing and Local Government[24] where he said that there must be consideration of "all the issues which are relevant to each individual case as it comes up for decision".

Thus, in *Att.-Gen., ex rel. Tilley v. Wandsworth L.B.C.*,[25] a resolution to refuse all applications for the care of children from "intentionally homeless" families was declared to be unlawful.

It is substance rather than form which matters. Thus, a perfunctory hearing with no exercise of discretion will not suffice. In *Sagnata Investments Ltd. v. Norwich Corp.*,[26] for example, the refusal of a permit for an amusement arcade in Norwich after a full hearing, but pursuant to a blanket policy, was held to be unlawful.

Apparent fetters on discretion

The exercise of discretion by a local authority is governed by the criteria set out by Lord Greene M.R. in *Associated Provincial Picture Houses Ltd v. Wednesbury Corp.*[27]   **12–006**

As a general rule, an authority must not prevent itself from being able to utilise any of the powers (or duties) entrusted to it by Parliament, for to do so constitutes a fetter on the discretion itself.

Instances of contractual fetters abound in the case law. The *locus classicus* is *Ayr Harbour Trustees v. Oswald*[28] where the House of Lords held that an agreement to acquire land could not lawfully include a covenant restraining the authority from interfering with that or nearby land in the future because such a covenant was incompatible with the authority's power of acquisition.[29]

On similar principles, a contract purporting to restrain an authority from making byelaws was held to be invalid as being incompatible with the original power to contract.[30] In *Stringer v. Minister of Housing and Local Government*[31] a formal agreement by a planning authority to discourage development near the Jodrell Bank radio telescope was held to be unlawful because it amounted to an advance decision to refuse planning permission irrespective of the merits of the future applications.

However, the general rule may be qualified. In *R. v. Hammersmith L.B.C., ex p. Beddowes*,[32] the Court of Appeal held that there is a difference between cases such as *Ayr Harbour* on the one hand and *Dowty Boulton Paul Ltd v. Wolverhampton Corp.*[33] on the other. In the former the original exercise of power was a renunciation of the very power purportedly exercised, whereas in the latter, exercise in one fashion created a conflict of

---

[24] [1970] 1 W.L.R. 1281 at p. 1298.
[25] [1981] 1 W.L.R. 854.
[26] [1971] 2 Q.B. 614.
[27] [1948] 1 K.B. 223.
[28] (1882) 8 App.Cas. 623.
[29] See *B.T.C. v. Westmorland C.C.* [1958] A.C. 126, *per* Viscount Simonds at p. 143.
[30] *Triggs v. Staines U.D.C.* [1969] 1 Ch. 10.
[31] [1970] 1 W.L.R. 1281.
[32] [1987] 1 Q.B. 1050.
[33] [1971] 1 W.L.R. 204.

powers. In *Beddowes* the Court of Appeal held that in the latter case, the preference of one power over another so as to extinguish the other, was permissible provided the decision otherwise complied with *Wednesbury* criteria.

The exercise of the first power to extinguish the second will, of course, be irrational where the second power is inconsistent with the first. So too, the fettering of a duty as opposed to a mere power is always unlawful.[34]

Fetters are not always contractual. It has already been seen how, in the context of local government, delegation and predetermined policies can operate as restraints on the unimpeded exercise of discretion. So too, a local authority may not restrict its decision-making powers by an estoppel, though it may do so by an adjudication *per rem judicatem.*

The decisions in this area are not easily reconciled. In *Southend-on-Sea Corp. v. Hodgson (Wickford) Ltd.*[35] where a borough engineer misrepresented the use and planning consent of an area of land to a subsequent purchaser of that land, a Divisional Court held that the borough was not estopped from serving an enforcement notice once it appreciated the true position. However, in *Lever Finance v. Westminster L.B.C.*[36] the Court of Appeal held that, where a planning officer told a developer that a proposed variation in detailed plans was not material and the developer acted on it, the planning authority was bound by that advice, because the officer had ostensible authority.

In *Western Fish Products v. Penwith D.C.*,[37] the Court of Appeal distanced itself from the wide principles espoused in *Lever Finance* and held that a local authority could only be estopped in two narrow cases. First, where the authority had delegated its decision-making function to the person making the representations, *e.g. Level Finance.* Second, where the authority had decided to waive a procedural irregularity in relation to the application as, for example, in *Wells v. Minister of Housing and Local Government.*[38] The general rule is that an authority cannot be estopped.[39]

ABUSING DISCRETION

12–007   The principles enunciated by Lord Greene M.R. in *Associated Provincial Picture Houses Ltd. v. Wednesbury Corp.*[40] require that an authority exercising a discretion must:

    (a)   take all relevant factors into account;
    (b)   exclude all irrelevant factors from its consideration;

---

[34] *Maritime Electric Co. Ltd v. General Dairies Ltd* [1937] A.C. 610.
[35] [1962] 1 Q.B. 416.
[36] [1971] 1 Q.B. 222.
[37] (1978) 77 L.G.R. 185, C.A.
[38] [1967] 1 W.L.R. 1000.
[39] See an application of the general principle in *Thrasyvoulou v. Secretary of State for the Environment* [1988] Q.B. 809.
[40] [1948] 1 K.B. 223 at pp. 228–230.

(c) reach a decision which is neither perverse nor irrational.

It is often difficult to isolate cases which fall exclusively into one category because a challenge will usually be mounted on more than one conceptual basis.

Relevant and irrelevant considerations

In *Prescott v. Birmingham Corp.*[41] the Court of Appeal held that a public transport scheme which was free for certain classes of individual was unlawful because the scheme failed to have regard to commercial realities. Similarly, in *Bromley L.B.C. v. G.L.C.*[42] the House of Lords held that a low-fare public transport scheme introduced by the G.L.C. was unlawful because the G.L.C. had failed to consider the economic consequences of such a subsidy.[43] Both cases may also be viewed as an application of the principles in *Roberts v. Hopwood*[44] that a council must act within its powers to pay employees wages and that it is outside those powers to pay wages out of philanthropic feelings.[45]

12–008

Another instance of an authority exceeding its powers because of an irrelevant consideration is afforded by the facts of *Hall & Co. Ltd v. Shoreham-by-Sea U.D.C.*[46] There the planning authority had imposed a condition requiring the developer to construct a road along a frontage so as to give the public a right of way. This condition was held unlawful because it did not fairly and reasonably relate to the development itself.

In the developing area of community care similar problems have arisen. In *R. v. Cleveland C.C., ex p. Cleveland Care Homes Association*[47] the Court granted judicial review to the operator of a registered residential care home, on the ground that the local authority had acted unreasonably in inserting into the contract it had made with the operator, conditions which nullified the legislative purpose of the National Health Service and Community Care Act 1990 and the Community Care (Residential Accommodation) Act 1992, which provisions had the effect of, *inter alia*, "necessarily involving the private sector in the provision of residential care". This decision is to be contrasted with that in *R. v. Newcastle City Council, ex p. Dixon*[48] where Auld J. held that the contracts made between local authorities and operators of Registered Homes were contracts entered into by the authorities on a commercial basis, that there was no public law duty on councils to the home owners, and that neither the 1948 National

---

[41] [1955] Ch. 210.
[42] [1983] 1 A.C. 768.
[43] *cf. R. v. Merseyside C.C., ex p. G.U.S.* (1982) 80 L.G.R. 639.
[44] [1925] A.C. 578.
[45] Compare *Roberts v. Hopwood* with the case of *Pickwell v. Camden L.B.C.* [1983] 1 Q.B. 962, where Camden entered into negotiations with striking workers and achieved a settlement which proved to provide better terms for the strikers than the settlement eventually agreed nationally. The Court held that the applicant District Auditor had failed to show that the council had acted in excess of its statutory powers.
[46] [1964] 1 W.L.R. 240.
[47] [1994] C.O.D. 221.
[48] [1994] 158 L.G.R. 441.

Assistance Act, nor the 1984 Registered Homes Act restrained local authorities, in terms of public law, in the terms of contracts they sought to rely on when making arrangements with the operators of residential care homes.

Some doubt has arisen as to whether the relevant considerations test applies in cases where the authority is not concerned with a decision-making process which requires it to weigh one factor against another, but is merely performing an administrative function.[49] This theme is developed in the speech of Lord Bridge in *Cocks v. Thanet D.C.*,[50] but it remains to be seen whether, in the context of local government, the distinction is more apparent than real. The better view is, probably, that whenever a local authority makes a decision the concept of relevant and irrelevant considerations is material.

In *R. v. Somerset C.C., ex p. Fewings*[51] the Court of Appeal considered whether councillor moral objections to stag hunting were a consideration relevant to the council's decision to ban hunting on its land. The Court, dismissing the council's appeal, held that a prohibition on hunting could only be justified under section 120(1)(b) of the Local Government Act 1972 if the council reasonably concluded that the prohibition was objectively necessary for the management of the herd or for the preservation or enhancement of the amenity of the area. That was not the case here.

The failure to consider a relevant factor, or the consideration of an irrelevant factor, will not *ipso facto* render the determination unlawful. The vital question is the effect on the quality of the decision itself.[52] The court will not act in vain and thus, if the reality is that absent the error the authority would still have made the same decision, the court will not intervene.[53]

Bad faith

12–009   It is, undoubtedly, an abuse of discretion for a local authority to act in bad faith. Bad faith consists of the dishonest use of power.[54] It is not synonymous with improper motive. Dishonesty is a subjective condition whereas improper motive may result from (for example) a genuinely mistaken view of the law.[55]

---

[49] See *R. v. Barnet & Camden Rent Tribunal, ex p. Frey Investments Ltd.* [1972] 2 Q.B. 342. See too *R. v. Derbyshire C.C., ex p. K, The Times* May 2, 1994.

[50] [1983] 2 A.C. 286.

[51] [1995] 1 All E.R. 513.

[52] *Pickwell v. Camden L.B.C.* [1983] Q.B. 962.

[53] See *R. v. Lewisham L.B.C., ex p. Shell UK Ltd.*, n. 60 below.

[54] See *Cannock Chase D.C. v. Kelly* [1974] 1 W.L.R. 1, *per* Megaw L.J. at p. 6, and Sir David Cairns at p. 11.

[55] Though an erroneous view of the law would be reviewable in itself.

Unreasonableness in local authority decision-making

As a residual basis for judicial review, the *Wednesbury* principle dictates **12–010** that local authorities must not exercise their powers arbitrarily, or so unreasonably that the exercise of discretion is clearly unjustifiable.

In *Wednesbury* itself, it was said that a decision was susceptible to review if it was so unreasonable that no reasonable authority could ever have come to it. There the Court of Appeal refused to interfere with the defendant authority's conditions on Sunday cinema performances because the most that could be said was that reasonable men could honestly hold different views about the conditions.[56]

A good illustration of the difficulties involved in determining which side of the line a decision falls is afforded by *Wheeler v. Leicester City Council.*[57] Forbes J. and the Court of Appeal had held that it was reasonable for the council to revoke a local rugby club's licence to use the council's recreational facilities so as to punish the club for undergoing a tour of South Africa contrary to the council's anti-apartheid policy.[58] However, on appeal, the House of Lords unanimously held that the decision to punish the club was unreasonable in the *Wednesbury* sense.[59] The club had done no wrong and it was unreasonable and an abuse of power to seek to punish them or impose the council's views upon them.

By contrast, in *R. v. Lewisham L.B.C., ex p. Shell UK Ltd*[60] where a council boycotted a company's goods because the company had links with South Africa and refused to sever them, the Court of Appeal held that this was not unreasonable in the *Wednesbury* sense, but declared the policy unlawful on other grounds.

As always, it will not be enough for the applicant to show that the local authority has been *Wednesbury* unreasonable in order to obtain judicial review relief. One such case is that of *R. v. Blackpool B.C., ex p. Red Cab Taxis Ltd,*[61] where Judge J. held that while the local council had attached a *Wednesbury* unreasonable condition to the granting of minicab licences, nonetheless judicial review would not, as a matter of discretion, lie, since the aggrieved minicab drivers had an alternative means of redress, namely pursuing the case through statutory appeals in the Magistrates' Court.

LOCAL AUTHORITIES IN THE POLITICAL ARENA

The position of local authorities is now largely regulated by statute.[62] **12–011** The mere presence of a political motive which does not conflict with a

---

[56] For an example of a case on the other side of the line, see *R. v. Hillingdon L.B.C., ex p. Royco Homes Ltd.* [1974] Q.B. 720, where a planning condition was struck down because no reasonable authority could possibly have imposed a similar condition.

[57] [1985] A.C. 1054.

[58] See particularly, Sir George Waller, n. 57 above at p. 1068A–C.

[59] See, *e.g.* Lord Roskill, n. 57 above at p. 1079A–D.

[60] [1988] 1 All E.R. 938.

[61] *The Times*, May 13, 1994.

[62] See, *e.g.* s.2, Local Government Act 1986 and also Local Government and Housing Act 1989.

statutory prohibition will not automatically render an exercise of power unlawful.

In *Secretary of State for Education v. Tameside M.B.C.*[63] the pursuit of an educational policy espoused by one political party did not, in the absence of some other illegality, render education decisions unlawful.[64] It has already been observed[65] that councillors can vote as they please even in accordance with party politics, provided their vote is bona fide in the interests of the community. This is further exemplified by *R. v. Greenwich L.B.C., ex p. Lovelace.*[66] There a council's standing orders gave it limited powers to alter the membership of a committee or sub-committee; the Court of Appeal held that it was lawful for a political group to use those powers to remove a councillor who had ceased to be a member of that political party. Similarly, if all material considerations are taken account of, the fact that the majority of a local planning authority is politically predisposed in favour of a proposed development will not disqualify the council from determining the application for planning permission.[67]

This is not to say that the pursuit of political objectives is permissible in every context. It may, in context, be an irrelevant consideration. In *R. v. Barnet L.B.C., ex p. Johnson,*[68] for example, the Court of Appeal held that where a council granted permission to use a public recreation ground for a fair, it was unlawful to impose a condition banning any political activity at the fair.

NATURAL JUSTICE

12–012   It is axiomatic that decisions of local authorities are susceptible to judicial review if there is a danger of bias.[69] Indeed, the rules preventing bias and self-interest are, in the case of local authorities, statutorily fortified.[70]

---

[63] [1977] A.C. 1014.

[64] See also *R. v. London Transport Executive, ex p. G.L.C.* [1983] Q.B. 484.

[65] fnn. 19 and 20 above.

[66] [1991] 1 W.L.R. 506.

[67] *R. v. Amber Valley D.C., ex p. Jackson* [1985] 1 W.L.R. 298.

[68] *The Independent*, August 17, 1990. See also: *Bromley L.B.C. v. Greater London Council* [1983] 1 A.C. 768 (*held*: political policy to reduce fares on London transport overrode discretion and, when implemented, was *ultra vires*). *R. v. Coventry Airport, ex p. Phoenix Aviation, The Times*, April 17, 1995 (*held*: no power to use discretion to submit to such rule).

[69] As in the case of magistrates, doubts existed as to whether the proper test is "reasonable suspicion" or "real likelihood". In *Steeples v. Derbyshire C.C.* [1985] 1 W.L.R. 256 Webster J. selected the latter test, whereas in *Hannam v. Bradford Corp.* [1970] 1 W.L.R. 937 Sachs L.J. preferred the less stringent "real likelihood" test. The "real danger" test enunciated by the House of Lords in *R. v. Gough* [1993] A.C. 646 seems, now, to be the test for all tribunals including *sembre* local authorities. For an analysis, see para. 2–018 *cf.* though, *R. v. Hereford and Worcester C.C., ex p. Wellington Parish Council, The Times*, April 7, 1995 (*held*: Gough inexplicable where real danger was inevitable: "closed minds" were then necessary).

[70] See L.G.A. 1972, s.94.

Similarly, local authorities are obliged to observe the other rules of natural justice. The elements of that duty will, however, vary according to the nature of the power being exercised.[71] The more draconian the power, the more comprehensive the requirements of natural justice. For example, generally speaking, a local authority must give an opportunity for a citizen to make prior representations where the decision will affect his livelihood.[72]

In *R. v. Birmingham City Council, ex p. Dredger and Paget*,[73] the Divisional Court granted an application for judicial review by market traders who claimed that they had a legitimate expectation of being consulted when the council, which had sole control of the regulation of the markets, implemented a fundamental change in the way that the market rents were levied on the traders. The Court held that the legitimate expectation extended both to the amount of the rental charges and the method of arriving at them. However, if there had been no express promise or a regular practice of consultation (which was admitted to exist) then it could not be said that the requirements of procedural fairness or natural justice demanded that the traders should be consulted in the matter of the determination of charges for the street market.

Licensing applications

The scope of natural justice in relation to licensing decisions of a local authority depends, very much, upon the subject matter of the application.[74] Being a quasi-judicial determination, procedural safeguards, where appropriate, should not be compared to the formality inherent in a court hearing,[75] **12-013**

Nevertheless, it will rarely be lawful to refuse the applicant a hearing.[76] Thus in *R. v. Wear Valley D.C., ex p. Binks*[77] where the council revoked a street trader's informal licence without giving any notice or even reasons for the decision, Taylor J. held that this was a breach of natural justice for three reasons. First, because the council were under a duty to notify the trader of their intention to revoke the licence. Second, because they failed to give any reasons for their decision. Third, because they failed to give her any opportunity to be heard before reaching a final decision. This case is useful as a contemporary exposition of the elements of natural justice in the context of local government licensing.

Audi alteram partem, where it applies to council committee licensing, probably requires at least the giving of notice of the substance of any objection and an opportunity to respond to such objection.[78] Ordinarily,

---

[71] See, *e.g. Ridge v. Baldwin* [1964] A.C. 40.
[72] See, *e.g. R. v. Liverpool Corp., ex p. Liverpool Taxi Owners Association* [1972] 2 Q.B. 299. For a recent example see *R. v. Enfield L.B.C., ex p. T. F. Unwin* (1989) 46 Building L.R. 1.
[73] [1993] C.O.D. 340.
[74] See *Russell v. Duke of Norfolk* [1949] 1 All E.R. 109, *per* Tucker L.J. at p. 18.
[75] See, *e.g.* Lord Loreburn L.C. in *Board of Education v. Rice* [1911] A.C. 179.
[76] *R. v. Reading B.C., ex p. Quietlynn* (1986) 85 L.G.R. 387.
[77] [1985] 2 All E.R. 699.
[78] *R. v. Huntingdon D.C., ex p. Cowan* [1984] 1 W.L.R. 501, *per* Glidewell J. at p. 508.

written representations will suffice, but there is no set formula. There may be situations where an oral hearing is desirable and an authority should decide on the form of representations in each case.[79] If the representations are to be written, it would appear that an opportunity to make representations must be extended not only to the applicant, but to all those whose interests are affected.[80]

The opportunity to make representations must be a genuine one. In *R. v. Barnsley M.B.C., ex p. Hook*[81] for example, certiorari lay to quash revocation of a market trader's licence where the prosecutor was allowed to remain present while the licensing subcommittee considered its decision, thus giving the appearance of unfairness.

In general, initial applications for local authority licences are less likely to require an applicant to be heard orally. The High Court is, on judicial review, concerned with whether there has been a genuine exercise of administrative discretion. If there has not, the decision will be capable of challenge on the usual basis.

It appears that the position will be otherwise where a person is seeking renewal or opposing early revocation. There will usually be a legitimate expectation that the licence holder will be given the right to be heard. This does not mean that the licence cannot be refused unless there has been a change of circumstances since the previous grant.[82]

Each case will turn on its own facts. It is instructive to compare the facts of *R. v. Gravesham B.C., ex p. Gravesham Association of Licensed Hackney Carriage Owners*[83] with those in *R. v. Liverpool Corp., ex p. Liverpool Taxi Owners' Association.*[84]

In *Gravesham* the High Court held that the mere competition brought by an increase in the numbers of taxi cab licences, did not require the council to hear representations in advance from the applicant. The council were not depriving the applicants of their livelihood and there was no legitimate expectation that, after the commencement of section 16 of the Transport Act 1985, they would be consulted.

Conversely, in the *Liverpool Taxi* case where the council had undertaken not to depart from its policy prior to the enactment of legislation, it was held that the undertaking created an expectation that, if it was to be departed from, an opportunity to be heard would first be afforded to the applicants.

Dismissal from local authority employment

12–014   The court will grant judicial review of dismissal decisions in relatively few situations. An employee's remedies will usually lie in the private law courts and tribunals. Judicial review will only be available where the case

---

[79] *ibid.*

[80] *R. v. Assistant Commissioner of Police of the Metropolis, ex p. Howell* [1986] R.T.R. 52.

[81] [1976] 1 W.L.R. 1052.

[82] *R. v. Birmingham City Council, ex p. Sheptonhurst Ltd* (1989) 87 L.G.R. 830, where the council declined on the basis that it was inappropriate.

[83] *The Independent,* January 14, 1987.

[84] [1972] 2 Q.B. 299.

involves a sufficient public interest. In *R. v. East Berkshire H.A., ex p. Walsh*[85] the Court of Appeal considered the necessary public element. There the applicant was a senior nursing officer who alleged that his dismissal was in breach of the rules of natural justice. The court held that such an allegation involved infringement of a private law right and had no public law element.[86] Purchas L.J. said: "In my judgment the inquiry ought to be directed towards the rights alleged to be infringed and the remedies sought rather than the status enjoyed, qua contract or appointment, by the applicant."

Thus, the public status of the post held is not relevant. The essential element to a public law claim is the presence of a restraint on the exercise by the public body of its powers of dismissal. This so-called "statutory injection" can be an express restraint on the power to dismiss employees[87] or even an unlawful sub-delegation of power.[88] In order to succeed, however, there must be some statutory underpinning. Thus, in *R. v. Derbyshire C.C., ex p. Noble*[89] a police surgeon was refused judicial review on the basis that his dismissal was rooted in contract and not the exercise of any statutory power *per se*.

Even where the dismissal is rooted in statute, the allegation must be that the statute creates a restriction on the public body as a public body and not merely as an employer generally.[90] However, where there is such a restriction, the employee will usually be entitled to the procedural protections afforded by the rules of natural justice.

Other cases requiring observance of natural justice

In *Breen v. Amalgamated Engineering Union*,[91] Lord Denning M.R. observed that where a person "has some right or interest, or legitimate expectation of which it would not be fair to deprive him without a hearing or reasons given, then these should be afforded him, according as the case may demand."

12–015

It has already been seen how this principle has been applied in local government licensing and unfair dismissal cases. Other areas where natural justice has been imported include those where there is a *lis inter partes*,[92] where property rights are affected,[93] and where there is a legitimate expectation of consultation prior to the implementation of a particular policy.[94]

In the present context, it remains to be seen whether Lord Denning M.R.'s observations in *Breen* will come to be seen as the high-water mark of

---

[85] [1985] Q.B. 152.
[86] *cf. Malloch v. Aberdeen Corp.* [1971] 1 W.L.R. 1478, *per* Lord Wilberforce at p. 1595.
[87] See, *e.g. Vine v. National Dock Labour Board* [1957] A.C. 488.
[88] See *ex p. Walsh* [1984] I.C.R. 743, *per* Lord Purchas at p. 767.
[89] [1990] I.C.R. 808.
[90] *Ridge v. Baldwin* [1964] A.C. 40, *per* Lord Reid at p. 65.
[91] [1971] 2 Q.B. 175 at p. 191.
[92] See *Hoggard v. Worsborough U.D.C.* [1962] 2 Q.B. 93.
[93] *Cooper v. Wandsworth Board of Works* (1863) 14 C.B. (N.S.) 180.
[94] As, *e.g.* in *R. v. Secretary of State for the Environment, ex p. Brent L.B.C.* [1982] Q.B. 593.

natural justice. In *R. v. Manchester City Council, ex p. King*[95] the Divisional Court seemed prepared to hold[96] that a proposed increase in street trading licence fees from £196 to £1,000 or £2,500, did not require the council to give market traders an opportunity to make advance representations, despite the fact that the increase in fees might force many of them out of business.

The courts are, nonetheless, adapting the rules of natural justice to the various functions local authorities perform. In *R. v. Wandsworth L.B.C., ex p. P*,[97] for example, where a short-term foster mother was accused of sexually abusing a child whilst in her care, and a decision was taken to remove her from the council's list of approved foster parents without sufficient notice of the allegations against her, or any opportunity to be heard, Ewbank J. held that the decision had been taken in breach of the principles of natural justice.

Similarly, the currently topical area of residential and community care is already providing case law on the nature of the obligation imposed on a local authority to consult when closing residential homes or making other fundamental changes to the scope of its residential care provision. In *R. v. Devon C.C., ex p. Baker*[98] the Court of Appeal had two appeals by permanent residents of two residential homes against the decision of Popplewell J. to dismiss applications for judicial review of the decisions of Devon and Durham County Councils respectively to close each of the said homes. The appeals raised questions of the appropriate consultation that had to take place, and the availability of a possible alternative remedy pursuant to section 7(D) of the Local Authority Social Services Act 1970 (as amended by the National Health Service and Community Care Act 1990). The Court of Appeal held that the consultation obligation was threefold and consisted of obligations:

    (a) to inform residents that the closure of the homes was under consideration well before a final decision was to be made;

    (b) to ensure that the residents had a reasonable time to put to the council their objections to the proposed closure;

    (c) that these objections, once received, should be considered by the council.

There was no individual right of residents to be consulted face to face by the council's representatives. In the Durham case, the notice on proposed closure was given too late, and insufficient time was allowed for representations in opposition to be made.

On the availability of an alternative remedy point, the Court of Appeal considered submissions from the local authorities that since section 7(D) of the 1970 Act provided that if the Secretary of State is satisfied that any local authority has failed to comply with any of its duties which are social services

---

[95] [1991] C.O.D. 422.
[96] Though in the event it was unnecessary to do so, because advance representations had in fact been made.
[97] [1989] C.O.D. 262.
[98] [1995] 1 All E.R. 73.

functions, he may make an order declaring the council to be in default with respect to that duty and may give appropriate directions to secure compliance. The Court of Appeal held that while the closure of the homes were part of the Councils' social services functions, it was not clear that the *consultation* in respect of these closures was part of such a function. In view of this, and as the issue was entirely one of law in a developing field more appropriate for consideration by the courts rather than the Secretary of State, the availability of the alternative statutory remedy did not preclude the application for judicial review.

The rules of natural justice are, however, not inflexible and much will depend upon the facts. In *R. v. Harrow L.B.C., ex p. D*[99] the High Court held that the exclusion of parents from a care conference convened to decide whether their children should be placed on the "at risk register", did not constitute a breach of the rules of natural justice because the parents had been given an opportunity to make written representations and a full and proper consideration of the children's interests would be precluded by their presence.

The limited nature of an applicant's "legitimate expectation" of being consulted when a local authority changes its policy with detrimental knock-on effects to the prospects of the applicant entering into a contract with the authority (for the conclusion of which negotiations were already well advanced) is demonstrated by the case of *R. v. Camden L.B.C., ex p. Hughes.*[1] The applicant had been given a chance to address councillors orally and in writing. She could have increased or amended her offer to contract. The local authority had taken counsel's advice and had agreed to compensation for the applicant. The authority's procedure was fair and the applicant's legitimate expectation had been met.

Great care must be observed when decisions concerning the suspension of councillors themselves are being taken. In *R. v. Portsmouth City Council, ex p. Gregory*[2] the High Court held that where investigations are conducted into alleged misconduct by a councillor, "Justice required fair notice of charges, proceedings that did not continue too long each day and, in a small community . . . a wholly independent judge".

It appears that cases of real urgency will permit a local authority, at least initially, to dispense with the rules of natural justice.

In *R. v. Birmingham C.C., ex p. Ferrero Ltd*[3] the Court of Appeal held that where there is a statutory power to issue a notice preventing the applicant supplying the public with a certain product, then a right to make advance representations could not be grafted onto the statute, particularly where the statute had its own appeal structure. This is to be contrasted with the position where there is no real urgency and the statute does not lay down an appeal procedure.[4]

---

[99] [1989] C.O.D. 368.
[1] [1994] C.O.D. 253.
[2] [1990] T.L.R. 196.
[3] [1993] 1 All E.R. 530, C.A.; (1991) 155 J.P.N. 522.
[4] See, *e.g. R. v. Secretary of State for Health, ex p. United States Tobacco International Inc.* [1992] Q.B. 353.

An authority should not usually be a judge in its own cause, but if the maxim *nemo judex in cause sua* is overcome by express statutory authority, the court will not intervene because there is no illegality.[5]

EXAMPLES OF JUDICIAL REVIEW AGAINST LOCAL AUTHORITIES

12–016   Where appropriate, Order 53 should be used to apply for relief against authorities for the following purposes:

(a) To quash an invalid decision. Certiorari will lie whether the decision is clearly *ultra vires*[6] or has been reached in contravention of natural justice.[7]

(b) To restrain the exercise of statutory powers. Here, prohibition is usually the appropriate remedy. A good example of the use of this order is shown by the facts of *R. v. Liverpool Corp., ex p. Liverpool Taxi Fleet Operators' Association*.[8]

(c) To enforce the proper exercise of a discretion. The case law is full of instances of the grant of mandamus in such circumstances. Frequently certiorari quashes the original decision and mandamus so as to compel the council to reconsider the problem. This occurred in *R. v. Rochdale M.B.C., ex p. Cromer Ring Mill*[9] where a council decision refusing a rate refund was quashed where discretion had been fettered by application of a fixed policy. In addition mandamus was granted requiring the council to redetermine the matter in the light of the court's judgment.

On judicial review, injunctions and declarations lie to achieve similar purposes to the prerogative orders though there may be situations where they are, in fact, more appropriate.[10] In *R. v. Bromley L.B.C., ex p. Lambeth L.B.C.*[11] judicial review was unusually sought not to challenge a decision, but on the contrary for a declaration that the decision was valid. Hodgson J. held that despite the non-availability of the prerogative orders, the Supreme Court Act 1981 gave the court jurisdiction to grant declarations in both positive and negative terms in judicial review proceedings.[12]

---

[5] See, *e.g. Wilkinson v. Barking Corp.* [1948] 1 K.B. 721.
[6] See, *e.g. R. v. Barnet L.B.C., ex p. Nilish Shah* [1983] 2 A.C. 309.
[7] See, *e.g. R. v. Barnsley M.B.C., ex p. Hook* [1976] 1 W.L.R. 1052.
[8] [1972] 2 Q.B. 299.
[9] [1982] 3 All E.R. 761.
[10] See, *e.g. R. v. G.L.C., ex p. Westminster C.C., The Times,* January 22, 1985.
[11] *The Times,* June 16, 1984.
[12] *cf.* the facts of *R. v. G.L.C., ex p. Bromley L.B.C., The Times,* March 27, 1984, where a different conclusion as to jurisdiction was reached.

OTHER METHODS OF CONTROL

Outside Order 53, local authorities may be controlled in the exercise of **12–017** their powers in a variety of ways. Applicants for judicial review should always consider the possibility of an alternative remedy.

For example, statutory rights of appeal should usually be utilised unless they are ineffectual.[13] There is also the possibility of private law proceedings[14] and of applying to the Ombudsman for Local Administration. Sometimes it will be more effective to take no immediate action but to mount an indirect challenge to the validity of a local authority decision by collateral means (*e.g.* by resisting possession proceedings by alleging unreasonable excess of discretion in fixing a rent increase).[15]

---

[13] See, *e.g. Stepney B.C. v. John Walker and Sons Ltd* [1934] A.C. 365. *cf. R. v. Paddington Valuation Officer, ex p. Peachey Corp. Ltd.* [1966] 1 Q.B. 380 (*Held*: prerogative orders were more suitable than statutory appeal where it was sought to impugn the validity of the whole rating list rather than merely challenging individual items).

[14] See, *e.g. Barrs v. Bethell* [1982] Ch. 294, where it was held that apart from judicial review proceedings and the audit procedure under the 1972 Local Government Act, a ratepayer was not entitled to sue a local authority or its members without the leave of the Attorney-General unless he could show either an interference with some private right or an interference with a public right from which he had suffered damage peculiar to himself.

[15] See *Wandsworth L.B.C. v. Winder* [1985] A.C. 461. See also: *R. v. Jenner* [1983] 1 W.L.R. 873.

13. HOUSING THE HOMELESS

APPLICATION OF ORDER 53

13–001   It is well established that decisions of housing authorities under Part III of the Housing Act 1985[1] may usually only be challenged by means of an application for judicial review.[2]

Proceedings by way of writ or originating summons are, in this context, likely to be struck out as constituting an abuse of process.[3]

THE SCHEME OF THE ACT

13–002   The Act provides for the responsibility, in carefully defined circumstances, of local authorities to house persons who are homeless or threatened with homelessness.

In *Cocks v. Thanet D.C.*[4] the plaintiff sought a declaration against the housing authority, alleging breach of its duty to secure permanent accommodation in respect of himself and his family under the 1977 Act. As a preliminary point, the council argued that the plaintiff was not entitled to proceed by way of action but was permitted only to apply for judicial review. Milmo J. ruled against this argument because he was bound by a previous decision of the Court of Appeal.[5] The council, thereupon, appealed directly to the House of Lords who allowed the appeal holding that the plaintiff's sole remedy was under Order 53.

Lord Bridge of Harwich delivered the leading speech. In the course of it he observed that:

> "it is inherent in the scheme of the Act that an appropriate public law decision of the housing authority is a condition precedent to the establishment of the private law duty".[6]

---

[1] Previously the Housing (Homeless Persons) Act 1977. Part III of the Housing Act 1985 came into force on April 1, 1986.

[2] See *Cocks v. Thanet D.C.* [1983] 2 A.C. 286, applying *O'Reilly v. Mackman* [1983] 2 A.C. 237. Before this there was uncertainty. *cf. Thornton v. Kirklees M.B.C.* [1979] Q.B. 626 and *De Falco v. Crawley B.C.* [1980] Q.B. 460 with *Lambert v. Ealing L.B.C.* [1982] 1 W.L.R. 550.

[3] *O'Reilly v. Mackman,* n. 2 above at pp. 274–275 and pp. 283–285. See also *Mohram Ali v. Tower Hamlets L.B.C.* [1993] Q.B. 407, *Tower Hamlets L.B.C. v. Abdi* (1993) 25 H.L.R. 80 and *Hackney L.B.C. v. Lambourne* (1993) 25 H.L.R. 172 (C.A.). For a criticism of the basis on which the last three cases were decided, see: Gordon and Barlow: "When is a Defence not a Defence?" New L.J., (1992) December 18.

[4] See n. 2 above.

[5] *i.e. De Falco v. Crawley B.C.,* n. 2 above.

[6] See n. 2 above, at p. 293.

By this is meant that the rights of an applicant to accommodation, and the correlative duties of the housing authority to house him, depend upon the determination of certain preliminary questions in the applicant's favour. It is the authority itself which is required to make decisions on these issues and so determine the scope of its own duties.

The initial decision-making function is, according to Lord Bridge, exclusively one of public law as is shown by the absence of any obligations in private law until the decision is made. If what appears to be a breach of statutory duty is, in fact, founded upon a defective decision, the applicant's complaint is really against alleged misuse of public powers. It is, therefore, only capable of being challenged through proceedings in judicial review.

THE DECISION-MAKING PROCESS

In order to challenge successfully an authority's decision under the Act   **13–003** an applicant, under Order 53, must establish invalidity not on the merits but on the process employed. As Lord Hailsham has remarked in a different context:

> "two reasonable [public bodies] can perfectly reasonably come to opposite conclusions on the same set of facts without forfeiting their title to be regarded as reasonable".[7]

In *Cocks v. Thanet*, Lord Bridge set out the relevant criteria to be applied in Order 53 applications under the 1977 Act (now Part III of the 1985 Act):

> "The power of decision being committed by the statute exclusively to the housing authority, their exercise of the power can only be challenged before the courts on the strictly limited grounds: (i) that their decision was vitiated by bias or procedural unfairness; (ii) that they reached a conclusion of fact which can be impugned on the principles set out in the speech of Lord Radcliffe in *Edwards v. Bairstow* [1956] A.C. 14[8]; or (iii) that, in so far as they have exercised a discretion (as they may be required to do in considering questions of reasonableness under section 17(1)(2) and (4))[9]; the exercise can be impugned on the principles set out in the judgment of Lord Greene M.R. in *Associated Provincial Picture Houses Ltd v. Wednesbury Corporation* [1948] 1 K.B. 223."[10]

The Court of Appeal has ruled that the court can substitute its own decision for that of the housing authority on certain issues.

In *R. v. Tower Hamlets L.B.C., ex p. Begum and Rahman*[11] Butler-Sloss L.J. held that the question of whether a person is an applicant within section

---

[7] *Re W (An Infant)* [1971] A.C. 682 at p. 700.
[8] *i.e.* the "no-evidence" rule. See *Re Islam (Tafazzul)* [1983] 1 A.C. 688 at pp. 717–718 (*per* Lord Lowry).
[9] Now s.60(1), (2) and (4) of the 1985 Act.
[10] See n. 2 above, at p. 292.
[11] [1993] 2 W.L.R. 9.

62 of the Act was not a matter for the discretion of the authority reviewable only on *Wednesbury* principles: rather it was a question of precedent fact. Consequently, the court was entitled to reach its own decision as to whether a person had applied for accommodation. Lord Donaldson of Lymington M.R. added that the question whether the authority had reason to believe that an applicant might be homeless or threatened with homelessness was also an issue on which the court was entitled to substitute its own conclusions for those of the authority, in accordance with the principles in *R. v. Secretary of State for the Home Department, ex p. Khawaja.*[12]

However, the House of Lords held on appeal that local authorities do not owe a duty under the Housing Act to persons who are totally mentally incapacitated and that, accordingly, it must be for the authority to evaluate the mental capacity of the applicant. Such an evaluation could be reviewed by the courts on *Wednesbury* principles alone.[13]

Generally, however, the courts give a wide degree of latitude to housing authorities in homelessness cases. In *R. v. Hillingdon L.B.C., ex p. Pulhofer*[14] Brightman L.J. expressed his dismay at the "prolific use" of judicial review in homelessness cases and urged the courts to exercise "great restraint" in giving leave to move for judicial review of the decisions of housing authorities.

Inquiries

13–004   Under the Act, a housing authority is required by section 62 to make such inquiries as are "necessary to satisfy themselves" before reaching certain determinations of fact (for which see below). This does not necessarily connote particularly extensive investigation. Paragraphs 4.1 to 4.10 of the Code of Guidance for Local Authorities[15] contain guidelines for housing authorities on the nature and extent of inquiries.

In *Lally v. Kensington and Chelsea L.B.C.*[16] Browne-Wilkinson J. distinguished between a duty to pursue inquiries "rigorously and fairly" and a much more detailed "CID-type" inquiry. The latter, he stated, was not appropriate to an Act being administered under great pressure. The same point was made in respect of an "already hard pressed local authority" in *Miller v. Wandsworth L.B.C.*[17]

---

[12] [1984] A.C. 74.

[13] [1993] 2 W.L.R. 609 (H.L.). Lord Slynn dissented from the majority of the House on the issue of whether a housing duty was owed to a totally mentally incapacitated person. This restriction of the ambit of persons to whom housing duties are owed was echoed by the Court of Appeal's decision in *R. v. Secretary of State for the Environment, ex p. Tower Hamlets L.B.C.* [1993] Q.C. 632 in which it was held that no duty was owed to house immigrants who had obtained entry by stating falsely that they had accommodation and that the housing authority was entitled to investigate the immigration status of an applicant for housing and determine whether the applicant was an illegal immigrant.

[14] [1986] A.C. 484 at 518.

[15] The 3rd edition of the Code was issued by the Secretary of State pursuant to s.71 of the Act in October 1991 and revised to include reference to the Asylum and Immigration Appeals Act 1993.

[16] *The Times*, March 27, 1980.

[17] *The Times*, March 19, 1980.

As perhaps an irreducible minimum, the applicant is entitled to such inquiries as are appropriate to the specific circumstances of the case. Thus, for example, the housing authority's inquiries must cover all questions relevant to determining priority need.[18]

This, of course, leaves the authority with considerable discretion. It may (to take one example) successfully argue for a lower standard of investigation where overseas applicants are concerned.[19] The authority's decision can be challenged on the basis of inadequacy of inquiries only if the inquiries which it is alleged that the authority should have made are ones which no reasonable council could have failed to make.[20]

However, in recent years the courts have evinced a greater readiness to enforce the duty to inquire. Thus, as part of the section 62 duty, basic issues must be put to the applicant. In *R. v. Ealing L.B.C., ex p. Chanter*[21] where the housing authority asked the applicant's sister whether the applicant had left their mother's house voluntarily, the court held that the authority had failed in its duty to make inquiries by omitting to put to the applicant the sister's statement that the departure was voluntary.[22] If the authority suspects that the applicant is not acting in good faith, this matter should ordinarily be put to the applicant.[23]

The courts have also, on occasions, defined the appropriate range of the authority's inquiries. So where an applicant claims that he sold his home to repay loans to relatives, the housing authority is obliged to inquire into the loans, their terms and all the surrounding circumstances so as to determine whether the repayments were necessary.[24] In *Patterson v. Greenwich L.B.C.*[25] the respondent decided to refer the applicant to Birmingham on the grounds of local connection under section 67 of the Act. In Birmingham the applicant had been violently and repeatedly assaulted by her boyfriend and was subject to a risk of domestic violence. She did not volunteer to the respondent any information as to her domestic history. However, the Court of Appeal held that the respondent breached its duty to

---

[18] *R. v. Ryedale D.C., ex p. Smith* (1983) 16 H.L.R. 66.

[19] *De Falco v. Crawley B.C.*, n. 2 above, at p. 484 (*per* Sir David Cairns). See also *R. v. Kensington and Chelsea L.B.C., ex p. Bayani* (1990) 22 H.L.R. 406 (C.A.).

[20] *R. v. Nottingham City Council, ex p. Costello* (1989) 21 H.L.R. 301. See, however, *R. v. Brent L.B.C., ex p. McManus* (1993) 25 H.L.R. 643 in which it was held that the authority should have made inquiries as to the psychiatric state of the applicant and her daughter and as to the effect of sectarian violence in the area of Belfast in which they had previously lived, on the family.

[21] (1992) *Legal Action* December.

[22] See also *R. v. Tower Hamlets L.B.C., ex p. Rouf* (1989) 21 H.L.R. 294 (failure by the authority to ask the applicant about those matters which were ultimately held against him).

[23] *R. v. City of Westminster, ex p. Ali and Bibi* (1993) 25 H.L.R. 109. But see *Hobbs v. Sutton L.B.C.* (1994) 26 H.L.R. 132 where the Court of Appeal held that *Rouf* did not establish that in every case where good faith arose the matter should be specifically put to the applicant.

[24] *R. v. Tower Hamlets L.B.C., ex p. Ullah* (1992) 24 H.L.R. 680 *per* Henry J. See also *R. v. Tower Hamlets L.B.C., ex p. Saber* (1992) *Legal Action* September (the housing authority made insufficient inquiries to establish whether the applicant knew about housing benefit and, if she did, why she failed to claim it).

[25] (1994) 26 H.L.R. 159.

make inquiries by failing to ask her whether there was any risk of domestic violence in Birmingham prior to the decision to refer.

Furthermore, any doubt or uncertainty resulting from inquiries carried out by the authority must be resolved in the applicant's favour.[26]

Giving a reasoned decision

13–005   Where any decision is made that has the effect of limiting the authority's housing obligations the Act provides (s.64(4)) that reasons must be given for the decision.

The reasons need not be full or closely argued. In *Lambert v. Ealing L.B.C.*[27] the housing authority gave, as its reason for not complying with the full housing duty, that the applicant had failed to secure permanent accommodation for himself and family when he came to this country from France.

The Court of Appeal effectively rewrote these reasons. Lord Denning M.R. said:

> "We do not analyse the housing department's reasons too closely in this court. As we said in the *De Falco* case, we look at the substance of the matter. The substance here is that the local authority were saying, 'When you left France, you made yourself intentionally homeless. We know that you have had those two 'holiday lets' since: but your original 'intentional homelessness' is still the cause of your being homeless now. We are not bound to house you permanently. All we are bound to do is to give you temporary accommodation until you find something for yourself.'"

However, in *City of Gloucester v. Miles,*[28] the Court of Appeal considered that, in order to comply with the requirement to state reasons, the notification of intentional homelessness should state: (1) that the authority are satisfied that the applicant for accommodation became homeless intentionally; (2) when he or she is considered to have become homeless; (3) why he or she is said to have become homeless at that time, i.e. what is the deliberate act or omission in consequence of which it is concluded that at that time he or she ceased to occupy accommodation which was available for his or her occupation; and (4) that it would have been reasonable for him or her to continue to occupy it.[29]

The ambit of the duty to give reasons in homelessness cases in the absence of an express statutory requirement has been reconsidered by Sir Louis Blom-Cooper Q.C. in *R. v. Lambeth L.B.C., ex p. Walters.*[30] The deputy judge held that there was a general duty to give reasons wherever the

---

[26] *R. v. Gravesham B.C., ex p. Winchester* (1986) 18 H.L.R. 207.
[27] See n. 2 above, at p. 554.
[28] (1985) 17 H.L.R. 292 (C.A.).
[29] See also *R. v. Hillingdon L.B.C., ex p. H* (1988) 20 H.L.R. 554 (failure to identify the deliberate act or omission in the decision letter).
[30] (1994) 26 H.L.R. 176.

legislative framework of the administrative process was infused with the concept of fair treatment to those potentially affected by administrative action. The authority should have given reasons for its decision that the accommodation offered in fulfilment of its full housing duty was suitable. The reasons should show whether it had directed its mind to the rival medical assessments of the applicant's son's condition. However, this approach was not endorsed by the Court of Appeal in *R. v. Kensington and Chelsea Royal London Borough Council, ex p. Grillo*.[30a]

The effect of a failure to provide proper reasons is that the decision is unlawful.[31]

Taking evidence

A housing authority will not be expected to have regard to categories of **13–006** admissible evidence as in a court of law.

In *R. v. Southampton City Council, ex p. Ward*,[32] McCullough J. emphasised that all that was required was for an authority to act reasonably. They need not, in particular, reject hearsay evidence[33] or require it to be confirmed by other information. There is, likewise, no need for all the information to be put to an applicant "chapter and verse" to give him an opportunity to deal with it before the authority may take such information into account. Nor is there any requirement that the applicant be interviewed by the decision-taker, rather than by more junior staff in the housing department.[34]

FOLLOWING A POLICY

It has already been seen that a decision-making body may not fetter its **13–007** discretion by rigid adherence to a pre-existing policy.

This is exemplified (indirectly) in relation to housing by *Att.-Gen. ex re Tilley v. Wandsworth L.B.C.*[35] There a resolution of a local authority that in cases of intentional homelessness (under the 1977 Act) in respect of a family with young children, assistance with alternative accommodation would not be provided under the Children and Young Persons Act 1963, was held to be unlawful. The Court of Appeal, affirming the decision of the trial judge, said that such resolution fettered the council's discretion to consider the individual circumstances of each child who came up for consideration. In *R. v. Harrow L.B.C., ex p. Carter*[36] the housing authority's strict policy of referring all cases where the homeless person was found to

---

[30a] *The Times*, May 13, 1995.
[31] *R. v. Tower Hamlets L.B.C., ex p. Ojo* (1991) 23 H.L.R. 488, *per* Steyn J.
[32] (1984) 14 H.L.R. 114.
[33] *R. v. Nottingham C.C., ex p. Costello*, n. 20 above at 308.
[34] *R. v. Sutton L.B.C., ex p. Hobbs, The Times*, October 13, 1992. See, also *R. v. Tower Hamlets L.B.C., ex p. Khatun, The Times*, December 8, 1994.
[35] [1981] 1 W.L.R. 854.
[36] *The Times*, November 3, 1992.

have a legitimate local connection elsewhere was held to amount to a fettering of discretion.

The application of this principle works both ways. Section 71 of the Act stipulates that the housing authority must have regard, in the exercise of its decision-making functions, to such guidance as may from time to time be given by the Secretary of State. The Code of Guidance contains a number of statements of general policy which place a fairly heavy onus on local authorities to comply with the full housing duty by giving a generous interpretation to expressions used in the Act.

Frequently it is argued that an authority has disregarded the Code, on the facts of a particular case. It is, nonetheless, apparent that all that is required is that the provisions of the Code be considered; they do not have to be applied. Rigid application of the Code is as much a fettering of discretion as pursuance, without discrimination, of a policy adverse to the applicant.

This was clarified in *De Falco v. Crawley B.C.*[37] Paragraph 2.18 of the then current Code of Guidance enjoined authorities, when assessing intentional homelessness, to consider only the most immediate cause of that homelessness, rather than events that may have taken place previously. The authority, in the event, considered the cause of the applicant's homelessness as emanating from a decision to leave Naples, rather than from more immediate events which had occurred in this country.

It was argued that the consideration of non-immediate factors meant that the authority had not had regard to the Code. Lord Denning M.R. dealt with it in this way:

> "I am quite clear that the code should not be regarded as a binding statute. The council, of course, had to have regard to the code ... but, having done so, they could depart from it if they thought fit. This was a case in which they were perfectly entitled to depart from it."[38]

THE CONTENT OF THE DECISION

13–008   In *Cocks v. Thanet D.C.*, Lord Bridge classified both the preliminary questions for determination, and the duties arising therefrom.

He identified the authority's public law functions as consisting of reaching decisions on the following questions:

  (a) Is the applicant homeless or threatened with homelessness?
  (b) If yes—does he have a priority need?
  (c) If yes—did he become homeless intentionally?

Judicial review is concerned not merely with the general decision-making process but also with the way in which a housing authority applies the

---

[37] See n. 2 above, at p. 478.
[38] n. 2 above, at p. 291.

relevant law. This is examined below in relation to the above questions. Before coming to this, however, it is necessary to understand the way in which public law decisions interlock with private law duties under Part III of the 1985 Act.

PUBLIC AND PRIVATE LAW CONTRASTED UNDER THE ACT

The following interrelationship subsists between public law decision-making and private law "executive functions" according to Lord Bridge in *Cocks v. Thanet.* **13–009**

(a) If a housing authority has reason to believe that the applicant may be homeless or threatened with homelessness, it must make such inquiries as are necessary to satisfy itself of the answers to each of the questions set out above ("the duty to inquire").[39]

(b) If it has reason to believe that he may be homeless and have a priority need, it must accommodate him pending the outcome of inquiries ("the temporary housing duty").[40]

(c) If, after appropriate inquiries, it is satisfied that there is homelessness/threatened homelessness, and priority need, but it is not satisfied that the applicant became homeless intentionally, it must provide suitable permanent accommodation ("the full housing duty").[41]

(d) If, after such inquiries, it is satisfied as to homelessness/threatened homelessness, but is also satisfied that there is both priority need and intentional homelessness, it must provide him with interim accommodation and with advice and assistance ("the limited housing duty").[42]

In Lord Bridge's view the various duties referred to are enforceable by action. If, however, the decision arrived at does not lead to a private law duty, an applicant's remedy lies solely at the level of public law against the quality of the particular decision.

This kind of demarcation brings its own difficulties. The duty to inquire, whilst expressed in mandatory form is, surely, inextricably bound up with the decision-making process. An allegation of lack of proper inquiry is one of the ways in which the quality of a decision may be attacked in public law. The problem stems from the fact that procedural and conceptual distinctions do not always coincide. This, it may be recalled, is one of the obstacles preventing a satisfactory definition of what is meant by "public law".

---

[39] 1985 Act, s.62.
[40] 1985 Act, s.63(1).
[41] 1985 Act, s.65(2).
[42] 1985 Act, s.65(3).

ASSESSING HOMELESSNESS/THREATENED HOMELESSNESS

13–010   Usually there is little room for dispute as to whether an applicant is homeless or threatened with homelessness.[43] Homelessness is, primarily, the absence of accommodation.[44] Threatened homelessness is the likelihood of a person becoming homeless within 28 days.[45]

Section 58(2) of the 1985 Act treats a person as having no accommodation if:

> "there is no accommodation which he, together with any other person who normally resides with him as a member of his family or in circumstances in which it is reasonable for that person to reside with him—
>
> (a) is entitled to occupy by virtue of any interest in it or by virtue of an order of the court, or
>
> (b) has an express or implied licence to occupy, or in Scotland has a right or permission or an implied right or permission to occupy, or
>
> (c) occupies as a residence by virtue of any enactment or rule of law giving him the right to remain in occupation or restricting the right of another person to gain possession."[46]

Section 58(2A) provides that a person "shall not be treated as having accommodation unless it is accommodation which it would be reasonable for him to continue to occupy".

Residual cases where a person having accommodation is still treated as being homeless are where:

(a) he cannot secure entry to it[47]; or

(b) it is probable that continued occupation will lead to violence or threats of violence from some other person residing there[48]; or

(c) the accommodation consists of a movable structure, vehicle or vessel designed or adapted for human accommodation[49] and there is no place where he is entitled or permitted to place it and reside in it.[50]

The above provisions reveal limited scope for reaching an unreasonable conclusion. There is, however, potential for straightforward human error.

---

[43] See *Cocks v. Thanet D.C.*, n. 2 above, at p. 291 E (*per* Lord Bridge).

[44] 1985 Act, s.58(1).

[45] 1985 Act, s.58(4). The most apposite example would be a court order for possession expiring in 28 days.

[46] In *R. v. Croydon L.B.C., ex p. Jarvis* (1994) 26 H.L.R. 194 the Court held that the authority was entitled to conclude that an applicant was not homeless in circumstances where her assured shorthold tenancy had expired and the landlord had served a notice seeking possession but where a possession order had not yet been obtained, even though it was plain that an order would be obtained if the applicant remained in the accommodation.

[47] 1985 Act, s.58(3)(a).

[48] 1985 Act, s.58(3)(b). *e.g.*, the battered wife.

[49] *e.g.* a caravan or houseboat.

[50] 1985 Act, s.58(3)(c). In *R. v. Chiltern D.C., ex p. Roberts et al.* (1991) 23 H.L.R. 384 travelling showmen were held to be neither homeless nor threatened with homelessness

An example of this occurred in *R. v. Waveney D.C., ex p. Bowers*.[51] The applicant was staying in an overnight shelter which, being overnight accommodation for homeless people on a day-to-day basis, afforded only the most basic facilities.

Stephen Brown J. held that the housing authority's decision that the applicant was homeless was wrong. The nature of the shelter and the fact that the applicant had no licence to use it took the case outside the Act.[52] Other cases suggest that purely temporary accommodation, even if technically occupied by virtue of a licence, will not prevent the applicant from being "homeless" within the statutory definition of that term.[53]

In *R. v. Hillingdon L.B.C., ex p. Puhlhofer*,[54] the House of Lords held that the physical conditions of the property could not be taken into account in determining whether the applicant was homeless, save where conditions were so bad that the term accommodation could not properly be used to describe them. In the light of this ruling the Act was amended: subsections 58(2A) and (2B) provide that the condition of the property may be taken into account in determining homelessness.

One element in the council's decision on homelessness/threatened homelessness should be to establish the material date. This is not important in determining whether the applicant is homeless, but it can become important to challenges on findings of intentionality (see below).

PRIORITY NEED

Section 59 of the Act lays down four exclusive[55] instances of priority need. These occur where a homeless person (or one who is threatened with homelessness):

13–011

    (a) is a pregnant woman or resides or might reasonably be expected to reside with a pregnant woman[56];

    (b) has dependent children who are, or who might reasonably be expected to be, residing with him[57];

---

whilst moving from fair to fair, residing in each fairground on a temporary basis. See also *R. v. Hillingdon L.B.C., ex p. Bax Legal Action*, December, 1992, in which the authority decided that the applicant had been homeless throughout the period he lived on a houseboat as he had no permanent place to moor it. The court held that as he had a licence to cruise and keep the boat on the relevant waterways he was not homeless within s.58(3)(c) and only became homeless when his houseboat was destroyed by fire.

[51] [1983] Q.B. 238 (C.A.) and *The Times*, May 25, 1982 (Stephen Brown J.).

[52] In fact, Stephen Brown J. dismissed the application for judicial review on other grounds, but the applicant's appeal was allowed and a declaration awarded. The Court of Appeal did not, further, consider the question of homelessness.

[53] See, especially, *R. v. Ealing L.B.C., ex p. Sidhu* (1982) 2 H.L.R. 45 and *Din v. Wandsworth L.B.C.* [1983] 1 A.C. 657 at 677 (*per* Lord Lowry). See, also *R. v. Royal Borough of Kensington and Chelsea, ex p. Ben-El-Mabrouk, The Times,* June 22, 1995, (*held*: 5th floor flat ever present fire which did not render applicants homeless).

[54] See n. 14 above.

[55] Although there may be further categories if specified by the Secretary of State: 1985 Act, s.59(3).

[56] 1985 Act, s.59(1)(a).

[57] 1985 Act, s.59(1)(b).

(c) is vulnerable (this vulnerability extending also to any person who resides or might reasonably be expected to reside with him) as a result of old age, mental illness or handicap, or physical disability or other special reason[58];

(d) is homeless or threatened with homelessness as a result of any emergency such as flood, fire or any other disaster.[59]

Judicial review may lie where an authority has misconstrued the Act. In *Re Islam (Tafazzul)*[60] the applicant had dependent children living with him but the authority decided that he did not have a priority need because it was not reasonable for those children to reside with him. The court decided that, whether or not the authority's estimation of what was reasonable was correct, it was an error of law to consider that question in relation to dependent children unless they were not, at the material time, residing with the applicant.

More common is the assertion that a housing authority has misapplied law to fact. The possession of a custody order, for example, is a wholly irrelevant consideration in determining priority need.[61]

Most of the definitions of priority need are clear-cut and the possible ambit of judicial interference is small. The issue of vulnerability may, however, cause problems.

In *R. v. Waveney D.C., ex p. Bowers*,[62] the Court of Appeal granted judicial review (by way of a declaration) of a council decision that the applicant was not a person in priority need.

The authority's decision seems to have been based on a literal application of the statutory criteria (old age, mental illness or handicap, physical disability, other special reason). The applicant was aged 59 and had slight brain damage which, together with a drinking problem, made limited supervision necessary. Considering these elements separately his condition did not bring him within the Act. Stephen Brown J., applying the *Wednesbury* principle, found it impossible to say that the council's decision was unreasonable.

Waller L.J. in the Court of Appeal took as the starting point an extended and more liberal interpretation of vulnerability as meaning "less able to fend for oneself so that injury or detriment will result when a less vulnerable man will be able to cope without harmful effects."[63] On that basis the applicant was clearly vulnerable, and his appeal against the initial refusal of judicial review was allowed.[64]

---

[58] 1985 Act, s.59(1)(c).

[59] 1985 Act, s.59(1)(d).

[60] See n. 8 above.

[61] *R. v. Ealing L.B.C., ex p. Sidhu*, n. 53 above.

[62] See n. 51 above.

[63] At pp. 244–245. This case places some reliance on the flexible approach required by para. 2–12 of the then Code of Practice.

[64] In *R. v. Lambeth L.B.C., ex p. Carroll* (1988) 20 H.L.R. 142 it was held that subnormality could constitute a mental handicap and that it was not necessary for there to be a recognisable psychotic illness in order to establish vulnerability.

In *R. v. Nithsdale D.C., ex p. Wilson*[65] the court held that the vulnerability of the applicant, who had been excluded from the parental home and subjected to sexual assault which left her nervous and unable to cope on the streets, was to be assessed by comparison with an average homeless person, that she was vulnerable for another special reason and that nothing odd or exceptional was required to establish vulnerability.[66]

INTENTIONAL HOMELESSNESS

This is, undoubtedly, the most fertile breeding ground for judicial review applications.   **13–012**

Section 60(1) of the 1985 Act provides that a person becomes homeless intentionally:

> "if he deliberately does or fails to do anything in consequence of which he ceases to occupy accommodation which is available for his occupation and which it would have been reasonable for him to occupy."[67]

Availability of occupation is defined (section 75) as meaning accommodation that is available for occupation not only by the applicant but also by "any other person who might reasonably be expected to reside with him".

Additional provisions govern the evaluation of deliberateness of conduct and reasonableness of continued occupation (section 60(3) and (4)); these are examined below.

It follows from the above provisions that before arriving at a decision that the applicant has made himself intentionally homeless an authority must consider whether:

(a) there has been a deliberate act or omission on the part of the applicant;

(b) there is a cesser of occupation[68];

(c) there is a causal relationship between these elements;

(d) the accommodation was, at the time of the conduct complained of, available for his occupation and it would have been reasonable for him to continue to occupy it.

Order 53 will be available if all these factors have not been adequately considered.

The applicant's conduct

There must be a deliberate act or omission on the part of the applicant. In this context, however, the word "deliberate" connotes something less than   **13–013**

---

[65] *Legal Action*, September, 1992.

[66] *cf. R. v. Bath C.C., ex p. Sangermano* (1985) 17 H.L.R. 94 it was held that language difficulties alone could not amount to some other special reason.

[67] Similar provisions (s.60(2)) deal with threatened intentional homelessness where an act/omission must have the "likely result" of forcing the applicant to vacate, etc.

[68] Or, in the case of threatened homelessness, that cesser of occupation is a likely result.

appreciation of the likely consequences of a particular course of behaviour.[69]

Obiter dicta by Lord Denning M.R. in *R. v. Slough B.C., ex p. Ealing L.B.C.*[70] had suggested that behaviour, however reprehensible, would fall outside the Act if an applicant did not deliberately intend, by reason of his conduct, to be evicted.

These observations were, however, disregarded by the Court of Appeal in *R. v. Salford City Council, ex p. Devenport.*[71] As Fox L.J. indicated, the Act contains no requirement that an applicant deliberately became homeless; only that he deliberately did or omitted to do something in consequence of which he ceased to occupy.

Examples of findings being upheld on this basis include: conduct resulting in eviction due to nuisance and annoyance to neighbours[72]; arrogance and rudeness leading to a request that the applicant vacate[73]; a wilful and/or persistent refusal to pay rent or mortgage arrears[74]; the failure by an evicted private tenant to take civil proceedings to secure re-entry and the failure by a cohabitant to use domestic remedies, *e.g.* ouster injunctions.

A wilful or persistent refusal or failure to pay rent may not amount to a deliberate act within the meaning of the section if the considered decision not to pay rent was caused by the applicant's lack of means. Thus, where a mother's means are insufficient to enable her to pay rent and maintain her children, her decision not to pay the rent may not be a deliberate act such as to justify a finding of intentional homelessness.[75]

The good faith proviso

13–014   A housing authority must consider the good faith defence afforded by section 60(3). This states that:

> "For the purposes of subsection (1) or (2) an act or omission in good faith on the part of a person who was unaware of any relevant fact shall not be treated as deliberate."

It is ignorance of a relevant fact, not its legal consequences, that falls within section 60(3). What amounts to a relevant fact seems to be a mixed question of law and fact. Certainly the authority has a large measure of discretion but it must apply the correct test. The question is whether the ignorance is in good faith, not whether it is reasonable.

---

[69] Since few people really become homeless intentionally. See Lord Lowry in *Din v. Wandsworth L.B.C.*, n. 53 above, at p. 679.

[70] [1981] Q.B. 801 at 809.

[71] (1983) 8 H.L.R. 54 (C.A.).

[72] *R. v. Salford C.C., ex p. Devenport, ibid.* See also *R. v. Hammersmith & Fulham L.B.C., ex p. P* (1990) 22 H.L.R. 21 (alleged criminal and anti-social behaviour leading to death threats from the I.R.A.).

[73] *Lazere v. Slough D.C.* reported in *Roof* (January 1981).

[74] *Robinson v. Torbay B.C.* [1982] 1 All E.R. 726, *R. v. Eastleigh B.C., ex p. Beattie (No. 2)* (1984) 17 H.L.R. 168.

[75] See *R. v. Wandsworth L.B.C., ex p. Hawthorne, The Times*, July 14, 1994.

Thus in *R. v. Hammersmith & Fulham L.B.C., ex p. Lusi*[76] the court held that the fact that the applicant had been misled as to business prospects which led him to move abroad constituted a relevant fact within section 60(3) and in *R. v. Wandsworth L.B.C., ex p. Rose*[77] certiorari was awarded to quash an adverse decision where the applicant came to England from Jamaica believing that her father would accommodate her. He had consented to this, but the accommodation became overcrowded. It was held that her unawareness of the true nature of her accommodation was a "relevant fact" for this purpose. On similar principles the good faith proviso was applied to an applicant who failed to discharge the mortgage instalments in the erroneous belief that the DHSS was making direct payments.[78]

Cesser of occupation

The housing authority must be satisfied that an applicant has ceased to occupy specific accommodation. Ordinarily, this will be a straightforward matter of fact. Judicial review may lie if this aspect is insufficiently considered.[79]   **13–015**

It is not immediately apparent whether the words "ceases to occupy" are to be equated with the concept of homelessness as defined in section 58. The fact of homelessness must be established prior to any investigation of intentionality. Thus it may be that it is unnecessary for the authority to do more than satisfy itself that the applicant is no longer occupying, even though he retains an interest in, or licence to occupy, particular accommodation.

The effect of such construction, however, severs the connection between "intentionality" and "homelessness". Perhaps, therefore, the expression "ceases to occupy" should be construed *ejusdem generis* with "homelessness".

The fact that a person who does not live in a house owned jointly with her mother and sisters voluntarily transfers her interest in the house to her mother cannot render her intentionally homeless as the transfer did not cause her to cease to occupy the accommodation. A deliberate act or omission which causes a person to cease to have the right to occupy accommodation is insufficient.[80]

---

[76] (1991) 23 H.L.R. 260. See also *R. v. Exeter City Council, ex p. Tranckle* (1994) 26 H.L.R. 244 (C.A.).

[77] (1983) 11 H.L.R. 197. See also *R. v. Winchester C.C., ex p. Ashton* (1992) 24 H.L.R. 48 (Q.B.D.) and 24 H.L.R. 520 (C.A.).

[78] *White v. Exeter C.C.* December 1981 L.A.G. Bul. 287. This is a county court decision but would probably be decided the same way on judicial review.

[79] But *cf. Lambert v. Ealing L.B.C.* (n. 2 above) where the authority does not seem to have properly thought out this point. As has been seen, the Court of Appeal simply rewrote its reasons.

[80] *R. v. Wandsworth L.B.C., ex p. Oteng* (1994) 26 H.L.R. 413.

Causality

13–016   Problems of causation frequently arise on judicial review. The principal issues, as the decided cases demonstrate, are whether:

    (a) the applicant is himself responsible for the consequences of someone else's conduct;

    (b) cause and effect are too remote.

The doctrine of acquiescence

13–017   Only the applicant may be the subject of a finding intentional homelessness.[81] Nonetheless the courts have not been slow to develop the doctrine of acquiescence whereby the applicant is held liable for the acts and omissions of another unless he has attempted to prevent such behaviour.[82] The principle is not confined to spouses and cohabitants: in *R. v. Salford City Council, ex p. Devenport* it was the behaviour of the applicant's children which led to the finding of intentionality.[83] If the applicant discovers the conduct too late to do anything about it, simple awareness of the acts/omissions in question does not amount to acquiescence.[84]

Child applicants cannot rely on the principle of non-acquiescence in the acts or omissions of their parents, as dependent children are not in priority need in their own right.[85]

Although the burden of establishing intentionality lies upon the authority, it would appear, from the acquiescence principle, that its only obligation is to investigate such evidence as is put before it.

If an applicant is unable to adduce any evidence, it seems that the housing authority is entitled to assume that he was a party to another's misconduct.[86] Decisions on this basis will be difficult to challenge since the policy of the Act "requires consideration of the family unit as a whole".[87]

Remoteness

13–018   The issue of remoteness occurs where an applicant has, at some time, become intentionally homeless but, thereafter, obtains accommodation.

Whether intervening accommodation breaks the chain of intentionality is not always easy to assess. In most cases it will be a question of fact but

---

[81] This flows from the wording of s.60.

[82] See especially *R. v. North Devon D.C., ex p. Lewis* [1981] 1 W.L.R. 328, *R. v. Swansea C.C., ex p. Thomas* (1983) 9 H.L.R. 64 and *R. v. Mole Valley D.C., ex p. Burton* (1988) 20 H.L.R. 479.

[83] n. 72 above.

[84] *R. v. East Northamptonshire D.C., ex p. Spruce* (1988) 20 H.L.R. 508 but *cf. R. v. Barnet L.B.C., ex p. O'Connor* (1990) 22 H.L.R. 486.

[85] *R. v. Oldham M.B.C., ex p. Garlick, R. v. Bexley L.B.C., ex p. Begum* [1993] 2 W.L.R. 609 (H.L.).

[86] *R. v. North Devon D.C., ex p. Lewis*, n. 82 above.

[87] *ibid.*, per Woolf J.

there may be situations where no reasonable authority could have come to a particular conclusion.[88]

Intervening accommodation is relevant only if "settled". It seems to be established that temporary or short-term accommodation is not settled and will not affect the chain of intentionality. Accommodation falling within this category has been held to include: a winter let not exceeding eight months[89]; a succession of short-term holiday lets[90]; and consecutive gypsy caravans for intermittent periods.[91]

It would appear that the test for settled accommodation is objective, despite indications in *Din* that the housing authority should consider the question of intervening accommodation subjectively. Thus, in *R. v. Purbeck D.C., ex p. Cadney*[92] the applicant sought to rely on a period of three months during which she had moved out of the matrimonial home to cohabit with someone else. She sought to argue that she had intended to stay permanently and that therefore these three months should count as a period of settled intervening accommodation. The court held that this was too subjective and that the authority was entitled to take the view that the intervening period was too precarious.

The question whether accommodation is settled is one of fact and degree. Although the length of residence is a highly relevant factor, there is no "magic" time before which the accommodation is not settled and after which it is.[93]

Available accommodation

Accommodation that the applicant has vacated (or is likely to be forced to vacate) must, at the material time,[94] be:

13–019

(a) available for his occupation; and
(b) accommodation which it would have been reasonable for him to continue to occupy.

Availability for occupation

Availability for occupation must, according to section 75 of the Act, be judged by whether it is available not merely for the applicant but also for any other person who might reasonably be expected to reside with him.

13–020

The impact of section 75 is sometimes overlooked and where this occurs judicial review will be obtainable. In *Re Islam (Tafazzul)*[95] for example, the housing authority made a finding of intentional homelessness where the

---

[88] As, *e.g.*, in *R. v. Basingstoke and Deane B.C., ex p. Bassett* (1983) 10 H.L.R. 94 at p. 125. (Council failed to consider marital breakdown as breaking the chain of causation).

[89] *Dyson v. Kerrier D.C.* [1980] 1 W.L.R. 1205.

[90] *Lambert v. Ealing L.B.C.*, n. 2 above.

[91] *Davis v. Kingston L.B.C., The Times*, March 28, 1981.

[92] (1985) 17 H.L.R. 534.

[93] See *R. v. Croydon L.B.C., ex p. Easom* (1993) 25 H.L.R. 262.

[94] *i.e.* at the time of the deliberate act or omission.

[95] See n. 8, above.

applicant arranged for his family to leave accommodation in Bangladesh and come to live with him in England. His accommodation in this country consisted of only two small rooms which was unsuitable for the family and, in consequence, a notice to quit was served.

In reaching its decision that the applicant was intentionally homeless, the authority took the view that it would have been reasonable for the applicant's family to continue to occupy their accommodation in Bangladesh. This decision was upheld by Glidewell J. and by the Court of Appeal (Ackner L.J. dissenting).[96]

Only Ackner L.J., in the Court of Appeal, applied what was then section 16 of the 1977 Act correctly to the facts. He stated that the English accommodation was never available for occupation by the family unit because it was unsuitable. This view was reiterated in the House of Lords by Lord Wilberforce, at his most succinct:

> "Put very briefly, the case is four square within the Act: the appellant was 'homeless': he was entitled to priority: he never had any 'available accommodation' within the meaning of section 16 which he could give up: section 17 [now section 60] could not be applied to his case. There is no answer to his claim."[97]

Reasonableness of continued occupation

13-021   The difficulty of succeeding in an application for judicial review in this context is illustrated by Lord Lowry's observation in *Din v. Wandsworth L.B.C.*[98] that an authority "may properly decide that it would have been reasonable for a person to continue to occupy ... even where it would also have been reasonable to leave".[99]

The reasonableness of continued occupation must be determined as at the time of the deliberate act or omission which led to cessation of occupation, rather than at the date on which the applicant left the property.[1]

Failure to consider reasonableness at all will, undoubtedly, lead to review.[2] So, too (depending on the circumstances), will the omission of

---

[96] In the Court of Appeal, Lord Denning M.R. thought that the accommodation abroad was occupied by the applicant through his family and that he was, therefore, ceasing to occupy accommodation for his own use. Sir Denys Buckley said that the applicant was directly responsible for ceasing to occupy the English accommodation by bringing his family here.

[97] At p. 708. See also *R. v. Westminster C.C., ex p. Ali* (1983) 11 H.L.R.. 83. *cf. R. v. Tower Hamlets L.B.C., ex p. Monaf* (1987) 19 H.L.R. 577 (Q.B.D.), (1988) 20 H.L.R. 529 (C.A.) in which the applicant had lived in the U.K. for a number of years during which time he made several visits to his family in Bangladesh. His last visit had lasted three years, at the end of which he brought his wife and children back with him. The authority decided that he was intentionally homeless and the court agreed that accommodation in Bangladesh had been available to him. The decision was quashed by the C.A. on different grounds (defects in the decision letters).

[98] See n. 53 above, at p. 679.

[99] For an example of the application of this principle, see *R. v. Gravesham B.C., ex p. Winchester*, n. 26 above.

[1] *R. v. Hammersmith and Fulham L.B.C., ex p. P*, n. 72 above.

[2] See, *e.g.*, *R. v. Eastleigh B.C., ex p. Beattie (No. 1)* (1983) 10 H.L.R. 94.

material factors.[3] However, in most instances, the disturbing of a decision will occur, under this head, by virtue of the residual principle in the *Wednesbury* case that no reasonable authority could have come to a particular view.

Thus in *R. v. South Herefordshire D.C., ex p. Miles*[4] a two-room, rat-infested hut without mains services was accommodation which an authority could consider reasonable in respect of two adults and two children, but which no reasonable authority could consider reasonable in respect of a third child. Yet in *R. v. Newham L.B.C., ex p. McIlory and McIlory*[5] the authority was entitled to decide that it would have been reasonable for the Catholic applicants who had been subjected to years of harassment by Protestants to have remained in occupation on the basis that they should have waited to see whether they would be rehoused by their landlords.

In *R. v. Croydon L.B.C., ex p. Graham*[6] the respondent authority concluded that the applicant, who had left the accommodation which she shared as a friend because she decided that she could not afford the rent, could have afforded to continue paying the rent. The Court of Appeal held that the reasonableness of her actions should not be judged on whether her income was sufficient to pay the rent. It was for the applicant to judge whether she would find it difficult to continue paying the rent. It was not necessarily unreasonable to seek to reduce her commitments. The respondent should have considered whether it was unreasonable to leave because it put her in a precarious and vulnerable position by reason of the accommodation to which she was moving. The Court of Appeal concluded that there was no material to justify such a finding.

Limitation on review: section 60(4)

When considering whether it would have been reasonable for a person to continue to occupy accommodation, section 60(4) of the 1985 Act provides that regard may be had to "the general circumstances prevailing in relation to housing in the district of the local housing authority to whom he applied for accommodation or assistance in obtaining accommodation". **13–022**

The court held in *R. v. Tower Hamlets L.B.C., ex p. Monaf*[7] that section

---

[3] The physical condition of a property is not the only factor to be taken into account in assessing the reasonableness of continued occupation. The availability of employment and benefits (*R. v. Hammersmith and Fulham L.B.C., ex p. Duro-Rama* (1983) 9 H.L.R. 71), the applicant's sense of isolation (*R. v. Swansea C.C., ex p. Hearn* (1991) 23 H.L.R. 372) and the applicant's financial position (*R. v. Hillingdon L.B.C., ex p. Tinn* (1988) 20 H.L.R. 305) are all relevant factors. In *R. v. Hillingdon L.B.C., ex p. Wilson* (1983) 12 H.L.R. 61, the court held that it was not reasonable to expect a woman to remain in accommodation in Australia in circumstances where she had no legal permission to remain and would shortly reach the stage of pregnancy when airlines would not permit her to fly. In *R. v. Brent L.B.C., ex p. Awua, The Independent,* July 25, 1995, the House of Lords held that council accommodation need not be "settled" before a reason is capable of being intentionally homeless by leaving it.

[4] (1985) 17 H.L.R. 82.

[5] (1991) 23 H.L.R. 570.

[6] (1994) 26 H.L.R. 286.

[7] (1988) 20 H.L.R. 529.

60(4) requires the authority to carry out a balancing act between the housing conditions in the authority's area and the accommodation which the applicant has ceased to occupy and the applicant's pattern of life. Such a comparison should, however, only be carried out where relevant to the case.[8]

An application for judicial review will lie where an authority has treated section 60(4) as exhaustive and failed to consider any other factors that might go to reasonableness.[9] Similarly there must actually be a scarcity of accommodation in the area in order for the authority to rely on this provision.[10] The authority need not provide detailed information on the nature and availability of accommodation in its area,[11] but it seems that they must have some evidence of the general circumstances prevailing in the area.[12]

Leaving before the making of a possession order

13–023   Particular problems occur where an applicant leaves accommodation before a court order for possession has been made against him.

In *Din v. Wandsworth L.B.C.*[13] the applicant had encountered difficulty in payment of rent and rates. He vacated the premises despite the housing authority's advice not to do so and before any demand for vacant possession. It was held that the authority decided correctly that it would have been reasonable for him to continue in occupation even though, subsequently, he would have become homeless anyway.

It does not follow that an applicant will always be expected to remain in occupation until the making of a possession order. *De minimis* prior departures should probably be ignored.[14] So, too, departures where possession will inevitably be obtained ought to be disregarded in estimating reasonableness.[15] Often, of course, the borderline will be a fine one.

LOCAL CONNECTION

13–024   A local authority's obligations may be modified if the housing authority takes the view that neither the applicant nor any person who might reasonably be expected to reside with him has any local connection. In certain circumstances it may be possible to transfer the burden of the obligation to provide the applicant with accommodation to another authority with whom the applicant does have such a local connection.[16]

---

[8] *R. v. Newham L.B.C., ex p. Tower Hamlets L.B.C.* (1991) 23 H.L.R. 62 (C.A.).

[9] *R. v. Hammersmith and Fulham L.B.C., ex p. Duro-Rama,* n. 3 above.

[10] See *Din v. Wandsworth L.B.C.,* n. 53 above, at p. 671 (*per* Lord Fraser).

[11] See *Tickner v. Mole Valley D.C.* August 1980 L.A.G. Bul. 187.

[12] See *R. v. Westminster C.C., ex p. Ali* (1983) 11 H.L.R. 83.

[13] See n. 53, above.

[14] See, *e.g., R. v. Mole Valley D.C., ex p. Minnett* (1983) 12 H.L.R. 49.

[15] *R. v. Portsmouth C.C., ex p. Knight* (1983) 10 H.L.R. 94 and *R. v. Surrey Heath B.C., ex p. Li* (1984) 16 H.L.R. 79. See also the Code of Guidance, para. 10–12.

[16] 1985 Act, ss.67 and 68.

The Court of Appeal concluded in *R. v. Tower Hamlets L.B.C., ex p. Abbas Ali*[17] that where an authority notifies by reason of section 67(2) of the Act another authority with whom there is a local connection, the first authority is under no duty by reason of section 65(2) to provide accommodation. Thus, where the second authority makes an offer of permanent accommodation which is refused (thereby discharging its duty under section 65(2)) and where the homeless person subsequently obtains a local connection with the original notifying authority, a duty is then imposed on the latter under section 65(2) and it cannot rely on the offer of accommodation made by the second authority as discharging that duty.

The term "local connection" is expressed by section 61 of the Act to refer to a connection with a particular area by reason of:

(a) voluntary normal residence (past or present);
(b) employment;
(c) family associations;
(d) any special circumstances.[18]

In *R. v. Eastleigh B.C., ex p. Betts*[19] the House of Lords emphasised that the fundamental question is whether a "local connection" exists. Residence and the other grounds stated in section 61 are irrelevant unless they are such as to give rise to a local connection. The housing authority may have regard to, but may not rigidly apply, the criteria for the interpretation of section 61(1) in the "Local Authority Agreement".

From the standpoint of judicial review, the decision in *Betts* makes it difficult to challenge a local authority's findings since there are no specific criteria for estimating local connection and it will, therefore, not always be easy to know what factors the authority have considered. In *R. v. Newham L.B.C., ex p. Tower Hamlets L.B.C.*[20] the Court of Appeal held that the referring authority's decision on intentionality could not found a referral if it was a decision that would be quashed in judicial review proceedings.[21]

SUITABLE ACCOMMODATION

The housing authority is under a duty to those who are homeless and in priority need to provide *suitable* permanent accommodation.[22] The **13–025**

---

[17] (1993) 25 H.L.R. 158.
[18] Service in the armed forces and residence by virtue of detention under the authority of an Act of Parliament are expressly excluded by s.60(2) and (3).
[19] [1983] 2 A.C. 613, followed in *R. v. Islington L.B.C., ex p. Adigun* (1988) 20 H.L.R. 600.
[20] See n. 8 above.
[21] Newham's decision was flawed because, *inter alia*, it failed to take account of the general housing circumstances prevailing in Tower Hamlets.
[22] 1985 Act, s.69(1). The duty can be discharged in stages (see *R. v. Brent L.B.C., ex p. MacWan* (1994) 26 H.L.R. 528). In order to discharge its duty the particular accommodation which is ultimately provided need not be indefinite (see *R. v. Brent L.B.C., ex p. Awua* n. 3 above). However, the full housing duty requires the provision of permanent accommodation albeit not necessarily in one place.

suitability of any accommodation offered to an applicant can only be challenged by way of judicial review.[23]

Obiter dicta of Simon Brown J. in *R. v. City of Westminster, ex p. Tansey*[24] and of the Court of Appeal in *Mohram Ali v. Tower Hamlets L.B.C.*[25] suggest that the question of suitability is a matter within the discretion of the housing authority and can be challenged only on *Wednesbury* principles. It was argued in the *Tansey* case that the suitability or otherwise of the accommodation was an issue of precedent fact which the court was entitled to decide for itself. The court rejected that contention. In the light of the House of Lord's decision in *R. v. Tower Hamlets L.B.C., ex p. Rahman and Begum*[26] it is unlikely that this conclusion can be successfully challenged.

In determining suitability, the authority must take into account Part IX (slum clearance), Part X (overcrowding) and Part XI (houses in multiple occupation) of the 1985 Act. This is not an exhaustive list of matters which the authority must consider. In particular, the authority must provide accommodation which is suitable for the needs of the applicant and any person who might reasonably be expected to reside with him.

Thus, in *R. v. Brent L.B.C., ex p. Omar*[27] the applicant, a political refugee, refused an offer of accommodation on the basis that the estate and premises in question reminded her of the prisons in which she had been tortured. She stated that she would rather commit suicide than live there. The authority erred in maintaining that it did not have to take her personal circumstances into account in determining the suitability of accommodation.[28]

Accommodation is not suitable unless it is at a rent which the applicant can afford, either from his own resources or with the benefit of such public assistance as is available to him.[29]

---

[23] See *Mohram Ali v. Tower Hamlets L.B.C.*, n. 3 above.

[24] (1988) 20 H.L.R. 520.

[25] See n. 3 above.

[26] See n. 11 above.

[27] (1991) 23 H.L.R. 446.

[28] This decision is consistent with the approach adopted by Nolan J. in *R. v. Ryedale D.C., ex p. Smith* (n. 17 above) in which the judge held that the accommodation which must be provided under the 1977 Act must be suitable or appropriate (although the Act did not, unlike the 1985 Act, specify this) and that the health of the applicant was a relevant consideration. In *R. v. Tower Hamlets L.B.C., ex p. Abdul Subhan* (1992) 24 H.L.R. 541 the court held that the possibility that the Bangladeshi applicant might suffer racial harassment was a material factor in assessing the suitability of the accommodation. In *R. v. Lewisham L.B.C., ex p. Dolan* (1993) 25 H.L.R. 68, it was held that although the authority was entitled to arrange for medical factors to be assessed by its qualified medical officers and non-medical/social factors to be assessed by its homelessness officers, the decision as to the suitability of the accommodation must be the result of a composite assessment of all the relevant material.

[29] *R. v. Tower Hamlets L.B.C., ex p. Kaur, Ali et al.* (1994) 26 H.L.R. 597.

REMEDIES

Interlocutory relief is normally available if the of convenience favours the   **13–026**
granting of such relief.[30] In *R. v. Cardiff City Council, ex p. Barry*[31] the
Court of Appeal stated that where the court grants leave to move for
judicial review of an authority's decision, the court should preserve the
status quo. Accommodation should usually be provided, as the balance of
convenience will generally favour the homeless applicant. In deciding
whether to grant interim relief, the public interest should also be
considered.[32] Notice should be given to the housing authority if the
applicant intends to apply for interim relief.[33] In *R. v. Brent L.B.C., ex p.
Okpala*[34] the Court of Appeal held that in cases of renewed applications for
leave to move for judicial review the Court of Appeal has inherent
jurisdiction to require the housing authority to house the applicant pending
the hearing of the renewed application.

As for final relief, in *Cocks v. Thanet D.C.*[35] Lord Bridge considered the
most appropriate remedy to seek in applications for judicial review of
decisions in the homelessness context. He observed that:

> "Even though nullification of a public law decision can, if necessary,
> be achieved by declaration as an alternative to an order of certiorari,
> certiorari to quash remains the primary and most appropriate
> remedy."

In some, instances, however, Lord Bridge recognised that mandamus
should be sought in parallel with certiorari. In general, certiorari alone was
required where an authority's decision was susceptible to challenge on
undisputed primary facts on the ground that no reasonable housing
authority, correctly directing itself in law, could be satisfied as to a
particular decision. In such circumstances, where the authority can, in
effect, reach only one decision, the court has power to grant an order
requiring the authority to provide accommodation. Where, however, a
decision was impugned on other grounds (*e.g.* applicant not fairly
heard/irrelevant factors considered), then "certiorari to quash and mandamus to redetermine will, in strictness, be the appropriate remedies."

It would appear that an applicant is also entitled to claim damages on an
application for judicial review if the housing authority is in breach of its full
housing duty.[36]

---

[30] See *American Cyanamid v. Ethicon* [1975] A.C. 396 (H.L.).
[31] (1990) 22 H.L.R. 261 (C.A.). *cf. R. v. Westminster C.C., ex p. Augustin* [1993] 1 W.L.R.
730, where the C.A. held that the applicant seeking to appeal from a refund of judicial
review in a homelessness case to the C.A. must be a prima facie case that the appeal would
succeed.
[32] *R. v. Kensington and Chelsea L.B.C., ex p. Hammell* [1989] Q.B. 518 at 531 E (C.A.).
[33] *ibid.* at 539 B–C.
[34] *Legal Action* September, 1992.
[35] See n. 2 above, at p. 295.
[36] *R. v. Lambeth L.B.C., ex p. Barnes* (1993) 25 H.L.R. 140. There is no right to damages for
breach of the duty to make inquiries—*R. v. Northavon D.C., ex p. Palmer The Independent*,
February 22, 1994.

14. COMMERCIAL JUDICIAL REVIEW

WHAT IS COMMERCIAL JUDICIAL REVIEW?

14–001   Many different types of applications for judicial review are concerned with money. Judicial review of decisions as to the allocation of milk quota by the Dairy Produce Quotas Tribunal, of decisions of the Inland Revenue Commissioners, of decisions relating to social security benefits or in respect of local authority financing: all these are instances of decision-making involving both commercial issues and substantial sums of money.

"Commercial judicial review" in the narrower sense is, however, essentially concerned with the supervision of those bodies responsible for the regulation of the financial market and of commercial activities. It embraces the decisions and actions of the Secretary of State for Trade and Industry,[1] the Stock Exchange,[2] the Director-General of Fair Trading,[3] the Panel on Take-overs and Mergers,[4] the Monopolies and Mergers Commission,[5] the Registered Designs Appeal Tribunal,[6] the Inland Revenue Commissioners,[7] the Securities and Investment Board and the various self-regulatory organisations (or "SROs") set up under the Financial

---

[1] See, *e.g. R. v. Secretary of State for Trade and Industry, ex p. Airlines of Britain Holdings plc, The Times,* December 10, 1992 (application to Court of Appeal for leave to move for judicial review of a decision by the Trade Secretary that Article 86 of the EEC Treaty did not apply to a proposed merger between British Airways and Dan Air).

[2] *e.g. R. v. International Stock Exchange of the United Kingdom and the Republic of Ireland, ex p. Elser (1982) Limited* [1993] 2 W.L.R. 70 (C.A.).

[3] *e.g. R. v. Director General of Fair Trading, ex p. Southdown Motor Services Limited, The Times,* January 19, 1993.

[4] *R. v. Panel for Take-overs and Mergers, ex p. Datafin plc* [1987] 1 Q.B. 815 (C.A.).

[5] *e.g. R. v. Monopolies and Mergers Commission, ex p. Elders IXL Limited* [1987] 1 W.L.R. 1221: *R. v. MMC ex p. National House Building Council, The Times,* January 25 1994, C.A.

[6] See *R. v. Registered Designs Appeal Tribunal ex p. Ford Motor Company Ltd, The Times,* March 9, 1994, Div.Ct.

[7] See *R. v. Inland Revenue Commissioners, ex p. SG Warburg & Co. Ltd, The Times,* April 25, 1994. Though note that in the *SG Warburg* case, Hidden J. held that even if (contrary to his primary finding) the I.R.C. had acted in a *Wednesbury* unreasonable sense, he would not have granted relief, since an appeal to the special or general commissioners would have achieved a just solution of the applicant's complaint. In so holding, the learned judge relied on *R. v. I.R.C., ex p. Opman International UK* [1986] 1 W.L.R. 568. See too *R. v. Inland Revenue Commissioners, ex p. Matrix-Securities Ltd* [1994] 1 W.L.R. 334.

Services Act 1986.[8] All these bodies share common goals: namely the protection of investors and the promotion of investor confidence.[9]

THE DECISION IN DATAFIN

The starting point for the consideration of a judicial review in the commercial arena is the decision of the Court of Appeal in *R. v. Panel on Take-overs and Mergers, ex parte Datafin plc.*[10] The judgment of Sir John Donaldson M.R. raises two important issues engaged in commercial judicial review: (i) the reviewability of self-regulatory organisations and (ii) the exercise of judicial restraint in the determination of substantive applications for judicial review involving such bodies.

14–002

The applicants, Datafin plc and Prudential Bache Securities Inc, who were involved in bidding to take over a company called McCorquodale plc, sought to challenge the decision of the Panel of Take-overs and Mergers that Norton Opax plc had not acted in concert with other parties in breach of the City Code on Take-overs and Mergers. Leave to move was refused by Hodgson J. and the Court of Appeal granted leave so that it could hear the substantive application and consider the issue of whether the Panel (which lacked any statutory, prerogative or common law powers— "performing its function without visible means of legal support"[11])—was susceptible to judicial review.

The Court rejected the argument advanced on behalf of the Panel that the source of the power was determinative of the reviewability of the body; rather it was the nature of the body's duties and functions that was material. Sir John Donaldson concluded that the Panel:

> "is without doubt performing a public duty and an important one . . . . The rights of citizens are indirectly affected by its decisions, some, but by no means all of whom, may in a technical sense be said to have

---

[8] *e.g. R. v. LAUTRO, ex p. Ross* [1993] 1 Q.B. 17; [1993] 1 All E.R. 545 (C.A.): *R. v. LAUTRO, ex p. Tee* [1993] C.O.D. 362 (two closely related cases on the scope of the duty of fairness owed by LAUTRO when serving intervention notices): *R. v. Investors' Compensation Scheme, ex p. Weyell and Veniard*; *R. v. Investors' Compensation Scheme, ex p. Last and Rowden* [1994] 1 All E.R. 602, [1994] C.O.D. 87: *Bank of Scotland v. Investment Management Regulatory Organisation Ltd (IMRO)* [1989] S.L.T. 432. *R. v. Securities and Investments Board, ex p. Independent Financial Advisers' Association*, The Times, May 18, 1995.

[9] Note, however, that decisions of the Insurance Ombudsman have recently been held *not* to be susceptible to judicial review. The Court held that the Bureau's powers were entirely derived from contract and could not be said to exercise government functions. The Insurance Ombudsman Bureau was established in 1981, not pursuant to the Financial Services Act 1986. Despite its being subsequently recognised by LAUTRO as performing a complaints investigation function under its rules, it could not be said that the Bureau had been "woven into a governmental system" (*per* Rose L.J.). See *R. v. Insurance Ombudsman Bureau, ex p. Aegon Life Assurance Ltd.*, The Times, January 7, 1994, which is, therefore in contrast to the Financial Services Act SRO cases at n. 8 above.

[10] n. 4 above.

[11] *ibid. per* Sir John Donaldson at p. 834.

assented to this situation, *e.g.* the members of the Stock Exchange. At least in its determination of whether there has been a breach of the code, it has a duty to act judicially and it asserts that its *raison d'être* is to do equity between one shareholder and another. Its source of power is only partly based upon moral persuasion and the assent of institutions and their members, the bottom line being the statutory powers exercised by the Department of Trade and Industry and the Bank of England. In this context I should be very disappointed if the courts could not recognise the realities of executive power and allowed their vision to be clouded by the subtlety and sometimes complexity of the way in which it can be exerted."[12]

Since *Datafin* there have been several applications for judicial review of decisions of bodies which, like the Panel for Take-overs and Mergers, are essentially self-regulatory in nature. Thus, in *R. v. Financial Intermediaries Managers and Brokers Regulatory Association, ex p. Cochrane*[13] it was accepted that FIMBRA's decisions were amenable to judicial review. In *R. v. Life Assurance and Unit Trust Regulatory Organization, ex p. Ross*[14] counsel for LAUTRO accepted that in this respect the Court of Appeal was bound by the decision in *Datafin* and that LAUTRO's decisions were, accordingly, reviewable.

LAUTRO's rules were subjected to judicial review in the case of *R. v LAUTRO, ex p. Kendall.*[15] LAUTRO had introduced a rule prohibiting its members from engaging as a company representative any person who owed more than £1,000 to any other member. The applicant sought the quashing of the rule on the grounds that it was unreasonable and/or that there had been a failure to take into account all reasonable considerations in its introduction. LAUTRO's justification for the rule was that it was for the protection of investors. The Court held that LAUTRO had taken into consideration the effect which the rule had on employees' ability to move from job to job. Had there not been evidence that LAUTRO had taken this into account, that would have been a ground for quashing the rule, but since there was such evidence, the application to quash the rule failed.

Similarly it has been assumed that the decision of the Commissioner appointed to hear an appeal from a decision of the Association of Futures Brokers and Dealers Limited, a self-regulatory organization, was within the realm of public law.[16]

INVESTORS' COMPENSATION SCHEME

14–003   The Investors' Compensation Scheme ("the Scheme") was set up under the Financial Services (Compensation of Investors) Rules 1990, pursuant to section 54 of the Financial Services Act 1986, and came into being on 28

---

[12] *ibid.* at 838.

[13] *The Times*, June 23, 1989; [1990] C.O.D. 33.

[14] n. 8 above.

[15] [1994] C.O.D. 169.

[16] *R. v. Association of Futures Brokers and Dealers Limited, ex p. Mordens Limited* [1991] C.O.D. 40.

August 1988. In *R. v. Investors Compensation Scheme ex p. Weyell*,[17] the Court of Appeal dealt with two cases arising out of the mis-selling of "Home Income Plans". The purpose of such plans was to release to investors some of the capital tied up in their homes, on which original mortgages had been wholly or mainly repaid. Under such plans, a loan was obtained from a lending institution secured by a mortgage on the investor's property. Much of the loan was invested in equity-linked single premium investment bonds and the balance, after deduction of fees, was made available to the investor. However, from about 1989, mortgage interests rate increased, and investment returns fell and/or property values dropped. The brokers who had advised the applicants in the taking out of the Home Income Plans were FIMBRA members. The investors claimed that these advisers had been in breach of contract, negligent, and had acted contrary to FIMBRA rules in the advice given to the investors. The claim against the Scheme arose because the brokers were unable themselves to satisfy the claims made against them.

The Court considered the question of whether the issues raised in the case were properly to be dealt with by way of judicial review. Counsel for both parties accepted that they were. However, the Court noted that in *R. v. FIMBRA*,[18] another Investors' Compensation Scheme case, the procedure adopted by the plaintiff (to which neither of the defendants objected) was originating summons rather than judicial review. In the *ex p. Weyell* case, Cresswell L.J. said:

> "In this case we are asked to proceed on facts which either are agreed or so far as the claims against defaulting firms are concerned are accepted for the purposes of these proceedings. On that basis and since both counsel were anxious for us to hear the applications, we accepted jurisdiction. We observe, however, that there may well come a stage at which an issue which arises on a claim by an investor against the compensation fund set up under s.54 may depend on the ascertainment of facts and will properly lie in the field of private law."

It cannot, therefore be taken necessarily to be the case that all such FIMBRA cases will properly be brought under the judicial review procedure. The comments in *ex p. Weyell* suggest that the decision of the best method of attempting to obtain legal redress will be a matter for an applicant's advisers to consider on a case-by-case basis.[19]

IS LLOYD'S AMENABLE TO JUDICIAL REVIEW?

In the light of the decision in *Datafin* and other cases, the amenability of the Corporation of Lloyd's to judicial review seemed probable. The

14–004

---

[17] n. 8 above.
[18] [1991] 4 All E.R. 398, [1992] Ch. 268.
[19] See, also on the Investors' Compensation Scheme, *R. v. Investors' Compensation Board, ex p. Bowden* [1995] 3 W.L.R. 289.

Divisional Court in *R. v. Corporation of Lloyd's ex p. Briggs*,[20] however, held otherwise.

Leave to move for judicial review of various decisions of the Corporation of Lloyd's relating to the requirement that Lloyd's "names" respond to cash calls and relating also to the manner of Lloyd's draw-down of names' deposits was granted by Potts J. Lloyd's applied successfully to the Divisional Court to set aside the grant of leave.

The primary ground given by Leggatt L.J. for setting leave aside was material non-disclosure on the part of the applicants at the hearing before Potts J. However, Leggatt L.J. also considered whether the powers which were the subject of the challenge were within the public domain, so as to render Lloyd's susceptible to judicial review. He concluded that the powers in question were exercisable solely by virtue of the contractual agreement of members of the society of Lloyd's to be bound by the decisions and directions of Lloyd's Council. There was, he held, an insufficiently public element in the relationship between Lloyd's and the names. The argument that Lloyd's, as a self-regulating body charged with the important responsibility of regulating the insurance market on behalf of all its members in the public interest, fulfils a role which but for its existence would be filled by a government body, was rejected. The Court held that Lloyd's' powers are derived from statute, which powers did not extend to any person in the insurance market save those who wished to operate in that section of the market governed by Lloyd's.

THE EXERCISE OF DISCRETION IN COMMERCIAL JUDICIAL REVIEW

14–005   The decision in Datafin is equally significant for its articulation of the approach which the courts should adopt in overseeing the decisions of financial institutions. Having decided the jurisdictional issue in favour of Datafin, the Court of Appeal rejected the substantive application. In so doing Sir John Donaldson M.R. made the following statement of principle:

"I wish to make it clear beyond a peradventure that in the light of the special nature of the panel, its functions, the market in which it is operating, the time scales which are inherent in that market and the need to safeguard the position of third parties, who may be numbered in thousands, all of whom are entitled to continue to trade upon an assumption of the validity of the panel's rules and decisions unless and until they are quashed by the court, I should expect the relationship between the panel and the court to be historic rather than contemporaneous. I should expect the court to allow contemporary decisions to take their course, considering the complaint and intervening, if at all, later and in retrospect by declaratory orders which would enable the panel not to repeat any error and would relieve individuals of the

---

[20] [1993] 1 Lloyd's Rep. 176, D.C.; *The Times*, July 30, 1992. In *R. v. Chairman of the Regulatory Board of Lloyd's, ex p. Macmillan, The Times*, December 14, 1994. Lloyd's did not contest its amenability to judicial review in the particular content.

disciplinary consequences of any erroneous finding of breach of the rules. This would provide a workable and valuable partnership between the courts and the panel in the public interest."[21]

This policy of judicial restraint has been echoed in the majority of commercial judicial review cases. Thus in *R. v. Stock Exchange, ex p. Else (1982) Ltd*, Sir Thomas Bingham M.R. emphasised that "the courts will not second-guess the informed judgment of responsible regulators steeped in knowledge of their particular market."[22]

Sir John Donaldson elaborated upon the advice proffered by the Court of Appeal in *Datafin* in the later case of *R. v. Panel on Take-overs and Mergers, ex p. Guinness plc*.[23] There he stated that the individual grounds for judicial review set out in the speech of Lord Diplock in *Council of Civil Service Unions v. Minister for the Civil Service*[24] were of limited utility in reviewing the decisions of a self-regulating body such as the Panel. He held that illegality was, generally, an inappropriate basis for review of a body which was both legislator and interpreter. Irrationality was as difficult to apply as it was for the Panel to judge what was or was not relevant.

Similar problems arose with regard to procedural impropriety as the procedures were of the Panel's own devising. Even the application of natural justice could cause problems as a determination of what was fair might depend on underlying value judgments as to, for example, appropriate time scales. The Master of the Rolls concluded that the court should "review the panel's acts and omissions more in the round than might otherwise be the case" and consider "whether something had gone wrong of a nature which required the intervention of the court". The Court duly held that the decision of the Panel to refuse an adjournment of a hearing into alleged breaches of the City code on Take-overs and Mergers by Guinness, although insensitive and unwise, had caused no actual injustice to Guinness. Consequently Guinness's appeal was dismissed.

THE ARGYLL CASE

The cautious approach articulated by *Lord Donaldson of Lymington* M.R. in *Datafin* and *Guinness* is vividly displayed in *R. v. Monopolies and Mergers Commission, ex p. Argyll Group plc*[25] which arose out of rival bidding for Distillers. In that case Guinness's proposal was referred by the Secretary of State for Trade and Industry to the Monopolies and Mergers Commission for inquiry and report under section 75 of the Fair Trading Act 1973. Before the Commission had organised, in accordance with its usual

14–006

---

[21] n. 4 above at p. 842.
[22] See n. 2 above, at pp. 82–83.
[23] [1990] 1 Q.B. 146 (C.A.).
[24] [1995] A.C. 374 (H.L.).
[25] [1986] 1 W.L.R. 763 (C.A.).

procedure, a group of members for the purposes of investigating the proposal, representatives of Guinness met with the chairman of the Commission. Information was provided as to certain of Distillers' activities which might not form part of a Guinness take-over. As a result the chairman decided that the proposal had been abandoned within the meaning of section 75(5) of the Act and recommended to the Secretary of State that the reference be laid aside. Guinness then made a revised bid for Distillers. The applicants, who were bidding in competition with Guinness, applied for judicial review of the Commission's decision that the proposal had been abandoned. Macpherson J. refused the application.

The Court of Appeal ruled that the decision on the abandonment of the proposal was correct, but that the chairman had no authority to take such a decision, nor did the Commission have the power under the Act tacitly to approve the chairman's decision. The decision had to be taken by a properly constituted group of members of the Commission. However, the Court declined in the exercise of its discretion to grant relief.

Sir John Donaldson M.R. based his decision to refuse relief on the "needs of public administration". He expressly relied on the following considerations:

(a) the group of members would have taken exactly the same decision as the chairman, and good administration was concerned with substance not form;

(b) speed of decision was vital in the financial arena and if relief were to be granted there would be further delay;

(c) the Secretary of State was the guardian of the public interest and had consented to the reference being laid aside[26];

(d) Argyll's interest was to prevent Guinness from putting in a bid—this was not an interest consistent with the purpose of the administrative process under the Act;

(e) the financial public was entitled to rely upon the finality of the decision and was entitled to decisiveness—third parties might already have relied on the validity of the various decisions.[27]

---

[26] See also *R. v. Monopolies and Mergers Commission, ex p. Visa International Service Association* [1990] C.O.D. 29. Hodgson J. stated that the Commission's report to the Secretary of State for Trade and Industry in relation to the possible existence of a monopoly of credit card services should not be read as if it were a statute or judgment and that the court should be slow to disable the Commission from recommending action considered to be in the public interest or to prevent the Secretary of State for Trade and Industry from acting thereon unless there were material and substantial errors of law. The *ex p. Visa International Service Association* case is further considered in *R. v. M.M.C. and the Secretary of State for Trade and Industry, ex p. Ecando* [1993] C.O.D. 89. See also *R. v. Investors Board, ex p. Bowden*, n. 9 above "the [Financial Services (Compensation of Investors)] Rules 1990 are not drawn with the tightness to be found in primary or secondary legislation and we approach the arguments with a caution against adopting the approach which is appropriate to the enactments".

[27] See also *R. v. Monopolies and Mergers Commission, ex p. Matthew Brown plc* [1987] 1 W.L.R. 1235 and *R. v. Monopolies and Mergers Commission, ex p. Elders IXL Ltd*, n. 5 above.

COMMERCIAL JUDICIAL REVIEW AS A "RESTRICTED AREA"

In "Should public law remedies be discretionary?"[28] Sir Thomas **14–007** Bingham M.R. considers the grounds upon which the courts may legitimately exercise their discretion to decline relief.

He identifies nine grounds: delay, standing, acquiescence, the conduct and motives of the applicant, the exhaustion of other remedies, the inevitability of the outcome, the fact that a remedy will serve no useful purpose, adverse public consequences and lastly what he terms "restricted areas", *i.e.* areas in which the courts are loathe to intervene, such as national security. He singles out as an example of a restricted area "the growing willingness of commercial opponents to pursue their policies by other means, namely by litigation".

In *R. v. The Institute of Chartered Accountants in England & Wales, ex p. Brindle*[29] the Institute appointed a Committee of Enquiry to investigate the activities of Price Waterhouse, accountants, as auditors of the failed Bank of Credit and Commerce International ("BCCI"). There was civil litigation also afoot against Price Waterhouse at the same time, initiated by, *inter alia*, the BCCI liquidators alleging negligence by the auditors. Price Waterhouse applied for, and obtained, judicial review of, *inter alia* the Committee's refusal to suspend its enquiry pending the outcome of the civil proceedings. This failure gave rise to a real risk of prejudice and injustice, especially given the coincidence of issues between the Committee of Enquiry's remit and the civil proceedings.

Whilst recognising that the courts were right not to declare financial regulation a "no-go" area in *Argyll* and *Datafin* Lord Justice Bingham concludes thus:

"It would seem to me wise for the courts to venture into this uncharted minefield with considerable circumspection lest the cure be more damaging to the wider investing public than the disease. I would expect the developing case law to define with greater precision the grounds upon which the court will exercise its discretion to refuse relief, but for the moment perhaps the courts have got the balance right."

In this area, as in no other save national security, the courts are acutely aware of "the danger of judges wrongly although unconsciously substituting their views for the views of the decision-maker".[30] This caution is, primarily, exercised out of consideration for the wider public interest as articulated in *Guinness*. Furthermore, the effectiveness of a self-regulatory body depends in the main on the perception by the market and by City institutions that the body in question is an authoritative decision-maker.

---

[28] [1991] P.L. 64.
[29] December 21, 1993, unrep.
[30] *per* Lord Keith in *R. v. Trade and Industry Secretary, ex p. Lonrho plc* [1990] 1 W.L.R. 525.

The quashing or doubting of its decisions by the courts can undermine its authority, with possibly severe consequences in a volatile market.

NATURAL JUSTICE AND THE CONTROL OF DISCIPLINARY PROCEDURES

14–008   It is plain from the decision of the Court of Appeal in *R. v. LAUTRO, ex p. Ross* that the courts are more comfortable dealing *ex post facto* with the familiar "disciplinary" aspects of decision-making in the commercial arena rather than with substantive decisions on the part of regulatory bodies.

Self-regulatory bodies are under a duty to act fairly, although in *Ross* the demands of that duty were minimised by considerations of urgency. Thus, in issuing an intervention notice which had the effect of preventing the applicant's company from conducting investment business, LAUTRO was entitled not to provide the applicant with the opportunity to make representations as LAUTRO had to act quickly so as to protect investors. However, the Court held that fair dealing required that LAUTRO afford the applicant the right to apply to set aside the decision or appeal against it.[31]

THE FUTURE OF COMMERCIAL JUDICIAL REVIEW

14–009   In 1989 Lord Alexander rejected the suggestion that there was a special principle of administrative law applicable to City activities. He stated firmly that "the broad principles of administrative law should apply consistently across the board".[32]

The present body of commercial case law does not bear out his conclusions. The courts afford an extremely wide margin of appreciation to those bodies which are concerned with the regulation of commercial activities.[33] However, recourse to judicial review will no doubt become more prevalent with the ever-increasing activity of the regulatory system in this sphere.

As Lord Justice Bingham's "uncharted minefield" becomes more familiar territory, the courts' reluctance to intervene too boldly in the affairs of the financial regulators will inevitably diminish.

---

[31] Mr Ross's application was, however, unsuccessful as the lack of opportunity to make representations after the issue of the notice was not one of the grounds of his application.

[32] "Judicial review and City regulators" [1989] 52 M.L.R. 640.

[33] See, *e.g. ex p. Bowden* at n. 9 above.

15. CIVIL LIBERTIES AND RELATED AREAS

PRISONERS AND THEIR RIGHTS

Undoubtedly, prisoners' rights continues to be one of the growth areas of judicial review. Over the last decade, the courts have been called upon to determine some difficult questions of principle concerning prisoners and their rights.

The right of access to the courts has caused particular problems. In *R. v. Secretary of State for the Home Department, ex p. Anderson*[1] a Divisional Court, applying *Raymond v. Honey*,[2] held that access to legal advisers was part of a prisoner's right to unimpeded access to the courts. The court ruled that prison rules which fettered such access more than was strictly necessary for proper administrative organisation were unlawful.

However, in *R. v. Secretary of State for the Home Department, ex p. Wynne*,[3] a majority of the Court of Appeal suggested, albeit technically *obiter*, that it was not unlawful for the Secretary of State to charge a prisoner who wanted to go to court to conduct his own litigation, and who was not legally aided, more than he could reasonably afford to pay for his transportation to court. Only Lord Donaldson of Lymington M.R. considered that a demand for a fee which was beyond the prisoner's means was tantamount to a denial of access to the courts and therefore unlawful. Although this case subsequently went to the House of Lords,[4] the House declined to resolve the conflict on this point, dismissing the appeal on the narrow basis that the prisoner had not made a specific application to be reimbursed for the cost of being brought to court.

In *R. v. Secretary of State for the Home Department, ex p. Leech*,[5] the Court of Appeal considered the *vires* of prison rules which allowed prison officers to read and stop correspondence between, *inter alia*, a prisoner and his solicitor. Rule 33(3) of the Prison Rules was drafted in extraordinarily wide terms:

> "Except as provided by these Rules, every letter or communication to or from a prisoner may be read or examined by the governor or an

---

[1] [1984] Q.B. 778. *cf. R. v. Governor of Brixton Prison and Another, ex p. Walsh* [1985] A.C. 154 (*held*: there is no duty on a governor to produce a prisoner to the magistrates' court to which he has been remanded).

[2] [1983] 1 A.C. 1.

[3] [1992] Q.B. 406.

[4] [1993] 1 W.L.R. 115.

[5] [1994] Q.B. 198, C.A.

officer deputed by him, and the governor may, at his discretion, stop any letter or communication on the ground that its contents are objectionable or that it is of inordinate length."

There have been several unsuccessful attempts to review the Home Secretary's refusal to refer cases to the Court of Appeal pursuant to section 17 of the Criminal Appeals Act 1968. Since s.17 gives the Home Secretary such a wide discretion, and requires him to look at a case "in the round after it had been right through the judicial process", the Court would be "very slow" to fault his reasons for not referring the case back to the Court of Appeal. The Secretary of State was entitled to have a policy for determining when referrals would be made, so long as (as was the case) each case was considered on its merits to see if it met the criteria of the policy or, if it did not, whether there was some other reason exceptionally to refer the case.[6] In *R. v. Secretary of State for the Home Department, ex p. H.*[7] the Divisional Court held that, in determining whether or not to refer a case under section 17, the Secretary of State was required to disclose sufficient material, on which his decision depended, to an applicant so as to enable him to make informed representations.

The application for judicial review succeeded on the basis that the rule was *ultra vires* section 47(1) of the Prisons Act 1952 in that it purportedly permitted the reading and stopping of confidential letters between prisoner and solicitor on wider grounds than merely to ascertain whether the letter was a bona fide solicitor/client communication. The court also held that the prisoner did have *locus standi* to bring the application, despite his being then held in a Scottish prison.

There have been a number of important cases in relation to the rights of life sentence prisoners.

The legality of the Home Secretary's "tariff" policy whereby, save in exceptional cases, a notional determinate sentence sufficient to meet the requirements of retribution and deterrence is decided by the Secretary of State prior to referring a life sentence case to the parole board for consideration was approved by the House of Lords in *Re Findlay*.[8] However, the *application* of the policy has given rise to successful challenges by way of judicial review.

In *R. v. Secretary of State for the Home Department, ex p. Handscomb*[9] a Divisional Court held that in determining the period which must elapse before which the parole board could review the tariff of a prisoner serving a discretionary life sentence, the Secretary of State was bound to accept either the recommendation of the trial judge or that of the Lord Chief

---

[6] See *R. v. Secretary of State for the Home Department, ex p. McCallion* [1993] C.O.D. 148. See also: *R. v. Secretary of State for the Home Department, ex p. Pegg* [1991] C.O.D. 46; *R. v. Secretary of State for the Home Department, ex p. Garland* [1989] C.O.D. 461; *R. v. Secretary of State for the Home Department, ex p. Cleeland* (October 8, 1987; unrep.)

[7] [1995] 1 W.L.R. 734.

[8] [1985] A.C. 318.

[9] (1987) 86 Cr.App.R. 59. The logic of this case was disapproved by the House of Lords in *R. v. Secretary of State, ex p. Doody* [1994] 1 A.C. 531 at p. 559B–C.

Justice. The logic of this case is not entirely free from difficulty. If it is for the Secretary of State to determine the review period, it must surely be unlawful for him to fetter himself to the judicial view. Nevertheless, this case is significant in that it discloses a willingness on the part of the judiciary to apply judicial review to ministerial decisions affecting prisoners convicted of very serious crimes.

R. v. Secretary of State, ex p. Walsh[10] was a case in which the Court of Appeal engrafted natural justice into this area, holding that a prisoner serving a discretionary life sentence was entitled to know the length of his tariff period.

In *R. v. Secretary of State, ex p. Doody,*[11] the House of Lords extended the reasoning of these cases and held that natural justice demanded that the Secretary of State was required to afford a prisoner serving a life sentence the opportunity to submit in writing representations as to the period that a prisoner should serve prior to the Home Secretary fixing the date of the prisoner's first parole review. Moreover, prior to the prisoner making any such written representations, the Home Secretary was obliged to tell him what the trial judge's recommendation (and that of the Lord Chief Justice) had been, and that while the Home Secretary was not obliged to accept the judiciary's view, he was required to give his reasons if and when he departed from it. Lord Mustill's speech ranges widely over the natural justice jurisprudence generally and the duty to give reasons in particular.[12]

A similar duty to give reasons was held to exist in the case of *R. v. Secretary of State for the Home Department, ex p. Duggan*[13] in respect of a prisoner's entitlement to reasons for the decision to maintain his Category A classification, which meant, *inter alia*, that he would not be considered for release on licence by the Parole Board. The Court held that although the initial classification may take place without disclosing to the prisoner the matters referred to (because speedy categorisation may be required) on each subsequent (approximately annual) assessment of classification, the prisoner was entitled to be given the gist of the material on which the decision was to be taken, to be given a chance to comment thereon, and to receive reasons for the eventual decision.

Natural justice has also been held to be relevant to consideration of a prisoner's case by the parole board.

---

[10] [1992] T.L.R. 230.

[11] [1994] 1 A.C. 531.

[12] Discretionary life sentence prisoners have similar statutory rights under the Criminal Justice Act 1991. For a case on the transitional provisions introduced under the 1991 Act, and the nature of the Secretary of State's obligations when deciding to issue a Certificate, see *R. v. Secretary of State for the Home Department, ex p. McCartney* [1994] C.O.D. 160.

The *Doody* decision in the House of Lords came just a little too late for the applicant in *R. v. Secretary of State for the Home Department, ex p. Van Der Vuurst De Vries* [1993] C.O.D. 502, in which the Court refused to criticise the Home Secretary's refusal to give his reasons for his decision to refuse a Dutch prisoner's request to be transferred to a prison in Kent so that his family might more conveniently visit him.

[13] [1994] C.O.D. 258.

In *R. v. Parole Board, ex p. Wilson*,[14] the Court of Appeal held that a prisoner subject to a discretionary life sentence of imprisonment was entitled to know the material before the parole board in order that he should be able to make adequate representations.[15] The same approach was taken in respect of a prisoner detained during Her Majesty's pleasure pursuant to section 33 of the Children and Young Persons Act 1933.[16]

To similar effect is the decision of the Divisional Court in *R. v. Secretary of State for the Home Department, ex p. Georghiades*.[17] There, a prisoner had been released on licence in 1976 with just a few years of his sentence to run. It was a condition of that licence that he keep in contact with his probation officer. By August 1976 he was in breach of that condition, because he had left the jurisdiction. The parole board was, *inter alia*, informed that the police wished to interview the prisoner in connection with a serious offence, and it recommended revocation of his licence. The Secretary of State proceeded to revoke it. In 1990 the prisoner returned to the jurisdiction and in 1992 he was arrested. The Secretary of State gave reasons for returning the applicant to prison, but did not tell the applicant of the material before the parole board in 1976.

The Divisional Court held that when a prisoner is given the reasons for the revocation of his licence, he is entitled to know the material which was placed before the parole board, so that he knows the case against him.[18]

Finally, there has been an important extension of judicial review to disciplinary decisions of prison governors. In *Leech v. Deputy Governor of Parkhurst Prison*[19] the House of Lords, whilst reaffirming the principle[20] that disciplinary decisions of Boards of Visitors are subject to the jurisdiction of the court and the rules of natural justice also clarified that the

---

[14] [1992] Q.B. 740. Contrast, though, the earlier decision of a Divisional Court in *R. v. Parole Board, ex p. Bradley* [1991] 1 W.L.R. 134 (*held*: discretionary lifer not entitled to see material before parole board; nor was the board required to provide reasons for its decision).

[15] *cf. R. v. Secretary of State, ex p. Creamer, ex p. Scholey* [1993] C.O.D. 162, in respect of *mandatory* life sentence prisoners, in which the Court (clearly reluctantly) held that the *Wilson* provisions did not apply to mandatory life sentences, on the authority of *Payne v. Lord Harris* [1981] 1 W.L.R. 754. *Payne* was overruled by the House of Lords in *ex p. Doody*, n. 11 above, and so presumably the *Creamer* case would now be decided differently.

[16] See *R. v. Secretary of State for the Home Department, ex p. Singh (Prem)* [1993] C.O.D. 501.

[17] [1992] T.L.R. 268.

[18] For other instances of judicial review against decisions of the Parole Board, see: *R. v. Parole Board, ex p. Lodomez* (1994) C.O.D. 525; *R. v. Parole Board, ex p. Gittens* (1992) C.O.D. 441; *R. v. Secretary of State for the Home Department, ex p. Edwards* (1994) C.O.D. 443; *R. v. Secretary of State for the Home Department, ex p. Pegg* (1994) *The Times*, August 11. *R. v. Secretary of State for the Home Department and the Parole Board, ex p. The Times*, July 26, 1995.

[19] [1988] A.C. 533.

[20] Previously laid down in *R. v. Board of Visitors of Hull Prison, ex p. St Germain* [1979] Q.B. 425. Of the many cases illustrative of the principle see, *e.g. R. v. Hull Prison Board of Visitors, ex p. St Germain (No. 2)* [1979] 1 W.L.R. 1401 (*held*: refusal by Board to permit witnesses to be called because of administrative inconvenience was unlawful); *R. v. Gartree Prison Visitors, ex p. Healy The Times*, November 14, 1984, (*held*: decisions refusing cross-examination or examination of a prisoner's witness were unlawful); *R. v. Secretary of State for the Home Department, ex p. Tarrant and Others* [1985] Q.B. 251 (*held*: Board of Visitors had a discretion to permit legal representation).

same principle applies to similar decisions of prison governors.[21] Further, in *R. v. Deputy Governor of Parkhurst Prison, ex p. Hague*,[22] the House expressly rejected the argument that the interference by the courts with the management of prisons was subversive of prison discipline.

REVIEWING POLICE POWERS

Order 53 provides a convenient procedure for those aggrieved both by decisions 1 of the police with regard to internal disciplinary procedures and also, more widely, by the exercise of (or failure to exercise) police powers.

15–002

Judicial review is, increasingly, utilised to ensure compliance with procedural fairness in disciplinary proceedings. Thus, in *R. v. Chief Constable of Merseyside Police, ex p. Calveley*[23] the Court of Appeal quashed disciplinary proceedings commenced against five police officers on the basis that an essential procedural protection had not been complied with.[24] Similarly, in *R. v. Chief Constable, ex p. Merrill*[25] the court quashed proceedings against a detective constable where the Chief Constable had erroneously concluded that service of a notice on the officer could be deferred until after the criminal trial of the complainant.

The remedy has also been used to correct errors of law occurring in the disciplinary process. In *R. v. Police Board, ex p. Madden*,[26] for example, a refusal by the Police Board to prefer disciplinary charges against an officer on the mistaken basis that the principle of double jeopardy prevented it from doing so because the D.P.P. had already decided not to prefer criminal charges on the same evidence, was quashed.

More commonly, judicial review is now widely employed to question the legality of police powers or policy.

In *Champion v. Chief Constable of Gwent*[27] a police constable who was elected to serve as a school governor applied to the Chief Constable for permission to sit on the school's sub-committee which appointed teachers. The Chief Constable not only refused permission but forbade him from sitting as a governor at all, on the basis that it might interfere with the impartial discharge of his police duties. The House of Lords held that such a conclusion either involved a necessary error of law or a perverse finding of fact, and quashed the decision.

---

[21] Thereby overruling *R. v. Deputy Governor of Camphill Prison, ex p. King* [1985] Q.B. 735, which suggested the contrary.

[22] [1991] 3 W.L.R. 340.

[23] [1986] Q.B. 424.

[24] Under reg. 7 of the Police (Discipline) Regulations 1977, officers should be cautioned and served with notice of the allegations against them as soon as reasonably practicable. This had not been done. Note, though, the observations of the court so far as the possibility of seeking an alternative remedy rather than judicial review. See also on police disciplinary tribunals, *R. v. Secretary of State for the Home Department, ex p. Barr* [1993] C.O.D. 346.

[25] [1989] 1 W.L.R. 1077.

[26] [1983] 1 W.L.R. 447.

[27] [1990] 1 W.L.R. 1.

In *R. v. Chief Constable of Lancashire, ex p. Parker*[28] the Divisional Court reviewed the execution of a search warrant by the police, where the police had failed to produce or supply a copy to the person whose premises were being searched. The court declared that the search was unlawful and, in consequence, so too was the seizure.

In *R. v. Chief Constable, ex p. C.E.G.B.*,[29] the Central Electricity Generating Board sought review of the Chief Constable's refusal to arrest demonstrators at one of the Board's potential nuclear power station sites. The Court of Appeal held that despite the fact that the police had the *power* to arrest protestors if there was a risk of a breach of the peace, the court would not compel them to do so. It is difficult to ascertain the correct principle upon which the Court refused relief. Lawton L.J. said[30]:

> "[The] application showed a misconception of the powers of chief constables. They command their forces but they cannot give an officer under command an order to do acts which can only lawfully be done if the officer himself with reasonable cause suspects that ... an arrestable offence has been committed .... The Chief Constable probably did order some of his constables to watch what was going on ... but what he could not do was to give unqualified orders to his officers to remove those who were obstructing the board's work."

Thus, Lawton L.J. refused relief on the narrow basis that the court cannot order the Chief Constable to issue an order which he has no power to issue and which, being a blanket order, would be unlawful. Templeman L.J. appeared to agree with this approach, when he said[31]:

> The Police are not bound in all circumstances to act every time there is breach of the law, criminal or civil. ... The court cannot tell the police how and when their powers should be exercised for the court cannot judge the explosiveness of the situation or deal with the individual problems which arise as a result of the activities of the obstructors."

Lord Denning M.R. decided the matter on a wider statement of principle that the decision was a policy decision with which the court should not interfere.[32]

It is difficult to reconcile this latter approach with the views of the other members of the Court of Appeal in *R. v. Commissioner of Police of the Metropolis, ex p. Blackburn*.[33]

This case involved an application for judicial review of a confidential instruction issued to senior officers of the Metropolitan Police requiring them to take no action against gaming clubs, contrary to the gaming laws, unless there were complaints of cheating, or they had

---

[28] [1993] 2 All E.R. 56.
[29] [1982] 1 Q.B. 458.
[30] At p. 474G.
[31] At 480G and 481B–C.
[32] At p. 472B–E.
[33] [1968] 2 Q.B. 118.

become the haunts of criminals.[34] The applicant sought reversal of this policy. The police argued that mandamus could not issue against it. The court unanimously held that, in principle, mandamus could issue.[35]

Salmon L.J. said[36]:

"In my judgment the police owe the public a clear legal duty to enforce the law—a duty which I have no doubt they recognise.... In the extremely unlikely event, however, of the police failing or refusing to carry out their duty, the court would not be powerless to intervene."

Salmon L.J. went on to postulate examples of policy directions as to prosecutions and where mandamus would lie. The better view might be to read Lord Denning M.R. as laying down no more than that if a policy decision satisfies *Wednesbury* criteria, then the courts will not intervene.[37]

A second issue arose in *Blackburn*. It was whether the applicant had sufficient *locus standi* for the remedy of mandamus.[38]

Edmund Davies L.J. voiced the general view of the Court when he said[39]:

"How and by whom the duty can be enforced is another matter, and it may be that a private citizen, such as the applicant, having no special or peculiar interest in the due discharge of the duty under consideration, has himself no legal right to enforce it."

Recently, with the devolution of control over criminal prosecutions from the police to the Crown Prosecution Service, applications for judicial review have been made against the C.P.S. with regard to its decisions to prosecute certain offenders. In *R. v. Chief Constable of Kent, ex p. L. (a minor)*,[40] Court held that a decision to prosecute a juvenile for a criminal offence was, in principle, susceptible to review, but only on *Wednesbury* grounds as, for example, in violation or disregard of a clear and settled policy. In *R. v. I.R.C., ex p. Mead*,[41] the court held that the court had a similar jurisdiction in relation to decisions to prosecute adults.

Another area in which judicial review has been of increasing importance has been in testing the limits of, and proper methods of employing, the new

---

[34] Crucially, before the hearing of the appeal, the police undertook to withdraw the policy direction and replace it with a new policy in favour of prosecution.
[35] However, in the light of the undertakings and the uncertainty in the law which had induced the policy direction in the first place, the court declined as a matter of discretion to grant relief.
[36] At p. 138G.
[37] See, *e.g. Holgate Mohammed v. Duke* [1984] 1 Q.C. 437, at p. 443B, *per* Lord Diplock, that the exercise of the power of arrest is reviewable on *Wednesbury* grounds.
[38] This point also engages the difficult question of whether section 31 of the Supreme Court Act 1981 permits a court to grant an injunction in lieu of mandamus, where there is insufficient standing for mandamus.
[39] At 149A.
[40] [1993] 1 All E.R. 758.
[41] [1993] 1 All E.R. 772. See, also: *R. v. Commissioner of Police of the Metropolis, ex p. P, The Times,* May 24, 1995 (*held*: caution administered in breach of Home Office Guidelines was perceptible to judicial review); *R. v. D.P.P. ex p. C., The Times,* March 7, 1994 (*held*: decision not to prosecute, contrary to guidelines, was susceptible to judicial review).

police powers under the Police and Criminal Evidence Act 1984 ("PACE") and the recent Criminal Justice Acts.[42] In *R. v. Director of the Serious Fraud Office, ex p. Johnson*[43] Auld J. held that a man, who had been charged with fraud, did not have locus standi to challenge the service on his wife of a notice under section 2(2) of the Criminal Justice Act 1987 requiring her to furnish information relating to the SFO's investigation of her husband. Further, the question of whether the spouse had a reasonable excuse for not complying with the notice was not susceptible to judicial review, being properly a matter for any court seised of proceedings against the spouse for failure to comply with the notice.

In *R. v. Chief Constable of South Wales, ex p. Merrick*[44] an application for judicial review was made in respect of a policy instituted by the respondent whereby solicitors were not allowed to consult with clients held in police custody at the Magistrates Court after 10 a.m. There was an issue as to whether section 58 of PACE applied to those in custody at Magistrates Courts after they had been remanded in custody. However, at common law a person held in custody was entitled to consult a solicitor at an early stage of the investigation provided this does not cause unreasonable delay or hindrance to the investigation of the crime. There was no significant difference so far as concerned securing to persons in custody the right to consult a solicitor between section 58(1) and the common law. It was proper to have a policy regulating access to those in custody, but the policy in this case was unlawful in imposing a blanket ban on contact after 10 a.m. The policy should have taken into account whether it was reasonably practicable to allow access immediately or within a period of time.

CORONERS

15–003   The High Court has a limited statutory power to review the decisions of coroners. Under section 13(2) of the Coroners Act 1988 the High Court can order an inquest to be held or, where an inquest has already been held, quash the inquisition (*i.e.* the verdict) and order a fresh inquest. This power can only be exercised where the court is satisfied that the coroner "refuses or neglects to hold an inquest which ought to be held"[45] or where it is necessary or desirable in the interests of justice that another inquest should be held.[46] The court will order a new inquest only where there is "a real risk that justice has not been done".[47]

In practice, judicial review is more widely used than this statutory

---

[42] For an example of an unsuccessful challenge to a police circular advising that there would be few circumstances in which the applicant would be properly admitted as solicitors' clerk at the interview of police suspects, see *R. v. Chief Constable of Leicestershire, ex p. Henning* [1994] C.O.D. 256.

[43] [1993] C.O.D. 58.

[44] [1994] 1 W.L.R. 663.

[45] s.13(1)(a).

[46] s.13(1)(b).

[47] *R. v. South London Coroner, ex p. Thompson, The Times,* July 9, 1982.

procedure. Applications under section 13 require the *fiat* of the Attorney-General.[48] Moreover, it is only the final verdict of the inquest that can be challenged under section 13. Judicial review, on the other hand, lies in respect of all interlocutory decisions of the coroner in addition to the verdict. An application for judicial review can be made at the same time as an application under the Coroners Act.[49] However, the court has said that where the Attorney-General's *fiat* has been obtained, it is preferable to proceed by way of section 13.[50] In *R. v. H.M. Coroner for Ceredigion, ex p. Wigley*,[51] an application was made both under section 13 and for judicial review. The court held that the test which the court had to apply in relation both to applications under section 13 of the Act and for judicial review was the same, threefold test, namely: (i) whether there were grounds to give rise to a consideration by the court of the exercise of its discretion as to whether there was a procedural irregularity, insufficiency of inquiry or the discovery of new facts or evidence, (ii) whether it was necessary or desirable in the interests of justice that another inquest should be held and (iii) whether there was a real possibility that a different verdict would be returned if a new inquest were held. The court, in dealing with criticisms of the coroner's procedure in that case, emphasised that a shorthand note should have been taken so as to prevent any later dispute as to what was said by any of the witnesses.

Prior to 1984 it was thought that judicial review of a coroner's decisions was available in very limited circumstances. In *R. v. Surrey Coroner, ex p. Campbell*[52] a Divisional Court held that, despite the decision of the House of Lords in *Anisminic v. Foreign Compensation Commission*,[53] the court could only order judicial review on the basis of error on the face of the inquisition, fraud by the coroner or an excess or refusal of jurisdiction. Errors of law within the jurisdiction, such as, as in *Campbell*, putting improper pressure on the jury to bring in a particular verdict, were not reviewable by the courts.

However, in *R. v. Greater Manchester Coroner, ex p. Tal*[54] the Divisional Court held that the decision in *Campbell* was plainly wrong, that the principle in *Anisminic* did apply to the coroner's court and that errors of law within the jurisdiction could be reviewed. The effect of *Tal* is, essentially, that all decisions taken by coroners are amenable to judicial review on the usual grounds. Coronial law is now a burgeoning area for judicial review. In *R. v. H.M. Coroner for Greater London, ex p. Koto*[55] the Court has

---

[48] In *R. v. Att.-Gen., ex p. Ferrante* (July 1, 1994; unrep.) it was held by Popplewell J. that refusal of the Attorney's *fiat* was not susceptible to judicial review. The case went to the C.A., but was decided on other grounds. See, also: *R. v. Attorney-General, ex p. Taylor and Another, The Times*, August 14, 1995 (*held*: Courts have no jurisdiction to review Attorney-General's decision not to bring proceedings for contempt of court).

[49] *Re Rapier*, dec'd [1988] Q.B. 26 at 29 *per* Woolf L.J.

[50] *R. v. West Berkshire Coroner, ex p. Thomas, The Times*, April 25, 1991.

[51] [1993] C.O.D. 364.

[52] [1982] Q.B. 661.

[53] [1969] 2 A.C. 147.

[54] [1985] Q.B. 67.

[55] See [1993] C.O.D. 444.

emphasised that judicial review will only exceptionally be available prior to the conclusion of an inquest.

Applications for judicial review of the decisions of coroners can be brought by anyone who has *locus standi*. In practice, most applications are brought by the family of the deceased.[56] It is probable that anyone who has a right to be represented at the inquest as a "properly interested person" under the Coroners Rules has sufficient interest for the purposes of Order 53. An application may be brought, for example, by a person who may be held responsible for the death of the deceased.[57]

Judicial review is available to challenge decisions other than the actual verdict such as a coroner's refusal to hold a post-mortem[58] or to hold an inquest,[59] a decision not to empanel a jury[60] and a decision to hold an inquest *in camera*.[61]

The grounds upon which certiorari will be granted to quash the verdict and a new inquest ordered[62] are various: where the jury sat for long periods without a break[63]; where the coroner refused to adjourn an inquest to allow evidence to be given of the medical treatment afforded a prisoner[64]; on the ground that the coroner wrongly refused to leave the verdict of lack of care to the jury[65] or wrongly left lack of care to the jury[66] and where the coroner

---

[56] See *R. v. H.M. Coroner for Greater London, ex p. Driscoll* [1994] C.O.D. 91, where the Court granted judicial review to two sisters of the deceased, who had been found by the coroner not to be "interested persons" within the meaning of rule 20(2)h of the Coroners Rules 1984. The Court held that the word "interested" should not be given a narrow or technical meaning and was not confined to a proprietary right or a financial interest in the estate of the deceased. However, the Court did recognise that there could be some cases in which a coroner could properly find that even a close relative was not a "properly interested person".

[57] *R. v. West London Coroner, ex p. Gray* [1988] Q.B. 467, *R. v. Birmingham Coroner, ex p. Secretary of State for the Home Department* (1990) *The Times*, August 6 (Home Secretary challenging a decision to leave to the jury lack of care as a possible verdict in respect of the death of a prisoner in custody).

[58] *R. v. H.M. Coroner for Greater London (Southern District), ex p. Ridley* [1985] 1 W.L.R. 1347.

[59] *R. v. Poplar Coroner, ex p. Thomas* [1993] 2 W.L.R. 547 (C.A.). See, too, *R. v. H.M. Coroner for South Glamorgan, ex p. Basoodeo Sujeeum* [1993] C.O.D. 366, where the Court refused to order an inquest into a death, originally recorded as being due to natural causes, when there had been a subsequent admission of negligence by the treating hospital in civil proceedings.

[60] *R. v. Inner London North District Coroner, ex p. Linnane* [1989] 1 W.L.R. 395.

[61] *R. v. McHugh, ex p. Trelford* (March 22, 1984; unrep.).

[62] For an example of a case where the general public interest in the holding of a fresh inquest weighed heavily with the court, see *R. v. H.M. Coroner for Solihull, ex p. Nutt* [1993] C.O.D. 449.

[63] *R. v. Southwark Coroner, ex p. Hicks* [1987] 1 W.L.R. 1624. See, too, *Re Inquest into the death of Roberto Calvi dec'd, The Times*, April 2, 1983. In *R. v. Birch, The Times*, March 27, 1992 it was said to be undesirable in a serious case [and what coroner's inquest is not serious?] to send a jury out after 3 p.m. save in exceptional circumstances.

[64] *ibid.*

[65] *ibid.* Guidelines for the circumstances in which a verdict of lack of care should be left to a jury are to be found in *R. v. H.M. Coroner for East Berkshire, ex p. Buckley* [1993] C.O.D. 96 in which it was held, *inter alia*, that counsel's submissions on the appropriate verdicts to leave to a jury were always submissions of law, and that the Coroner, even if of the view that no reasonable jury could have found a lack of care, should have heard counsel's submissions.

[66] *R. v. Birmingham Coroner, ex p. Secretary of State for the Home Department*, n. 9 above.

retired with the jury whilst the verdict was under consideration.[67]

The court has no power to substitute in appropriate circumstances for a wrong verdict the verdict which the jury must on a proper direction have found: a fresh inquest must be ordered.[68]

As with other areas of judicial review, the courts will not interfere with the merits of the coroner's decision. Thus in *R. v. Poplar Coroner, ex p. Thomas*[69] the Court of Appeal held that the coroner had been perfectly entitled to reach the conclusion that a person who died during an asthma attack, in circumstances in which there was a possibility that the delay in the arrival of the ambulance had contributed to the death, had not died an "unnatural death" within section 8(1)(a) of the Coroners Act 1988 and declined to interfere with the decision.

In *R. v. H.M. Coroner for Inner London, ex p. Dallaglio and Lockwood Croft*[70] an application was made by relatives of two of those killed in the *Marchioness* pleasure boat disaster on the Thames, challenging the decision of the coroner not to resume an adjourned inquest into the deaths. The disaster occurred on August 20, 1989. The coroner's inquest had been opened and adjourned in the weeks following the disaster. The coroner planned to hold the inquest in two parts, the first relating to the time and cause of death of the deceased, and the second relating to eyewitness and technical evidence relating to the collision on the river. Part one of the enquiry had not been completed when the whole matter was adjourned yet again, pending various criminal proceedings arising out of the accident. When these were completed, in late June 1992, the coroner had to decide whether or not there was "sufficient cause" to resume his enquiry, pursuant to section 16(3) of the Coroners' Act 1988. The coroner decided that there was not.

The basis of the applicants' application for judicial review was the coroner's alleged bias (although it should be noted that the applicants disavowed any suggestion of conscious bias on the part of the coroner). In short, what the applicants had to do was show (*per* Simon Brown L.J.)[71]:

> "in the first instance an appearance of bias and then on an examination of all the facts a real possibility that the Coroner may unconsciously have felt resentful towards them in such a way as to have influenced his approach to their case for a resumption [of the inquest]."

The Court did not in terms deal with the question of whether the coroner, in deciding whether or not to resume an action, was obliged to canvass the views of the relatives of the deceased. However, "having done so he was clearly bound to deal fairly and judicially with their views".

---

[67] *R. v. Wood, ex p. Anderson* [1928] 1 K.B. 302.

[68] *ibid.*

[69] n. 11 above.

[70] [1994] 4 All E.R. 139.

[71] Following the guidelines in bias cases set out by the House of Lords in *R. v. Gough* [1993] A.C. 646.

Simon Brown L.J. summed up his conclusions on bias in the following way:

"I find myself in the last analysis unable to discount the real possibility that the Coroner unconsciously allowed himself to be influenced against the appellants ... by a feeling of hostility towards them."

The Court remitted the matter to a coroner for a different district to decide whether the inquest should be resumed,[72] although the Court was careful to state that the new coroner might well come to the conclusion that there was not sufficient cause to restart the inquest, especially in view of the further time which had by now elapsed from the initial adjournment. Such a decision, not to restart the inquest, if made properly and with proper regard being paid to all points of view, would be very difficult to challenge on any further judicial review proceedings.

The Court of Appeal clearly regretted that a public inquiry had not been held into the *Marchioness* disaster, and warned the applicants that even if they were successful in having an inquest held, it would not be able to address all their concerns, many of which were much more appropriate for the much more wide-ranging investigation of a public inquiry.[73]

MENTAL HEALTH AND COMMUNITY CARE

15–004   The Mental Health Act 1983 provides a code for the admission, detention, treatment and discharge of persons suffering from mental disorders. In *Black v. Forsey*[74] the House of Lords held that Scotland's equivalent to the 1983 Act (the Mental Health (Scotland) Act 1984) comprehensively lays down the powers of hospital authorities to detain patients and that such authorities enjoy no common law power to detain.[75]

Part II of the 1983 Act identifies the grounds upon which persons may be admitted to hospital (whether for assessment under section 2, for treatment under section 3 or in cases of emergency under section 4),[76] determines

---

[72] *cf. R. v. H.M. Coroner for South Yorkshire, ex p. Stringer* [1994] C.O.D. 176, where the Court held that even had it found the applicants' complaints persuasive, in any event it would not have exercised its discretion to order a fresh inquest into the deaths of the applicants' relatives in the Hillsborough soccer stadium disaster in April 1989. Criticisms of the police had already been made in the Taylor report, and there was no evidence to base a criticism of the emergency services. It would also not be in the interests of witnesses to investigate the tragedy once again. See also *R. v. H.M. Coroner for Western District of East Sussex, ex p. Homberg* [1994] C.O.D. 279.

[73] *cf. R. v. Coroner for North Humberside, ex p. Jamieson* [1995] Q.B. 1. for observations by the C.A. on the limited nature of a coroner's inquest.

[74] (1987) S.L.T. 681.

[75] Private individuals retain a common law power to detain in cases of emergency persons of unsound mind who are a danger to themselves or others.

[76] For the relationship between discharges after s.2 admission and admission shortly thereafter under s.3, *R. v. Managers of South Western Hospital, ex p. M* [1993] Q.B. 683.

who may make an application for a patient to be admitted and how such an application should be made. Various requirements must be complied with in order for admissions to be validly made: in particular, recommendations from medically qualified practitioners are necessary. Part II also deals with guardianship, the reclassification of patients (i.e. as suffering from a mental disorder different from that in respect of which the patient was admitted) and leave of absence for patients from hospital.

Part III of the Act is concerned with persons who are the subject of criminal proceedings or who have been sentenced for criminal offences. Provision is made in respect of such persons for remand to a mental hospital, hospital orders (i.e. authorising admission to and detention in a hospital) and restriction orders (restricting discharge of the patient from hospital).

Under Part V of the Act, applications may be made to a Mental Health Review Tribunal in respect of, *inter alia*, admissions to hospital and guardianship. The tribunal's function is to review the justification(s) for the patient's continued detention or guardianship or, where the patient has been conditionally discharged, to review the continued imposition of conditions. It was made clear by the Court of Appeal in *R. v. Hallstrom, ex p. Waldron*[77] that the tribunals have no jurisdiction to determine whether a patient has been wrongly admitted. The tribunals have the power under sections 72 and 73 of the Act to discharge patients from hospital.[78]

There are a number of other provisions in the Act concerning, *inter alia*, the management and control of the property and affairs of the patient, the functions of the local authorities and consent to treatment. However, the majority of the applications for judicial review which come before the courts involve the scheme for admission and detention in Parts II and III of the Act or refusals to discharge by mental health review tribunals.

Implementation of the scheme contained in Parts II, III and V of the Act involves decision-making by a variety of bodies and persons, including medical practitioners, hospital authorities, the Mental Health Review Tribunal and the Secretary of State for the Home Department. Judicial review lies in respect of decisions made by these persons or bodies at all stages of dealing with mentally disordered persons, *i.e.* from admission to discharge and recall.

Thus, in *R. v. Hallstrom, ex p. W (No. 2)*[79] McCullough J. granted an application for judicial review of the recommendations of two doctors under section 3 of the Act that the applicant be detained for treatment. The applicant had refused treatment. The doctors believed that the treatment was necessary and accepted that it could be provided to the patient in the community with the patient's consent. The recommendation for detention was made on the basis that detention was the only way in which the treatment could be provided. McCullough J. held that a patient could only

---

[77] [1986] 1 Q.B. 824 at 846.
[78] As to the content of these sections, see *R. v. Canons Park Mental Health Review Tribunal, ex p. A* [1994] 3 W.L.R. 630.
[79] [1986] 2 All E.R. 306.

be detained under section 3 of the Act if the treatment necessitated detention as an in-patient and that, accordingly, the recommendations were *ultra vires*.

In *R. v. Ealing District Health Authority, ex p. Fox*[80] Otton J. granted judicial review of the failure by a health authority to provide aftercare services for a patient whose conditional discharge from a mental hospital had been deferred by the mental health review tribunal until adequate arrangements for aftercare had been made.

The fundamental principle to which regard should be had by the courts in determining applications for judicial review in the area of mental health was articulated by McCullough J. in *R. v. Hallstrom, ex p. W. (No. 2)* as follows:

"Parliament is presumed not to enact legislation which interferes with the liberty of the subject without making it clear that this was its intention. ... It goes without saying that, unless clear statutory authority to the contrary exists, no one is to be detained in hospital or to undergo medical treatment or even to submit himself to a medical examination without his consent. This is as true of a mentally disordered person as of anyone else."[81]

However it is evident that the courts on occasions take a more restrictive view especially where it is perceived that the patient is a danger to the public. In *R. v. Secretary of State for the Home Department, ex p. K.*[82] the Court of Appeal had no hesitation whatsoever in upholding the decision of the Secretary of State to recall to hospital a patient who would shortly be released from prison, even though the tribunal which had last considered his case concluded on unanimous medical evidence that he was no longer suffering from any mental disorder and even though there had been no change of circumstances since the tribunal's decision. It is plain from the list of factors which the Court of Appeal stated should be taken into account that the concern for public safety was given considerable weight.

Proceedings in mental health review tribunals have primarily been challenged in judicial review proceedings on the basis of breach of natural justice.[83] A tribunal's refusal to direct a discharge has been successfully challenged on the basis that the tribunal gave "wholly inadequate" reasons.[84] In *R. v. Oxford Regional Mental Health Review Tribunal, ex p. Secretary of State for the Home Department*[85] the House of Lords ruled that there had been a breach of natural justice in a case

---

[80] [1993] 1 W.L.R. 373.

[81] n. 4 above, at 314.

[82] [1990] 3 W.L.R. 755.

[83] Alternatively the tribunal can be required to state a case for determination by the High Court on a point of law under s.78(8) of the Act. Judicial review, however, permits "a broader consideration of the issues" and offers "a much more comprehensive range of reliefs" (*per* Nolan J. in *Bone v. Mental Health Review Tribunal* [1985] 3 All E.R. 330 at 334).

[84] *R. v. Mental Health Review Tribunal, ex p. Clatworthy* [1985] 3 All E.R. 699.

[85] [1988] A.C. 120 (H.L.).

where the tribunal conditionally discharged a patient under a deferred order without informing the Secretary of State for the Home Department of the hearing. In *R. v. Secretary of State for the Home Department, ex p. Didlick*,[86] the Court considered the principles governing restriction orders, and held that merely allowing conditions attaching to a discharge to lapse was not the same as securing for the former patient an absolute discharge, so that the power subsequently to issue a warrant of recall remained.

One area in which judicial review may have an important role to play is the provision of care to mentally disordered and other vulnerable persons living in the community. Under the National Health Service and Community Care Act 1990 the responsibility for the assessment of the needs of the mentally ill and for the provision of services to the mentally ill falls upon the social services departments of local authorities. Those affected by deficiencies in the assessment procedure or the failure to provide adequate community care may have to seek redress through judicial review.[87]

In *R. v. North Yorkshire C.C., ex p. Hargreaves*,[88] judicial review was granted of an offer of placements for respite care under the community care regime. The Court held that the local authority had a duty to take account of the preferences of both carer and service user, and that it had wrongly assumed that the two were synonymous.

In *R. v. Gloucestershire County Council, ex p. M and others*,[89] a Divisional Court held that local authorities were under a duty to make arrangements under s.2 of the Chronically Sick and Disabled Persons Act 1970 once it had decided that such arrangements were necessary to meet the needs of a disabled person. In so deciding, however, it could take its financial resources into account.

---

[86] [1993] C.O.D. 412.

[87] See *R. v. Secretary of State for Health, ex p. Alcohol Recovery Project* [1993] C.O.D. 344, where the Court rejected the application, *inter alia*, on the grounds of delay in making an application. That the Court did so despite the application for leave being made on December 23 in respect of a decision taken on October 2, less than three months before, is a salutary reminder to applicants that the rules impose an obligation to make an application promptly, and that three months' delay in applying will, in some cases, prove to be too long. For two contrasting decisions on the powers of community care authorities to impose terms in contracts with the operators of residential homes, see *R. v. Newcastle-upon-Tyne Council, ex p. Dixon* [1994] C.O.D. 217, and *R. v. Cleveland C.C., ex p. Cleveland Care Homes Association* [1994] C.O.D. 221. In *Cleveland* it was argued for the council that the matter was one of private contract law and hence not amenable to judicial review. The Court disagreed on the basis that, *inter alia*, the availability of preferred accommodation for potential residents was sufficiently related to the purpose of the 1990 legislation to provide the necessary statutory underpinning.

[88] *The Times*, November 9, 1994.

[89] *The Times*, June 21, 1995.

16. MISCELLANEOUS AREAS OF REVIEW

JUDICIAL REVIEW OF STATUTORY TRIBUNALS

16–001 The term "statutory tribunal" means no more than the establishment of a public body by Act of Parliament to perform certain administrative functions. There are countless examples of such tribunals in existence, each with their constituent Act and internal procedure. Examples include: the Lands Tribunal,[1] the Social Security Commissioners,[2] Rent Assessment Committees,[3] and less well-known bodies such as the Dairy Produce Quota Tribunal.[4] The textbooks on administrative law usually devote much space to these entities because they form the backbone of effective administration. In the context of judicial review, however, they play a less prominent role, since their decisions are frequently subject to appeal.

Their jurisdiction is strictly controlled by the enabling Acts, as can be seen from the structure of decision-making in immigration law, already encountered.[5] In particular, there is a wide difference in the system of appeals from primary decisions. Some statutes permit no appeal whatsoever,[6] others allow appeals to specified internal bodies (Employment Appeal Tribunals, Immigration Appeal Tribunals), or to courts.[7] The nature of the appeal may include empowering the tribunal in question to determine the validity of subordinate regulations.[8]

Notwithstanding the diversity of these procedures, judicial review will lie against decisions defective in the respects enumerated in Chapter 2, provided that Order 53 is considered to be legally convenient and provided, also, that there is no relevant preclusive clause.[9]

The following are instances of Order 53 remedies being granted against statutory tribunals: certiorari against the decision of a rating committee where it failed to disclose an expert report which had a causative effect on

---

[1] The Lands Tribunal Act 1949.
[2] Social Security Act 1992, s.23.
[3] Landlord and Tenant Act 1987, s.31.
[4] See *R. v. Dairy Produce Quota Tribunal, ex p. P. A. Cooper & Sons* [1993] C.O.D. 277—a duty to give reasons case.
[5] See Chap. 11.
[6] Betting, Gaming and Lotteries Act 1963, s.29.
[7] Aircraft and Shipbuilding Industries Act 1977, Sched. 7.
[8] See *Chief Adjudication Officer v. Foster* [1993] A.C. 754.
[9] These matters are considered in more detail in paras. 2–033 and 6–011.

the assessment[10]; mandamus against a valuation panel that wrongfully declined jurisdiction[11]; and a declaration against a tribunal that unlawfully suspended a docker from work without pay.[12]

Sometimes judicial review will be the only appropriate method of obtaining relief. The most obvious situation is where no appeal lies as, for example, in *Bland v. Chief Supplementary Benefit Officer*,[13] where the Court of Appeal held that a Commissioner's refusal of leave to appeal from the decision of an inferior tribunal was not a "decision" for the purpose of the legislation governing appeal.

A further, curious, instance of judicial review being the only available remedy is where a party actually has a decision in its favour but objects to some part of the reasoning. This occurred in *G.L.C. v. Secretary of State for the Environment and Harrow L.B.C.*[14] There, the applicants sought leave to move for judicial review of the reasoning of the planning inspector. Woolf J. (as he then was) gave leave on the basis that the applicants could not appeal, as they were not truly "aggrieved" for the purposes of the appeal provision.

Similarly, Order 53 rather than appeal will be appropriate where the tribunal has taken some step which is antecedent to the actual decision.[15]

Judicial review will be used against statutory tribunals predominantly to challenge the legality of decisions (as opposed to their merits)[16] and in particular, the violation of natural justice.[17] Listed tribunals under the Tribunals and Inquiries Act 1992 are required "to furnish a statement, either written or oral, of the reasons for the decision if requested, on or before the giving or notification of the decision." Certiorari and mandamus will lie if no intelligible reasons are provided.[18]

Statutory time limit and ouster clauses have already been discussed (see para. 6–011). The Tribunal and Inquiries Act 1992 makes special provision for pre-1958 ouster clauses. Section 12 thereof provides that such clauses, inserted in statutes before August 1, 1958 "shall not have effect so as to prevent the removal of the proceedings into the High Court

---

[10] *R. v. Westminster Assessment Committee, ex p. Grosvenor House (Park Lane) Ltd* [1941] 1 K.B. 53.

[11] *R. v. West Norfolk Valuation Panel, ex p. H. Prins Ltd* (1975) 73 L.G.R. 206.

[12] *Barnard v. National Dock Labour Board* [1953] 2 Q.B. 18.

[13] [1983] 1 W.L.R. 262. See also, *ex p. Stevenson* [1892] 1 Q.B. 609.

[14] [1985] J.P.L. 868.

[15] See, *e.g. R. v. Camden L.B.C., ex p. Comyn Ching Co. (London) Ltd* (1984) 47 P. & C.R. 1417; *Islington L.B.C. v. Secretary of State for the Environment* (1982) 43 P. & C.R. 300.

[16] As in *Paddington Valuation Officer, ex p. Peachey Property Corporation Ltd* [1966] 1 Q.B. 380.

[17] *R. v. Deputy Industrial Injuries Commissioner, ex p. Jones* [1962] 2 Q.B. 677. *R. v. Vaccine Damage Tribunal, ex p. Loveday*, The Times, April 20, 1985.

[18] See, *e.g. R. v. Industrial Injuries Commissioner, ex p. Howarth* (1968) 4 K.I.R. 621; *Iveagh (Earl) v. M.H.L.G.* [1964] 1 Q.B. 395. Note that reasons will not necessarily subject a decision to review merely because they reflect an irrelevant consideration, if the decision would have been the same in any event. See *R. v. Broadcasting Complaints Commission, ex p. Owen* [1985] Q.B. 1153.

by order of certiorari or to prejudice the powers of the High Court to make orders of mandamus."

The implication seems to be that clauses after that date may be intended to have exclusory effect.[19]

PUBLIC INQUIRIES

16-002   The statutory public inquiry is a traditional administrative procedure for ensuring that policies are submitted for objection by those likely to be affected. Typical areas include town and country planning and compulsory purchase legislation.

Judicial review does not usually arise in relation to inquiries because, generally, appeals lie only on a point of law to the High Court and there is a time limit of (usually) six weeks. This type of statutory review will, effectively, preclude judicial review after the statutory period has expired (see para. 6–011).

Order 53 will, however, be available where the Secretary of State unreasonably refuses to hold a public inquiry. In *R. v. Secretary of State for the Environment, ex p. Binney*[20] Webster J. held that the decision not to hold an inquiry should be made only where the minister could be reasonably satisfied that one was unnecessary because: (i) he could properly weigh up any two or more conflicting public issues, and (ii) all those with the right to make representations would necessarily have taken those into account. Applying those principles, certiorari was granted to quash a decision not to hold a public inquiry into the proposed alteration of the A34 trunk road between Winchester and Newbury.

In most other cases, complaints against legality or breaches of natural justice at inquiries will be made through the statutory machinery by way of appeal to the High Court.[21] The principles applied are, however, similar to those applied on judicial review.[22] Because a public inquiry is not a *lis inter partes*, it is essential for the minister to have regard to the public interest; if he does not, an order may be quashed on *Wednesbury* principles.[23] The rules of natural justice are especially apposite to such proceedings.[24] The minister is required to consider all objections, but this must be construed with reference to the subject matter of the inquiry.[25] As with tribunals,

---

[19] This may not, in fact, be so. See, *e.g. R. v. Preston Supplementary Benefits Appeal Tribunal, ex p. Moore* [1975] 1 W.L.R. 624 at p. 628.

[20] *The Times*, October 8, 1983. See also *Niarchos (London) Ltd v. Secretary of State for the Environment* (1981) 79 L.G.R. 264 (unreasonable decision to reopen inquiry quashed under Ord. 53).

[21] Judicial review may sometimes lie instead of the statutory procedure. See below.

[22] See para. 6–009.

[23] See, *e.g. Prest v. Secretary of State for Wales* (1983) 81 L.G.R. 193.

[24] See, *e.g. Errington v. Minister of Health* [1935] 1 K.B. 249, supplemented, now, by statutory rules made under the Tribunal and Inquiries Act 1992.

[25] *Bushell v. Secretary of State for the Environment* [1981] A.C. 75; *R. v. London Regional Passenger Committee, ex p. Brent L.B.C. The Times*, May 23, 1985.

reasons must be given for decisions by virtue of section 10 of the Tribunals and Inquiries Act 1992.

PLANNING CASES

As with immigration law, planning cases fall within a statutory scheme of quasi-judicial tribunals and inquiries. It follows that judicial review will lie where the statutory scheme provides no, or no equally convenient, remedy.[26] In the Town and Country Planning Act 1990, Parliament has preserved the extensive appellate structure created by the 1971 Act.

16–003

On that basis judicial review lies both from certain decisions of local planning authorities and of the Secretary of State (including a decision to decline jurisdiction to hear an appeal).[27]

As against a local planning authority, review will, for example, lie (on *C.C.S.U.* principles) against a decision to grant planning permission,[28] to issue a stop notice[29] to refuse to accept a valid application for permission[30] and to declare that planning permission has lapsed.[31] However, review will not lie where an applicant seeks merely to affirm his own interest in the property at the expense of other developers.[32]

As against the Secretary of State judicial review may, for example, lie of a decision not to call in an application for planning permission for the Secretary of State's consideration[33] and of a decision not to order a fresh planning inquiry.[34]

A particular difficulty which arises in the context of planning law is *locus standi*. It appears that those whose property interests may be directly affected by the grant of planning permission will possess standing to challenge a decision.[35] However, pressure groups seeking to preserve sectors of the environment will not always be treated so favourably.[36]

---

[26] As to this see, *e.g. R. v. Hillingdon L.B.C., ex p. Royco Homes Ltd* [1974] 1 Q.B. 720, (*held*: judicial review was, in the circumstances, more convenient than the statutory appeal system provided). *cf., however: R. v. Epping Forest D.C., ex p. Green* [1993] C.O.D. 81, (*held*: the decision in *Royco* was exceptional and applied only where there was a clear-cut error of law).

[27] See *Lenlyn v. Secretary of State for the Environment* [1985] J.P.L. 482; *R. v. Secretary of State for the Environment, ex p. JBI Financial Consultants* [1989]1 P.L.R. 1.

[28] *R. v. South Hertfordshire D.C., ex p. Felton* [1991] J.P.L. 633.

[29] *R. v. Secretary of State for the Environment, ex p. Hillingdon L.B.C.* [1986] 2 All E.R. 273.

[30] *R. v. Elmbridge B.C., ex p. Oakimber* [1991] 3 P.L.R. 35.

[31] *R. v. Elmbridge B.C., ex p. Health Care Corp. Ltd* [1991] 3 P.L.R. 63.

[32] *See R. v. Peterborough C.C., ex p. London Brick Property* [1988] 1 P.L.R. 27.

[33] *R. v. Secretary of State for the Environment, ex p. Middlesbrough B.C.* [1988] 3 P.L.R. 52.

[34] *R. v. Secretary of State for the Environment, ex p. Fielder Estates* [1988] 3 P.L.R. 62.

[35] See *R. v. Torfaen B.C., ex p. Jones* [1986] J.P.L. 686.

[36] *R. v. Secretary of State for the Environment, ex p. Rose Theatre Trust* [1990] 1 Q.B. 504. But note the growing ambit of standing in the environmental challenges brought by pressure groups referred to in para. 4–007.

EDUCATION

16–004   Parents, governors and local education authorities have, in recent years, had frequent recourse to judicial review in challenging decisions taken in the educational arena, such as the expulsion of pupils,[37] the removal of governors,[38] and the refusal to provide free transport to school.[39]

The High Court is most often invited to exercise its power of judicial review in the following three areas: (i) the assessment of, and provision for, special educational needs; (ii) the criteria for the admission of children to particular schools; and (iii) the reorganisation of schools (in particular the acquisition of grant-maintained status).

Special educational needs

16–005   Under section 167 of the Education Act 1993 an LEA is under an obligation, where it is of the opinion that a child has special educational needs (*i.e.* learning difficulties) which call for the LEA to determine the special educational provision that should be made, to assess those needs. If the LEA, after making the assessment, is of the opinion that it should determine the special educational provision that should be made for the child, the LEA must make a "statement" in respect of that child and in accordance with the provisions of section 168 of the 1993 Act.

Challenges have been brought by parents in respect of the refusal to make a statement,[40] the inadequacy of the provision specified in the statement,[41] the failure to make available the special educational provision detailed in the statement,[42] the failure of an LEA to pay for the travelling expenses of a child with special educational needs to attend the school of his parents' choice, when the LEA said that those needs could be met at a school closer to the child's home (to which travelling expenses would be paid),[43] and the failure to allow a further appeal to the Appeal Committee where changes have been made to the original statement.[44]

In *R. v. Hereford and Worcester C.C., ex p. Lashford*[45] it was argued, by the parents of a child with special educational needs, that an LEA was obliged to make a statement in respect of a child whom it had assessed as having such needs. The Court of Appeal rejected their argument and stated that an

---

[37] *R. v. Board of Governors of London Oratory School, ex p. Regis* (February 4, 1988; unrep.); *R. v. Headmaster of Fernhill Manor School, ex p. Brown, The Times,* June 5, 1992.

[38] *R. v. Brent L.B.C., ex p. Assegai, The Times,* June 18, 1987.

[39] *R. v. Devon C.C., ex p. G* [1989] A.C. 573; *R. v. Rochdale M.B.C., ex p. Schemet* [1993] C.O.D. 113.

[40] *R. v. Hereford and Worcester C.C., ex p. Lashford* [1987] 1 F.L.R. (C.A.).

[41] *R. v. Secretary of State for Education and Science, ex p. E, The Times,* May 9, 1991.

[42] *R. v. Secretary of State for Education and Science, ex p. L.* 86 L.G.R. 13.

[43] See *R. v. Essex C.C., ex p. C* [1993] C.O.D. 398.

[44] See *R. v. Clwyd C.C., ex p. A* [1993] C.O.D. 35.

[45] See n. 40, above.

LEA need only make a statement in respect of a child with special educational needs if the LEA had determined, in its discretion, that it was necessary to make special educational provision. The respondent LEA was entitled to hold the view that the child's needs were already adequately met in the school which the child attended.

Provision is made in section 169 of the 1993 Act for parents to appeal to a Special Educational Needs Tribunal from the determinations of the LEA not to make a statement,[46] or as to the content of the statement.[47] These appeals must be pursued before an application for judicial review is made.[48] Once they have been pursued, however, an application for judicial review may lie, as in *R. v. Secretary of State for Education, ex p. S*[49] or, more probably, a statutory appeal from the decision of the Tribunal to the High Court.[50]

In *S.* the Secretary of State in considering an appeal under the then prevailing law (section 8(6) of the 1981 Education Act) obtained expert advice from a school inspector. He did not, however, disclose the substance of this advice to the appellant or his family. This failure, so it was argued, so departed from the requirements of fairness as to vitiate the decision. The Court agreed. Sedley J. held that if fairness dictated that the Secretary of State disclose the advice if he was thinking of adopting it wholesale (the Secretary of State had conceded that there was a duty of disclosure if and only if the expert report raised something new which the Secretary of State was minded to accept) it equally dictates disclosure where the advice is capable of materially influencing the Secretary of State's evaluation.

The admission of pupils

An increasing number of applications for judicial review are made by parents who wish to challenge refusals by schools or LEAs to admit their children to particular schools. Section 6(2) of the Education Act 1980 imposes a duty upon an LEA and upon the governors of a county or voluntary school to comply with any preference expressed by parents for a particular school for their children. Section 6(3) provides that there is no such duty in the following situations: (a) if compliance with the preference would prejudice the provision of efficient education or the efficient use of resources[51]; (b) if the preferred school is an aided or special agreement school and compliance with the preference would be incompatible with any

16–006

---

[46] s.169 Education Act 1993. Delay in issuing a statement is potentially susceptible to judicial review but any application is likely to be superseded by the issuing of such statement; see *R. v. Gloucestershire C.C., ex p. P* [1994] E.L.R. 334.

[47] s.170 Education Act 1993. For a case upholding an appeal on the sufficiency of the statement, see *Re L* [1994] E.L.R. 16.

[48] *R. v. Salford C.C., ex p. L, The Times,* April 17, 1992 (Popplewell J.).

[49] [1994] C.O.D. 200.

[50] See s.181(2) Education Act 1993 clarifying that the Special Educational Needs Tribunal is a tribunal falling within the appeal provisions of the Tribunals and Inquiries Act 1992, s.11(1).

[51] In *R. v. Governors of the Hasmonean High School, ex p. N and E* [1994] E.L.R. 343, the test under s.6(3)(a) of the 1980 Act was held *not* to have been misapplied.

arrangements for the preservation of the character of the school between the local education authority and the governors; or (c) if the arrangements for admission are based on selection by reference to ability or aptitude and compliance with the preference would be incompatible with such a selection procedure.

In *R. v. Bishop Challoner School, ex p. Choudhury*[52] the applicants were the parents of children, one Hindu and one Muslim, who had been refused admission to a voluntary aided Roman Catholic school which had more applicants for admission than it could accommodate without prejudicing the provision of efficient education. The school operated an admissions policy based, in order of priority, on the following categories: baptised Catholics, the children of baptised Catholics, practising Christians and other Christians. The applicants argued that the school was bound to comply with parental preferences, that it could not rely on s.6(3)(b) of the 1980 Act because no arrangements had been entered into between the LEA and the governors and that s.6(3)(a) did not entitle the school, in choosing (as it had to) which applications to reject, to rely on an admissions policy designed to preserve the character of the school. The applicants claimed that such a policy could only be taken into account under s.6(3)(b).

The House of Lords rejected this contention, holding that where the number of applicants to a school exceeds the number of places (as envisaged in s.6(3)(a)) the school must have an admissions policy of some kind in order to determine who to accept or reject. The school was entitled to choose as its policy criteria which were designed to preserve the character of the school.

The High Court has held that certain admissions policies are unlawful. Thus a policy operating in relation to over-subscribed schools which gave precedence to Greenwich residents over children living outside the borough was declared *ultra vires* by the Court of Appeal because it conflicted with the duty in s.6(5) of the 1980 Act to give effect to parental preference regardless of whether the child came from the local education authority's area.[53]

The *Greenwich* decision was further considered in *R. v. Bromley L.B.C., ex p. C*,[54] in which the applicants challenged the policy which Bromley had adopted in the light of the *Greenwich* case, namely that, in relation to over-subscribed schools, children would be accorded priority as follows: children with a brother or sister at the school, proximity of the school and the accessibility of an alternative school, but with the proviso that the council would depart from the results of the application of these criteria if and to the extent that it was necessary in order to comply with its duties under sections 7 and 8 of the Education Act 1944 (*i.e.* to ensure the availability of sufficient education in the LEA's area). A Divisional Court held that the effect of section 6(5) of the 1980 Act was that the authority

---

[52] [1992] 3 W.L.R. 99.
[53] *R. v. Shadow Education Committee of Greenwich L.B.C., ex p. Governors of John Ball Primary School* (1989) 88 L.G.R. 589 (C.A.).
[54] *The Times,* June 6, 1991.

could in no circumstances favour children living within its area, despite sections 7 and 8, and that the proviso was accordingly unlawful.

Reorganisation

The proposals of LEAs for the reorganisation of local schools have **16–007** frequently been the subject of legal challenge. Sections 12 and 13 of the Education Act 1980 contain the machinery by which an LEA should effect such a reorganisation. Proposals to close, establish or significantly alter schools must be published and submitted to the Secretary of State. Objections may be submitted to the LEA which must be passed on to the Secretary of State. If no objections are received the LEA can go ahead.[55] If, on the other hand, there are objections, approval is required. The Secretary of State may approve, reject or modify the proposals.

There is no statutory obligation to consult prior to the formulation of proposals by an LEA, although the Secretary of State has expressed in circulars his expectation that there will be consultation. This has received the imprimatur of the High Court: in *R. v. Brent L.B.C., ex p. Gunning*[56] the applicants (parents of schoolchildren in Brent) argued that the LEA's attempts at consultation with local parents had been wholly inadequate. Hodgson J. had no hesitation in holding that the parents had a legitimate expectation that they would be consulted. He held that a proper consultation must take place whilst the proposals were still at a formative stage, that the proposer must give sufficient reasons for any proposal to permit intelligent consideration and response, that adequate time must be given for consideration and response and that the product of consultation must be taken into account by the LEA in finalising any statutory proposals.

Other grounds of challenge to reorganisation proposals include the failure to consider a report from the LEA contrary to Schedule I, Part II, para. 7 of the Education Act 1944.[57] As to the Court of Appeal's determination of a potential conflict between an education authority's desire to close a single sex boys' school (when a single sex girls' school elsewhere in the authority's area continued to thrive) and its obligations under the Sex Discrimination Act 1975, see *Kingsbury v. Northampton Education Department*.[58]

The Education Reform Act 1988 added a new dimension to the issue of reorganisation. The Act created a new category of "grant-maintained schools", which are funded by the Department of Education and Science and are independent of LEA control. A number of schools have applied for grant-maintained status since the Act came into force. In *R. v. Secretary of State for Education and Science, ex p. Avon C.C.*[59] the LEA submitted

---

[55] Unless the proposals fall within s.12(4) of the 1980 Act or unless the Secretary of State exercises his power under s.12(5)(a) to give notice to the LEA that approval will be required.
[56] (1986) 84 L.G.R. 168.
[57] *R. v. Kirklees M.B.C., ex p. Molloy* (1987) 86 L.G.R. 115 (C.A.).
[58] [1994] C.O.D. 114.
[59] [1990] 88 L.G.R. 716, *(No. 2)* (1990) 88 L.G.R. 737 (C.A.).

proposals for reorganisation to the Secretary of State under section 12 of the 1980 Act. Under the proposals, Beechen Cliff Boys School would be converted into a sixth form college. The governors of the school applied for grant-maintained status under section 62 of the 1988 Act. The Secretary of State rejected the LEA's proposals and acceded to the governors' application.

An application for judicial review of the Secretary of State's decision was successfully brought by the LEA. Hutchinson J. held that the Secretary of State had misconstrued section 73 of the 1988 Act[60] in giving the governors' application priority rather than weighing the application against the LEA's proposals equally in the balance and that he had failed to take into consideration the consequences of his decision for the remainder of the schools in Bath.

The Secretary of State reconsidered the application and the proposals and reached the same decision. On this occasion his reasons for reaching that decision were carefully elaborated. The LEA brought a second application for judicial review which was, unusually, heard by the Court of Appeal. It was argued on behalf of the applicant that the Secretary of State had again treated the governors' application as paramount, that he had set out three alternatives for the LEA to consider which he wrongly regarded as feasible, and that he had failed to take into account the problems which the LEA would face by reason of their duties under the Sex Discrimination Act 1975.

The Court of Appeal refused the application, holding that the Secretary of State was perfectly entitled to adopt a policy of preferring applications for grant-maintained status provided that it was rigidly applied, that there was no evidence upon which the Court could find that he was *Wednesbury* unreasonable in considering the alternative options feasible and that the Secretary of State had had sufficient regard to any difficulties which the LEA might face under the Sex Discrimination Act. The Court of Appeal concluded by describing the application as a "misconceived" attempt to ask the Court to intervene in what was essentially a dispute as to educational policy.

It seems that judicial restraint is likely to be the keynote in any future applications under Order 53 in respect of the acquisition of grant-maintained status.[61]

---

[60] Under s.73, where both applications by schools for grant-maintained status and proposals by LEAs for reorganisation are made, the Secretary of State must consider both proposals together on their merits.

[61] It is submitted that *R. v. Governors of Astley High School, ex p. Northumberland C.C.* [1994] C.O.D. 27 is an example of such restraint.

TAX AND JUDICIAL REVIEW

In *R. v. I.R.C., ex p. Preston*[62] the House of Lords reaffirmed the principle **16–008** that tax authorities are not immune from the process of judicial review. However, review will not generally lie where there is a statutory appeal route.[63] There are, however, a number of exceptions to this general rule.

In *ex p. Preston* itself, Lords Scarman and Templeman postulated examples where the commissioners might manipulate events so as to deprive the taxpayer of a tactical advantage in any later appeal. They suggested that in such cases judicial review would be available to prevent an abuse of power.

Similarly, Order 53 is the appropriate route where the validity of tax regulations themselves are being challenged as invalid.

The most recent and celebrated example of this is *R. v. I.R.C., ex p. Woolwich Equitable Building Society*.[64] There, the building society successfully challenged certain parts of the Income Tax (Building Societies) Regulations 1986, on the basis that they were *ultra vires*. This resulted in the I.R.C. being held liable to repay tax recovered from the society under the invalid regulations.[65]

In *R. v. Commissioner for the Special Purposes of the Income Tax Acts, ex p. Stipplechoice Ltd*[66] the Court of Appeal, somewhat surprisingly, appeared prepared to accept that because the Commissioner's decision to allow the revenue to issue an out-of-time assessment could not be appealed until an assessment was actually made, judicial review was available. This is novel, because the assessment itself would have provided a suitable form of challenge to the decision. The argument which found favour was apparently that the costs of appealing the assessment would not be recoverable, whereas those of an Order 53 application would.

Interlocutory decisions, from which there is no appeal, are in principle reviewable. Thus, in *R. v. General Commissioners for St Marylebone, ex p. Hay*,[67] the court was prepared to assume jurisdiction over a decision of the Commissioners whereby the applicant was refused permission to reopen his appeal.[68]

Similarly, in *Kovak v. Morris*,[69] the Court of Appeal held that the appropriate way to challenge the decision of tax Commissioners on the

---

[62] [1985] A.C. 835.
[63] See, *e.g. R. v. IRC, ex p. S.G. Warburg & Co. Ltd* [1994] S.T.C. 518. Tax assessments may not be altered except initially by appeal to the Commissioners and thereafter by way of case stated to the High Court. See s.29, 56 T.M.A. 1970.
[64] [1990] 1 W.L.R. 1400.
[65] *Woolwich Equitable Building Society v. I.R.C.* [1992] 3 W.L.R. 229.
[66] [1985] STC 248.
[67] [1983] STC 346.
[68] Although the challenge was ultimately unsuccessful.
[69] (1985) 58 TC 493.

basis of irregularities at the hearing is by way of judicial review.[70] However, this is only so where the irregularities are such that they would not give rise to a right of appeal.[71]

In *R. v. I.R.C., ex p. M.F.K. Underwriting Agents Ltd*[72] it was held by the Court of Appeal that the court would only consider reviewing the revenue's decision to go back on a previous assurance if the applicant could establish that (1) he had been full and frank in the material he had provided the revenue with, so as to enable them to determine his application, (2) he made it clear that he wanted a full and considered response from the revenue, (3) the response given was clear and unambiguous, (4) the revenue indicated that it would not depart from its response, (5) he relied upon that response. This decision was applied by the House of Lords in *R. v. I.R.C., ex p. Matrix-Securities Ltd.*[73]

All the remedies usually available in an Order 53 application are available to be utilised in tax matters. For example, at some time, all of the prerogative orders have been made against tax authorities. In *R. v. Ward, ex p. Stipplechoice Ltd (No. 3)*,[74] certiorari went to quash the Special Commissioner's decision after he refused an adjournment following amendment to the assessment under appeal by the inspector. Mandamus is an unusual remedy to seek in the tax arena. It will not issue against the Crown. It may not issue against the Crown's servants (but see para. 3–015). However, if the duty is towards the applicant himself, the order will issue. Such a situation arose in *Special Commissioners v. Pemsel*[75] and *R. v. Brixton I.T.C.*[76] Similarly, prohibition will lie to prevent an excess of jurisdiction by the commissioners.[77] Only in the most limited circumstances will the doctrine of proportionality be applied to (VAT) penalties provided for by national law.[78]

In the past there has been difficulty in obtaining interim relief against the Crown or Crown servants. This has already been discussed (see para. 3–020).

---

[70] The facts of this case are unusual. The Commissioners refused the taxpayer's application for an adjournment in order to present them with accounts. However, the taxpayer had failed to submit income tax returns for the last 14 years and the commissioners refused the adjournment.

[71] See *R. v. Brentford General Commissioners, ex p. Chan* (1985) 57 TC 651. Approved in *R. v. Special Commissioners, ex p. Napier* [1988] STC 573.

[72] [1990] 1 W.L.R. 1545. See, also *R. v. I.R.C., ex p. Unilever Plc* [1994] S.T.C. 841 (*held*: Revenue Practice of allowing submission of informal or late tax relief claims, created a legitimate expectation that the practice would continue subject to contrary notification).

[73] [1994] 1 W.L.R. 334.

[74] [1989] STC 93.

[75] [1891] A.C. 531

[76] (1913) 6 TC 195.

[77] *R. v. Swansea I.T.C., ex p. English Crown Spelter Co. Ltd* [1925] 2 K.B. 250.

[78] *Commissioners of Customs and Excise v. P. & O. Steam Navigation Company* [1993] C.O.D. 164.

BROADCASTING AND COMMUNICATIONS

There have been an increasing number of cases involving judicial review **16–009**
of the bodies charged with regulating the broadcasting and communications industries.

For example, the premium rate telephone lines watchdog body, the Independent Committee for the Supervision of Telephone Information Services, has been held to be amenable to judicial review.[79] The Broadcasting Complaints Commission has also been the subject of several cases.[80]

The Broadcasting Complaints Commission was created by the Broadcasting Act 1980 to examine and adjudicate upon complaints arising from programmes broadcast on commercial or BBC television. In particular, the Commission's role is to consider allegations of unjust or unfair treatment in programmes, or the unwarranted infringement of privacy in, or in connection with, the obtaining of material included in such programmes.[81] One question currently exercising the courts is the proper limit to be imposed upon the category of legitimate complainants to the Commission. Does *locus standi* lie only with those actually portrayed in programmes entitled to complain, or may complaints be made by, for example, lobby groups who have an interest in the subject matter of a broadcast programme? The 1990 Act states that complaints may be made by an individual or a body of persons, whether or not incorporated, but that complaints cannot be entertained unless made by "the person affected" or by a person authorised by him to make the complaint on his behalf.[82] "Persons affected" by unjust and unfair treatment are defined by section 150 of the Act as being, "participant[s] in the programme ... who was the subject if that treatment or a person who, whether such a participant or not, had a direct interest in the subject matter of that treatment." It is submitted, therefore, that the direct interest must be a direct interest in the unfair treatment meted out to the participant, not a direct interest in the subject matter of the programme itself.[83]

---

[79] See *R. v. ICSTIS, ex p. Firstcode Limited* [1993] C.O.D. 325. See also, *R. v. Independent Television Commission, ex p. TSW Ltd, The Times,* March 30, 1992, involving an unsuccessful challenge to television decisions.

[80] See *R. v. Broadcasting Complaints Commission, ex p. Lloyd* [1993] C.O.D. 137—"the Commission's procedures were informal, and they were mercifully not obstructed by lawyers or rigid rules", *per* Macpherson J. See also *R. v. BCC, ex p. Granada Television Ltd, The Times,* December 16, 1994; *R. v. BCC; ex p. BBC, The Times,* February 24, 1995 and the cases referred to in n. 83 below. Note that the BCC is soon to be merged with the Broadcasting Standards Council.

[81] See s.143 Broadcasting Act 1990.

[82] Separate provision is made for the bringing of complaints on behalf of the recently deceased. See s.144(2) of the 1990 Act.

[83] It is submitted that the court's approach in *R. v. BCC, ex p. Owen* [1985] 1 Q.B. 1153 supports the foregoing analysis. That was a complaint brought by Dr David Owen, the then Leader of the SDP. The basis of his complaint was that his party had been unfairly treated. The Court accepted that he could bring a complaint, but was at pains to emphasise the limited and personal nature of the scope to bring a complaint to the BCC. Contrast, though, Law's J.'s approach in *R. v. BCC, ex p. BBC, The Times,* May 26, 1994. See, also,

The BCC's procedure for considering complaints made to it is set out in the 1990 Act. A hearing is not necessary,[84] but if the decision is taken to hold a hearing, it must be in private, and all parties involved must be given an opportunity to attend and be heard.[85]

The growth of satellite television poses problems for United Kingdom regulators in attempting to apply U.K. standards to broadcasts received in this country but originating overseas. For broadcasts originating in other European Union countries, the potential for conflict between EU law and (purely) domestic law is clear. Indeed, just such a conflict occurred in the case of *R. v. Secretary of State for the National Heritage, ex p. Continental Television*[86] where the question which arose was whether or not the Secretary of State had power to proscribe pornographic satellite television broadcast directly by satellite from another Member State of the EU. The case was referred to the European Court, on the construction of Directive 89/552, but the interest of the case from a judicial review standpoint is the Court's refusal to countenance any interim injunction to the effect of the Secretary of State's order by statutory instrument pending the European Court's determination.

FURTHER CATEGORIES OF REVIEW

16–010   Unlike public policy, the categories of review are not closed. Part 3 of this book has concentrated on most of the principal categories, but it is by no means exhaustive. Likely areas of future growth include environmental judicial review[87] and the process of compulsory competitive tendering.

Order 53 has been, and will continue to be, invoked by infinitely contrasting groups—by students and teachers, by those seeking licences as well as by those attempting to prevent licences from being granted, by councils against ministers and by ministers against councils.

Factual categories are, however, only helpful as illustrations of general principle. What is clear is that the law relating to judicial review has continued to develop apace in recent years, and that the ongoing development of new and interesting areas of review shows no sign of abating.

Schiemann J. in *R. v. BCC, ex p. Channel Four Television Corporation, The Times,* January 4, 1995 (*held*: "direct interest" should be broadly).

[84] *ibid.*, s.145(1).

[85] *ibid.*, s.145.

[86] See [1993] C.O.D. 421, upheld by the Court of Appeal at [1994] C.O.D. 121.

[87] See, *e.g.* Woolf "Are the Judiciary Environmentally Myopic?" (1992) 4 J.Env.L. 1, 6–8. Of the many cases, see: *R. v. Secretary of State for Transport, ex p. Richmond-upon-Thames L.B.C. and Others (No. 1)* [1994] 1 W.L.R. 74; *(No. 2) The Times,* December 29, 1994; *R. v. HM Inspectorate of Pollution, ex p. Greenpeace Ltd* [1994] 1 W.L.R. 570; *R. v. Avon C.C., ex p. Terry Adams Ltd The Times,* January 20, 1994, *R. v. Secretary of State for Foreign and Commonwealth Affairs, ex p. the World Development Movement Limited* [1995] 1 W.L.R. 386.

APPENDICES

Order 53 of the Rules of the Supreme Court

ORDER 53

APPLICATIONS FOR JUDICIAL REVIEW

Cases appropriate for application for judicial review

1.—(1) An application for—   **A–01**

(a) an order of mandamus, prohibition or certiorari, or
(b) an injunction under section 30 of the Act restraining a person from acting in any office in which he is not entitled to act,

shall be made by way of an application for judicial review in accordance with the provisions of this Order.

(2) An application for a declaration or an injunction (not being an injunction mentioned in paragraph (1)(b)) may be made by way of an application for judicial review, and on such an application the Court may grant the declaration or injunction claimed if it considers that, having regard to—

(a) the nature of the matters in respect of which relief may be granted by way of an order of mandamus, prohibition or certiorari,
(b) the nature of the persons and bodies against whom relief may be granted by way of such an order, and
(c) all the circumstances of the case,

it would be just and convenient for the declaration or injunction to be granted on an application for judicial review.

Joinder of claims for relief

2. On an application for judicial review any relief mentioned in rule 1(1)   **A–02**
or (2) may be claimed as an alternative or in addition to any other relief so mentioned if it arises out of or relates to or is connected with the same matter.

Grant of leave to apply for judicial review

A–03 3.—(1) No application for judicial review shall be made unless the leave of the Court has been obtained in accordance with this rule.

(2) An application for leave must be made *ex parte* to a judge by filing in the Crown Office—

(a) a notice in Form No. 86A containing a statement of
  (i) the name and description of the applicant,
  (ii) the relief sought and the grounds upon which it is sought,
  (iii) the name and address of the applicant's solicitors (if any) and
  (iv) the applicant's address for service; and
(b) an affidavit which verifies the facts relied on.

(3) The judge may determine the application without a hearing, unless a hearing is requested in the notice of application, and need not sit in open court; in any case, the Crown Office shall serve a copy of the judge's order on the applicant.

(4) Where the application for leave is refused by the judge, or is granted on terms, the applicant may renew it by applying—

(a) in any criminal cause or matter, to a Divisional Court of the Queen's Bench Division;
(b) in any other case, to a single judge sitting in open court or, if the Court so directs, to a Divisional Court of the Queen's Bench Division:

Provided that no application for leave may be renewed in any non-criminal cause or matter in which the judge has refused leave under paragraph (3) after a hearing.

(5) In order to renew his application for leave the applicant must, within 10 days of being served with notice of the judge's refusal, lodge in the Crown Office notice of his intention in Form No. 86B.

(6) Without prejudice to its powers under Order 20, rule 8, the Court hearing an application for leave may allow the applicant's statement to be amended, whether by specifying different or additional grounds or relief or otherwise, on such terms, if any, as it thinks fit.

(7) The Court shall not grant leave unless it considers that the applicant has a sufficient interest in the matter to which the application relates.

(8) Where leave is sought to apply for an order of certiorari to remove for the purpose of its being quashed any judgment, order, conviction or other proceedings which is subject to appeal and a time is limited for the bringing of the appeal, the Court may adjourn the application for leave until the appeal is determined or the time for appealing has expired.

(9) If the Court grants leave, it may impose such terms as to costs and as to giving security as it thinks fit.

(10) Where leave to apply for judicial review is granted, then—

(a) if the relief sought is an order of prohibition or certiorari and the Court so directs, the grant shall operate as a stay of the proceedings to which the application relates until the determination of the application or until the Court otherwise orders;

(b) if any other relief is sought, the Court may at any time grant in the proceedings such interim relief as could be granted in an action begun by writ.

Delay in applying for relief

4.—(1) An application for leave to apply for judicial review shall be made **A–04** promptly and in any event within three months from the date when grounds for the application first arose unless the Court considers that there is good reason for extending the period within which the application shall be made.

(2) Where the relief sought is an order of certiorari in respect of any judgment, order, conviction or other proceeding, the date when grounds for the application first arose shall be taken to be the date of that judgment, order, conviction or proceeding.

(3) The preceding paragraphs are without prejudice to any statutory provision which has the effect of limiting the time within which an application for judicial review may be made.

Mode of applying for judicial review

5.—(1) In any criminal cause or matter, where leave has been granted to **A–05** make an application for judicial review, the application shall be made by originating motion to a Divisional Court of the Queen's Bench Division.

(2) In any other such cause or matter, the application shall be made by originating motion to a judge sitting in open court, unless the Court directs that it shall be made—

(a) by originating summons to a judge in chambers; or

(b) by originating motion to a Divisional Court of the Queen's Bench Division.

Any direction under sub-paragraph (a) shall be without prejudice to the judge's powers under Order 32, rule 13.

(3) The notice of motion or summons must be served on all persons directly affected and where it relates to any proceedings in or before a court and the object of the application is either to compel the court or an officer of the court to do any act in relation to the proceedings or to quash them or any order made therein, the notice or summons must also be served on the clerk or registrar of the court and, where any objection to the conduct of the judge is to be made, on the judge.

(4) Unless the Court granting leave has otherwise directed, there must be at least 10 days between the service of the notice of motion or summons and the hearing.

(5) A motion must be entered for hearing within 14 days after the grant of leave.

(6) An affidavit giving the names and addresses of, and the places and dates of service on, all persons who have been served with the notice of

motion or summons must be filed before the motion or summons is entered for hearing and, if any person who ought to be served under this rule has not been served, the affidavit must state that fact and the reason for it; and the affidavit shall be before the Court on the hearing of the motion or summons.

(7) If on the hearing of the motion or summons the Court is of opinion that any person who ought, whether under this rule or otherwise, to have been served has not been served, the Court may adjourn the hearing on such terms (if any) as it may direct in order that the notice or summons may be served on that person.

Statements and affidavits

A–06   6.—(1) Copies of the statement in support of an application for leave under rule 3 must be served with the notice of motion or summons and, subject to paragraph (2), no grounds shall be relied upon or any relief sought at the hearing except the grounds and relief set out in the statement.

(2) The Court may on the hearing of the motion or summons allow the applicant to amend his statement, whether by specifying different or additional grounds or relief or otherwise, on such terms, if any, as it thinks fit and may allow further affidavits to be used if they deal with new matters arising out of an affidavit of any other party to the application.

(3) Where the applicant intends to ask to be allowed to amend his statement or to use further affidavits, he shall give notice of his intention and of any proposed amendment to every other party.

(4) Any respondent who intends to use an affidavit at the hearing shall file it in the Crown Office as soon as practicable and in any event, unless the Court otherwise directs, within 56 days after service upon him of the documents required to be served by paragraph (1).

(5) Each party to the application must supply to every other party on demand and on payment of the proper charges copies of every affidavit which he proposes to use at the hearing, including, in the case of the applicant, the affidavit in support of the application for leave under rule 3.

Claim for damages

A–07   7.—(1) On an application for judicial review the Court may, subject to paragraph (2), award damages to the applicant if—

    (a) he has included in the statement in support of his application for leave under rule 3 a claim for damages arising from any matter to which the application relates, and

    (b) the Court is satisfied that, if the claim has been made in an action begun by the applicant at the time of making his application, he could have been awarded damages.

(2) Order 18, rule 12, shall apply to a statement relating to a claim for damages as it applies to a pleading.

Application for discovery, interrogatories, cross-examination etc.

8.—(1) Unless the Court otherwise directs, any interlocutory application **A–08** in proceedings on an application for judicial review may be made to any judge or a master of the Queen's Bench Division, notwithstanding that the application for judicial review has been made by motion and is to be heard by a Divisional Court.

In this paragraph "interlocutory application" includes an application for an order under Order 24 or 26 or Order 38, rule 2(3) or for an order dismissing the proceedings by consent of the parties.

(2) In relation to an order made by a master pursuant to paragraph (1) Order 58, rule 1, shall, where the application for judicial review is to be heard by a Divisional Court, have effect as if a reference to that Court were substituted for the reference to a judge in chambers.

(3) This rule is without prejudice to any statutory provision or rule of law restricting the making of an order against the Crown.

Hearing of application for judicial review

9.—(1) On the hearing of any motion or summons under rule 5, any **A–09** person who desires to be heard in opposition to the motion or summons, and appears to the Court to be a proper person to be heard, shall be heard, notwithstanding that he has not been served with notice of the motion or the summons.

(2) Where the relief sought is or includes an order of certiorari to remove any proceedings for the purpose of quashing them, the applicant may not question the validity of any order, warrant, commitment, conviction, inquisition or record unless before the hearing of the motion or summons he has lodged in the Crown Office a copy thereof verified by affidavit or accounts for his failure to do so to the satisfaction of the Court hearing the motion or summons.

(3) Where an order for certiorari is made in any such case as is referred to in paragraph (2) the order shall, subject to paragraph (4) direct that the proceedings shall be quashed forthwith on their removal into the Queen's Bench Division.

(4) Where the relief sought is an order of certiorari and the Court is satisfied that there are grounds for quashing the decision to which the application relates, the Court may, in addition to quashing it, remit the matter to the Court, tribunal or authority concerned with a direction to reconsider it and reach a decision in accordance with the findings of the Court.

(5) Where the relief sought is a declaration, an injunction or damages and the Court considers that it should not be granted on an application for judicial review but might have been granted if it had been sought in an action begun by writ by the applicant at the time of making his application, the Court may, instead of refusing the application, order the proceedings to continue as if they had been begun by writ; and Order 28, rule 8, shall apply

as if, in the case of an application made by motion, it had been made by summons.

Saving for person acting in obedience to mandamus

A–10   10. No action or proceeding shall be begun or prosecuted against any person in respect of anything done in obedience to an order of mandamus.

Proceedings for disqualification of member of local authority

A–11   11.—(1) Proceedings under section 92 of the Local Government Act 1972 must be begun by originating motion to a Divisional Court of the Queen's Bench Division, and, unless otherwise directed, there must be at least 10 days between the service of the notice of motion and the hearing.

(2) Without prejudice to Order 8, rule 3, the notice of motion must set out the name and description of the applicant, the relief sought and the grounds on which it is sought, and must be supported by affidavit verifying the facts relied on.

(3) Copies of every supporting affidavit must be lodged in the Crown Office before the motion is entered for hearing and must be supplied to any other party on demand and on payment of the proper charges.

(4) The provisions of rules 5, 6 and 9(1) as to the persons on whom the notice is to be served and as to the proceedings at the hearing shall apply, with the necessary modifications, to proceedings under the said section 92 as they apply to an application for judicial review.

Consolidation of applications

A–12   12. Where there is more than one application pending under section 30 of the Act, or section 92 of the Local Government Act 1972, against several persons in respect of the same office, and on the same grounds, the Court may order the applications to be consolidated.

Appeal from judge's order

A–13   13. No appeal shall lie from an order made under paragraph (3) of rule 3 on an application for leave which may be renewed under paragraph (4) of that rule.

Meaning of "Court"

A–14   14. In relation to the hearing by a judge of an application for leave under rule 3 or of an application for judicial review, any reference in this Order to "the Court" shall, unless the context otherwise requires, be construed as a reference to the judge.

APPENDIX B

Relevant Sections of the Supreme Court Act 1981

Orders of mandamus, prohibition and certiorari

29.—(1) The High Court shall have jurisdiction to make orders of mandamus, prohibition and certiorari in·those classes of cases in which it had power to do so immediately before the commencement of this Act.   **B–01**

(2) Every such order shall be final, subject to any right of appeal therefrom.

(3) In relation to the jurisdiction of the Crown Court, other than its jurisdiction in matters relating to trial on indictment, the High Court shall have all such jurisdiction to make orders of mandamus, prohibition or certiorari as the High Court possesses in relation to the jurisdiction of an inferior court.

(4) The power of the High Court under any enactment to require justices of the peace or a judge or officer of a county court to do any act relating to the duties of their respective offices, or to require a magistrates' court to state a case for the opinion of the High Court, in any case where the High Court formerly had by virtue of any enactment jurisdiction to make a rule absolute, or an order, for any of those purposes, shall be exercisable by order of mandamus.

(5) In any enactment—

   (a) references to a writ of mandamus, of prohibition or of certiorari shall be read as references to the corresponding order; and
   (b) references to the issue or award of any such writ shall be read as references to the making of the corresponding order.

Injunctions to restrain persons from acting in offices in which they are not entitled to act

30.—(1) Where a person not entitled to do so acts in an office to which this section applies, the High Court may—   **B–02**

   (a) grant an injunction restraining him from so acting; and
   (b) if the case so requires, declare the office to be vacant.

(2) This section applies to any substantive office of a public nature and permanent character which is held under the Crown or which has been created by any statutory provision or royal charter.

Application for judicial review

B–03   **31.**—(1) An application to the High Court for one or more of the following forms of relief, namely—

    (a) an order of mandamus, prohibition or certiorari;

    (b) a declaration or injunction under subsection (2); or

    (c) an injunction under section 30 restraining a person not entitled to do so from acting in an office to which that section applies,

shall be made in accordance with rules of court by a procedure to be known as an application for judicial review.

(2) A declaration may be made or an injunction granted under this subsection in any case where an application for judicial review, seeking that relief, has been made and the High Court considers that, having regard to—

    (a) the nature of the matters in respect of which relief may be granted by orders of mandamus, prohibition or certiorari;

    (b) the nature of the persons and bodies against whom relief may be granted by such orders; and

    (c) all the circumstances of the case,

it would be just and convenient for the declaration to be made or the injunction to be granted, as the case may be.

(3) No application for judicial review shall be made unless the leave of the High Court has been obtained in accordance with rules of court; and the court shall not grant leave to make such an application unless it considers that the applicant has a sufficient interest in the matter to which the application relates.

(4) On an application for judicial review the High Court may award damages to the applicant if—

    (a) he has joined with his application a claim for damages arising from any matter to which the application relates; and

    (b) the court is satisfied that, if the claim had been made in an action begun by the applicant at the time of making his application, he would have been awarded damages.

(5) If, on an application for judicial review seeking an order of certiorari, the High Court quashes the decision to which the application relates, the High Court may remit the matter to the court, tribunal or authority concerned, with a direction to reconsider it and reach a decision in accordance with the findings of the High Court.

(6) Where the High Court considers that there has been undue delay in making an application for judicial review, the court may refuse to grant—

    (a) leave for the making of the application; or

    (b) any relief sought on the application,

if it considers that the granting of the relief sought would be likely to cause substantial hardship to, or substantially prejudice the rights of, any person or would be detrimental to good administration.

(7) Subsection (6) is without prejudice to any enactment or rule of court

which has the effect of limiting the time within which an application for judicial review may be made.

★   ★   ★   ★

Power of High Court to vary sentence on certiorari

43.—(1) Where a person who has been sentenced for an offence—   **B–04**

  (a) by a magistrates' court; or
  (b) by the Crown Court after being convicted of the offence by a magistrates' court and committed to the Crown Court for sentence; or
  (c) by the Crown Court on appeal against conviction or sentence,

applies to the High Court in accordance with section 31 for an order of certiorari to remove the proceedings of the magistrates' court or the Crown Court into the High Court, then, if the High Court determines that the magistrates' court or the Crown Court had no power to pass the sentence, the High Court may, instead of quashing the conviction, amend it by substituting for the sentence passed any sentence which the magistrates' court or, in a case within paragraph (b), the Crown Court had power to impose.

(2) Any sentence passed by the High Court by virtue of this section in substitution for the sentence passed in the proceedings of the magistrates' court or the Crown Court shall, unless the High Court otherwise directs, begin to run from the time when it would have begun to run if passed in those proceedings; but in computing the term of the sentence, any time during which the offender was released on bail in pursuance of section 37(1)(d) of the Criminal Justice Act 1948 shall be disregarded.

(3) Subsections (1) and (2) shall, with the necessary modifications, apply in relation to any order of a magistrates' court or the Crown Court which is made on, but does not form part of, the conviction of an offender as they apply in relation to a conviction and sentence.

APPENDIX C

Relevant Practice Directions

PRACTICE DIRECTION (CROWN OFFICE LIST: UNCONTESTED PROCEEDINGS) [1982] 1 W.L.R. 979

C–01 The following practice direction was given by Lord Lane C.J. on June 11, 1989:

Where the parties are agreed as to the terms on which civil proceedings entered in the Crown Office List, including applications for judicial review, appeals by way of case stated and statutory appeals, can be disposed of and require an order of the court to put these terms into effect, they should hand into the Crown Office a document (together with two copies thereof) signed by the parties setting out the terms of the proposed agreed order and a short statement of the matters relied upon as justifying the making of the order, authorities and statutory provisions relied on being quoted. Where practicable, copies of statutory instruments which are relevant should be annexed to the document.

The Crown Office will then submit the document to a judge and, if he is satisfied that an order can be made, he will cause the proceedings to be listed for hearing and the order will be announced in open court without the parties or their representatives having to attend.

If, on the information originally provided and any information subsequently provided at the judge's request, the judge is not satisfied that it is proper for the order to be made, he will cause the proceedings to be listed for hearing in the normal way.

It is hoped that wherever possible parties and their advisers will take advantage of this direction and provide sufficient information to enable the judge to be satisfied as to the propriety of making an order without hearing the parties, since the direction is designed to save the expense to the parties and the time of the court.

PRACTICE DIRECTION (JUDICIAL REVIEW: APPEALS) [1982] 1 W.L.R.
1375

The following Practice Direction was given by Lord Lane C.J. and Sir John   **C–02**
Donaldson M.R. on November 2, 1982:

A refusal in a non-criminal cause or matter by a Divisional Court of the
Queen's Bench Division or by a single judge to grant leave to apply for
judicial review is appealable to the Court of Appeal. Heretofore the practice
has been for the Court of Appeal to hear the substantive application if it
grants leave: *R. v. Industrial Injuries Commissioner, Ex parte Amalgamated
Engineering Union* [1966] 2 Q.B. 21. There were, at the time of its
introduction, good reasons for the practice. Those reasons no longer exist,
except in the rare case where the reason for the refusal was that the court
was bound by a previous decision of the Divisional Court or a single judge.

In future if, following a refusal by the Divisional Court or a single judge,
the Court of Appeal grants leave to apply for judicial review, the
substantive application should be made to the Divisional Court unless the
Court of Appeal otherwise orders. The Court of Appeal will not normally
so order unless the court below is bound by authority or for some other
reason an appeal to the Court of Appeal is inevitable.

PRACTICE DIRECTION (EVIDENCE: DOCUMENTS) [1983] 1 W.L.R.
922; [1983] 3 All E.R. 33

The following practice direction was made by Lord Lane C.J. on June 21,   **C–03**
1983:

This practice direction applies to the Court of Appeal and to all divisions
of the High Court. Any affidavit, exhibit or bundle of documents which
does not comply with R.S.C., Ord. 41 and this direction may be rejected by
the court or made the subject for an order for costs.

Affidavits

1. *Marking*

At the top right hand corner of the first page of every affidavit, and also
on the backsheet, there must be written in clear permanent dark blue or
black marking: (i) the party on whose behalf it is filed; (ii) the initials and
surname of the deponent; (iii) the number of the affidavit in relation to the
deponent; and (iv) the date when sworn.

For example: "2nd Dft: E. W. Jones: 3rd: 24.7.82."

2. *Binding*

Affidavits must not be bound with thick plastic strips or anything else
which would hamper filing.
f

Exhibits

3. *Markings generally*

Where space allows, the directions under paragraph 1 above apply to the first page of every exhibit.

4. *Documents other than letters*

(i) Clearly legible photographic copies of original documents may be exhibited instead of the originals provided the originals are made available for inspection by the other parties before the hearing and by the judge at the hearing.

(ii) Any document which the court is being asked to construe or enforce, or the trusts of which it is being asked to vary, should be separately exhibited, and should not be included in a bundle with other documents. Any such document should bear the exhibit mark directly, and not on a flysheet attached to it.

(iii) Court documents, such as probates, letters of administration, orders, affidavits or pleadings, should never be exhibited. Office copies of such documents prove themselves.

(iv) Where a number of documents are contained in one exhibit, a front page must be attached, setting out a list of the documents, with dates, which the exhibit contains, and the bundle must be securely fastened. The traditional method of securing is by tape, with the knot sealed (under the modern practice) by means of wafers; but any means of securing the bundle (except by staples) is acceptable, provided that it does not interfere with the perusal of the documents and it cannot readily be undone.

(v) This direction does not affect the current practice in relation to scripts in probate matters, or to an affidavit of due execution of a will.

5. *Letters*

(i) Copies of individual letters should not be made separate exhibits, but they should be collected together and exhibited in a bundle or bundles. The letters must be arranged in correct sequence with the earliest at the top, and properly paged in accordance with paragraph 6 below. They must be firmly secured together in the manner indicated in paragraph 4 above.

(ii) When original letters, or original letters and copies of replies, are exhibited as one bundle, the exhibit must have a front page attached, stating that the bundle consists of so many original letters and so many copies. As before, the letters and copies must be arranged in correct sequence and properly paged.

6. *Paging of documentary exhibits*

Any exhibit containing several pages must be paged consecutively at centre bottom.

7. *Copies of documents generally*

It is the responsibility of the solicitor by whom any affidavit is filed to ensure that every page of every exhibit is fully and easily legible. In many cases photocopies of documents, particularly of telex messages, are not. In all cases of difficulty, typed copies of the illegible document (paged with "a" numbers) should be included.

8. *Exhibits bound up with affidavit*

Exhibits must not be bound up with, or otherwise attached to, the affidavit itself.

9. *Exhibits other than documents*

The principles are as follows. (i) The exhibit must be clearly marked with the exhibit mark in such a manner that there is no likelihood of the contents being separated; and (ii) where the exhibit itself consists of more than one item (*e.g.*, a cassette in a plastic box), each and every separate part of the exhibit must similarly be separately marked with at least enough of the usual exhibit mark to ensure precise identification.

This is particularly important in cases where there are a number of similar exhibits which fall to be compared. Accordingly:

(a) The formal exhibit marking should, so far as practicable, be written on the article itself in an appropriate manner (*e.g.*, many fabrics can be directly marked with an indelible pen), or, if this is not possible, on a separate slip which is securely attached to the article in such a manner that it is not easily removable. (N.B. Items attached by Sellotape or similar means are readily removable). If the article is then enclosed in a container, the number of the exhibit should appear on the outside of the container unless it is transparent and the number is readily visible. Alternatively, the formal exhibit marking may be written on the container or, if this is not possible, on a separate slip securely attached to the container. If this is done, then either—(i) the number of the exhibit and, if there is room, the short name and number of the case, the name of the deponent and the date of the affidavit must be written on the exhibit itself and on each separate part thereof; or (ii) all these particulars must appear on a slip securely attached to the article itself and to each separate part thereof.

(b) If the article, or part of the article, is too small to be marked in accordance with the foregoing provisions, it must be enclosed in a sealed transparent container of such a nature that it could not be reconstituted once opened, and the relevant slip containing the exhibit mark must be inserted in such container so as to be plainly visible. An enlarged photograph or photographs showing the relevant characteristics of each such exhibit will usually be required to be separately exhibited.

10. *Numbering*

Where a deponent deposes to more than one affidavit to which there are exhibits in any one matter, the numbering of such exhibits should run consecutively throughout, and not begin again with each affidavit.

11. *Reference to documents already forming part of an exhibit*

Where a deponent wishes to refer to a document already exhibited to some other deponent's affidavit, he should not also exhibit it to his own affidavit.

12. *Multiplicity of documents*

Where, by the time of the hearing, exhibits or affidavits have become numerous, they should be put in a consolidated bundle, or file or files, and be paged consecutively throughout in the top right hand corner, affidavits and exhibits being in separate bundles or files.

Bundles of documents generally

13. The directions under 5, 6 and 7 above apply to all bundles of documents. Accordingly they must be (i) firmly secured together, (ii) arranged in chronological order, beginning with the earliest, (iii) paged consecutively at centre bottom, and (iv) fully and easily legible.

14. Transcripts of judgments and evidence must not be bound up with any other documents, but must be kept separate.

15. In cases for trial where the parties will seek to place before the trial judge bundles of documents (apart from pleadings) comprising more than 100 pages, it is the responsibility of the solicitors for all parties to prepare and agree one single additional bundle containing the principal documents to which the parties will refer (including in particular the documents referred to in the pleadings) and to lodge such bundle with the court at least two working days before the date fixed for the hearing.

PRACTICE DIRECTION (UNCONTESTED PROCEEDINGS: CROWN OFFICE LIST (APPLICATIONS OUTSIDE LONDON): JUDICIAL REVIEW) [1983] 1 W.L.R. 925

C–04 The following practice was made by Lord Lane C.J.

Uncontested applications in criminal causes or matters

1. *Practice Direction (Crown Office List: Uncontested Proceedings)* [1982] 1 W.L.R. 979 of June 11, 1982, deals with the disposal of uncontested *civil* proceedings entered in the Crown Office List (including applications for judicial review) without the attendance at the court of the parties or their legal advisers where the parties are agreed as to the terms on which the proceedings could be disposed of and an order of the court is required to

put the terms into effect. The same practice will from now on apply to *criminal* causes or matters entered in the Crown Office List, save that where a judge is satisfied that the order can be made, the proceedings will be listed for hearing in open court before a Divisional Court rather than a single judge without the parties or their representatives having to attend. Parties are reminded of the importance of complying with the requirements of the earlier direction since the objects of saving time and the cost of attendance at court can only be achieved if the court is given sufficient information to enable a decision to be made as to whether or not to make the order.

Applications made outside London

2. Proceedings which are required to be entered in the Crown Office List should wherever practicable be commenced in London. Where the urgency makes it necessary for an application in respect of such proceedings to be made outside London, the Crown Office should be consulted prior to making the application, if necessary by telephone, and the application should be made in accordance with any arrangements made by the Crown Office for its hearing outside London. The application should be confined to those matters which have to be dealt with urgently and as soon as the application has been dealt with, the proceedings should be continued in London and further applications should be heard and directions given in London.

Delay in applying for leave to apply for judicial review

3. Where an application for leave to apply for judicial review under R.S.C., Ord. 53 is not made promptly and in any event within three months from the date when grounds for the application first arose as required by R.S.C., Ord. 53, r. 4, the application should set out the reasons for the delay.

If the consent of a proposed respondent to an extension of time has been obtained such consent should be submitted with the application. If a proposed respondent has not consented to an extension he shall on notice to the applicant have the right to apply promptly in open court to set aside any leave or direction which is given. Such an application to set aside will not always be necessary since in any event on the substantive hearing a respondent will be entitled to rely on delay in making the application as a ground for opposing the grant of relief.

PRACTICE DIRECTION (CROWN OFFICE LIST) [1987] 1 W.L.R. 232;
[1987] 1 ALL E.R. 368

The following Practice Direction was made by Lord Lane C.J. on February 3, 1987: **C–05**

This practice direction applies to the Crown Office list, the elements of which are described in the *Practice Direction (Trials in London)* [1981] 1 W.L.R. 1296 given on July 31, 1981.

1. As from March 2, 1987 the following arrangements will apply to the listing of cases included in the Crown Office list.

2. The head clerk, under the direction of the Master of the Crown Office, will arrange the Crown Office list into the following parts.

3. *Part A: cases not ready to be heard*

Cases where leave has yet to be obtained, or the time limits for the filing or lodging of notices, affidavits or other documents have not expired and where, in consequence, a case is not yet ready to be heard.

4. *Part B: cases ready to be heard*

In cases where the time limits mentioned in Part A have expired it will be assumed that all parties are ready to be heard. When a case enters Part B the applicant or his solicitors will be informed by letter. It will be the responsibility of the applicant or his solicitors to forward a copy of that letter to (i) the clerk to counsel instructed by the applicant and (ii) any respondent to the case or his solicitor who should inform the clerk to counsel instructed by him. It will be the responsibility of counsel's clerks to inform the head clerk, *in writing*, of counsel's time estimate for the case and of any alteration thereto.

5. The head clerk will make arrangements for hearing dates to be fixed, drawing cases from Part B in order of entry so far as is practicable. While the head clerk will give as much notice as possible of the date fixed for hearing he cannot undertake to accommodate the wishes of applicants, respondents, their solicitors or counsel. The occasional need to list cases at short notice may mean that parties are unable to be represented by the counsel of their first choice. In particular it should be remembered that the cases listed in the Crown Office list take precedence, so far as the attendance of counsel is concerned, over cases listed for hearing in the Crown Court unless a Divisional Court or a judge otherwise directs.

6. *Part C: cases stood out*

Where a case appears in Part B, or Part E (see post), and any party to the case is of the opinion that he is not ready to be heard he may apply to the Master of the Crown Office to have the matter stood out into Part C. Where the Master of the Crown Office accedes to such an application he may do so on such terms as he thinks fit. Where he declines to direct that the matter be stood out into Part C application may be made to a Divisional Court or a judge, as the case may be, by way of notice of motion.

7. *Part D: the expedited list*

Cases entered in this list will be listed for hearing as soon as practicable. In cases other than those where a Divisional Court or a judge has directed that a case be considered for expedition, application for inclusion in Part D should be made in the first instance to the Master of the Crown Office but where he declines to direct its inclusion in Part D, application may be made to a Divisional Court or a judge, as the case may be, by way of notice of motion.

8. *Part E: cases listed for hearing*

This part of the list will contain those cases where a date for hearing has been fixed.

9. As from March 2, 1987 the Daily Cause List will, in relation to the Crown Office list, contain only such cases as are to be heard on the next sitting day.

10. A copy of Parts, B, C, D and E of the Crown Office List may be inspected in the Crown Office.

11. In the practice direction the expression "applicant" includes "appellant" where the context so requires and the expression "judge" means a judge hearing cases in the Crown Office list.

PRACTICE NOTE (CROWN OFFICE LIST) [1987] 1 ALL E.R. 1184

The following Practice Note was made by Mann J. on April 3, 1987.   **C–06**

I make the following observations with the approval of Watkins L.J. The practice direction handed down by Lord Lane C.J. on February 3, 1987 (*Practice Note* [1987] 1 All E.R. 368, [1987] 1 W.L.R. 232) prescribed the arrangements which as from March 2, 1987 apply to the listing of cases included in the Crown Office list. Part B of that list contains cases ready to be heard. Part D is the expedited list. The pressure on both of those parts is great. Particularly is it so when the case is to be heard by the single judge. In regard to both parts it is the responsibility of counsel's clerks to inform in writing the head clerk of counsel's time estimate for a case and of any variation in an estimation previously given. Dealing with the list is critically dependant on the reasonable accuracy of estimates. Plainly precision is impossible but there have been a number of cases recently where the estimate can be described only as an ill-judged underestimate. In the interests of the dispatch of business and of those who have business in this court, close attention must be paid to the reality of an estimate. I emphasise, should there be a belief to the contrary, that underestimation secures no advantage in the listing of a case.

PRACTICE NOTE, THE TIMES, NOVEMBER 4, 1987

Practice Note: Crown Office Lists

The following Practice Note was given by Mann J. on November 2, 1987:   **C–07**

Counsel should assist the court by complying with the active case letter from the Crown Office requiring the lodging in the office of a list of issues, a list of propositions of law, a chronology and a list of persons concerned.

Mann J. said a letter was sent by the Crown Office requiring the lodging in the Crown Office of a list of issues, a list of propositions, a chronology and a list of persons concerned.

It was very regrettable that the letter was more honoured in its breach than in the observance. The honouring of the letter would expedite the business of the court, not only to the benefit of the court, but also to the Bar and litigants.

A day would come when a party would have his case adjourned for not having observed the letter. Unless it was honoured, the system would not work.

It was quite hopeless to present, as his Lordship had been presented at the weekend, with some 400 pages of documents for a case due to begin the following Monday without any form of guidance. The letter from the Crown Office in that particular case had been sent on April 1, 1987.

PRACTICE NOTE (JUDICIAL REVIEW: AFFIDAVIT IN REPLY)
[1989] 1 W.L.R. 358

C–08   The following Practice Note was made by Watkins L.J. on March 7, 1989:

With effect from March 7, 1989 and by virtue of rule 7 of the Rules of the Supreme Court (Amendment) 1989 the period allowed to a respondent in judicial review proceedings for filing an affidavit in reply under Order 53, r. 6(4) will be increased from 21 days to 56 days.

This follows a general acceptance that the period of 21 days was unrealistically short and therefore, in many cases, unenforceable. The period substituted cannot be so characterised. It has been set realistically, having regard to the interests of both applicants and respondents, and as such must be strictly adhered to. Although there is provision for extending this period—see Ord. 3, r. 5—it must be clearly understood that extensions of time will be granted only in circumstances which are wholly exceptional and for the most compelling reasons. For all practical purposes respondents would be well advised to treat the period of 56 days as absolute.

Thus, in any case in which the notice of motion and other documents referred to in Order 53, r. 6(1) are served upon a respondent on or after March 7, that respondent has 56 days in which to file in the Crown Office any affidavit in reply.

The Crown Office will not accept respondents' affidavits outside the 56 day period unless an extension of time has first been obtained.

Applications for extension of time will be considered in the first instance by the Master of the Crown Office. An appeal against his decision will lie to a judge hearing cases in the Crown Office List.

Where a judge directs an expedited hearing by entering a case in Part D of the Crown Office List (see Lord C.J.'s *Practice Direction (Crown Office List)* [1987] 1 W.L.R. 232) applicants should have in mind the need to invite the judge to abridge the 56 day period where the circumstances of the case so require.

Delays in lodging respondents' affidavits have hitherto caused severe prejudice to applicants and consequent damage to the administration of justice. The amendment to Order 53, r. 6(4) and the procedure set out in this practice note will prevent the continuance of this difficulty.

PRACTICE DIRECTION (JUDICIAL REVIEW: APPEALS)
[1990] 1 W.L.R. 51

The following Practice Direction was made by Lord Lane C.J. and by Lord Donaldson of Lymington M.K. on December 15, 1989:   **C–09**

Practice Direction (Judicial Review: Appeals) [1982] 1 W.L.R. 1375 given on November 2, 1982, provides that where, in a non-criminal cause or matter, the Court of Appeal grants a renewed application for leave to move for judicial review, the substantive application should be made to the Divisional Court, save where the Court of Appeal reserves the application to itself. Henceforth, save again where the Court of Appeal reserves the application to itself, the application should be set down in the Crown Office List to be heard by a single judge, unless a judge nominated to try cases in that list directs that the application is to be heard by a Divisional Court of the Queen's Bench Division.

PRACTICE DIRECTION (CROWN OFFICE LIST) (No. 2)
[1991] 1 W.L.R. 280

The following Practice Direction was given by Watkins L.J., Alliot and Cresswell JJ. on March 18, 1991:   **C–10**

Striking out for want of prosecution

1. Further to the *Practice Direction (Crown Office List)* [1987] 1 W.L.R. 232 cases which are approaching the top of Part B of the Crown Office List must be confirmed as active by the applicant, or the appellant, as the case may be. The Crown Office will seek written confirmation that the case is active and if such confirmation is not received within two weeks of the request from the Crown Office the matter will be listed before the court to show cause as to why it should not be struck out for want of prosecution.

Withdrawal of solicitors

2. Where a solicitor ceases to act for a party and the party has not given notice of change of solicitors in accordance with R.S.C., Ord. 67, r. 1 the solicitor may apply to the court, by way of summons to the Master of the Crown Office, for an order declaring that the solicitor has ceased to act for that party: R.S.C., Ord. 67, r. 6.

3. If no such order is obtained, the solicitor must be regarded as

continuing to act and notice of listing dates, etc. will be given to the solicitor, whose responsibility it will be to brief counsel to appear before the court.

Ex parte applications for leave to apply for judicial review

4. With effect from April 9, 1991 applications for leave to apply for judicial review will be listed on the footing that the application will take no more than 20 minutes, and any reply by a respondent who attends such an application will take no more than 10 minutes. Where counsel considers that the hearing of the application will require more than the time allowed he should provide a written estimate and a special fixture must be arranged.

PRACTICE DIRECTION (CROWN OFFICE LIST: PREPARATION
FOR HEARINGS)
[1994] 1 W.L.R. 1551

C–11   The following Practice Direction was given by Lord Taylor of Gosforth C.J. on October 25, 1994:

The following arrangements will take effect immediately.

Applications for leave to apply for judicial review and for leave to appeal under section 289 of the Town and Country Planning Act 1990

Where the documents in support of an application for leave exceed 10 pages, they must be paginated and indexed in a convenient bundle. In addition, a list must be provided of the pages essential for reading by the court. Where only part of a page needs to be read, that part should be indicated, by side lining or in some other way, but not by highlighting.

Substantive hearings

As a case reaches the top of Part B of the Crown Office List the applicant/appellant's solicitors will be informed by letter that the case is likely to be listed, at short notice, with effect from a date specified in the letter (the "warned date"). It is the responsibility of the applicant/appellant's solicitors to inform the respondent and all interested parties of the likelihood of the case being listed at short notice.

In cases where a fixed date is given, it is the responsibility of the applicant/appellant's solicitors to inform the respondent and all interested parties of the fixed date.

The applicant/appellant's solicitors are also responsible for providing a paginated, indexed, bundle for the use of the court. The bundle must be lodged with the Crown Office at least *five* clear working days before the warned date or, where a fixed date has been given, at least *five* clear working days before the fixed date.

Advocates are required to lodge skeleton arguments in the Crown Office.

Advocates for the applicant must lodge, and serve, their skeleton arguments at least *five* clear working days before the warned date or the fixed date, as appropriate. Advocates for the respondent or other party wishing to be heard must lodge, and serve, their skeleton arguments at least *three* clear working days before the warned date or the fixed date, as appropriate. The skeleton argument must quote the Crown Office reference number and the warned date or the fixed date, as appropriate, and contain (a) the time estimate for the complete hearing, including delivery of judgment (whether or not an estimate has been given earlier); (b) a list of issues; (c) a list of propositions of law to be advanced (together with the authorities relied upon in support, with page references to passages relied upon); (d) a chronology of events (with reference to the paginated bundle prepared for the court); (e) a list of the essential documents for advance reading by the court, with page references to passages relied upon; (f) a list of dramatis personae where the number of people who feature in the documents warrants it.

The above time limits must be strictly observed. Failure to do so may result in adjournment and may be penalised in costs. Advocates may however supplement their skeleton arguments up to one working day before the hearing.

Where a case is due to be listed for hearing before a Divisional Court *two* copies of the skeleton argument and paginated bundle are required. Where the case is due to be listed for hearing before a single judge only one copy of each is required.

Amendment of grounds and further affidavits

Any notice of intention to seek leave to amend the grounds or relief or to rely upon further affidavits must be given to the other party or parties and the Crown Office, together with the proposed amendments or affidavits, no later than *five* clear working days before the warned date or the fixed date, as appropriate. If notice is not given at that time, the court will be reluctant to exercise its powers to allow amendment or the use of further affidavits, save in exceptional circumstances.

APPENDIX D

Crown Office Materials Exemplified by a Case Study

SPECIMEN NOTICE OF APPLICATION FOR LEAVE TO APPLY FOR JUDICIAL REVIEW (FORM 86A)

In the High Court of Justice
Queen's Bench Division
Crown Office List

D–01   In the matter of an application by Charles Nutfield for leave to apply for Judicial Review (Ord 53, r.3)

And in the matter of section 72 of the Mental Health Act 1983.

Applicant's Ref No	Notice of Application for leave to apply for Judicial Review (Ord 53, r.3)	Crown Office Ref No

This form must be read together with Notes for Guidance obtainable from the Crown Office

To the Master of the Crown Office, Royal Courts of Justice, Strand, London, WC2A 2LL

Name, address and description of Applicant	Charles Nutfield, Derby Unit, Horton Hospital, Epsom, Surrey. Patient.
Judgment, order, decision or proceeding in respect of which relief is sought	Decision of the Mental Health Review Tribunal dated May 22, 1995 that the applicant not be discharged from liability to be detained.

RELIEF SOUGHT

(1) Certiorari to quash the said decision. Further or alternatively,

(2) Remission under Order 53, r. 9(4) directing the said Mental Health Review Tribunal ("the tribunal") to reconsider matter and reach a decision in accordance with the findings of the Court. Further or alternatively,

(3) Mandamus requiring the tribunal to hear the applicant's application under the Mental Health Act 1983 according to law. Further or alternatively,

(4) Mandamus requiring the tribunal to give proper, intelligible and adequate reasons for its decision. Further or alternatively,

(5) A declaration that where treatment is likely to result in deterioration of a patient's condition, such patient is entitled to be discharged under section 72(1)(b)(i) of the Mental Health Act 1983. Further or alternatively,

(6) A declaration that where treatment is not likely to alleviate or prevent a deterioration of a patient's condition, such patient is entitled to be discharged under section 72(1)(b)(i) of the Mental Health Act 1983.

(7) The applicant seeks an expedited hearing of the substantive application for judicial review (if leave to move is granted) together with an Order abridging time for service of the Respondent's evidence to seven days or such further period as the Court deems appropriate.

(8) The applicant seeks an oral hearing of the application for leave.

Name and address of the
applicant's solicitors or, if no
solicitors acting, the address for
service of the applicant

Signed ....

Leyton & Co.,
Epsom Court,
Epsom,
Surrey.

GROUNDS ON WHICH RELIEF IS SOUGHT

A. LEGAL MATRIX

1. Liability to detention under section 3 of the Mental Health Act 1983 (all section numbers herein refer to the 1983 Act) requires (*inter alia*), in the case of a person suffering from "psychopathic

disorder or mental impairment" that "medical treatment in a hospital" "is likely to alleviate or prevent a deterioration of his condition", (see section 3(2)(b)). There is no equivalent requirement in the case of a person classified as suffering from "mental illness".

2. Similarly, renewal of a patient's detention under section 20 depends (*inter alia*) in the case of a person suffering from psychopathic disorder upon the condition that medical treatment in a hospital "is likely to alleviate or prevent a deterioration of his condition". There is no compulsory equivalent condition in the case of a person classified as suffering from mental illness (see section 20(4)).

3. Section 72 provides, so far is is believed to be material, as follows:
"(1) Where application is made to a Mental Health Review Tribunal by or in respect of a patient who is liable to be detained under this Act, the tribunal may in any case direct that the patient be discharged, and ...

> **(b) the tribunal shall direct the discharge of a patient liable to be detained otherwise than under section 2 above if they are satisfied—**
>> **(i) that he is not then suffering from mental illness, psychopathic disorder, severe mental impairment or mental impairment or from any of those forms of disorder of a nature or degree which makes it appropriate for him to be liable to be detained in a hospital for medical treatment; or**
>> **(ii) that it is not necessary for the health or safety of the patient or for the protection of other persons that he should receive such treatment ...**

(2) In determining whether to direct the discharge of a patient detained otherwise than under section 2 above in a case not falling within paragraph (b) of subsection (1) above, the tribunal shall have regard—

> **(a) to the likelihood of medical treatment alleviating or preventing a deterioration in the patient's condition ...".**

4. Thus: the Mental Health Act invests the tribunal with a general discretion to direct the discharge of a patient "in any case". It imposes a *duty* on the tribunal to direct discharge where either of the criteria specified in section 72(b)(i) or (ii) are satisfied. In determining whether to exercise its general discretion (where not under a duty to discharge) the tribunal is *required, inter alia,* to "have regard to the likelihood of medical treatment alleviating or preventing a deterioration of the patient's condition".

5. Foreshadowing the submissions of law (see below) the applicant contends, in outline, that:

(a) It cannot be appropriate that a patient should be liable to be detained in a hospital for medical treatment where such treatment is likely to cause a deterioration in his condition. But more:

(b) It cannot be appropriate that a patient should be liable to be so detained where treatment is unlikely to alleviate or prevent a deterioration of his condition. Further:

(c) In performing its duty and/or exercising its general discretion under section 72, no reasonable tribunal could fail to direct discharge in circumstances where treatment was either causing a deterioration in a patient's condition or else did not meet the criteria for admissibility or renewal of detention, namely that such treatment was likely to alleviate or prevent a deterioration of a patient's condition.

B. FACTUAL BACKGROUND

6. The applicant is, currently, liable to be detained under section 3 of the Mental Health Act 1983 at Derby Ward, Horton Hospital, Epsom in Surrey.

7. The applicant is aged 45. He was made liable to section 3 detention on October 2, 1994 and transferred from St Luke's Woodside Hospital to the Derby Unit of Horton Hospital aforesaid on March 13, 1995: the latter is an interim secure unit which accepts referrals from other hospitals.

8. On or about April 1, 1995 the applicant's liability to detention was renewed under section 20. His classification of mental disorder was, both at the time of original admission under section 3 and at the time of the said renewal, that of "mental illness". However, shortly before the tribunal hearing (see below) his consultant determined that he should be reclassified as suffering from "psychopathic disorder" as being a borderline personality disorder.

9. The tribunal hearing took place on May 22, 1995 (for the material and evidence before the tribunal, see exhibit "N.A.M.1" exhibited to the affidavit sworn in support of the present application). The most material evidence is believed to be that set out in paragraphs 5 and 6 below.

10. Dr O.S. Loose, a consultant psychiatrist, stated in his report dated May 21, 1995 *inter alia* as follows:

(1) The applicant met the criteria for "psychopathic disorder" as defined in section 1(2).

(2) The most suitable form of treatment was "milieu therapy". However, such treatment could not be provided in the context of a section under the Mental Health Act and required a patient to act co-operatively.

(3) The only forms of treatment which would alleviate the applicant's condition required the applicant's active co-operation which he was, currently, unwilling to give.

(4) Whilst if the applicant were to be discharged from hospital "there would undoubtedly be further episodes of self-harm and other risky behaviours", further detention "will merely erode his already precarious confidence and ability to cope with the world".

(5) The applicant did not meet the criterion for admission to hospital under section 3(1)(b) and it was, therefore, appropriate for the tribunal to discharge him from liability to detention under section 3.

11. Dr Loose gave oral evidence to similar effect to that contained in his said report.

12. Dr David Smith (consultant at the Henry Rollin Unit at Horton Hospital) prepared a short report indicating his view that none of the criteria under section 72(1)(b)(i)–(iii) applied and that the applicant ought not to be discharged. In oral evidence to the tribunal Dr Smith observed that the deterioration that Dr Loose believed would ensue from further detention was "a stage that his [the applicant's] condition would go through" before potential improvement.

C. THE TRIBUNAL DECISION

13. The tribunal was not satisfied that any of the criteria in section 72(b) were met (for which see below). It did not, however, consider it likely that treatment was alleviating or preventing a deterioration of the applicant's condition (see answer to question 8 at "N.A.M.1").

14. The tribunal's written reasons for not directing that the applicant be discharged (exhibited as "N.A.M.1") amount, in the applicant's submission, to the following:

(1) The tribunal was satisfied that "psychopathic disorder" was the correct classification.

(2) The only appropriate medical treatment which might alleviate the applicant's disorder would be psychotherapy in a group setting but this required the co-operation of the applicant which he was unwilling to give.

(3) The evidence of the RMO (Dr Smith) that the applicant's mental condition might deteriorate for a time (if detained) was accepted. It was also accepted that there was evidence that the applicant's mental condition had deteriorated whilst being detained.

(4) There was also evidence that the applicant's mental condition had deteriorated during a period of obsession (over Dr Sallon).

(5) The applicant's said deterioration might "in due course" give way to subsequent alleviation of the applicant's mental condition and he might then be willing to co-operate with appropriate therapy. Until that time it was necessary that the applicant should continue to be detained under medical supervision.

D. SUBMISSIONS OF LAW

15. The applicant submits that:

    (a) the tribunal misdirected itself in determining that it was appropriate for the applicant to be liable to be detained in a hospital for medical treatment: in the light of its own findings it was under a duty to direct discharge under section 72(b)(i);

    (b) (in any event) the tribunal, by virtue of its said findings, acted unlawfully in not directing the applicant's discharge by virtue of its statutory discretion under sections 72(1) and (2);

    (c) (in any event) the tribunal's reasoning was defective thereby rendering its said decision unlawful.

16. As to (a) the applicant advances the following propositions:

    (1) Given the tribunal's finding that: (a) it was not likely that medical treatment was alleviating or preventing a deterioration of the applicant's condition, and (b) there was evidence that the applicant's condition had deteriorated during such treatment, no reasonable tribunal could have found it appropriate for the applicant to be liable to be detained in a hospital for such treatment to be continued. Further:

    (2) The speculation that the applicant's deterioration *might* at some unspecified time (and for no attributed reason) "give way to subsequent alleviation" was an immaterial consideration to take into account when determining the appropriateness of the applicant being liable to be detained in a hospital for continued medical treatment.

    (3) As a matter of law, treatment that is proved to cause deterioration in a patient's mental condition cannot render it appropriate for such patient to remain liable to be detained for the continuation of such treatment. Alternatively:

    (4) Treatment that is found to be unlikely to alleviate or prevent such deterioration cannot render it appropriate for such patient to remain liable to be detained for the continuation of such treatment. So far as is necessary the applicant will argue that *R. v. Mersey Mental Health Review Tribunal, ex p.* D, *the Times*, April 13, 1987 (to contrary effect) is "plainly wrong" and/or decided *per incuriam* and, therefore, not binding.

17. As to (b) the applicant contends that even if the tribunal was not under a duty to direct discharge, no reasonable tribunal could have failed to direct discharge under its general discretion given: (a) its own findings (see above), and (b) the evidence of Dr Loose (not ostensibly rejected by the tribunal) that further detention would merely erode the applicant's already precarious confidence and ability to cope with the world, and that the applicant did not meet the criteria necessary for admission to hospital under section 3.

18. As to (c) the applicant contends that the tribunal's reasons were manifestly defective and/or in breach of the requirement to provide a reasoned decision under r. 23 of the Mental Health Review Tribunal Rules 1983 (S.I. 1983 No. 942) in that:

   (1) The tribunal's reasons for failing to direct discharge were not "adequate and intelligible" (see: *Re Poyser and Mills' Arbitration* [1964] 2 Q.B. 467, p. 478, per Megaw J.) given its finding that continued treatment was unlikely to alleviate or prevent a deterioration of the applicant's condition and that deterioration had occurred during the course of such treatment. Further, the tribunal gave no reason for its speculation that the applicant's condition might "in due course" give way to subsequent alleviation.

   (2) The tribunal's reasons do not enable the applicant to know whether the case advanced on his behalf by an independent psychiatrist, Dr. Loose, had been accepted or rejected in whole or in part or (if rejected) the reason therefore (see: *R v. Mental Health Review Tribunal, ex p. Clatworthy* [1985] 3 All E.R. 699, p. 704, per Mann J.).

   (3) The tribunal's reasoning does not enable one to read from it the issue to which the reasons are directed (see: *R v. Mental Health Review Tribunal, ex p. Pickering* [1986] 1 All E.R. 99, p. 104, per Forbes J.) given the tribunal's acceptance that psychotherapy in a group setting on a voluntary basis (necessarily outside section 3 detention) was the only appropriate medical treatment for alleviation of the applicant's condition but the ostensibly contrary reasoning that it was necessary that the applicant should continue to be detained for nursing care under medical supervision.

19. It is submitted that there is no true alternative remedy available to the applicant. The logic of the tribunal's findings in this case compel a direction that he be discharged. In a case involving liberty of the subject an applicant ought not, as a matter of principle, to be exposed to the risk of different findings by a freshly constituted tribunal or to the risk of misapplication of the law as, *ex hypothesi*, in the present case. Further, and in any event, if the substantive application for judicial review is ordered to be expedited a new tribunal hearing will take place earlier than would be the case if the

applicant has to await a listing for such hearing (see affidavit filed in support of the present application).

MICHAEL RITCHIE

AFFIDAVIT IN SUPPORT OF APPLICATION FOR LEAVE TO APPLY FOR JUDICIAL REVIEW

N.A.M.1: _____
Filed on behalf of
the applicant.

In the High Court of Justice   D–02
Queen's Bench Division   Crown Office Ref
Crown Office List

CO/

In the matter of an application by Charles Nutfield for leave to apply for Judicial Review (Ord. 53, r. 3).

And in the matter of section 72 of the Mental Health Act 1983.

AFFIDAVIT

I, NICHOLAS ANDREW MACKINTOSH, of Leyton & Co., Epsom Court, Epsom, Surrey, Solicitor, MAKE OATH and say as follows:—

1. I am a Solicitor of the Supreme Court, and an Assistant Solicitor employed by Leyton & Co, of Epsom Court, aforesaid. I hold the conduct of this case on the applicant's behalf and I am duly authorised by the applicant to make this affidavit in support of his application for leave to move for judicial review of a decision of the Mental Health Review Tribunal dated May 22, 1995, directing that the applicant not be discharged from liability to be detained under section 3 of the Mental Health Act 1983.

2. Unless otherwise stated the facts and matters deposed to herein are within my knowledge or else derived from documentation made available to me in my aforesaid capacity.

3. I have read a copy of the notice of application (Form 86A) and I confirm that the factual content thereof is true and accurate.

4. There is now produced and shown to me marked "N.A.M.1" a copy of the tribunal's decision. I invite the Court to consider Question 8 and the answer thereto together with the handwritten reasoning that follows.

5. There is further produced and shown to me marked "N.A.M.2" a copy of the documentary material before the tribunal consisting of the following:

311

(1) Psychiatric report dated May 11, 1995 by Dr G. Field.
(2) Undated social circumstances report from Islington Council.
(3) Part 'A' statement.
(4) Form 22: Reclassification document.
(5) Psychiatric report dated May 21, 1995 by Dr O. Loose.
(6) Supplementary psychiatric report dated May 22, 1995 by Dr D. Smith.

6. Finally, there is further produced and shown to me marked "N.A.M.3" a copy of my notes of evidence at the tribunal hearing that took place on May 22, 1995, and in respect of which I represented the applicant. I prepared these notes at the earliest practicable opportunity.

7. The detailed background is well set out in the material before the tribunal. For the benefit of the Court, however, I would like to make the following additional observations:

(1) On being transferred to the Derby Unit the clinical diagnosis on the applicant was that of reactive depression in the context of an impulsive personality. This came within the definition of "mental illness" under the Mental Health Act 1983.

(2) On April 20, 1995 I represented the applicant at a meeting of the Hospital Managers with a view to the Managers reviewing the appropriateness of the applicant's detention pursuant to their powers under section 23 of the 1983 Act. At that time the Hospital Managers were newly appointed non-executive directors of the new Riverside Mental Health Trust. At that stage the applicant was still diagnosed as suffering from mental illness. I am informed by Dr Smith and believe that he was asked by the managers to provide information to them at a meeting of the managers that took place the day after the meeting at which I represented the applicant. The applicant was not informed of this and had no opportunity to hear what Dr James told the managers or to make representations thereon. This is clearly contrary to paragraph 22 of the Code of Practice annexed to the Mental Health Act itself and, in my respectful opinion, elementary principles of natural justice. However, because of the proximity of the tribunal hearing on May 22 I did not take matters further beyond writing to the managers to express my disquiet.

(3) Shortly before the tribunal hearing the position changed dramatically in that Dr Smith, the applicant's consultant psychiatrist, decided that the applicant's classification should be changed from mental illness to that of psychopathic disorder. The difference between a classification of "mental illness" and that of "psychopathic disorder" has extremely important consequences in the context of the statutory regime under the Mental Health Act in that (in respect of psychopathic disorder but not mental illness) for admission to hospital under section 3 or renewal under section 20 the "treatability" test must be satisfied, namely that for admission to hospital or renewal of authority of detention the

treatment provided in hospital must be likely to alleviate or prevent deterioration of a patient's condition.

(4) So important was this change of classification that I decided that a report should be obtained from an independent consultant psychiatrist. I refer the Court to Dr Loose's report which indicates in the clearest terms that the treatability test is not satisfied in the applicant's case.

(5) As can be seen from my notes of the tribunal hearing, Dr Loose was sympathetic to Dr Smith's dilemma that to discharge the applicant could have harmful consequences. He formed the view, nonetheless, that continued detention would cause the applicant's condition to deteriorate still further and that the only treatment that would help the applicant was voluntary psychotherapy outside the compulsory nature of liability to detention under section 3.

(6) The tribunal appears to accept Dr Loose's evidence but to speculate that the applicant's condition might improve in the future to the point where he would be willing to undertake such therapy. I am advised by Counsel that this approach may be unlawful.

8. In the present case the applicant, having entered a further period of detention, is entitled to apply for a new tribunal hearing. However, I am informed by the tribunal and believe that although the applicant may be able to obtain a further tribunal hearing within 8 weeks of such application in practice, hearings often take longer than this to arrange. By way of contrast, I am further informed by the tribunal and believe that a tribunal hearing would be arranged as a matter of urgency in the week following a successful application to the High Court for judicial review. Further, I rely upon the legal argument on alternative remedy set out in form 86A at paragraph 19.

9. In all the circumstances I respectfully invite the Court to grant the present application.

SWORN etc

SPECIMEN SKELETON ARGUMENT FOR THE APPLICANT

Ex p. Nutfield

SKELETON ARGUMENT OF APPLICANT

B = Bundle of Documents.

1. INTRODUCTION

(a) This is an application for judicial review of a decision of the **D–03** Mental Health Review Tribunal ("the tribunal") dated May 22, 1995 that the applicant not be discharged from liability to be detained (for the decision see: B/21–24). Leave to move was granted by Mr Justice Wise on June 30, 1995 after an oral hearing, (B/B): expedition was ordered and time for service of the respondent's evidence abridged to 14 days.

(b) The application is brought by Mr Charles Nutfield, a patient currently liable to be detained under section 3 of the Mental Health Act 1983. His case raises an important point of construction under the 1983 Act. (Section numbers herein refer to the 1983 Act unless otherwise stated.)

(c) In essence, the tribunal found that Mr Nutfield no longer satisfies the conditions necessary to justify either his admission to hospital under section 3 or renewal of her detention under section 20. Notwithstanding this the tribunal, believing itself to be exercising its powers under section 72(b)(i) according to law, refused to discharge him on the basis that his condition (psychopathic disorder) was of a nature or degree which made it appropriate for him to be liable to be detained.

(d) It is the applicant's primary submission that the criteria regulating both admission to hospital and renewal of detention must apply equally to the tribunal's consideration of whether it is appropriate for a patient to be liable to be detained. Put shortly: continued liability to detention cannot be appropriate where the conditions justifying admission have fallen away ("the construction issue").

(e) It is, further, contended that:

(1) the tribunal acted unlawfully/irrationally in not directing the applicant's discharge insofar as it was entitled to exercise any discretion under sections 72(1) and 72(2) given the tribunal's own findings in respect of the effect that treatment was having on Miss Andrews ("the illegality/irrationality issue"); and/or,

(2) the tribunal's reasoning is defective and, necessarily, renders its decision unlawful ("the reasons issue").

2. LEGAL REGIME

(a) Liability to detention under section 3 requires (*inter alia*), in the case of a person suffering from "psychopathic disorder or mental impairment" that "medical treatment in a hospital" "is likely to alleviate or prevent a deterioration of his condition", (see section 3(2)(b)), (referred to below as "the treatability test"). There is no equivalent requirement in the case of a person classified as suffering from "mental illness".

(b) Similarly, renewal of a patient's detention under section 20 depends (*inter alia*) in the case of a person suffering from psychopathic disorder upon the condition that medical treatment in a hospital "is likely to alleviate or prevent a deterioration of his condition". There is no compulsory equivalent condition in the case of a person classified as suffering from mental illness, (see section 20(4)).

314

(c) Section 72 provides, so far is is believed to be material, as follows:
"(1) Where application is made to a Mental Health Review Tribunal by or in respect of a patient who is liable to be detained under this Act, the tribunal may in any case direct that the patient be discharged, and ...

    (b) the tribunal shall direct the discharge of a patient liable to be detained otherwise than under section 2 above if they are satisfied—

        (i) that he is not then suffering from mental illness, psychopathic disorder, severe mental impairment or mental impairment or from any of those forms of disorder of a nature or degree which makes it appropriate for him to be liable to be detained in a hospital for medical treatment; or

        (ii) that it is not necessary for the health or safety of the patient or for the protection of other persons that he should receive such treatment ...

    (2) In determining whether to direct the discharge of a patient detained otherwise than under section 2 above in a case not falling within paragraph (b) of subsection (1) above, the tribunal shall have regard—

(a) to the likelihood of medical treatment alleviating or preventing a deterioration in the patient's condition ...".

(d) Thus: the Mental Health Act invests the tribunal with a general discretion to direct the discharge of a patient "in any case". It imposes a *duty* on the tribunal to direct discharge where either of the criteria specified in section 72(b)(i) or (ii) are satisfied. In determining whether to exercise its general discretion (where not under a duty to discharge) the tribunal is *required, inter alia*, to "have regard to the likelihood of medical treatment alleviating or preventing a deterioration of the patient's condition".

(e) Mr Nutfield is not a restricted patient. However, as developed below, the provisions of the MHA 1983 relating to restricted patients are relevant to the legal argument. Section 73 deals with the discharge of restricted patients admitted under sections 37/41. Such patients, if suffering from psychopathic disorder, may only be admitted to hospital under a hospital order if the treatability test is satisfied (see section 37(2)(a)(i)). The discharge criteria for all restricted patients in section 73(1) refer, materially, only to section 72(b)(i)/(ii): restricted patients do not fall within the general discretionary powers of a tribunal under sections 72(1) and 72(2). Thus (at the point of consideration of discharge by a tribunal), the treatability test can only be applied to restricted patients suffering from psychopathic disorder under the provisions of section 72(1)(b).

315

(f) Finally, section 145(1) defines 'medical treatment' as including "nursing, and also ... care, habilitation and rehabilitation under medical supervision".

3. PSYCHOPATHIC DISORDER UNDER THE MHA 1959 AND 1983

(a) The Percy Commission (para. 356) considered that there was insufficient justification for special compulsory powers in relation to *adult* psychopaths except where their conduct constituted a criminal offence. Further, the Commission recognised that even in respect of non-adult persons suffering from psychopathic disorder "the circumstances in which the use of compulsion is justifiable are ... limited" (*ibid*, para. 353) but that "there is a strong case for authorising the use of compulsion to ensure training *or treatment in hospital*" (*ibid*, para. 354: emphasis added). The MHA 1959 implemented these proposals except that it sub-divided the Commission's definition of psychopathic disorder into: (i) subnormality and (ii) psychopathic disorder. Thus:

(b) Section 4(4) MHA 1959 defined 'psychopathic disorder' as "a persistent disorder or disability of mind (whether or not including sub-normality of intelligence) which results in abnormally aggressive or seriously irresponsible conduct on the part of the patient, *and requires or is susceptible to medical treatment*" (emphasis added). And:

(c) Section 26(2) MHA 1959 provided, so far as is material, that: "An application for admission for treatment may be made in respect of a patient on the grounds—(a) that he is suffering from mental disorder, being— ... (ii) in the case of a patient under the age of 21 years, psychopathic disorder or subnormality; and (b) that it is necessary in the interests of the patient's health or safety or for the protection of other persons that the patient should be so detained". Finally:

(d) Section 123(1) MHA 1959 provided, so far as is material, that: "Where application is made to a Mental Health Review Tribunal by or in respect of a patient who is liable to be detained under this Act, the tribunal may in any case direct that the patient be discharged, and shall so direct if they are satisfied—(a) that he is not then suffering from mental illness, psychopathic disorder, subnormality or severe subnormality; or (b) that it is not necessary in the interests of the patient's health or safety or for the protection of other persons that the patient should continue to be liable to be detained ...".

(e) In its "Review of the Mental Health Act 1959" (Cmnd. 7320) the Government (paras. 2.38 *et seq.*) recognised that age limits for persons suffering from psychopathic disorder were, to some extent, arbitrary. Nonetheless, the importance of retaining the treatability criterion for those suffering from psychopathic disorder was emphasised in the Government White Paper "Reform of Mental Health Legislation" (Cmnd. 8405) which, after summarising the recommendations of the Butler Committee set up to review the operation of the MHA 1959, para. 1.26 states as follows:

"... the Government accepts that the [new] Act should establish a clear requirement that psychopaths should only be detained under compulsory powers where there is a good prospect of benefit from treatment. The present definition of psychopathic disorder includes the wording 'and requires or is susceptible to medical treatment'. The Government proposes that this should be omitted from the definition in section 4 of the [1959] Act, since it does not seem appropriate as part of a definition, but that a 'prospect of benefit from treatment' requirement should instead be incorporated into the criteria for compulsory admission and renewal of detention".

(f) There ensued first the Mental Health (Amendment) Act 1982 and, thereafter, the Mental Health Act 1983 (see above).

4. THE FACTS

(a) The applicant is, currently, detained under section 3 of the Mental Health Act 1983 at Derby Ward, Horton Hospital, Epsom in Surrey.

(b) The applicant is aged 45. He was made liable to section 3 detention on October 2, 1994 and transferred from St Luke's Woodside Hospital to the Derby Unit of Horton Hospital aforesaid on March 13, 1995: the latter is an interim secure unit which accepts referrals from other hospitals.

(c) On or about April 1, 1995 the applicant's liability to detention was renewed under section 20. His classification of mental disorder was, both at the time of original admission under section 3 and at the time of the said renewal, that of "mental illness". However, shortly before the tribunal hearing (see below) his consultant determined that he should be reclassified as suffering from "psychopathic disorder" as being a borderline personality disorder.

(d) The tribunal hearing took place on May 22, 1995 (for the material and evidence before the tribunal, see exhibit "N.A.M.2" B/26–40, and "N.A.M.3" B/42–50). The most material evidence is believed to be that set out in paragraphs (e) and (g) below.

(e) Dr O.S. Loose, a consultant psychiatrist, stated in his report dated May 21, 1995 *inter alia* as follows:

(1) The applicant met the criteria for "psychopathic disorder" as defined in section 1(2).

317

(2) The most suitable form of treatment was "milieu therapy". However, such treatment could not be provided in the context of a section under the Mental Health Act and required a patient to act co-operatively.

(3) The only forms of treatment which would alleviate the applicant's condition required the applicant's active co-operation which he was, currently, unwilling to give.

(4) Whilst if the applicant were to be discharged from hospital "there would undoubtedly be further episodes of self-harm and other risky behaviours", further detention "will merely erode her already precarious confidence and ability to cope with the world".

(5) The applicant did not meet the criterion for admission to hospital under section 3(1)(b) and it was, therefore, appropriate for the tribunal to discharge him from liability to detention under section 3.

(f) Dr Loose gave oral evidence to similar effect to that contained in his said report.

(g) Dr David Smith (consultant at the Henry Rollin Unit at Horton Hospital) prepared a short report indicating his view that none of the criteria under section 72(1)(b)(i)–(iii) applied and that the applicant ought not to be discharged. In oral evidence to the tribunal Dr Smith observed that the deterioration that Dr Loose believed would ensue from further detention was "a stage that his [the applicant's] condition would go through" before potential improvement.

5. TRIBUNAL DECISION

(a) The tribunal was not satisfied that any of the criteria in section 72(b) were met (for which see below). It did not, however, consider it likely that treatment was alleviating or preventing a deterioration of the applicant's condition (see answer to question 8 at "N.A.M.1", B/22).

(b) The tribunal's written reasons for not directing that the applicant be discharged (exhibited as "N.A.M.1", B/21–24) amount, in the applicant's submission, to the following:

(1) The tribunal was satisfied that "psychopathic disorder" was the correct classification.

(2) The only appropriate medical treatment which might alleviate the applicant's disorder would be psychotherapy in a group setting but this required the co-operation of the applicant which he was unwilling to give.

318

(3) The evidence of the RMO (Dr Smith) that the applicant's mental condition might deteriorate for a time (if detained) was accepted. It was also accepted that there was evidence that the applicant's mental condition had deteriorated whilst being detained.

(4) There was also evidence that the applicant's mental condition had deteriorated during a period of obsession (over Dr Sallon).

(5) The applicant's said deterioration might "in due course" give way to subsequent alleviation of the applicant's mental condition and he might then be willing to co-operate with appropriate therapy. Until that time it was necessary that the applicant should continue to be detained under medical supervision.

6. THE CONSTRUCTION ISSUE

(a) The tribunal found that the treatability test was not satisfied: Mr Nutfield could not, on that finding, have been admitted under section 3 and his detention could not have been renewed under section 20. It follows, inevitably, that it cannot have been appropriate for Mr Nutfield to be liable to be detained. This is a straightforward question of construction of the words "appropriate ... to be liable to be detained" in section 72(1)(b)(i). The proposition is that:

(b) The criteria for mandatory discharge in section 72(1)(b)(i) and (ii) necessarily match the criteria for admission to hospital and renewal of detention under sections 3, 20 and 37.

(c) This reflects (generally):

(1) the rationale of Mental Health *Review* Tribunals;

(2) the fact that there are no sensible criteria supporting (mandatory) appropriateness of continued liability to detention other than continued justification of the criteria underpinning detention/renewal of detention;

(3) the significance of the phrase "liable to be detained".

(d) Specifically (in the context of psychopathic disorder) it reflects:

(1) the treatability test being: (i) part of the MHA 1959 Act definition of "psychopathic disorder" itself (see above), an (ii) the justification for the detention and renewal of detention of those suffering from psychopathic disorder under the MHA 1983;

319

(2) the fact that unless the treatability test is contained in section 72(1)(b)(i) restricted patients suffering from psychopathic disorder (whose admission under section 37 *depends* upon such test being satisfied) cannot have that test applied at any point by a tribunal.

(e) But more: there is, in any event, a presumption against imposition of a statutory impairment of liberty of the person without clear words (see Bennion on 'Statutory Interpretation' Second edition, p. 578 and the examples therein cited). On the tribunal's finding Mr Nutfield was not suffering from psychopathic disorder at all within the meaning of that term in the MHA 1959. He could not have been admitted under section 26(2) MHA 1959 *and he would have been entitled to be discharged under section 123(1) of the 1959 Act.* But if that is right the Respondent is driven to submit that Parliament intended completely different consequences to follow as the result of the treatability test being taken out of the statutory definition of 'psychopathic disorder' and placed, instead, as part of the liability to detention criteria in the MHA 1983. This is a manifestly impossible position and is disavowed by the Government itself (see para. 3(e) above and the extract from Cmnd. 8405 there cited).

(f) On analysis it is plain that:

(1) the fact that section 72(1)(b)(i) refers to the appropriateness of continued liability to detention is shorthand for the discrete statutory criteria justifying detention or continued detention of patients suffering from different forms of mental disorder contained elsewhere in the Act;

(2) the statutory intent (in the context of psychopathic disorder) is only to permit detention where the treatability test is satisfied.

(g) *R. v. Mersey Mental Health Review Tribunal, ex p. D, The Times,* April 13, 1987 (a decision of a Divisional Court) held (see transcript, pp. 6H–7A) as follows:

"It is to be observed that there is no requirement that the medical treatment envisaged in sections 72 and 73 should be such medical treatment as might have the effect of alleviating or improving the condition of the applicant. It is simply medical treatment as so defined in section 145, namely, care and habilation and rehabilitation under medical supervision."

(h) But that decision must be seen in context. It is clear that it did not, on analysis, address the construction issue at all. The transcript (p. 5D/E) shows that the Divisional Court accepted the tribunal's finding under section 72(b)(i) and rejected the submission (plainly incorrect) that detention *per se* could not constitute medical treatment (see transcript, p. 6D/F). What the Divisional Court did *not* address, however, was the meaning to be given to the phrase "appropriate . . . to be liable to be detained" which, as the construction argument seeks to demonstrate, necessarily import the treatability test into section 72(1)(b)(i) in respect of those patients suffering from psychopathic disorder.

(i) Thus, the decision in *Ex p. D* is:

    (1) not binding on this court in terms of ratio; or,

    (2) was decided *per incuriam*; or,

    (3) is "plainly wrong" (see: *R. v. Greater Manchester Coroner, ex p. Tal* [1985] QB 67).

7. THE ILLEGALITY/IRRATIONALITY ISSUE

(a) If, contrary to the applicant's submissions in terms of construction, the tribunal had a discretion whether or not to discharge it cannot be "appropriate" for a person suffering from psychopathic disorder to be liable to be detained where the treatability test is no longer satisfied. If that is right, the tribunal ought to have directed discharge in any event.

(b) Axiomatically, the statutory discretion in section 72(1) and (2) must be exercised in accordance with the policy and objects of the MHA 1983 (see: *Padfield v. Minister of Agriculture, Fisheries and Food* [1968] AC 997). But once it is accepted (as it must be) that Parliament did not intend to submit those suffering from psychopathic disorder to continued treatment under detention where the treatability test was not satisfied it follows that a finding (as here) that such test was not satisfied must in law and on *Wednesbury* rationality principles lead to a direction for discharge.

(c) Further: the tribunal's own reasoning should have lead to a direction that Mr Nutfield should be discharged because:

    (1) it accepted that the only effective treatment was treatment outside hospital, and:

    (2) it did not find that detention in hospital would be likely to prevent deterioration (indeed it accepted that for an unspecified length of time such detention might *cause* deterioration).

(d) The tribunal appears to have "reasoned" the matter thus: if the applicant was detained in hospital he *might* at some unspecified time come to co-operate with a group therapy imperative.

(e) Such approach is, it is submitted, entirely unlawful. It is so for (at least) three reasons, being that:

(1) treatability (for those suffering from psychopathic disorder) is couched in terms of probability not possibility;

(2) the monitoring of a patient's condition in the hope that a projected course of treatment would eventually permit a tribunal to order discharge is contrary to the intended statutory regime (see: *R. v. Mental Health Review Tribunal, ex p. Secretary of State for the Home Department, The Times,* March 25, 1987);

(3) detention in hospital for an ulterior purpose, namely the consent to treatment outside hospital is, similarly, outside the purposes of the statute (*cf: R. v. Hallstrom, ex p.* W [1986] 2 W.L.R. 883).

8. THE REASONS ISSUE

(a) The applicant contends that the tribunal's reasons were manifestly defective and/or in breach of the requirement to provide a reasoned decision under r. 23 of the Mental Health Review Tribunal Rules 1983 (S.I. 1983 No. 942) in that:

(1) The tribunal's reasons for failing to direct discharge were not "adequate and intelligible" (see: *Re Poyser and Mills' Arbitration* [1964] 2 Q.B. 467, p. 478, per Megaw J.) given its finding that continued treatment was unlikely to alleviate or prevent a deterioration of the applicant's condition and that deterioration had occurred during the course of such treatment. Further, the tribunal gave no reason for its speculation that the applicant's condition might "in due course" give way to subsequent alleviation.

(2) The tribunal's reasons do not enable the applicant to know whether the case advanced on his behalf by an independent psychiatrist, Dr Frank, had been accepted or rejected in whole or in part or (if rejected) the reason therefor (see: *R. v. Mental Health Review Tribunal, ex p. Clatworthy* [1985] 3 All E.R. 699, p. 704, per Mann J.).

(3) The tribunal's reasoning does not enable one to read from it the issue to which the reasons are directed (see: *R. v. Mental Health Review Tribunal, ex p. Pickering* [1986] 1 All E.R. 99, p. 104, per Forbes J.) given the tribunal's acceptance that psychotherapy in a group setting on a voluntary basis (necessarily outside section 3 detention) was the only appropriate medical treatment for alleviation of the applicant's condition but the ostensibly contrary reasoning that it was necessary that the applicant should continue to be detained for nursing care under medical supervision.

MICHAEL RITCHIE

MISCELLANEOUS CROWN OFFICE FORMS

1. FORM JRJ. NOTIFICATION OF DECISION ON INITIAL APPLICATION FOR LEAVE TO APPLY FOR JUDICIAL REVIEW   **D–04**

Crown Office Ref

In the High Court of Justice
Queens Bench Division
Crown Office List   CO/21/93

In the matter of an application for Judicial Review

The Queen—v.—Mental Health Review Tribunal

Ex parte **Nutfield**

Application for leave to apply for Judicial Review
NOTIFICATION of the first Judge's decision (Order 53 r. 3)

Following:

☐ consideration of the documents only;   **or**

☐ consideration of the documents **and** oral submissions by the applicant or counsel
[   ] in open court.

Order by the Honourable Mr Justice Dense

Observations for the applicant:

leave refused

Dated 17/6/95   Signed I. Dense

Where leave to apply has been granted, applicants and their legal advisers are reminded of their obligation to reconsider the merits of their application in the light of the respondent's affidavit.

323

Notes for the applicant

Sent/Handed to the applicant/
the applicant's solicitors
on (date):

(1) Where the Judge has refused leave an
applicant or his solicitor may renew
his application by completing and
returning form 86B within 10 days of
the service upon him of this notice.
The application may not be renewed
in a non-criminal cause or matter if
the Judge has heard oral argument.

(2) If leave has been granted the
applicant or his solicitor must within
14 days from the grant of leave:
a) serve on all person directly
affected
—copy Notice of Motion in form
86 together with Form 86A,
supporting affidavits and exhibits;
b) enter in the Crown Office the
original Notice of Motion in form
86, together with:
—2 copies; £50 fee; affidavit of
service.

Applicant's Ref No.

**Judge's observations to the Crown Office
(Not for the applicant)**

**D–05   2. FORM 86B. NOTICE OF RENEWAL OF APPLICATION FOR
LEAVE TO APPLY FOR JUDICIAL REVIEW**

Crown Office Ref

**In the High Court of Justice
Queens Bench Division
Crown Office List**

CO/21/93

In the matter of an application for Judicial Review

The Queen—v.—Mental Health Review Tribunal

Ex parte Nutfield

Notice of RENEWAL of application for leave to apply for Judicial Review (Order 53 rule 3(5))

To the Master of the Crown Office, Royal Courts of Justice, Strand, London WC2A 2LL

The applicant renews his application for leave to apply for Judicial Review

Signed   Leyton & Co.   Dated   18/6/95

Applicant's Ref No. NAM/1   Tel. No. 01812403   Fax No.

This notice must be lodged in the Crown Office within **10 days** of the service on the applicant or his solicitor of notice that the original application for leave has been refused.

Form 86B

For Office use only   **Acknowledgment of Renewal and date of hearing**

Received in the Crown Office on:

19/6/95

The Master of the Crown Office acknowledges receipt of your Notice of Renewal, the hearing of which has been fixed for

the 30th day of June 1995 at 10.30 o'clock

Where Counsel is being instructed it is the responsibility of solicitors to ensure that Counsel is informed of this date.

Information as to the venue may be obtained from the Crown Office on the day before the hearing.

D–06 3. NOTIFICATION OF DECISION ON RENEWED APPLICATION FOR LEAVE TO APPLY FOR JUDICIAL REVIEW

Crown Office Ref

In the High Court of Justice
Queens Bench Division
Crown Office List   CO/21/93

In the matter of an application for Judicial Review

      The Queen—v.—Mental Health Review Tribunal

      Ex parte **Nutfield**

      Renewed application for leave to apply for Judicial Review following an oral hearing NOTIFICATION of the Court's decision

Order by ~~the Divisional Court of the Queen's Bench Division, or the~~ Honourable Mr Justice Rock

leave to move

Where leave to apply has been granted, applicants and their legal advisers are reminded of their obligation to reconsider the merits of their application in the light of the respondent's affidavit.

Counsel: M. Ritchie

Date: 4/7/95   Crown Office Associate:

Notes for the applicant

(1) If the Court or Judge has refused leave this decision is final as far as this Court is concerned. The Notes for Guidance deal in outline with rights of appeal.

(2) If leave has been granted the applicant or his solicitor must within 14 days from the grant of leave:
   a) serve on all persons directly affected
      —copy Notice of Motion in form 86 together with Form 86A, supporting affidavits and exhibits;
   b) enter in the Crown Office the original Notice of Motion in form 86, together with:
      —2 copies; £50 fee; affidavit of service.

Sent/Handed to the applicant/ the applicant's solicitors on (date):

Applicant's Ref No.

---

4. NOTICE OF MOTION AFTER OBTAINING LEAVE TO APPLY FOR JUDICIAL REVIEW   D–07

Crown Office Ref

**In the High Court of Justice
Queens Bench Division
Crown Office List**

CO/21/93

In the matter of an application for Judicial Review

The Queen—v.—Mental Health Review Tribunal

Ex parte **Nutfield**

Learning Resources
Centre

Notice of Motion for Judicial Review (Order 53 rule 5)

Take Notice that pursuant to the leave of a ~~Divisional Court of the Queen's Bench Division~~ given on 30/6/95 the Court will be moved as soon as Counsel can be heard on the applicant's behalf for an order for relief in the terms, and on the grounds, set out in Form 86A, herewith.

327

And that the costs of and occasioned by this motion be the applicant's

And take notice that on the hearing of this motion the applicant will use the affidavit and exhibits, copies of which accompany this notice.

And also take notice that the Divisional Court of the Queen's Bench Division (or the Honourable Mr Justice   ) by order dated   directed that all proceedings in (*or* on) the said   be stayed until after the hearing of this motion or further order.]

Dated the 5th day of July 1995

To   The Treasury Solicitor   Signed   N.A. Makintosh

Solicitor for   of Leyton & Co.
The respondent

Solicitor for the applicant

Ref No.   NAM/1
Tel. No.
Fax. No.

Important

1. Any respondent who intends to use an affidavit at the hearing should inform the Crown Office of his intention within 10 days of the service of this notice.
2. Any such affidavit must be filed in the Crown Office as soon as practicable and in any event within 56 days of service.
3. This notice must be filed in the Crown Office within 14 days after the grant of leave to move and must be accompanied by an affidavit of service; see the Notes for Guidance obtainable from the Crown Office, Royal Courts of Justice, Strand, London WC2A 2LL.

ACTIVE CASE LETTER FROM THE CROWN OFFICE

CROWN OFFICE
Royal Courts of Justice
Strand
London WC2A 2LL

Telephone: 0171–936 6297

FAX: 0171–936 6802 DX: 44450 STRAND

Messrs Leyton & Co   Your reference:
Epsom Court
Epsom
Surrey   Our reference: CO/21/93

Date: January 27, 1995

Dear Sirs,

Re: R. v MENTAL HEALTH REVIEW TRIBUNAL, ex p. NUTFIELD

The above matter has been listed for hearing on July 27, 1995. **D–08**
You should therefore instruct counsel to attend. It is your responsibility to notify the respondent and all interested parties of this date. A copy of this letter should be served by you upon the respondent and upon any interested party as soon as possible.

Papers for the Court

You are reminded of the need to comply with the Practice Note issued by the Lord Chief Justice on July 21, 1983 and reported at [1983] 3 All E.R. 33 and the Practice Direction issued by the Lord Chief Justice on October 25, 1994 in relation to the composition and pagination of bundles of documents. The paginated bundle prepared for the use of the Court must be lodged with the Crown Office at least *five* clear working days before the date fixed for hearing.

Advocates are required to lodge skeleton arguments in the Crown Office. Advocates for the applicant must lodge, and serve, skeleton arguments at least *five* clear working days before the hearing date. Advocates for the respondent or other party wishing to be heard must lodge, and serve, skeleton arguments at least *three* clear working days before the hearing date. The skeleton argument must quote the Crown Office reference number and the hearing date and must contain

- (a) the time estimate for the complete hearing, including delivery of judgment (whether or not an estimate has been given earlier);
- (b) a list of issues;
- (c) a list of propositions of law to be advanced (together with the authorities relied upon in support, with page references to passages relied upon);
- (d) a chronology of events (with reference to the paginated bundle prepared for the court);
- (e) a list of the essential documents for advance reading by the Court, with page references to passages relied upon;
- (f) a list of *dramatis personae* where the number of people who feature in the documents warrants it.

The above time limits must be strictly observed. Failure to do so may result in adjournment and may be penalised in costs. Advocates may, however, supplement their skeleton arguments up to one working day before the hearing.

All copy documents in this case will be destroyed (as confidential waste) two working days after the final decision of the High Court unless a written request for the documents is received by the Crown Office before the expiry of that period.

Withdrawal or Settlement

Should it be your client's intention not to proceed with this matter, you should obtain the consent of all parties to the matter being withdrawn. Such consent should indicate the terms of any agreed order that the parties would wish the Court to make and in any event should deal with the question of costs. The case will only be taken out of the list when a notice of withdrawal/consent order with a provision for costs signed by all parties has been received in this office.

If there is a possibility that the case will settle, but no final agreement has been reached, you should apply by summons, forthwith, to the Master of the Crown Office to have the case stood out into Part C of the Crown Office List (see the Practice Direction issued by the Lord Chief Justice on February 3, 1987 and reported at [1987] 1 W.L.R. 232 and [1987] 1 All E.R. 368).

Yours faithfully,

Miss A Hearn
Listing Officer

NB: It is the duty of the parties to notify the Crown Office of any problems which may affect the listing of the above-mentioned case, *e.g.* whether special facilities for disabled access are required.

CROWN OFFICE NOTES FOR GUIDANCE

THE CROWN OFFICE LIST

NOTES FOR GUIDANCE

APPLICATIONS FOR JUDICIAL REVIEW

D–09 GENERAL These notes, issued at the direction of the Lord Chief Justice, are not intended to be exhaustive but merely to offer an outline of the procedure to be followed. Applicants and their legal advisers should consult Order 53 of the rules of the Supreme Court as amended by S.I. 1980 No. 2000 for a full account.

1. LEGAL AID

Neither the Court nor the Crown Office has power to grant legal aid which may only be obtained from the Law Society. Application should be made to the appropriate Area Committee whose address will be found in the telephone directory, or through a Solicitor, who may prepare an application for the Committee's consideration, under the Green Form Scheme.

2. TIME

(a) Applications for leave to apply for Judicial Review must be made as soon as possible after the date of the judgment order, decision or other proceeding in respect of which relief is sought but in any event within the period of three months allowed by Order 53 rule 4.

(b) The Court can extend or abridge time wherever a time limit is fixed by the Rules but will only exercise this power where it is satisfied there are very good reasons for doing so. If an extension or abridgement of time is sought grounds in support of that application must be filed and verified by affidavit: Order 3 rule 5(1).

3. FEES

A fee of £20.00 is payable on lodging an application for leave to apply for Judicial Review. A further £80.00 is payable, if leave is granted, on entering an affidavit of service and notice of motion, total £100.00. Cheques should be made payable to HM Paymaster General. Personal cheques are not accepted unless supported by a bankers cheque guarantee card presented in the Fees Room at the time of lodging the application.

4. FORM OF APPLICATION

Applications for leave to move for Judicial Review must be made in Form 86A and must be supported by an affidavit verifying the facts relied on: Order 5 rule 3(2). In addition to the original documents, the applicant must provide two copies, where the application is to be considered by a Divisional Court, and one copy in a civil case where the application is to be considered by a single Judge.

N.B. Where the documents in support of an application

for leave exceed 10 pages, they must be paginated and indexed in a convenient bundle. In addition, a list must be provided of the pages essential for reading by the Court. Where only part of a page needs to be read, that part should be indicated, by side lining or in some other way, but not by highlighting.

5. LEAVE TO MOVE

Ex parte applications for leave to move for Judicial Review will be considered in one of two ways:

(a) Unless the applicant otherwise requests in his notice of application, the papers in the case will be placed before a Judge who will decide whether to grant leave to move without hearing any oral submissions. The purpose of this procedure is to ensure that applications may be dealt with speedily and without unnecessary expense. Applicants or their Solicitors will be informed of the Judge's decision on Form JRJ. If leave is refused an applicant or his solicitor may renew the application in a criminal cause or matter to the Divisional Court and otherwise to a single Judge sitting in open Court, by completing and returning Form 86B within 10 days of the notice of refusal being served upon him.

(b) If the notice of application contains such a request it may proceed directly to an oral hearing before a Judge in open Court. Where the Judge refuses leave an applicant or his solicitor may, in a criminal cause or matter *only*, renew his application for hearing by a Divisional Court by completing and lodging Form 86B within 10 days of the notice of refusal being served upon him. In a civil matter the Judge's decision is final so far as his Court is concerned. Paragraph 10 of these notes deals in outline with rights of appeal. At an oral hearing an applicant may appear in person or be represented by Counsel. The name of Counsel must be given to the Crown Office as soon as it is known. The Crown Office will inform an applicant or his legal advisers, as the case may be, of the date fixed for any oral hearing: Order 53 rule 3(3)(4) and (5).

6. NOTICE OF MOTION

Where leave is granted the applicant or his solicitor must, within 14 days from the grant of leave, serve a notice of motion in Form 86 (together with a copy of the order granting leave) on all persons directly affected and enter a copy in the Crown Office together with an affidavit of service. The latter must give the names and addresses of, and the places and dates of service on, all persons who have been served with the notice of motion. If any person who ought to have been served has not been served the affidavit must state that fact and the reason for it: Order 53 rule 5(5) and (6).

7. RESPONDENTS

A party upon whom a notice of motion is served may, if he wishes, file an affidavit in reply but must inform the Crown Office of his intention of doing so as soon as practicable, and must file it as soon as practicable and in any event within 56 days after service, having given notice thereof to the applicant. He may be represented at the hearing and all parties who file affidavits will be informed of the date fixed for hearing.

8. HEARING OF MOTION

When an application is ready to be heard it will be entered in Part B of the Crown Office List, see the Practice Direction at [1987] 1 W.L.R. 232 and [1987] 1 All E.R. 368, and the applicant or his solicitor informed. While the Crown Office will give as much notice as possible of the date fixed for hearing it cannot undertake to accommodate the wishes of applicants, respondents, their Solicitors or Counsel; in particular the occasional need to list cases at short notice may mean that parties are unable to be represented by the Counsel of their first choice. Applications in criminal causes or matters will be heard by a Divisional Court consisting of two or more Judges. Civil cases will generally be heard by a single Judge sitting in open Court but may be heard by a Divisional Court where the Court so directs: Order 53 rule 5(1) and (2).

9. EXPEDITION

Where leave to apply for Judicial Review has been granted, and an applicant believes that he has grounds for an expedited hearing of his application, he may apply by summons to the Master of the Crown Office to have his case entered in the Expedited List, Part D of the Crown Office List, see the Practice Direction referred to in paragraph 8 above.

10. COSTS

It is a general rule that the party which loses is ordered to pay the costs of the other side.

11. APPEALS

A. CRIMINAL MATTERS

    (i) *Substantive application*
        The Administration of Justice Act 1960 provides:

    "S1(1) Subject to the provisions of this section, an appeal shall lie to the House of Lords, at the instance of the defendant or the prosecutor—
        (a) from any decision of a Divisional Court of the Queens Bench Division in a criminal cause or matter;

        (b) . . .

        (2) No appeal shall lie under this section except with the leave of the Court below or of the House of Lords; and such leave shall not be granted unless it is certified by the court below that a point of law of general public importance is involved in the decision and it appears to that court or to the House of Lords, as the case may be, that the point is one which ought to be considered by that House."

    (ii) Where leave has been refused by the Divisional Court there is no right of appeal.

B. CIVIL MATTERS

    (i) In a *Substantive application* in a civil matter appeal lies with leave of the Court to the Court of Appeal Civil Division.
    (ii) An *ex parte* application for leave which has been refused by a Judge after a hearing may be renewed to the Court of Appeal Civil Division within seven days.

12. ADVICE

    If in doubt about any procedural matter applicants, respondents or their advisers should direct their enquiries to the Crown Office, telephone number: 0171–936 6205.

The Crown Office
Royal Courts of Justice
Strand   January 12, 1981
London WC2A 2LL   (revised October 25, 1994)

APPENDIX E

Procedural Tables

PROCEDURAL TABLES

APPLYING FOR LEAVE TO APPLY FOR JUDICIAL REVIEW IN A CRIMINAL CAUSE OR MATTER

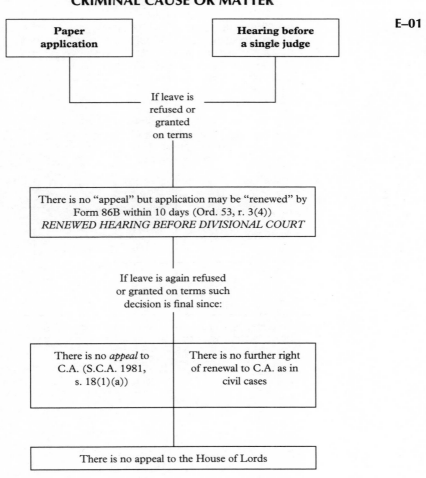

E–01

APPLYING FOR LEAVE TO APPLY FOR JUDICIAL REVIEW IN A CIVIL CAUSE OR MATTER

E–02

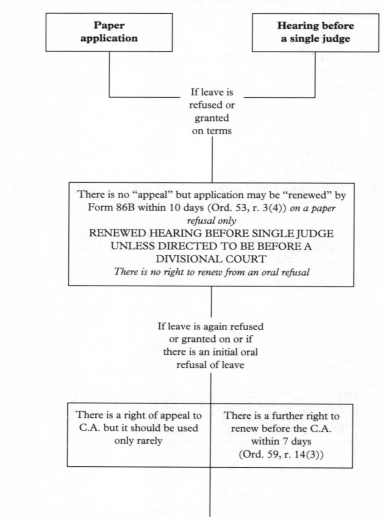

Paper application		Hearing before a single judge

If leave is
refused or
granted
on terms

There is no "appeal" but application may be "renewed" by Form 86B within 10 days (Ord. 53, r. 3(4)) *on a paper refusal only*
RENEWED HEARING BEFORE SINGLE JUDGE UNLESS DIRECTED TO BE BEFORE A DIVISIONAL COURT
There is no right to renew from an oral refusal

If leave is again refused
or granted on or if
there is an initial oral
refusal of leave

There is a right of appeal to C.A. but it should be used only rarely	There is a further right to renew before the C.A. within 7 days (Ord. 59, r. 14(3))

There is no further right of appeal or renewal to the House of Lords

LEAVE—FULL HEARING: PRACTITIONER CHECK LIST

Applicant	Respondent
On the application for leave consider asking for: – a stay of proceedings if seeking certiorari or prohibition or interim relief if seeking other remedies (Ord. 53, r. 3/10). – expedited hearing with an order for abridgment of time for service of respondent's evidence: – other directions *e.g.* bail; – amendment of Form 86A	Usually the respondent will not be present at the application for leave. If served with papers, however, or if the respondent is made aware of a prospective application for leave then consider: – contacting the Crown Office and finding out whether it is a paper or oral hearing; – if on paper, asking the Crown Office to seek directions from the court as to the matter being listed for oral hearing; – if oral, finding out the date and time of the hearing and attending on an "opposed *ex parte*" basis.
After the grant of leave: – serve 86A, motion and affidavit within 14 days; – lodge affidavit of service, motion and affidavit with Crown Office in same time; – if seeking certiorari and not done before, lodge order, *etc.*, complained of with Crown Office before hearing; – provide realistic time estimate when asked to do so by Crown Office; – consider serving affidavit in answer to respondents; – make any necessary interlocutory application; – review merits; – if settling, comply with uncontested proceedings Practice Directions; – lodge bundle of documents and skeleton arguments, 5 clean working days before the hearing.	After the grant of leave; – on receipt of 86A, *etc.*, consider applying to strike out or set aside the judicial review application; – comply with R.S.C. as to time for service of respondent's evidence which is usually 56 days from service unless abridgment of time has been ordered (the Crown Office will refuse to accept late affidavits); – provide realistic time estimate when asked to do so by Crown Office; – consider serving affidavit if any matters arise out of any further affidavit by applicant; – make any necessary interlocutory application; – review merits; – if settling, comply with uncontested proceedings Practice Direction; – agree content of bundle with applicant.

APPENDIX F

Relevant Extracts from Law Commission Paper "Administrative Law: Judicial Review and Statutory Appeals" Law Com. No. 226

PART XIII
SUMMARY OF CONCLUSIONS AND RECOMMENDATIONS

F–01   In this section we set out a summary of our conclusions and recommendations for reform of the procedures of judicial review and statutory appeals.

GENERAL CONSIDERATIONS
Case-load and delay

F–02   With regard to issues of case-load and delay, we believe that there are a number of underlying principles which must be taken into account if the procedural framework is to be effective. We consider that the system should:

(a) ensure the efficient despatch of business so as to minimise delay;

(b) avoid, so far as practicable, inconsistencies as between different judges in the exercise of discretion, particularly in the operation of the filter to exclude hopeless applications (at present the leave stage); and

(c) be robust enough to ensure not only that the present delays can be reduced to an acceptable level, but that there is no danger of a return to anything resembling the unacceptable position which existed up to the middle of 1993. (Paragraph 2.28)

We also believe that consideration should be given to the question of how to:

(d) address the access to justice issues raised by those concerned by the concentration of judicial review in London and the South-East; and

(e) avoid the perceived dangers in the present use of deputy high court judges in the exercise of the Crown Office's jurisdiction. (Paragraphs 2.28; Appendix C)

338

Homelessness

The provision of an internal review cannot be regarded as a proper substitute for a right of appeal to a court or an independent tribunal. We recommend the creation of a right of appeal on a point of law to a court or independent tribunal in homelessness cases. (Paragraphs 2.26, 2.27)

PROCEDURAL EXCLUSIVITY

We believe that the present position whereby a litigant is required to proceed by way of Order 53 only when (a) the challenge is on public law and no other grounds; i.e. where the challenge is solely to the validity or legality of a public authority's acts or omissions and (b) the litigant does not seek either to enforce or defend a completely constituted private law right is satisfactory. (Paragraph 3.15)

F–03

Transfer into and out of Order 53

It is recommended that the existing rule be amended so as to enable an action commenced by writ to be transferred into Order 53 and to continue as an application for judicial review provided the plaintiff satisfies the criteria for the granting of leave or, on our recommendation, for an application being allowed to proceed to a full judicial review. Further, the judge should be empowered to order proceedings brought under Order 53 to continue as if they had begun by writ, provided he or she is satisfied that the remedy sought is suitable for transfer into one of the forms of relief available in an action begun by writ. (Paragraphs 3.21, 3.19, Draft Order 53 rule 11(1)(2))

Transfer to the High Court and certification

We propose that any party to an action should be able to apply by summons to the district judge or master to transfer the action to the High Court on the ground that it raises issues of public law. It is envisaged that if the district judge or master considers the case a suitable one then it could be "certified as fit for a nominated judge if available" and transferred to the High Court, either, in a case solely raising public law issues, to the Crown Office List, or in a "mixed" case to the Queen's Bench Division. (Paragraph 3.23)

THE INITIAL STAGE OF THE APPLICATION

A new Form 86A

We recommend that Form 86A should be amended to ask the applicant to provide information concerning: (i) any relief sought, including interlocutory relief; (ii) any alternative remedies; (iii) whether the respondent has been asked to consider the complaint or reconsider the decision; (iv) the reasons for any delay; and (v) the date of any application for legal

F–04

aid (if relevant), the date when it was granted or refused and, if granted, the number of the legal aid certificate. (Paragraph 4.3; Appendix B)

A "request for information procedure"

We recommend that a "request for information" procedure should be introduced to be used at the discretion of the application judge. (Paragraph 4.9; Appendix B)

Notification of the decision

We recommend that if the application is not allowed to proceed to a substantive hearing (in the present terminology, if leave is *refused*) the application judge should complete the amended Form JRJ, to state that he or she has considered the application and should provide reasons for refusing to allow the application to proceed to a substantive hearing. (Paragraph 4.12)

FILTERING OUT HOPELESS APPLICATIONS: LEAVE OR PRELIMINARY CONSIDERATION

F–05 We recommend that the filtering stage of an application for judicial review should be known as the "preliminary consideration" rather than the leave stage. (Paragraph 5.8; Draft Order 53 rule 3)

We recommend that all applications for preliminary consideration should, in the first instance, be determined entirely on paper, unless the application falls within a recognised category for which an oral hearing might be necessary. We further recommended that the following categories should be so recognised: (i) where the application includes a claim for immediate interim relief; (ii) where on the basis of the written material it appears to the Crown Office or the judge that a hearing is desirable in the interests of justice. (Paragraph 5.11; Draft Order 53 rules 3(6) and 3(7))

Criteria for permitting an application to proceed to a substantive hearing

We recommend that it should be stated in the Rules that unless either the facts or the propositions relied upon by the applicant disclose a serious issue which ought to be determined, or that there ought for some other reason to be a substantive hearing, an application for judicial review should not be allowed to proceed beyond the preliminary consideration. (Paragraph 5.15; Draft Order 53 rule 3(5)(a))

Standing

We recommend that an application should not be allowed to proceed to a substantive hearing unless the court is satisfied that the applicant has been or would be adversely affected, or the High Court considers that it is in the public interest for an applicant to make the application. (Paragraph 5.22; Draft Bill, clause 1, new section 31B(1))

Time limits

We recommend:—

(a) that the time limit in applications for judicial review should be prescribed in rules of court (Draft Bill, clause 1, new section 31(B)(2)) and should be three months from the date when grounds for the application first arose (Draft Order 53, rule 2(1));

(b) that the court may refuse an application made within the three month time limit if the application is not sufficiently prompt and, that if the relief sought was granted, on an application made at this stage, it would be likely to cause substantial hardship to, or substantially prejudice the rights of, any person or be detrimental to good administration (Draft Order 53, rule 2(2));

(c) that an application may be made after the end of the period of three months if the court is satisfied that there is a good reason for the application not to have been made within that period, and that if the relief sought was granted, on an application made at this stage, it would not be likely to cause substantial hardship to, or substantially prejudice the rights of, any person or be detrimental to good administration (Draft Order 53, rule 2(3)).

We also suggest that the court should take account of the fact that an alternative remedy was being pursued as a good reason why an application made after 3 months should be allowed to proceed to a substantive hearing. (Paragraph 5.35)

Unincorporated associations

We recommend that unincorporated associations should be permitted to make applications for judicial review in their own name through one or more of their members applying in a representative capacity where the court is satisfied that the members of the applicant association have been or would be adversely affected or are raising an issue of public interest warranting judicial review, and that the members of the association are appropriate persons to bring that challenge. (Paragraph 5.41, Draft Order 53 r. 1(2))

INTERIM RELIEF

We recommend that there should be statutory provision for interim relief **F–06** against ministers in their official capacity and against government departments in judicial review proceedings. (Paragraph 6.13; Draft Bill, clause 1, new section 31B(5))

Interim relief prior to the preliminary consideration

We recommend that it be made clear in the Rules that there is jurisdiction to grant interim relief before it has been decided in the preliminary consideration of an application to allow it to proceed to a substantive hearing. (Paragraph 6.17; Draft Order 53, rule 5(1))

The form of interim relief

We recommend that there should be provision for interim injunctions, interim declarations and stays of proceedings before courts and tribunals in proceedings by way of judicial review. (Paragraph 6.27; Draft Bill, clause 1, new section 31A(4)(a); Draft Order 53 rule 5)

INTERLOCUTORY PROCEDURES

F–07 We do not make any recommendations for reform of the rules on discovery. (Paragraph 7.12)

REMEDIES

Nomenclature

F–08 The latin titles of the orders be replaced so that the prerogative orders the court would have power to make in judicial review proceedings would be called: a mandatory order, a prohibiting order, and a quashing order. (Paragraph 8.3; Draft Bill, clause 1, new sections 31(1) and 31(3))

Title of cases

The description of judicial review cases should be reformed by Practice Direction so that they are titled, "In the matter of an application for judicial review: *ex parte Applicant, R. v Respondent*". (Paragraph 8.4)

Claims for Restitution and in Debt, and Interest

We recommend that, as is the case for damages, the court may order restitution in judicial review proceedings provided such restitution would have been granted in an action begun by writ. (Paragraph 8.5; Draft Bill, clause 1, new section 31B(3); Draft Order 53 rules 1 and 8)

We also recommend that, as is the case for damages and is proposed for restitution, the court may award a liquidated sum in judicial review proceedings provided such an award would have been made in an action begun by writ. (Paragraph 8.7; Draft Bill, clause 1, new section 31B(3); Draft Order 53 rule 8)

Advisory declarations

We recommend that explicit provision be made for the High Court to make advisory declarations in the exercise of its supervisory jurisdiction by way of judicial review. (Paragraph 8.12; Draft Bill, clause 1, new section 31A(4)(b))

We also recommend that where the judge is satisfied that the application is for an *advisory* declaration, he should also be satisfied that the point concerned is one of general public importance, before he makes the advisory declaration or, at the initial (*i.e.* leave) stage, allows the application to proceed to a substantive hearing. (Paragraph 8.14; Draft Bill, clause 1, new section 31A(5))

Power to make substitute orders

We recommend that the court should be empowered to substitute its own decision for the decision to which the application relates (Draft Bill, clause 1, new section 31(4)(b)) provided that: (i) there was only one lawful decision that could be arrived at; and (ii) the grounds for review arose out of an error of law. We also recommend that the power to substitute its own decision should be limited to cases involving the decisions of courts and tribunals. (Paragraph 8.16; Draft Bill, clause 1, new section 31(5))

RENEWED APPLICATIONS AND APPEALS

We recommend that it be stated in the Rules that any application by a **F–09** respondent to set aside an order that an application for judicial review may proceed should be made not later than 28 days beginning with the day on which the respondent is served with the notice of application. (Paragraph 9.4, Draft Order 53 rule 17(3))

We also recommend that no appeal lie to the Court of Appeal from an order made following an application to have an application for judicial review set aside. (Paragraph 9.5, Draft Order 53, r. 17(4))

We also recommend that it be made clear in the Rules that access to the Court of Appeal to challenge an order setting aside a decision to allow a preliminary application to proceed is by way of a renewal of the original application. (Paragraph 9.6, Draft Order 53 rule 17(4))

COSTS

We propose that in those cases where an oral hearing is required the **F–10** court should have the power to make a costs order in favour of either applicant or respondent.

We recommend that costs should be available from central funds where a case is allowed to proceed to a substantive hearing on the basis of either a public interest challenge or for the purpose of seeking an advisory declaration. (Paragraph 10.6; Draft Bill, clause 1, new section 31B(4))

We also recommend that the Civil Legal Aid (General) Regulations 1989 be amended to enable the Board to consider the wider public interest in having the case heard. (Paragraph 10.9)

HABEAS CORPUS

We do not make any proposals for reform, but we do urge that a wide **F–11** review of habeas corpus appeal provisions be undertaken to enable a unified appeal system to be achieved. (Paragraph 11.32)

STATUTORY APPEALS

Crown Office Rules

We recommend that all public law procedures should be consolidated **F–12** into one set of Crown Office Rules. This should be done, however, in co-ordination with Lord Woolf's review of civil rules and procedures, and we do not propose that these rules are drafted until the results of that review are known. (Paragraph 12.2)

The High Court's powers on appeals by way of case stated

We recommend amendment of the Supreme Court Act 1981 so as to confirm statutorily the powers of the High Court on case stated appeals from the Crown Court. (Paragraph 12.9; Draft Bill, clause 2)

We consider that existing procedures for appeals to the High Court by way of case stated should be replaced in due course by provisions for appeal on a point of law. No new case stated provisions should be created in the future. (Paragraph 12.10)

Statutory Review

We recommend that a model "application to quash" provision should be used in future for statutory review provisions. (Paragraph 12.14; Appendix E)

Intervention

We recommend that Order 55 be amended so as to allow for intervention by a third party (which may include a Minister of government department) in a statutory appeal providing that the court is satisfied that the third party is a proper person to be heard. (Paragraph 12.19)

Time limits and power to extend time

A list should be maintained in the proposed Crown Office Rules of those statutory appeals where [for good reasons] a different time limit applies, the rest being limited to 28 days in any provision of general effect. (Paragraph 12.20)

When time starts to run in statutory appeals

We recommend that the date from which time should be calculated for statutory appeals is the date of posting (plus a stated number of days), and that this provision should be included in the Rules. (Paragraph 12.21)

Power to extend time

We recommend that in future the availability or otherwise of an extension of time should be set out clearly in the proposed Crown Office Rules. (Paragraph 12.22)

Interim suspension and stay of orders pending appeal

We recommend that the types of appeal where Parliament has provided by statute that the entering of an appeal should act as a stay on the order or decision in question should be listed in the Crown Office Rules. (Paragraph 12.23)

Other interlocutory provisions

We propose that interlocutory provisions should be made clear and accessible, in whatever way is most effective, so that appellants may be confident of the procedure in their particular case. This might be done by the inclusion of such provisions in the proposed Crown Office Rules. (Paragraph 12.24)

The orders which can be made on appeal

We consider harmonisation desirable in principle, at least for statutory appeals, although not for statutory review, and recommend that in future such a provision should be formulated as part of the Crown Office Rules. (Paragraph 12.25)

Allocation of business to the different divisions of the High Court

A Chancery Division judge should be assigned from time to time to sit as an additional judge in VAT cases in the Crown Office List as Family Division Judges are now regularly appointed as additional Queen's Bench judges to hear judicial review cases with a family law element. The effect of this change on the efficient dispatch of VAT appeals should be closely monitored, and if the situation does not improve, more radical changes, such as a transfer of the whole of this jurisdiction to the Chancery Division, should be considered. (Paragraph 12.29)

DRAFT FORMS

Application for Judicial Review (Preliminary consideration)

In the High Court of Justice   *Crown office Ref:*
Queens Bench Division
Crown Office List

In the matter of an application for Judicial Review

Ex parte

The Queen – v –

You must read the notes for guidance obtainable from the Crown Office. Send the completed form to the Master of the Crown Office, Royal Courts of Justice, Strand, London WC2A 2LL.

The Applicant	Name	
	Address	
	Description	
Legal Aid Date: *(if any)*	Application	
	Date: granted	
	Date: refused	
	Certificate No	
Service *Give the name and address of solicitors for applicant or (if solicitors not acting for the applicant the address at which the applicant is to be served)*	Name	
	Address	
	Ref.	
	Tel No	
	Fax No	
Respondent(s)	Name	
	Address	
Decision *give details including* • *date* • *judgment decision or* • *other proceedings in which relief is sought*		

Relief sought	
Grounds on which relief is sought *(please include an outline of any propositions of law, supported by any authorities and indicate if interlocutory relief is sought)* *Grounds must be supported by an affidavit which verifies the facts relied on. Where grounds have been settled by Counsel they must be signed by Counsel.*	

347

Alternative remedies *(Please identify any alternative remedies provided by the relevant statute. If these have not been pursued please state why not)*	
Review by respondent(s) *(Please state if the proposed respondent(s) has been asked to consider the complaint made or reconsider the decision in question, if appropriate. If so, please provide details.)*	
Delay *(Please give reasons for any relevant delay)*	

Signed

Dated

Application for Judicial Review (Request for information)

In the High Court of Justice   *Crown office Ref:*
Queens Bench Division
Crown Office List

In the matter of an application for Judicial Review

Ex parte

The Queen – v –

An application for Judicial Review has been lodged with the Crown Office by the above named Applicant. A copy of this form 86A is attached.

The Hon. Mr Justice
is considering whether this application should be allowed to proceed to a full hearing.

Please answer the questions on this form and return within 14 days of receipt of the information from the applicant to the Master of the Crown Office, Royal Courts of Justice, Strand, London WC2A 2LL. At the same time you must send a copy of this form when completed to the Applicant. You will find the Applicants address on the front of the attached form.

Take Notice: The Judge has directed that the Applicant (or his solicitors) should send copies of the affidavit(s) and exhibits to you.

Information which The Court Requests	
1. Before reaching the decision which is the subject of challenge, did you offer the applicant the opportunity to make representations to you? • *state yes or no* • *if no state your reasons*	
2. Has the decision which is the subject of challenge been reviewed internally? • *state yes or no* • *if yes state by whom and when*	

3. Do you submit that there is any alternative remedy which the applicant should have pursued or should now pursue before making an application to seek judicial review?
   - *state yes or no*
   - *if yes state what this is*

4. Do you support the case proceeding to a substantive hearing?
   - *state yes or no*
   - *if no state your reasons*

5. Supplementary information
   - *Please answer the following information*

(please continue on another sheet if necessary)

This request for information is signed on behalf of the Head of the Crown Office

signature   *stamp*

date

Application for Judicial Review (Notification of the decision)

In the High Court of Justice   *Crown office Ref:*
Queens Bench Division
Crown Office List

In the matter of preliminary consideration for Judicial Review

Ex parte

The Queen – v –

Order by the Honourable Mr Justice

Judge's order

The judge made the decision after consideration of the following:

□ *Consideration of the documents only:*	□ *Consideration of the documents and oral submissions:*	□ *by Applicant or*	□ *Counsel in open court*

Notes for applicant
1. *Where a substantive hearing has been granted, applicants and their legal advisors are reminded of their obligations to reconsider the merits of their application in the light of the respondent's affidavit.*

2. *Where the Judge has refused to allow the application to proceed an applicant or his solicitor may renew his application by completing and returning Form 86A within 10 days of the service upon him of this notice. The application may not be renewed in a non-criminal cause or matter if the Judge has heard oral argument.*

3. *If the Judge has allowed the application to proceed to a substantive hearing the applicant or his solicitor* **must within 14 days** *from the grant of leave:*

● *Serve on all persons directly affected – copy Notice of Motion together with Form 86A supporting affidavits and exhibits;*

● *enter in the Crown Office in the original Notice of Motion, together with 2 copies: £50. fee; affidavit of service.*

Sent/Handed to the applicant/the applicant's solicitors on

Date:

Applicant's Ref No.

Judge's Notes to the applicant

If this application is renewed

I consider/do not consider (*delete as appropriate*)
that notice should be served on the respondent

**Judge's observations to the
Crown Office**
(Not for applicant)

Index—Judicial Review